Code X 2/6.00

Morris Marina Owners Workshop Manual

by J H Haynes
Member of the Guild of Motoring Writers

and B L Chalmers-Hunt
TEng (CEI), AMIMI, AMIRTE, AMVBRA

Models covered

All models Marina Mk 1 & 2

Covers manual and automatic gearbox versions of above

ISBN 0 900550 73 2

HAYNES PUBLISHING GROUP
SPARKFORD YEOVIL SOMERSET ENGLAND
distributed in the USA by
HAYNES PUBLICATIONS INC
861 LAWRENCE DRIVE
NEWBURY PARK
CALIFORNIA 91320
USA

Acknowledgements

Thanks are due to the British Leyland Motor Corporation (Austin/Morris Division) for their permission to use certain line illustrations in this manual, to Castrol Limited for lubrication details and to some franchised garages who have helped with practical technical information. Thanks are also due to the Champion Sparking Plug Company who supplied the illustrations showing the various spark plug conditions. The bodywork repair photographs used in this manual were provided by Lloyds Industries Limited who supply 'Turtle Wax', 'Dupli-color Holts', and other Holts range products.

Last, but not least, thanks must go to all those people at Sparkford who assisted in the production of this manual, particularly Brian Horsfall, Tim Parker, Peter Strasman, Lee Saunders and John Austin.

About this manual

Its aims

The aim of this Manual is to help you get the best value from your car. It can do so in several ways. It can help you decide what work must be done (even should you choose to get it done by a garage), provide information on routine maintenance and servicing, and give a logical course of action and diagnosis when random faults occur. However, it is hoped that you will make full use of the Manual by tackling the work yourself. On simpler jobs it may even be quicker than booking the car into a garage, and having to go there twice, to leave and collect it. Perhaps most important, a lot of money can be saved by avoiding the costs the garage must charge to cover its labour and overheads.

The Manual has drawings and descriptions to show the function of the various components so that their layout can be understood. Then the tasks are described and photographed in a step-by-step sequence so that even a novice can do the work.

Its arrangement

The manual is divided into Thirteen Chapters, each covering a logical sub-division of the vehicle. The Chapters are each divided into consecutively numbered Sections and the Sections into paragraphs (or sub-sections), with decimal numbers following on from the Section they are in, eg 5.1, 5.2, 5.3 etc.

It is freely illustrated, especially in those parts where there is a detailed sequence of operations to be carried out. There are two forms of illustration: figures and photographs. The figures are numbered in sequence with decimal numbers, according to their position in the Chapter: eg Fig. 6.4 is the 4th drawing/illustration in Chapter 6. Photographs are numbered (either individually or in related groups) the same as the Section or sub-section of the text where the operation they show is described.

There is an alphabetical index at the back of the manual as well as a contents list at the front.

References to the 'left' or 'right' of the vehicle are in the sense of a person facing forwards in the driver's seat.

Whilst every care is taken to ensure that the information in this manual is correct no liability can be accepted by the authors or publishers for loss, damage or injury caused by any errors in, or omissions from, the information given.

Contents

Introduction to the Morris Marina 1.3

See Supplement for introduction to the later models

The Morris Marina 1.3 together with the Marina 1.8 (the subject of another manual) were launched in April 1971 at the start of the British Leyland Motor Corporation sales drive through the Austin/Morris Division, as a replacement for the ageing Austin A60 and Morris Oxford. Nothing startling in terms of engineering design was introduced for they then, as now, used the 'A' and 'B' series BMC engines, Morris Minor front suspension and solid rear axle suspended on leaf springs connected by a Triumph Toledo type gearbox. Not surprisingly they work very well; not surprisingly from an engineering point of view, but surprisingly from a customer point of view. While it is obviously an unrepentant two or four door family saloon it is also a driver's car and a good one at that.

The 1.3 appears with a four door saloon body and a two door coupe both in De Luxe and Super De Luxe states of trim. Where there are differences between the two we will call them the saloon and the coupe.

These are well balanced cars, perhaps better balanced than the larger engined Marina and whilst they are undoubtedly the economy models they are no mean performers either. This can well be described as a good BLMC model.

Main overall dimensions

Length	Saloon	13 ft 10 1/8 in	(4.219 m)
	Coupé	13 ft 7 1/8 in	(4.143 m)
Width	Saloon	5 ft 4 1/16 in	(1.635 m)
	Coupé	5 ft 4 3/8 in	(1.640 m)
Height	Saloon	4 ft 8 1/8 in	(1.425 m)
	Coupé	4 ft 7 3/8 in	(1.406 m)
Wheelbase		8 ft	(2.438 m)
Weight	Saloon	1936 lbs	(878 kg)
	Coupé	1870 lbs	(848 kg)

Morris Marina 1.3 Coupe Deluxe (Mk 1)

Morris Marina 1.3 Super 2-door (Mk 2)

Ordering spare parts

Always try to obtain genuine British Leyland parts from a franchised BLMC garage. Use the Unipart system too, if you can. It obviously makes good sense to go straight to a franchised garage even though you can order parts through any garage for they will be more familiar with your car than most, and there is a better chance that they can supply you ex stock.

When ordering new parts it is essential that the storeman has full information about your particular model of Marina. He cannot guarantee to supply you with the correct part unless you give him your model and car and body numbers and in the case of engine, gearbox or rear axle parts, their relevant numbers. If possible take the part to be replaced along too.

If you are going to use the extensive BLMC exchange scheme make sure that the component which you wish to exchange is clean and complete before placing it on the parts counter.

The car and body numbers are located on two plates fixed to the left hand bonnet lock platform.

The engine number is afixed to the cylinder block on its right hand side.

The gearbox number is stamped on the right hand side.

The rear axle number is stamped on the outside face of the differential casing joint flange.

A typical Marina 1.3 car number could be MA4S9S 107618M

M	–	Morris
A	–	'A' series engine
4S	–	4 door (2S is 2 door)
9	–	Model series
S	–	Super De Luxe
107618	–	Serial number
M	–	BLMC internal reference suffix

Routine maintenance

Maintenance should be regarded as essential for ensuring safety and desirable for the purpose of obtaining economy and performance from the car. By far the largest element of the maintenance routine is visual examination.

The maintenance instructions listed are those recommended by the manufacturer. They are supplemented by additional maintenance tasks which, from practical experience, need to be carried out.

The additional tasks are indicated by an asterisk and are primarily of a preventative nature — they will assist in eliminating the unexpected failure of a component.

Weekly, before a long journey, or every 250 miles (400 Km)

1 Remove the dipstick and check the engine oil level which should be up to the 'MAX' mark. Top up the oil in the sump with Castrol GTX. On no account allow the oil to fall below the 'MIN' mark on the dipstick. The distance between the 'MAX' and 'MIN' marks corresponds to approximately 1.5 pints (0.85 litre).

2 Check the battery electrolyte level and top up as necessary with distilled water. Make sure that the top of the battery is always kept clean and free of moisture. See Chapter 10.

3 Inspect the level of water in the translucent plastic reservoir. This should be maintained at the required level mark by adding soft water, such as rain water, via the screwed cap. If the reservoir is empty, remove the radiator filler plug, completely fill the radiator and replace the filler plug. Remove the reservoir screwed cap and half fill the reservoir. Refit the cap. Check for leaks. See Chapter 4.

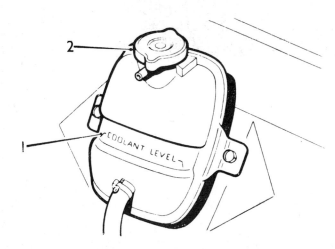

2 COOLANT RESERVOIR

1 Level mark, 2 Pressure cap

4 Check the tyre pressures with an accurate gauge and adjust as necessary. Make sure that the tyre walls and treads are free of damage. Remember that the tyre tread should have a minimum of 1 millimetre depth across three quarters of the total width of the tread.

5 Refill the windscreen washer container with soft water. Add an anti-freezing solution satchet in cold weather to prevent freezing (do not use ordinary anti-freeze). Check that the jets operate correctly.

6 Remove the wheel trims and check all wheel nuts for tightness but take care not to overtighten.

Every 6000 miles (10000 Km) or 6 months

Complete the service items in the weekly service check as applicable, plus:

1 Run the engine until it is hot and then place a container of 8 pints (4.55 litres) under the engine sump drain plug located on the right hand side at the rear of the sump (Fig RM 1/4). Remove the drain plug and its copper sealing washer. Allow the oil to drain out for 10 minutes. Whilst this is being done unscrew the old oil filter cartridge located on the right hand side of the engine and discard. Smear the rubber seal on a new cartridge with a little oil and refit it to the filter head. Screw it on and tighten hand tight only. Clean the oil filler cap in petrol and wipe dry. Check the drain plug copper sealing washer and if damaged fit a new one. Refit the drain plug and sealing washer. Refill the engine with 6½ pints (3.7 litres) of Castrol GTX and clean off any oil which may have been split over the engine or its components. Run the engine and check the oil level. The interval between oil changes should be reduced in very hot or dusty conditions or during cool weather with much slow or stop/start driving.

2 Wipe the top of the carburettor suction chamber and unscrew and withdraw the oil cap. Top up the dashpot with fresh Castrol GTX to raise the level to ½ inch (13 mm) above the top of the hollow piston rod. Push the damper assembly back into position and screw the cap firmly into position.

3 Check the carburettor adjustment as described in Chapter 3, Section 17.

4 Carefully examine the cooling and heater systems for signs of leaks. Make sure that all hose clips are tight and that none of the hoses have cracked or perished. Do not attempt to repair a leaking hose, always fit new. Generally inspect the exterior of the engine for signs of water leaks or stains. The method of repair will depend on its location. This check is particularly important before filling the cooling system with anti-freeze as it has a greater searching action than pure water and is bound to find any weak spots.

5 The fan belt adjustment must be tight enough to drive the dynamo (or alternator) without overloading the bearings, including the water pump bearings too. The method of adjusting the fan belt is described in Chapter 2, Section 2. It is correct when it can be pressed in ½ inch (13 mm) under moderate hand pressure at the mid point of its longest run from the dynamo/alternator to the crankshaft pulley.

6 Lubricate the accelerator control linkage cable and pedal fulcrum with a little engine oil.

7 Inspect the steering rack rubber boots for signs of leaking which, if evident, must be rectified as described in Chapter 11.

8 Lubricate the two nipples on each of the front swivel pins

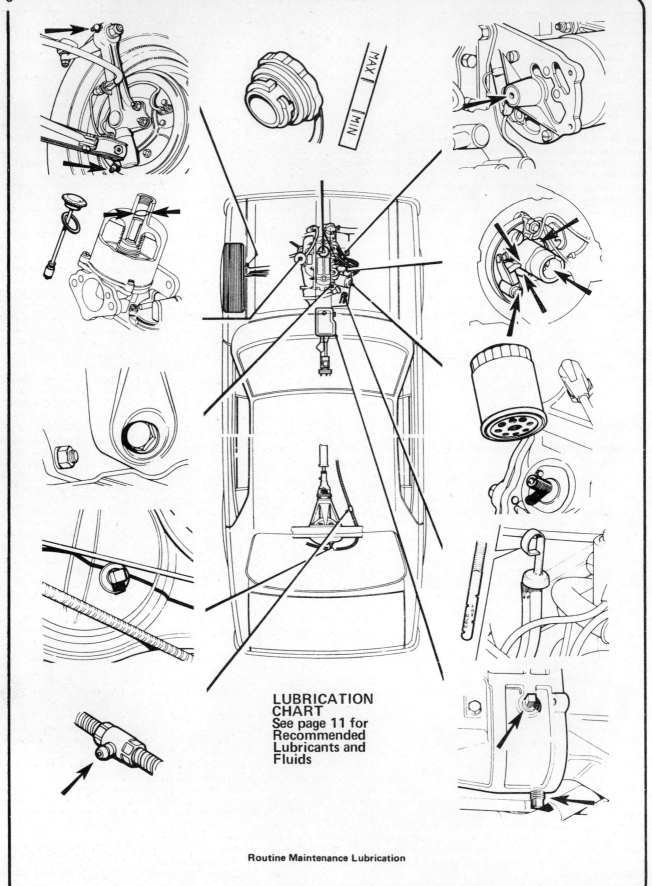

LUBRICATION CHART
See page 11 for Recommended Lubricants and Fluids

8

with several strokes of the grease gun filled with Castrol LM Grease (Fig RM 1/10).

9 Inspect all steering ball joints for signs of wear, leaking rubber boots and securing nuts for tightness. If a ball joint rubber boot has failed the whole assembly should be renewed. See Chapter 11.

10 Check the front wheel alignment. For this special equipment is necessary therefore leave this to the local BLMC garage. See Chapter 11, Section 24.

11 Wipe the top of the brake and clutch master cylinder and unscrew the caps. Check the level of hydraulic fluid in the reservoirs and top up, if necessary to the marks on the exterior of the reservoir with the recommended fluid. Make sure the cap breather vent is clean and then refit the cap. Take care not to spill any hydraulic fluid on the paintwork as it acts as a solvent. (Fig RM 3).

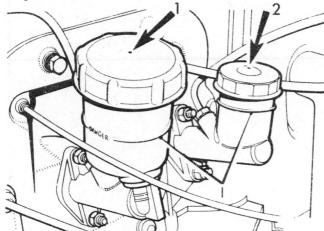

FIG RM 3 BRAKE AND CLUTCH MASTER CYLINDER RESERVOIRS

1 Brake master cylinder reservoir, 2 Clutch master cylinder reservoir

12 Check the adjustment of the handbrake and footbrake. If travel is excessive refer to Chapter 9 and adjust the footbrake and then the handbrake if its travel is still excessive.

13 Refer to Chapter 9 and inspect the brake linings and pads for wear and the front discs and rear drums for scoring.

14 Carefully examine all brake hydraulic pipes and unions for signs of leakage and flexible hoses for signs of perishing. Make sure that the front brake flexible hoses are not in contact with any body or mechanical component when the steering is turned through both locks.

15 Lubricate the nipple on the handbrake cable using a grease gun filled with Castrol LM Grease

16 Lubricate all moving parts of the handbrake system with Castrol GTX.

17 From cars numbered 43892 to 45000 and 48101 and any cars prior to that if fitted with a grease nipple on the propeller shaft front universal joint lubricate the nipple with 3 to 4 strokes of the grease gun filler with Castrol LM Grease.

18 Refer to Chapter 4, Section 11 and remove the spark plugs. Clean, adjust, if necessary, and replace.

19 Refer to Chapter 4, Section 2 and clean and adjust the distributor contact breaker points.

20 Spring back the two clips and remove the distributor cap. Lift off the rotor arm. Apply a few drops of thin oil over the screw in the centre of the cam spindle and on the moving contact breaker pivot. Apply a smear of grease to the cam surface. Remove any excess oil or grease with a clean rag. Apply a few drops of oil through the holes in the contact breaker base plate to lubricate the automatic timing control.

21 Refer to Chapter 4, Section 10 and check the ignition timing. Adjust if necessary.

22 Wipe the area around the gearbox level/filler plug. Unscrew

the plug and check the level of oil which should be up to the bottom of the threads. Top up if necessary using Castrol Hypoy and refit the plug. Wipe away any spilled oil (fig RM 1/6).

23 Wipe the area around the rear axle level/filler plug. Unscrew the plug and check the level of oil which should be up to the bottom of the threads. Top up if necessary using Castrol Hypoy and refit the plug. Wipe away any spilled oil (Fig RM 1/7).

24 **Automatic transmission:** With the vehicle standing on level ground, apply the handbrake and move the selector to the 'P' position. Start the engine and allow to run at idle speed for a minimum of 2 minutes. With the engine still running withdraw the dipstick from the filler tube to be found at the rear of the engine compartment. Wipe the dipstick and quickly replace and withdraw the dipstick again. Check the level of oil and top up if necessary with Castrol TQF. Take great care not to overfill (Fig RM 1/13).

25 Generally check the operation of all lights and electrical equipment. Renew any blown bulbs with bulbs of the same wattage rating and rectify any electrical equipment fault. See Chapter 10.

26 Check the battery electrolyte specific gravity as described in Chapter 10, Section 3. Clean the battery terminals and smear them with vaseline (petroleum jelly) to prevent corrosion.

27 Check the alignment of the headlights and adjust if necessary. See Chapter 10.

28 Check the condition of the windscreen wiper blades and fit new if the blade end has frayed, softened or perished. They should be renewed every 12 months.

29 Apply a few drops of engine oil through the oil hole in the dynamo commutator end bearing (Fig RM 1/9).

30 Generally check the exhaust system for signs of leaks. Apply a little Holts Silencer Seal or Gum Gum to small blow holes. If badly corroded the system must be renewed. Check all exhaust mountings for tightness.

31 Carefully examine all clutch and fuel lines and unions for signs of leakage and flexible hoses for signs of perishing. Check the tightness of all unions and renew any faulty lines or hoses

32 Lubricate all door, bonnet and boot lid locks, hinges and controls with Castrol Everyman.

33 Inspect the seat belts for damage to the webbing. Check that all seat and seat belt mountings are tight.

34 Make sure that the rear view mirror is firm in its mounting and is not crazed or cracked.

35 Wash the bodywork and chromium fittings and clean out the interior of the car. Wax polish the bodywork including all chromium and bright metal trim. Force wax polish into any joints in the bodywork to prevent rust formation.

36 If it is wished change over the tyres to equalise wear.

37 Balance the wheels to eliminate any vibration especially from the steering. This must be done on specialist equipment.

38 Lubricate the washer around the wiper spindles with several drops of glycerine.

Every 12,000 miles (20,000 Km) or 12 months

Complete the service items in the 6000 mile service check as applicable plus:

1 To fit a new air cleaner element, unscrew the wing nut and lift away the cover, body and element which should be discarded. Wipe out the container and fit a new element. Replace the cover. Make sure that the sealing ring between the air cleaner body and carburettor is not damaged or perished. Refit the air cleaner to the carburettor and secure with the fibre washer and nut. During warm weather position the air cleaner intake away from the exhaust manifold or during cold weather move the air intake close to the exhaust manifold (Fig RM 4).

2 Remove the oil filler cap and filter assembly on the top of the rocker cover and fit a new one.

3 Refer to Chapter 1, Section 58 and check the valve rocker clearances. Adjust as necessary.

4 Refer to Chapter 11, Section 3 and adjust the front wheel bearing end float.

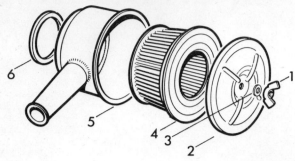

AIR CLEANER COMPONENTS

*1 Wing nut, 2 Sealing washer, 3 Top cover, 4 Element
5 Body, 6 Sealing ring*

5 Inspect the ignition H T leads for cracks or deterioration. Replace as necessary.
*6 Examine the dynamo brushes, replace them if worn and clean the commutator. See Chapter 10, Section 9 and 10.

Every 24,000 miles (40,000 Km) or 18 months

Complete the service items in the 6000 and 12,000 mile service check as applicable plus:
*1 Examine the hub bearings for wear and replace as necessary. See Chapter 11, Section 2.
*2 Check the tightness of the battery earth lead on the body.
*3 Renew the condenser in the distributor. See Chapter 4, Section 4.
*4 Remove the starter motor, examine the brushes and replace as necessary. Clean the commutator and starter drive. See Chapter 10.
*5 Test the cylinder compressions, and if necessary remove the cylinder head, decarbonise, grind in the valves and fit new valve

springs. See Chapter 1.
6 Completely drain the brake hydraulic fluid from the system. All seals and flexible hoses throughout the braking system should be examined and preferably renewed. The working surfaces of the master cylinder, wheel and caliper should be inspected for signs of wear or scoring and new parts fitted as necessary. Refill the hydraulic system with recommended brake fluid. See Chapter 9, Section 3.

Every 36,000 miles (60,000 Km) or 3 years

Complete the service items in the 6000 and 12000 mile service as applicable plus:
1 If a brake servo unit is fitted, pull back the filter dust cover and withdraw the end cap. The filter is located in the servo unit housing where the pushrod passes through from the brake pedal. Cut off the old filter element. Cut through the new filter in a diagonal manner to the centre hole and fit it over the pushrod and into the housing. Replace the end cap and dust cover.

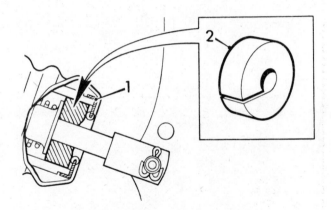

BRAKE SERVO UNIT AIR FILTER

1 End cap, 2 Filter element

Quick reference capacities and dimensions

Engine sump capacity (with filter)	6½ pints (3.7 litres)
Manual gearbox capacity	1½ pints (0.85 litres)
Automatic gearbox (top up from MIN to MAX on dipstick) ...	1 pint (0.57 litres)
Rear axle capacity	1¼ pints (0.71 litres)
Cooling system (with heater)	7½ pints (4.26 litres)
Windscreen washer bottle	3 pints (1.7 litres)
Valve clearances	0.012 inch (0.30 mm) COLD
Plug gap	0.025 inch (0.64 mm)
Contact breaker gap	0.014 to 0.016 inch (0.36 to 0.41 mm)
Negative earth	
Firing order	1 3 4 2
Maximum towing weight	1680 lb (762 kg)

Recommended lubricants and fluids

COMPONENT	TYPE OF LUBRICANT OR FLUID	CORRECT CASTROL PRODUCTS
ENGINE	Multigrade. To API SE specification	Castrol GTX
GEARBOX	High quality EP90 gear oil	Castrol Hypoy B90
REAR AXLE	High quality EP90 gear oil	Castrol Hypoy B90
GREASE POINTS	Multi-purpose high melting point lithium based grease	Castrol LM Grease
DISTRIBUTOR	See text for details of application	Vaseline petroleum jelly and Castrol LM Grease
COOLING SYSTEM	Anti-freeze solution complying with BS 3151 or 3152	Castrol Anti-freeze
BRAKE AND CLUTCH HYDRAULIC SYSTEMS	Hydraulic fluid conforming to SAE J1703D	Castrol Girling Universal Brake and Clutch Fluid
AUTOMATIC TRANSMISSION	High quality automatic transmission fluid BLMC type F	Castrol TQF

Castrol GRADES

Castrol Engine Oils

Castrol GTX

An ultra high performance SAE 20W/50 motor oil which exceeds the latest API MS requirements and manufacturers specifications. Castrol GTX with liquid tungsten† generously protects engines at the extreme limits of performance, and combines both good cold starting with oil consumption control. Approved by leading car makers.

Castrol XL 20/50

Contains liquid tungsten†; well suited to the majority of conditions giving good oil consumption control in both new and old cars.

Castrolite (Multi-grade)

This is the lightest multi-grade oil of the Castrol motor oil family containing liquid tungsten†. It is best suited to ensure easy winter starting and for those car models whose manufacturers specify lighter weight oils.

Castrol Grand Prix

An SAE 50 engine oil for use where a heavy, full-bodied lubricant is required.

Castrol Two-Stroke-Four

A premium SAE 30 motor oil possessing good detergency characteristics and corrosion inhibitors, coupled with low ash forming tendency and excellent anti-scuff properties. It is suitable for all two-stroke motor-cycles, and for two-stroke and small four-stroke horticultural machines.

Castrol CR (Multi-grade)

A high quality engine oil of the SAE-20W/30 multi-grade type, suited to mixed fleet operations.

Castrol CRI 10, 20, 30

Primarily for diesel engines, a range of heavily fortified, fully detergent oils, covering the requirements of DEF 2101-D and Supplement 1 specifications.

Castrol CRB 20, 30

Primarily for diesel engines, heavily fortified, fully detergent oils, covering the requirements of MIL-L-2104B.

Castrol R 40

Primarily designed and developed for highly stressed racing engines. Castrol 'R' should not be mixed with any other oil nor with any grade of Castrol.

†Liquid Tungsten is an oil soluble long chain tertiary alkyl primary amine tungstate covered by British Patent No. 882,295.

Castrol Gear Oils

Castrol Hypoy (90 EP)

A light-bodied powerful extreme pressure gear oil for use in hypoid rear axles and in some gearboxes.

Castrol Gear Oils (continued)

Castrol Hypoy Light (80 EP)

A very light-bodied powerful extreme pressure gear oil for use in hypoid rear axles in cold climates and in some gearboxes.

Castrol Hypoy B (90 EP)

A light-bodied powerful extreme pressure gear oil that complies with the requirements of the MIL-L-2105B specification, for use in certain gearboxes and rear axles.

Castrol Hi-Press (140 EP)

A heavy-bodied extreme pressure gear oil for use in spiral bevel rear axles and some gearboxes.

Castrol ST (90)

A light-bodied gear oil with fortifying additives

Castrol D (140)

A heavy full-bodied gear oil with fortifying additives.

Castrol Thio-Hypoy FD (90 EP)

A light-bodied powerful extreme pressure gear oil. This is a special oil for running-in certain hypoid gears.

Automatic Transmission Fluids

Castrol TQF
(Automatic Transmission Fluid)

Approved for use in all Borg-Warner Automatic Transmission Units. Castrol TQF also meets Ford specification M2C 33F.

Castrol TQ Dexron®
(Automatic Transmission Fluid)

Complies with the requirements of Dexron® Automatic Transmission Fluids as laid down by General Motors Corporation.

Castrol Greases

Castrol LM

A multi-purpose high melting point lithium based grease approved for most automotive applications including chassis and wheel bearing lubrication.

Castrol MS3

A high melting point lithium based grease containing molybdenum disulphide.

Castrol BNS

A high melting point grease for use where recommended by certain manufacturers in front wheel bearings when disc brakes are fitted.

Castrol Greases (continued)

Castrol CL

A semi-fluid calcium based grease, which is both waterproof and adhesive, intended for chassis lubrication.

Castrol Medium

A medium consistency calcium based grease.

Castrol Heavy

A heavy consistency calcium based grease.

Castrol PH

A white grease for plunger housings and other moving parts on brake mechanisms. It must NOT be allowed to come into contact with brake fluid when applied to the moving parts of hydraulic brakes.

Castrol Graphited Grease

A graphited grease for the lubrication of transmission chains.

Castrol Under-Water Grease

A grease for the under-water gears of outboard motors.

Anti-Freeze

Castrol Anti-Freeze

Contains anti-corrosion additives with ethylene glycol. Recommended for the cooling systems of all petrol and diesel engines.

Speciality Products

Castrol Girling Damper Oil Thin

The oil for Girling piston type hydraulic dampers.

Castrol Shockol

A light viscosity oil for use in some piston type shock absorbers and in some hydraulic systems employing synthetic rubber seals. It must not be used in braking systems.

Castrol Penetrating Oil

A leaf spring lubricant possessing a high degree of penetration and providing protection against rust.

Castrol Solvent Flushing Oil

A light-bodied solvent oil, designed for flushing engines, rear axles, gearboxes and gearcasings.

Castrollo

An upper cylinder lubricant for use in the proportion of 1 fluid ounce to two gallons of fuel.

Everyman Oil

A light-bodied machine oil containing anti-corrosion additives for both general use and cycle lubrication.

Chapter 1 Engine

Contents

Specifications

Manufacturers type number	12 v
	4 cylinder
Bore	70.61 mm (2.78 in)
Stroke	81.28 mm (3.2 in)
Capacity	1275 cm^3 (77.8 in^3)
Firing order	1 3 4 2
Valve operation	overhead by pushrod
Compression ratio	8.8:1 High 8.0:1 Low
Cranking pressure: HC	190 lb/sq in (13.4 kg/cm^2)
LC	170 lb/sq in (12 Kg/cm^2)
Torque HC	69 lb ft at 2500 rpm
LC	65.5 lb ft at 2600 rpm
Brake mean effective pressure	134 lb/in^2 at 2500 rpm (High compression)
	127 lb/in^2 at 2600 rpm (Low compression)

Crankshaft	Forged steel
Main journal dia.	2.0012 to 2.0017 in (50.830 to 50.843 mm)
Minimum regrind dia.	1.912 to 1.9617 in (49.815 to 49.827 mm)
Crankpin journal dia.	1.7497 to 1.7504 in (44.442 to 44.460 mm)
Minimum regrind dia.	1.7097 to 1.7102 in (43.426 to 43.439 mm)
Crankshaft end thrust	Thrust washers at centre main bearing
Crankshaft end float	0.002 to 0.003 in (0.051 to 0.076 mm)

Main bearings ... ...
    Length ... ...
    Diametrical clearance ... ...
    Undersizes ... ...

3 thin wall type of VP3 lead-indium or NFM/3B
0.975 to 0.985 in (24.765 to 25.019 mm)
0.002 to 0.0003 in (0.0251 to 0.076 mm)
0.010 in 0.020 in 0.030 in 0.040 in (0.254 mm 0.508 mm 0.762 mm 1.016 mm)

Connecting rods ... ...
    Length between centre ... ...

Horizontally split big end, plain small end
5.748 to 5.757 in (145.1 to 146 mm)

Big-end bearings ... ...
    Length ... ...
    Diametrical clearance ... ...
    End-float on crankpin ... ...

Thin wall; steel backed, copper-lead, indium plated
0.840 to 0.050 in (21.33 to 29.59 mm)
0.0017 to 0.0032 in (0.04 to 0.08 mm)
0.006 to 0.010 in (0.15 to 0.25 mm)

Gudgeon pin ... ...
    Fit in piston ... ...
    Fit in connecting rod ... ...
    Diameter (outer) ... ...

Pressed in connecting rod
Hand push-fit
0.0008 to 0.0015 in (0.02 to 0.04 mm) interference
0.8123 to 0.8125 in (20.63 to 20.64 mm)

Pistons ... ...
    Clearance of skirt in cylinder: Top ... ...
                           Bottom ... ...

    Gudgeon pin bore ... ...
    Oversizes available ... ...
    Width of ring grooves: Top ... ...
                  Second ... ...
                  Third ... ...
                  Oil control ... ...

Aluminium solid skirt dished crown
0.0029 to 0.0037 in (0.07 to 0.09 mm)
0.0012 to 0.0022 in (0.03 to 0.06 mm)
4 - 3 compression, 1 oil control
0.8126 to 0.8128 in (20.64 to 29.65 mm)
+ 0.010 in (+0.254 mm) +0.020 in (+ 0.508 mm)
0.064 to 0.065 in (1.625 to 1.651 mm)
0.064 to 0.065 in (1.625 to 1.651 mm)
0.064 to 0.065 in (1.625 to 1.651 mm)
0.1578 to 0.1588 in (4.01 to 4.03 mm)

Piston rings
    Compression: Top ... ...
               Second and third ... ...
    Width: Top, second and third ... ...
    Fitted gap: Top ... ...
               Second and third ... ...
    Ring to groove clearance: Top, second and third ... ...

chrome
tapered cast iron
0.0615 to 0.0625 in (1.57 to 1.60 mm)
0.011 to 0.016 in (0.28 to 0.41 mm)
0.008 to 0.013 in (0.20 to 0.33 mm)
0.0015 to 0.0035 in (0.04 to 0.09 mm)

    Oil control ... ...
    Fitted gap: rails ... ...
               side spring ... ...

Apex
0.010 to 0.040 in (0.254 to 1.02 mm)
0.012 to 0.028 in (0.30 to 0.70 mm)

Camshaft ... ...
    Journal diameters: Front ... ...
                   Centre ... ...
                   Rear ... ...
    Bearing liner inside diameter (finished): Front ... ...
                                      Centre ... ...
                                      Rear ... ...
    Bearings ... ...
    Diametrical clearance ... ...
    End thrust ... ...
    End-float ... ...
    Drive ... ...
    Timing chain ... ...
    Cam lift ... ...

Forged steel
1.6655 to 1.6660 in (42.304 to 42.316 mm)
1.62275 to 1.62325 in (41.218 to 41.231 mm)
1.37275 to 1.37350 in (34.866 to 34.889 mm)
1.652 in (41.98 mm)
1.61 in (40.89 mm)
1.36 in (34.52 mm)
White metal lined, steel bracket
0.001 to 0.002 in (0.02 to 0.05 mm)
Taken on locating plate
0.0003 to 0.007 in (0.07 to 0.18 mm)
Duplex chain and gear from crankshaft
0.375 in (9.52 mm) pitch x 52 pitches
0.318 in (8.07 mm)

Rocker gear
    Rocker shaft: Dia. ... ...
    Rocker arm: Bore ... ...
                 Brush inside diameter (finished) ... ...

0.5615 to 0.5625 in (14.26 to 14.29 mm)
0.686 to 0.687 in (17.44 to 17.45 mm)
0.5630 to 0.5635 in (14.3 to 14.31 mm)

Tappets ... ...
    Outside diameter ... ...
    Length ... ...

Bucket type
0.81125 to 0.81175 in (20.60 to 20.62mm)
1.495 to 1.505 in (37.97 to 38.23 mm)

Valves
    Seat angle: inlet ... ...
             exhaust ... ...
    Head diameter: inlet ... ...
                 exhaust ... ...
    Stem diameter: inlet ... ...
                 exhaust ... ...

45°
45°
1.307 to 1.312 in (33.2 to 33.21 mm)
1.1515 to 1.1565 in (29.24 to 29.37 mm)
0.2793 to 0.2798 in (7.09 to 7.11 mm)
0.2788 to 0.2793 in (7.08 to 7.09 mm)

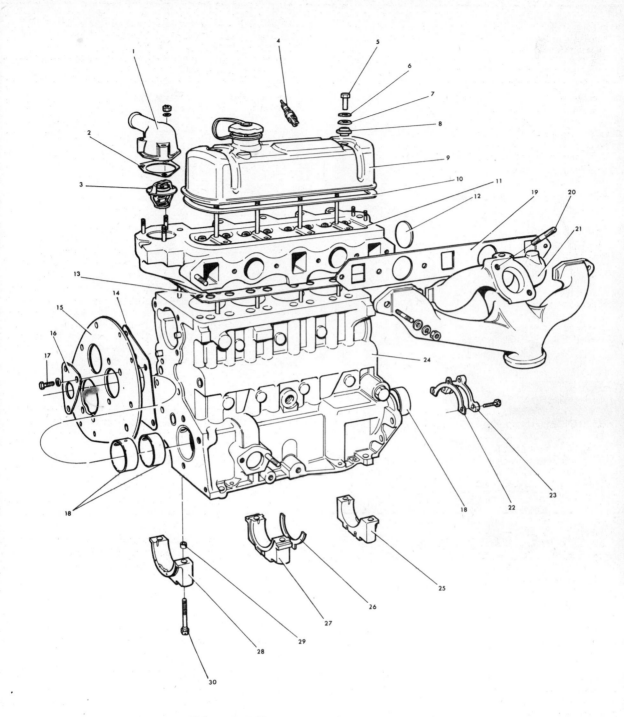

FIG.1.1 ENGINE - BLOCK AND CYLINDER HEAD

1 Water outlet	9 Rocker cover	17 Bolt - thrust plate retaining	24 Cylinder block
2 Gasket	10 Gasket	18 Camshaft bushes	25 Rear main bearing cap
3 Thermostat	11 Cylinder head	19 Manifold gasket	26 Thrust washer - crankshaft
4 Spark plug	12 Core plug	20 Stud	27 Centre main bearing cap
5 Shaped nut	13 Cylinder head gasket	21 Combined inlet and ex-	28 Front main bearing cap
6 Plain washer	14 Gasket	haust manifold	29 Dowel
7 Shaped washer	15 Front plate	22 Gasket	30 Bolt - main bearing cap re-
8 Sealing washer - rubber	16 Camshaft thrust plate	23 Rear cover	taining.

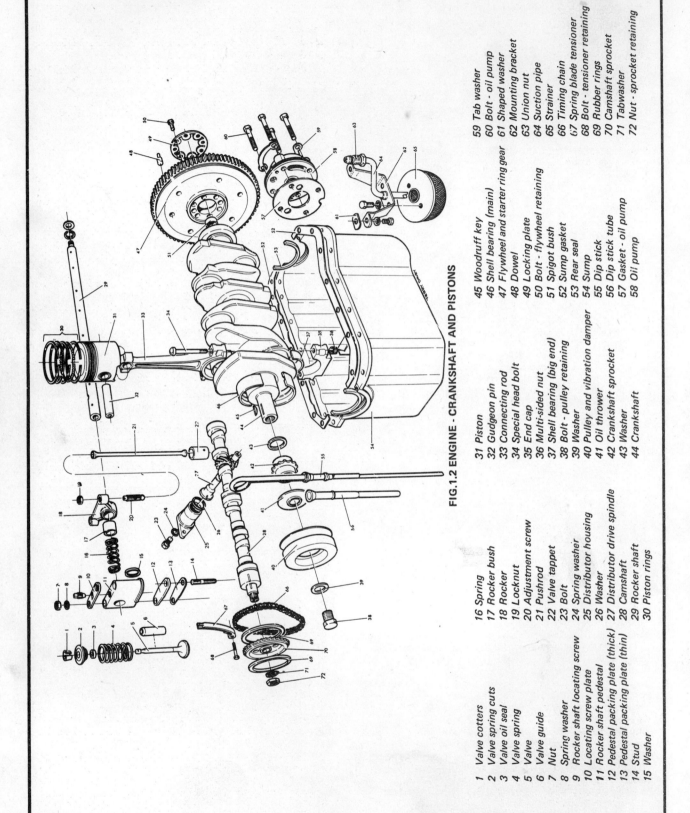

FIG.1.2 ENGINE - CRANKSHAFT AND PISTONS

1 Valve cotters
2 Valve spring cuts
3 Valve oil seal
4 Valve spring
5 Valve
6 Valve guide
7 Nut
8 Spring washer
9 Rocker shaft locating screw
10 Locating screw plate
11 Rocker shaft pedestal
12 Pedestal packing plate (thick)
13 Pedestal packing plate (thin)
14 Stud
15 Washer

16 Spring
17 Rocker bush
18 Rocker
19 Locknut
20 Adjustment screw
21 Pushrod
22 Valve tappet
23 Bolt
24 Spring washer
25 Distributor housing
26 Washer
27 Distributor drive spindle
28 Camshaft
29 Rocker shaft
30 Piston rings

31 Piston
32 Gudgeon pin
33 Connecting rod
34 Special head bolt
35 End cap
36 Multi-sided nut
37 Shell bearing (big end)
38 Bolt - pulley retaining
39 Washer
40 Pulley and vibration damper
41 Oil thrower
42 Crankshaft sprocket
43 Washer
44 Crankshaft

45 Woodruff key
46 Shell bearing (main)
47 Flywheel and starter ring gear
48 Dowel
49 Locking plate
50 Bolt - flywheel retaining
51 Spigot bush
52 Sump gasket
53 Rear seal
54 Sump
55 Dip stick
56 Dip stick tube
57 Gasket - oil pump
58 Oil pump

59 Tab washer
60 Bolt - oil pump
61 Shaped washer
62 Mounting bracket
63 Union nut
64 Suction pipe
65 Strainer
66 Timing chain
67 Spring blade tensioner
68 Bolt - tensioner retaining
69 Rubber rings
70 Camshaft sprocket
71 Tabwasher
72 Nut - sprocket retaining

Stem to guide clearance - inlet and exhaust   ... ...   0.0015 to 0.0025 in (0.04 to 0.08 mm)
Valve lift: Inlet and exhaust   ... ...   0.318 in (8.07 mm)

Valve springs

Free length   ... .   1.95 in (49.13 mm)
Fitted length   ... .   1.383 in (35.13 mm)
Load at fitted length   ... .   79.5 lb (36.03 Kg)
Load at top of lift   ... .   124 lb (56.3 Kg)
Number of working coils 4½

Valve timing

Timing marks : positions   ... .   Dimples on camshaft and crankshaft wheels
Rocker clearance cold : Running ... ...   0.012 in (0.305 mm)
            Timing   ... ...   0.021 in (0.533 mm)
Inlet valve : opens   ... .   5º B T D C
        closes   ... .   45º B B D C
Exhaust valve : opens   ... ...   51º B B D C
          closes   ... ...   21º A T D C

Lubrication   ... .   Wet sump pressure fed
System pressure : running ... ...   70 lb/in^2 (4.92 Kg/cm^2)
               idling   ... ...   15 lb/in^2 (1.05 Kg/cm^2)
Oil pump   ... .   Internal gear, splined drive from camshaft
        outer ring end float ... ...   0.005 in (0.127 mm)
        inner rotor end float   ... ...   0.005 in (0.127 mm)
        outer ring to pump body diametrical clearance   ...   0.010 in (0.254 mm)
        rotor lobe clearance   ... ...   0.006 in (0.152 mm)
Capacity   ... .   1.75 gal (8 litres) per minute at 1000 rpm
Oil filter   ... .   Full flow: screw on, disposable cartridge type
By pass valve opens ... .   8 to 12 lb/in^2 (0.56 to 0.84 Kg/cm^2)
Oil pressure relief valve   ... ...   70 lb/in^2 (4.92 Kg/cm^2)
Relief valve spring : free length   ... ...   2.86 in (72.64 mm)
              fitted length ... ...   2.156 in (54.77 mm)
              load at fitted length   ... ...   13 to 14 lb ft (5.90 to 6.36 Kg f)

Torque Wrench Settings

	lb f ft	Kg f m
Big end cap nuts	35	4.8
Main bearing cap bolts	60	8.3
Cylinder head nuts:		
Up to 1975	40	5.5
1975 on	50	6.9
Rocker shaft bracket nuts	25	3.4
Gearbox adaptor plate bolts	25	3.4
Flywheel securing bolts	40	5.5
Sump securing bolts	6	0.8
Oil pump securing bolts	9	1.2
Crankshaft pulley bolt	70 to 80	9.68 to 11.06
Manifold nuts	15	2.07
Rocker cover retaining nuts	4	0.55
Tappet chest side covers	3 to 4	0.41 to 0.55
Thermostat housing nuts	8	1.11
Timing cover ¼ in bolts	6	0.83
Timing cover 5/16 in bolts	14	1.94
Water pump bolts	17	2.35
Crankshaft rear oil seal retainer bolts	25	3.5
Camshaft nut	60 to 70	8.30 to 9.68
Distributor clamp bolt	2.5	0.35
Water pump pulley set screws	18	2.49
Heater outlet adaptor	6 to 8	0.83 to 1.11
Thermal transmitter	16	2.21
Oil relief valve dome nut	40 to 45	5.53 to 6.22
Propeller shaft retaining bolt nuts	28	3.8

1 General description

The 1275 cc engine is a four cylinder overhead valve type fitted with a single S U carburettor.

Two valves per cylinder are mounted vertically in the cast iron cylinder head and run in pressed in valve guides. They are operated by rocker arms and pushrods from the camshaft which is located at the base of the cylinder bores in the left hand side of the engine.

The cylinder head has all fire siamesed inlet and exhaust parts on the left hand side. Cylinders 1 and 2 share an inlet port as do cylinders 3 and 4. Cylinders 1 and 4 have individual exhaust ports and cylinders 2 and 3 share an exhaust port.

The cylinder block and upper half of the crankcase are cast together and a pressed steel sump is bolted to the underside. Attached to the rear of the engine backplate is the clutch, bell housing and gearbox.

The dished crown pistons are made from anodised aluminium and have a solid skirt. Three compression and one oil control ring are fitted to each piston.

At the front of the engine is a single or double row chain driving the camshaft via the camshaft and crankshaft sprockets. The chain is tensioned by a spring loaded slipper type tensioner which automatically adjusts for chain stretch. The camshaft is supported by three steel backed white metal bearings. If these are replaced it is necessary to ream the bearings in position.

The overhead valves are operated by means of rocker arms mounted on the rocker shaft running along the top of the cylinder head. The rocker arms are actioned by pushrods and tappets which in turn rise and fall in sequence with the lobes on the camshaft. The valves are held closed by small springs.

The static and dynamically balanced forged steel crankshaft is supported by three renewable main bearings. Crankshaft end float is controlled by four semi-circular thrust washers two of which are located on either side of the centre bearing.

The centrifugal water pump and radiator cooling fan are driven, together with the dynamo or alternator, from the crnakshaft pulley wheel by a rubber/fabric 'fan' belt. The distributor is mounted towards the rear on the right hand side of the cylinder block and advances and retards the ignition timing mechanically and by vacuum. The distributor is driven at half crankshaft speed by a short shaft and skew gear from a skew gear on the camshaft. The oil pump is mounted at the rear of the engine and driven from the rear of the camshaft.

Bolted to the rear end of the crankshaft is the flywheel, to which is bolted the diaphragm spring clutch. Mounted on the circumference of the flywheel is the starter ring gear into which the starter motor drive engages when starting the engine.

2 Major operations with engine in place

The following major operations can be carried out to the engine with it in place in the car:
1 Removal and replacement of the cylinder head assembly.
2 Removal and replacement of sump.
3 Removal and replacement of the big end bearings.
4 Removal and replacement of the pistons and connecting rods.
5 Removal and replacement of the timing chain and gears.
6 Removal and replacement of the camshaft.

3 Major operations with engine removed

The following major operations must be corried out with the engine out of the car and on a bench or floor:
1 Removal and replacement of the main bearings.
2 Removal and replacement of the crankshaft.
3 Removal and replacement of the oil pump.
4 Removal and replacement of the flywheel.

4 Methods of engine removal

There are two methods of engine removal: complete with clutch and gearbox or without the gearbox. Both methods are described.

It is easier if a hydraulic trolley jack is used in conjunction with two axle stands, so that the car can be raised sufficiently to allow easy access underneath the car. Overhead lifting tackle will be necessary in both cases.

There is, however, one more method of removing the engine and gearbox. This is to first release all controls, cables, pipes and propeller shaft, then the engine and gearbox should be supported by lifting tackle or trolley jack and the mountings removed. The engine and gearbox can then be lowered to the floor with the lifting tackle or trolley jack. The front of the car should be jacked up high and the engine and gearbox drawn forwards. Using this method (possibly removing the cylinder head as well) can eliminate the need for hoist and may be of use in a confined space.

NOTE: Cars fitted with automatic transmission necessitating engine and transmission removal should have the transmission removed FIRST as described in Chapter 6, Section 9. The transmission is itself heavy.

5 Engine removal with gearbox

1 The complete unit can be removed easily in about three hours or less.
2 With the help of an assistant open and take the weight of the bonnet and undo and remove the four bolts, spring and plain washers. Carefully lift the bonnet up, releasing the prop, and then over the front of the car. Store in a safe place where it will not be scratched (photo).
3 Remove the expansion tank cap and radiator filler plug. Slacken the bottom hose clip and remove the hose from the radiator. Catch the coolant in a suitable container.
4 Undo and remove the cylinder block drain plug located towards the rear left hand side of the engine (photo). Try to catch any coolant left. Try also to keep the floor dry.
5 Disconnect the negative and then the positive battery terminals and tuck the leads to the rear of the battery (photo).
6 Slacken and remove all the coolant hoses left connected between the engine and radiator and the heater:
    Top hose at thermostat elbow end (photo A).
    Bottom hose heater connection (photo B).
    Bottom hose at water pump (photo C and D).
    Expansion tank hose (photo E).
7 It will be found easier to work in the engine compartment if the bonnet support is removed. Using a screwdriver ease the clip from the support and unhook the support from its bracket on the front panel (photo).
8 Slacken the rear heater hose clip from the union on the top rear of the cylinder head. Pull off the hose and tuck back out of the way (photo).
9 Undo and remove the two bolts, plain and spring washer securing the top radiator support brackets to the front panel (photo).
10 Undo and remove the two bolts, plain and spring washers that secure the top radiator support brackets to the side panels (photo). Lift away the two top support brackets, carefully detaching the rubber insert from the mounting peg on the radiator (photo).
11 The radiator may now be lifted upwards and away from the car (photo). Photo 5.11B shows the rubber insert in one of the two lower radiator mounting brackets.
12 Slacken the accelerator cable to linkage clamp bolt and withdraw the accelerator inner cable (photo).
13 Using two open ended spanners slacken the choke control cable clamping nut and withdraw the inner cable (photo). Carefully release the two cables from the outer cable support bracket and withdraw (photo).

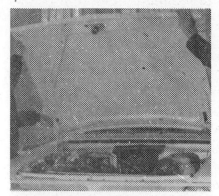
5.2. Two people are needed

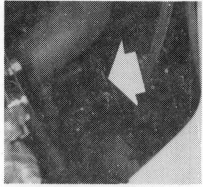
5.4. Note the flow of coolant

5.5. Negative (-) terminal to earth

5.6A. Always use a large enough screw-driver

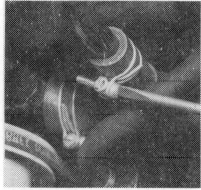
5.6B. Manipulate the hoses to clear the screwdriver

5.6C. Hold the clip to stop it slipping

5.6D. Pull firmly but not fearcely

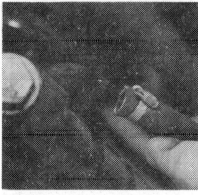
5.6E. Use a jubilee type clip to replace this one

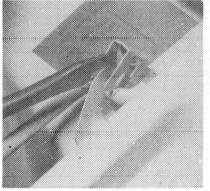
5.7. A wide blade is needed

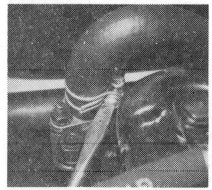
5.8. Slide the clip upwards before pulling the hose

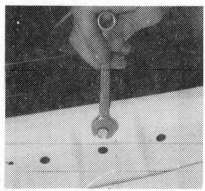
5.9. Try not to scratch the paint

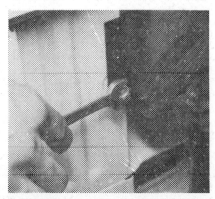
5.10A. An open-end or ring will do

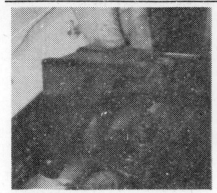

5.10B. Pull off the rubber grommet

5.11A. Mind the fan blades

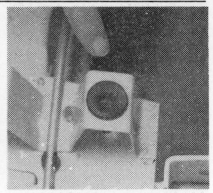

5.11B. Renew if perished

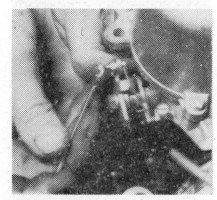

5.12. Use a spanner, not pliers!

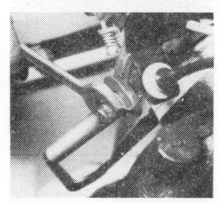

5.13A. Use two open-enders

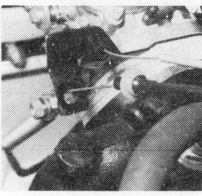

5.13B. A firm pull will release

14 Detach the accelerator linkage spring from its lower attachment (photo).

15 Slacken the clip securing the hose to the carburettor body and carefully detach the hose (photo). Then pull the fuel hose from the union on the carburettor float chamber (photo). Plug the end with a pencil to stop dirt ingress. Also disconnect the fuel tank feed pipe from the pump inlet union.

16 Undo and remove the wing nut and fibre washer securing the air cleaner body to the carburettor (photo), and lift away the air cleaner lid, element and body (photo).

17 Undo and remove the two nuts and spring washers securing the carburettor to the inlet manifold studs (photo), and ease the carburettor away from the inlet manifold (photo).

18 Lift the metal shield away from the inlet manifold (photo).

19 Undo and remove the two exhaust manifold to down pipe clamp nuts (photo) and lift away the two halves of the clamp (photo).

20 Slacken the hose clip at the inlet manifold union and ease off the hose (photo).

21 Undo and remove the six nuts and large washers securing the inlet/exhaust manifold to the side of the cylinder head. Note that the second nut from the front also secures the heater pipe support, (photo). Draw the manifold away from the cylinder head studs and lift away (photo). Tie the exhaust downpipe to the left hand wing valance.

22 Working under the car, undo and remove the one nut and bolt that secures the braided earth cable to the engine (photo).

23 Mark the spark plug H T cables to ease refitting in the correct order and disconnect from the spark plugs. Then release the HT cable from the centre of the ignition coil, spring back the two clips securing the distributor cap to the distributor boyd and lift away the distributor cap and HT leads. (photo). Disconnect the LT wiring to the distributor, ignition coil, oil pressure, switch and thermal transmitter.

24 Working under the car undo and remove the one bolt and spring washer securing the speedometer cable retainer to the

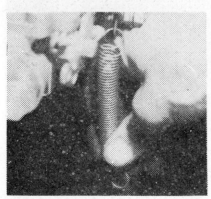

5.14. Try not to overstretch

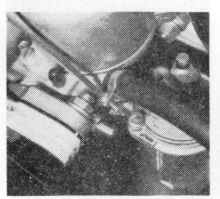

5.15A. A long phillips screwdriver

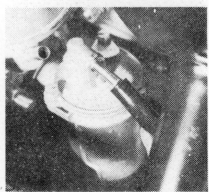

5.15B. Again a firm pull will release

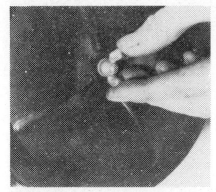
5.16A. Recover the washer underneath

5.16B. This is a clean filter

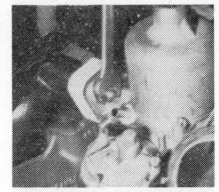
5.17A. Use an open-ender only

5.17B. Use both hands to pull off square

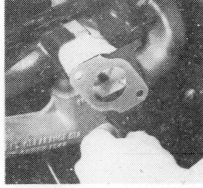
5.18. Release carefully

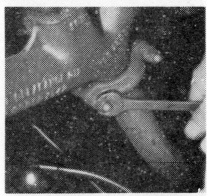
5.19A. A ring spanner may be better

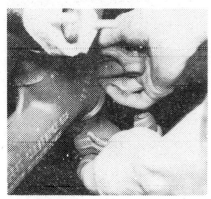
5.19B. Undo both bolts

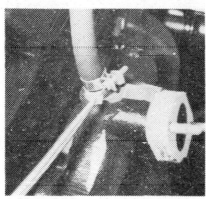
5.20. Release this hose now

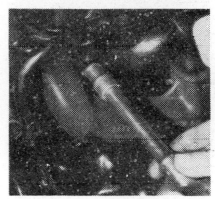
5.21A. A socket is most suitable

5.21B. Pull off square

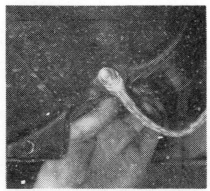
5.22. Two spanners are needed

5.23. Lift the clips

gearbox extension housing (photo). Lift away the retainer and withdraw the speedometer cable. Tuck the end of the cable back out of the way so it is not damaged.

25 Using a hydraulic jack support the weight of the gearbox. Mark the gearbox and propeller shaft mating flanges to ease re-fitting in their original positions. Undo and remove the four self locking nuts and bolts (photo).

26 Undo and remove the two bolts, spring and plain washers securing the gearbox mounting bracket to the underside of the body (photo). Then undo and remove the one bolt and spring washer securing the mounting bracket to the underside of the gearbox (photo). Lift away the mounting, disconnect the clutch hydraulic pipe from the slave cylinder.

27 Place a rope sling or chain around the engine and support its weight using an overhead hoist. Make sure that there is no possibility of these slipping when the unit is being removed as it has to be lifted out at a steep angle.

28 Undo and remove the two nuts, bolts and spring washers securing the engine mountings to the body shell brackets (photo).

29 If the gearbox is to be separated from the engine when away from the vehicle undo and remove the two bolts and spring washers securing the sump extension bracket to the underside of the clutch bellhousing now (photo).

30 Unscrew and remove the self tapping screws securing each carpet finisher to the door sill. Lift away the finisher and carpet-ing so exposing the gear change lever rubber moulding retaining plate (photo).

31 Undo and remove the self tapping screws securing the gear change lever rubber moulding retaining plate to the floor panel (photo). Lift away the plate. Then slide the rubber moulding and foam sleeve up the gear change lever (photo). Note that sealer is used under the rubber moulding flange.

32 Turn the gear change lever retaining cup in an anti-clockwise direction so releasing the bayonet fixing (photo). Ease the gear change lever up, at the same time being prepared to depress the plunger and spring in the fulcrum ball (photo). Recover the plunger and spring from the fulcrum ball (photo).

33 Check that no controls, cables or pipes have been left connected to the engine or gearbox and that they are safely tucked to one side where they will not catch as the unit is being removed.

34 Lower the jack supporting the weight of the gearbox and commence raising the engine. Note the steep angle that must be attained to ensure clearance of the body. Continue raising the engine until the rear of the sump is clear of the front cross member. The rear of the gearbox can now be lifted by hand over this cross member as either the car is pushed rearwards or the hoist is drawn away from the engine compartment (photo). Lower the unit to the ground, away from the car.

35 Check that the engine compartment and floor area around the car are clear of loose nuts and bolts as well as tools.

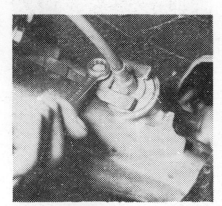
5.24. Use a ring spanner

5.25. This will be fairly tight

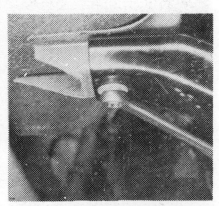
5.26A. This nut may be corroded

5.26B. This one will probably be oily

5.28. Check the mounting for slop

5.29. Release at this stage

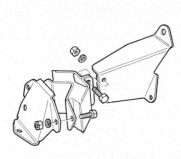
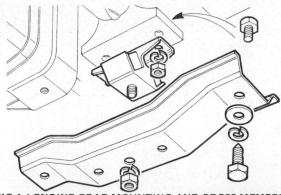

FIG.1.3 ENGINE FRONT MOUNTING　　　**FIG.1.4 ENGINE REAR MOUNTING AND CROSS MEMBER**

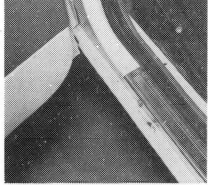

5.30. It is difficult to put back, release carefully!

5.31A. Self tapping

5.31B. A sliding fit only

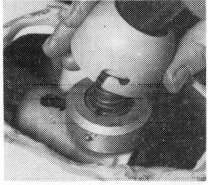
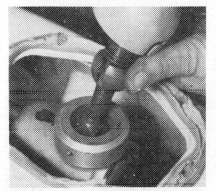
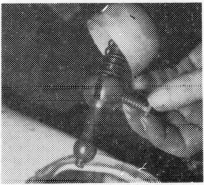

5.32A. Bayonet type fit

5.32B. Pull up straight and true

5.32C. Carefully place on one side

5.34. Note the steep angle necessary

6 Engine removal less gearbox

1 If it is necessary to remove only the engine, leaving the gearbox in position, the engine can be removed in about two and three quarter hours.

2 Follow the instructions given in Section 5 paragraphs 2 to 23 inclusive.

3 Using a hydraulic jack support the weight of the gearbox.

4 Undo and remove the nut and washer securing the heavy duty cable to the rear of the starter motor. Undo and remove the two nuts, bolts and spring washers that secure the starter motor to the engine back plate and gearbox bell housing and lift away the starter motor.

5 Place a rope sling or chains around the engine and support its weight using an overhead hoist.

6 Undo and remove the remaining nuts, bolts and spring washers securing the engine back plate to the gearbox bell housing. Then undo and remove the two nuts, bolts and spring washers securing the engine mountings to the main body member brackets.

7 Check that no controls, cables or pipes have been left connected to the engine and that they are safely tucked to one side where they will not be caught as the unit is being removed.

8 Raise the engine slightly to enable the engine mountings to clear their mounting brackets and move it forwards until the clutch is clear of the first motion shaft. Continue lifting the unit taking care not to damage the front valance and grille. Then lower the engine to the ground.

9 To complete, clear out any loose nuts and bolts and tools from the engine compartment and the floor area.

7 Separating the engine from the gearbox

1 With the engine and gearbox on the floor undo and remove the one remaining nut, bolt and spring washer securing the starter motor to the engine back plate and gearbox bell housing and lift away the starter motor.

2 Undo and remove the remaining nuts, bolts and spring washers securing the clutch bell housing to the engine back plate.

3 Carefully draw the gearbox rearwards, detaching it from the dowel located at the top rear of the engine block. It is important that the gearbox is not allowed to hang on the first motion shaft for its weight will bend it.

8 Dismantling the engine - general

1 It is obviously best to mount the engine on a dismantling stand, but as this is not likely to be available, stand the engine on a strong bench to be at a comfortable working height. It can be dismantled on the floor but it is not desirable.

2 During the dismantling process take great care to keep the exposed parts free from dirt. Firstly, thoroughly clean down the outside of the engine, removing all traces of oil and congealed dirt. Use paraffin or Gunk. The latter will make the job much easier for, after the solvent has been applied and allowed to stand for a time, a water can be used to wash off the solvent with all the dirt. If the dirt is thick and deeply embedded, work the solvent into it with a wire brush. Finally, wipe down the exterior of the engine with a rag and only then, when it is quite clean, should the dismantling process begin. As the engine is stripped, clean each part in a bath of paraffin or petrol.

3 Never immerse parts with oilways in paraffin (for example, the crankshaft). To clean them, wipe down carefully with a petrol dampened cloth. Oilways can be cleaned out with nylon pipe cleaners. If an airline is available, all parts can be blown dry and the oilways blown through as an added precaution.

4 Re-use of old engine gaskets is false economy and will lead to oil and water leaks, if nothing worse. Always use new gaskets throughout. However, do not throw the old gaskets away, for it happens that an immediate replacement may not be found and the old gasket is then very useful as a template. Hang up the old gaskets as they are removed, on a suitable hook.

5 To strip the engine it is best to work from the top down. The underside of the crankcase when supported on wood blocks acts as a firm base. When the stage where the crankshaft and connecting rods have to be removed, is reached, the engine can be turned on its side and all other work carried out with it in this position.

6 Wherever possible, replace nuts, bolts and washers finger tight from wherever they were removed. This helps avoid loss and muddle later. If they cannot be replaced lay them out in such a fashion that it is clear from whence they came.

9 Removing ancillary engine components

Before basic engine dismantling begins it is necessary to strip it of ancillary components as follows:

Dynamo or alternator
Distributor
Thermostat
Oil filter cartridge
Inlet/exhaust manifold and carburettor
Mechanical fuel pump

It is possible to strip all these items with the engine in the car if it is merely the individual items that require attention. Presuming the engine to be out of the car and on the bench, and that the item mentioned is still on the engine, follow this procedure:

1 Slacken off the dynamo/alternator retaining bolts and remove the unit with its adjustment link.

2 To remove the distributor first disconnect the vacuum advance/retard pipe from the side of the distributor, (not fitted to 1.3 H C engine). Undo and remove the two screws with spring and plain washers that secure the distributor clamp flange to the cylinder block and lift away the distributor and clamp flange.

3 Remove the thermostat cover by undoing and removing the three nuts and spring washers which hold it in position. Lift away the cover and gasket, followed by the thermostat itself.

4 Remove the oil filter cartridge by simply unscrewing it from the side of the cylinder block.

5 Undo and remove the six nuts and washers that secure the inlet/exhaust manifold assembly to the side of the cylinder head. If the carburettor is still mounted on the inlet manifold release it from the petrol feed pipe from the pump. Lift off the manifold assembly and recover the gasket.

6 Remove the mechanical fuel pump by unscrewing the two retaining nuts and spring washers which hold it to the block. Release it from the petrol feed pipe to the carburettor float chamber and lift away.

The engine is now stripped of all ancillary components and is ready for major dismantling to begin.

10 Cylinder head removal - engine in car

1 Drain the cooling system as described in Chapter 2.

2 Detach the distributor vacuum pipe from the carburettor.

3 Undo and remove the two rocker cover securing bolts, lifting brackets and washers and lift away the rocker cover and its gasket.

4 Slacken the by pass hose clip at the water pump end of the hose (photo).

5 Undo and remove the three nuts and spring washers securing the thermostat cover to the top of the cylinder head. Lift the cover from the three studs and recover the gasket. The thermostat may now be lifted out from its location.

6 Detach the thermal transmitter cable from the unit on the side of the cylinder head (photo).

7 Slacken the hose clips and remove the breather hose and fuel hose from the carburettor. Then undo and remove the two nuts and spring washers securing the carburettor to the inlet manifold. Lift the carburettor from the studs and recover the metal heat shield.

8 Undo and remove the one manifold nut that secures the metal heater pipe support bracket. Slacken the hose clips on either end

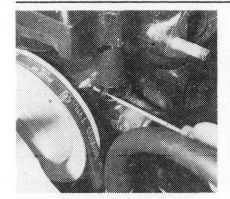

10.4 Use a thin blade screwdriver here

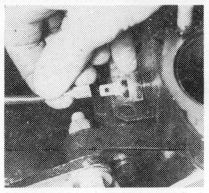

10.6. Clean off first before releasing

10.11. This is a lock nut

10.12. Use a socket if possible

10.14. Lift up straight

10.15. Always keep the pushrods in order

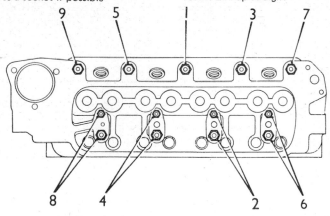

FIG.1.5 CYLINDER HEAD NUT LOOSENING SEQUENCE

10.16. Be patient and careful

of the metal heater pipe and detach the hoses. Lift away the metal heater pipe. Recover the one manifold washer from the stud. Undo and remove the two nuts securing the exhaust manifold to downpipe clamp. Part and lift away the two halves of the clamp. Undo and remove the remaining nuts and washers securing the manifold assembly to the side of the cylinder head. Lift away the manifold assembly and recover the gasket.

9 Slacken the heater hose clip on the union at the rear of the cylinder head. Pull the hose off the union.

10 Mark the spark plug H T leads to ensure correct refitting and detach the leads from the spark plugs. Spring back the distributor cap spring clips and lift off the distributor cap. Place to one side of the engine compartment.

11 Slacken the eight nuts securing the rocker shaft pedestals to the cylinder head in a progressive manner. Remove the eight nuts and washers (photo).

12 Slacken the remaining cylinder head nuts on a progressive manner, in the order shown in Fig.1.5 (photo).

13 Recover the locking tab from no 2 rocker shaft bracket.

14 Lift the rocker shaft from the top of the cylinder head (photo).

15 Remove the push rods, keeping them in the order in which they were removed (photo). The easiest way to do this is to push them through a sheet of thin card in the correct sequence.

16 The cylinder head can now be removed by lifting upwards. If the head is jammed, try to rock it to break the seal. Under no circumstances try to prise it apart from the block with a screwdriver or cold chisel as damage will be done to the faces of the head or block. If the head will not readily free, turn the engine over using the starter motor as the compression in the cylinders will often break the cylinder head joint. If this fails to work, strike the head sharply with a plastic headed or wooden hammer, or with a metal hammer onto a piece of wood on the head. Under no circumstances hit the head directly with a metal hammer as this may cause the iron casting to fracture. Several sharp taps with a hammer at the same time pulling upwards should free the head. Lift the head off and place on one side (photo).

11 Cylinder head removal - engine on bench

The sequence for removal of the cylinder head with the engine on the bench is basically identical to the later operations for removal with the engine in the car. Refer to Section 10 and follow the instructions given in paragraphs 2 to 5, 7 to 10, 12, and 14 to 20.

12 Valve removal

1   The valves are easily removed from the cylinder lead. Compress each spring in turn with a valve spring compressor until the two halves of the collets can be removed. Release the compressor and lift away the two collets, spring top caps, the spring oil seal (inlet valves only) and the valve (Fig.1.6).

2   If, when the valve spring compressor is screwed down, the valve spring top cup refuses to free and expose the split collet, do not continue to screw down on the compressor as there is a likelihood of damaging it. Gently tap the top of the tool directly over the cap with a light hammer. This should free the cap. To avoid the compressor jumping off the valve retaining cap when it is tapped, hold the compressor firmly in position with one hand.

3   It is essential that the valves are kept in their correct sequence unless they are so badly worn that they are to be renewed. If they are going to be reused, place them in a sheet of card having eight holes numbered 1 to 8 corresponding with the relative positions. Also keep the valve springs, caps etc in this same order.

13 Valve guide - removal

Valve guide removal is a simple task but it is not recommended that you should do this because their replacement is too difficult to do accurately. Leave their removal and insertion to a specialist engineering shop.

14 Rocker assembly - dismantling

1   To dismantle the rocker assembly, release the rocker shaft locating screw, remove the split pins, flat and spring washers from each end of the shaft and slide from the shaft the shims, pedestals, rocker arms and rocker spacing springs.

2   From the end of the shaft undo the plug which gives access to the inside of the rocker which can now be cleaned of sludge etc. Ensure the rocker arm lubricating holes are clear.

15 Timing cover, gears and chain - removal

The timing cover, gears and chain can be removed with the engine in the car provided the radiator and fan belt are removed. The procedure for removing the timing cover, gears and chain is otherwise the same irrespective of whether the engine is in the car or on the bench.

1   Bend back the locking tab of the crankshaft pulley locking washer under the crankshaft pulley retaining bolt, and with a large socket remove the bolt and lock washer (Fig.1.7).

2   Placing two large screwdrivers or tyre levers behind the crankshaft pulley wheel at 180° to each other, carefully lever off the pulley. It is preferable to use a proper extractor if this is available, but damage will not occur if care is taken.

3   Remove the woodruff key from the crankshaft nose with a pair of pliers and note how the groove in the pulley is designed to fit over it. Place the woodruff key in a glass jar for it is a very small. Store carefully.

4   Unscrew the bolts holding the timing cover to the block. NOTE: that three different sizes of bolt are used, and that each block makes use of a large flat washer as well as a spring washer.

5   Pull off the timing cover and gasket. With the timing cover off take off the oil thrower. Note which way round the oil

thrower is fitted.

6   Undo and remove the pivot screw and plain washer retaining the tensioner to the front engine plate. Lift away the tensioner and the second plain washer.

7   To remove the camshaft and crankshaft timing wheel complete with chain, first bend back the camshaft gear retaining nut lock washer and unscrew the nut and lift away the nut and lock washer. Ease each wheel forward a little at a time levering behind each gearwheel in turn with two large screwdrivers or tyre levers at 180° to each other. If the gear wheels are locked solid then it will be necessary to use a proper gearwheel and pulley extractor, and if one is available this should be used anyway in preference to levers. With both gearwheels safely off, remove the woodruff keys from the crankshaft and camshaft with a pair of pliers and place them in a jar for safe keeping. Note the number of very thin packing washers behind the crankshaft gearwheel and remove them very carefully.

16 Camshaft - removal

The camshaft can be removed with the engine on the bench or in the car. If the camshaft is to be removed with the engine in the car, the radiator and fan belt must be removed after the cooling system has been drained. The timing cover, gears and chain, must be removed as described in Section 15. It is also necessary to remove the distributor drive shaft as described in Section 17. With the drive gear out of the way; proceed:

1   Undo and remove the three bolts and spring washers which hold the camshaft locating plate to the block. The bolts are normally covered by the camshaft gearwheel (Fig.1.8). Remove the plate. Recover the tappets if they are still in place and keep in the correct order as fitted in the engine.

2   The camshaft can now be withdrawn. Take great care to remove the camshaft gently, and in particular ensure that the cam peaks do not damage the camshaft bearings as the shaft is pulled forward.

17 Distributor drive - removal

To remove the distributor drive with the sump still in position it is necessary first to remove one of the tappet cover bolts. With the distributor and the distributor clamp plate already removed, this is achieved as follows:

1   Unscrew the single retaining bolt and spring washer to release the distributor housing. With the distributor housing removed, if the sump is still in position, screw into the end of the distributor drive shaft a 5/16 inch UNF bolt. A tappet cover bolt is ideal for this purpose. The drive shaft can then be lifted out, the shaft being turned slightly in the process to free the shaft skew gear from the camshaft skew gear (Fig.1.9).

2   If the sump has already been removed then it is a simple matter to push the drive shaft out from inside the crankcase.

18 Sump, piston, connecting rod and big end bearing - removal

The sump, pistons and connecting rods can be removed with the engine still in the car or with the engine on the bench. If in the car, proceed as for removing the cylinder head with the engine in the car. If on the bench proceed as for removing the cylinder head with the engine out of the car. The pistons and connecting rods are drawn up out of the top of the cylinder bores.

1   Undo and remove the two bolts plain and spring washers securing the sump connecting plate to the gearbox bellhousing if the engine is still in the car (Fig.1.10).

2   Undo and remove the bolts and spring washers holding the sump in position. Lift away the sump and gasket.

3   Unscrew the oil suction pipe at the cylinder block.

4   The two bolts holding the oil cleaner support bracket (one on the centre and one on the rear main bearing caps) should now be unscrewed. The bracket complete with the strainer can now

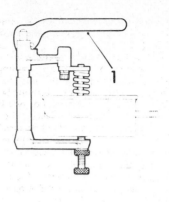

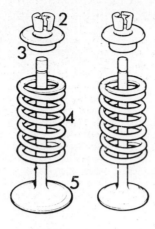

FIG.1.6 VALVE REMOVAL

1	Universal valve spring	3	Top cup
	compressor	4	Spring
2	Collets	5	Valve

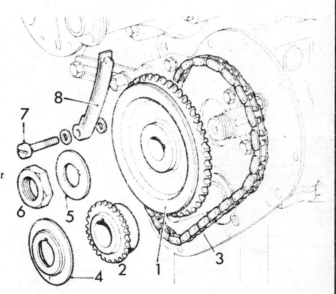

FIG.1.7 TIMING GEAR AND CHAIN ASSEMBLY

1	Camshaft gear	5	Lock washer
2	Crankshaft gear	6	Nut
3	Timing chain	7	Tensioner retaining bolt
4	Oil thrower	8	Tensioner

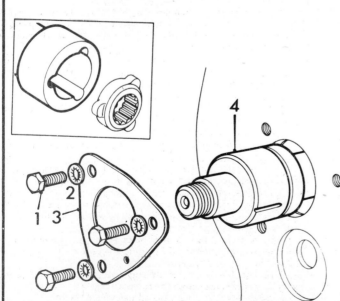

FIG.1.8 CAMSHAFT RETAINING PLATE

1	Plate securing bolt	4	Camshaft front end
2	Shakeproof washer		Inset: Oil pump end of cam-
3	Retaining plate		shaft and coupling

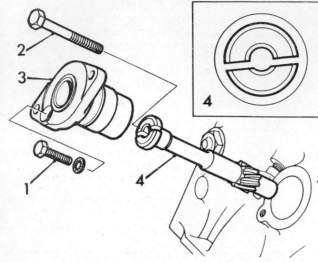

FIG.1.9 DISTRIBUTOR DRIVE SHAFT AND HOUSING

1   Distributor housing securing
   bolt and shakeproof washer
2   0.312 inch UNF bolt, 3.5
   inch (90 mm) long for shaft
   removal

3   Distributor drive housing
4   Distributor drive shaft
Inset: Final fitted position of
slot.

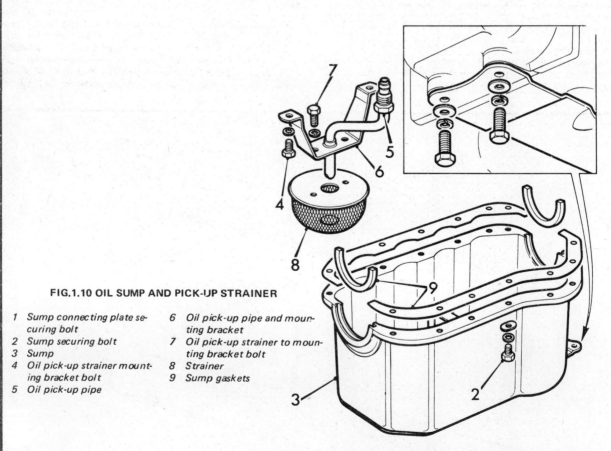

FIG.1.10 OIL SUMP AND PICK-UP STRAINER

1   Sump connecting plate securing bolt
2   Sump securing bolt
3   Sump
4   Oil pick-up strainer mounting bracket bolt
5   Oil pick-up pipe

6   Oil pick-up pipe and mounting bracket
7   Oil pick-up strainer to mounting bracket bolt
8   Strainer
9   Sump gaskets

be lifted away giving access to the big end bolts.

5   Undo and remove the big end cap retaining nuts using a socket and remove the big end caps one at a time, taking care to keep them in the right order and the correct way round. Also ensure that the shell bearings are also kept with their correct connecting rods and caps for inspection. Normally, the numbers 1 to 4 are stamped on adjacent sides of the big end caps and connecting rods, indicating which cap fits on which rod and which way round the cap fits. If no numbers or lines can be found then scratch mating marks across the joint from the rod to the cap with a sharp screwdriver. One line for connecting rod number 1, two for connecting rod number 2 and so on. This will ensure there is no confusion later for it is most important that the caps go back in the position on the connecting rods from which they were removed.

If the big end caps are difficult to remove they may be gently tapped with a soft hammer.

6   To remove the shell bearings, press the bearing opposite the groove in both the connecting rod and the connecting rod cap, and the bearings will slide out easily.

7   Withdraw the pistons and connecting rods upwards and ensure they are kept in the correct order, for replacement in the same bore. Refit the connecting rod caps and bearings to the rods for inspection and correct re-location.

19 Gudgeon pin - removal

A press type gudgeon pin is used and requires a special BLMC tool number 18G 1150 with adaptor 18G 1150A to remove and replace the pin. This tool is shown in Fig.1.11 and must be used in the following manner:

1   Securely hold the hexagonal body in a firm vice and screw back the large nut until it is flush with the end of the main centre screw.

Well lubricate the screw and large nut as they have to withstand high loading. Now push the centre screw in until the nut touches the thrust race.

2   Fit the adaptors number 18G 1150A onto the main centre screw with the piston ring cutaway positioned uppermost. Then slide the parallel sleeve with the groove end first onto the centre screw.

3   Fit the piston with the 'FRONT' OR 'V' mark on towards the adaptor on the centre screw. This is important because the gudgeon pin bore is offset and irreparable damage will result if fitted the wrong way round. Next fit the remover/replacer bush on the centre screw with the flange end towards the gudgeon pin.

4   Screw the stop nut onto the main centre screw and adjust it until approximately 0.032 inch (0.8 mm) end play ('A' in Fig.1.11) exists, and lock the stop nut securely with the lock screws. Now check that the remover/replacer bush and parallel sleeve are positioned correctly in the bore on both sides of the piston. Also check that the curved face of the adaptor is clean and slide the piston onto the tool so it fits into the curved face of the adaptor with the piston rings over the cut away.

5   Screw the large nut up to the thrust race and holding the lockscrew turn the large nut with a ring spanner or long socket until the piston pin is withdrawn from the piston.

20 Piston ring removal

1   To remove the piston rings, slide them carefully over the top of the piston, taking care not to scratch the alloy off the piston. Never slide them off the bottom of the piston skirt. It is very easy to break piston rings if they are pulled off roughly. This operation should be done with extreme caution. It is helpful to use an old 0.020 inch feeler gauge, to ease their removal.

2   Lift one end of the piston ring to be removed out of its groove and insert the end of the feeler gauge under it. Turn the feeler

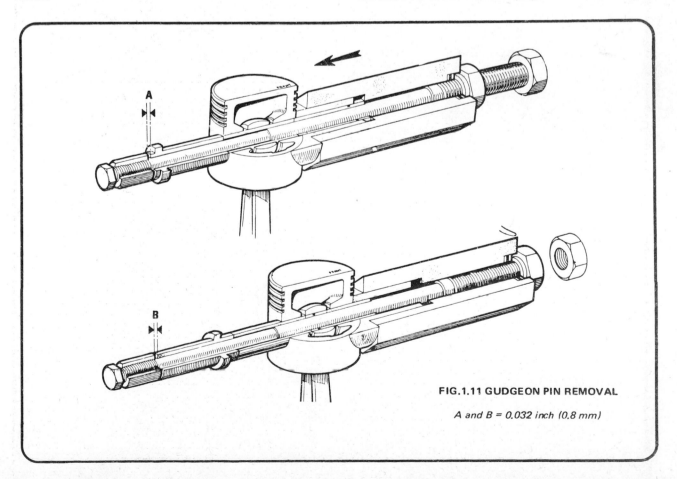

FIG.1.11 GUDGEON PIN REMOVAL

A and B = 0.032 inch (0.8 mm)

gauge slowly round the piston and as the ring comes out of its rests on the land above. It can then be eased off the piston with the feeler gauge stopping it from slipping into any empty grooves if it is any but the top piston ring that is being removed.

21 Flywheel and engine back plate - removal

Having removed the clutch (see chapter 5) the flywheel and engine back plate can be removed. It is only possible for this operation to be carried out with the engine out of the car.
1 Undo and remove the six bolts securing the flywheel to the end of the crankshaft. Lift away the shaped lock washer and the flywheel (Fig.1.12).
2 Some difficulty may be experienced in removing the bolts by rotation of the crankshaft every time pressure is put on the spanner. Lock the crankshaft in position while the bolts are removed with a wooded wedge placed between the crankshaft and the side of the block inside the crankcase.

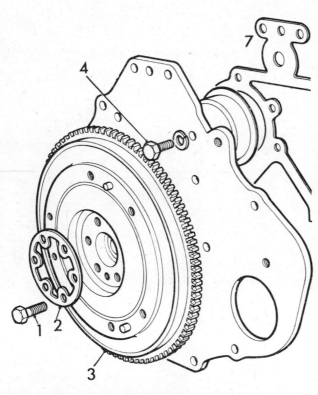

FIG.1.12 ENGINE BACKPLATE AND FLYWHEEL

1 Flywheel securing plate
2 Lock washer
3 Flywheel
4 Backplate securing bolt
5 Backplate
6 Oil pump cover
7 Gasket

3 The engine back plate is held in position by a number of bolts and spring washers of varying size. Release the bolts noting where the different size bolts fit then place them together to avoid their becoming lost. Lift away the back plate from the block complete with the paper gasket.

22 Crankshaft and main bearing - removal

Drain the engine oil, remove the timing gears and remove the sump, the oil gauze filter and suction pipe, the big end bearings, flywheel and engine backplate as already described. Removal can only be attempted with the engine on the bench.
1 Undo and remove the six bolts securing the main bearing caps to the cylinder block. Then remove the two bolts which hold the front main bearing cap against the engine front plate
2 Remove the main bearing caps and the bottom half of each bearing shell, taking care to keep the bearing shells in the right caps. When removing the centre bearing cap, note the bottom semi-circular halves of the thrust washers, one half lying on either side of the main bearing. Lay them with the centre bearing along the correct side.
3 Slightly rotate the crankshaft to free the upper halves of the bearing shells and thrust washers which should now be lifted away and placed over the correct bearing cap.
4 Remove the crankshaft by lifting it away from the crankcase.

23 Lubrication system - description

A force feed system of lubrication is fitted with oil circulated around the engine from the sump below the cylinder block. The level of engine oil in the sump is indicated by the dipstick which is fitted on the right hand side of the engine. The optimum level is indicated by the maximum mark. The level of oil in the sump, ideally, should neither be above or below this line. Oil is replenished via the filler cap in the front of the rocker cover.

The oil pump is mounted at the end of the crankcase and is driven by the crankshaft. It is of Holborn Eaton concentric rotor type and is of the non draining variety to allow rapid pressure build up when starting from cold.

Oil is drawn from the sump through a gauge screen in the oil scratiner and is sucked up the pick-up pipe and drawn into the oil pump. From the oil pump it is forced under pressure along a gallery on the right hand side of the engine, and through drillings to the big end, main and camshaft bearings. A small hole in each connecting rod allows a jet of oil to lubricate the cylinder wall with each revolution.

From the camshaft front bearing oil is fed through drilled passages in the cylinder block and head to the front rocker pedestal where it enters the hollow rocker shaft. Holes drilled in the hollow rocker shaft allow for lubrication of the rocker arms, the valve stems and pushrod ends. This oil is at a reduced pressure to the oil delivered to the crankshaft bearings. Oil from the front camshaft bearing also lubricates the timing gears and timing chain. Oil returns to the sump by various passages, the tappets being lubricated by oil returning via the push rod drillings in the block.

A full flow cartridge type filter is fitted and oil passes through this filter before it reaches the main oil gallery. The oil is passed directly from the oil pump to the filter.

24 Oil filter - removal and replacement

The external oil filter is of the disposable cartridge type and is located on the right hand side of the engine (Fig. 1.13).

To renew the oil filter unscrew the old cartridge from the filter head and discard it. Smear the seal on the new filter with a little oil and position it on the filter head. Screw it on and tighten with the hands only. Do not attempt to tighten with a spanner or strap wrench. If the filter proves to be excessively tight it can be pierced and tapped off.

25 Oil pressure relief valve - removal and replacement

To prevent excessive oil pressure - for example when the engine oil is thick and cold - an oil pressure relief valve is built into the right-hand side of the engine at the rear. The relief valve is identified externally by a large 9/16 inch domed hexagon nut (Fig.1.14).

To dismantle the valve unscrew the domed nut and remove it complete with sealing washer. The relief spring and valve can then be easily extracted.

In position the valve fits over the opposite end of the relief valve spring resting in the dome of the hexagon nut, and bears against a machining in the block. When the oil pressure exceeds 70 lb/sq in (4.92 Kg/cm^2), the valve is forced off its seat and the oil bypasses it and returns via a drilling directly into the sump.

Check the tension of the spring by measuring its length. If it is shorter than 2.86 inch (72.64 mm) it should be replaced with a new spring.

Examine the valve for signs of fitting which, if evident, it should be carefully lapped in using cutting paste. Remove all traces of paste when a good seating has been obtained.

Reassembly of the relief valve is the reverse sequence to removal.

26 Oil pump - removal and dismantling

Oil pump removal is an operation which can only be carried out with the engine out of the car. Prior to removing the pump it is necessary to remove the clutch, flywheel, and engine backplate. The oil pump is connected to the camshaft via a shaped coupling inserted in the rear of the camshaft.

1 Bend back the locking tabs on the four securing bolts that hold the pump to the block. (Fig.1.15). Unscrew the bolts and remove them complete with shaped tab washers.

2 The oil pump cover can now be removed, complete with drive shaft and inner rotor and coupling.

3 To dismantle the oil pump undo the one screw securing the two halves of the pump body together. Carefully ease the pump cover from the two dowels on the pump body and lift out the rotors.

27 Engine - examination and renovation - general

With the engine stripped and all parts thoroughly cleaned, every component should be examined for wear. The following items should be checked and, where necessary, renewed or renovated as described later.

28 Crankshaft - examination and renovation

1 Examine the crankpin and main journal surfaces for signs of scoring or scratches, check the ovality of the crankpins at different positions with a micrometer. If more than 0.001 inch (0.0254mm) out of round, the crankpins will have to be reground. It will also have to be reground if there are any scores or scratches are present. Also check the journals in the same fashion.

2 Centre main bearings are prone to failure. This is not always immediately apparent, but slight vibration in an otherwise normally smooth engine and a very slight drop in oil pressure under normal conditions are clues. If the centre main bearing is suspected of failure it should be investigated immediately by dropping the sump and removing the centre main bearing cap. Failure to do this will result in a badly scored centre main journal. If it is necessary to regrind the crankshaft and fit new bearings an engineering works will be able to decide how much metal to grind off and be able to supply the correct undersize shells to fit.

3 While you're examining the crankshaft, don't forget the gearbox input shaft spigot bush at the rear end. The input shaft should be a snug fit in the bush, but if there's wear evident

you'll have to tap the bush 9/16 in UNF and screw in a suitable bolt; by pulling on the bolt head you'll be able to draw out the bush. When fitting the replacement, press it in until the end is flush with the counterbore.

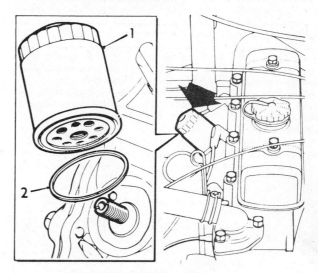

FIG.1.13 ENGINE OIL FILTER

1 Oil filter cartridge   2 Sealing ring

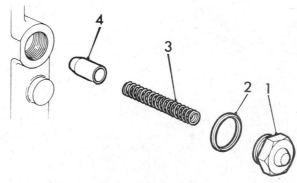

FIG.1.14 OIL PRESSURE RELIEF VALVE

1 Dome nut   3 Spring
2 Sealing washer   4 Valve

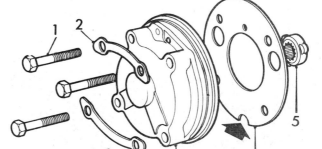

FIG.1.15 OIL PUMP REMOVAL

1 Oil pump securing bolt   4 Gasket. Note cutout
2 Tab washer   5 Oil pump coupling
3 Oil pump

29 Big end and main bearings - examination and renovation

1 Big end bearing failure is usually accompanied by a noisy knocking from the crankcase and a slight drop in oil pressure. Main bearing failure is accompanied by vibration which can be quite severe as the engine speed rises and falls, and a drop in oil pressure.

2 Bearings which have not broken up, but are badly worn will give rise to low oil pressure and some vibration. Inspect the big ends, main bearings and thrust washers for signs of general wear, scoring, fitting and scratches. The bearings should be a matt grey in colour. With lead — indium bearings should a trace of copper colour be noticed the bearings are badly worn, for the lead bearing has worn away to expose the indium underlay. Renew the bearings if they are in this condition or if there is any sign of scoring or fitting.

3 The undersizes available are designed to correspond with re-grind sizes ie 0.010 bearings are correct for a crankshaft regrind — 0.010 undersize. The bearings are infact slightly more than the stated undersize as running clearances have been allowed for during their manufacture.

4 Very long engine life can sometimes be achieved by changing big end bearings at 30,000 miles and main bearings at 50,000 miles, irrespective of bearing wear. Normally, crankshaft wear is infinitesimal and regular changes of bearings may ensure mileages of between 100,000 and 120,000 miles before crankshaft regrinding becomes necessary. Crankshafts normally have to be reground because of scoring due to bearing failure.

5 Once dismantled only refit new bearing shells. It is false economy to replace old bearings even if they have run for only an hour!

30 Cylinder bores - examination and renovation

1 The cylinder bores must be examined for taper, ovality, scoring and scratches. Start by carefully examining the top of the bores. If they are worn fractionally a very slight ridge will be found on the thrust side. This marks the top of the piston travel. You will have a good indication of the bore wear prior to dismantling the engine, or removing the cylinder head; Excessive oil consumption accompanied by blue smoke from the exhaust is a sure sign of worn cylinder bores and piston rings.

2 Measure the diameter of the bore just under the ridge with a micrometer and compare it with the diameter at the bottom of the bore, which is not subject to such wear. If the difference between the two measurements is more than 0.006 inch (0.1524 mm) then it will be necessary to fit a 'ring set' or to have the cylinders rebored and fit oversize pistons and rings. If no micrometer is available remove the rings from one piston and place the piston in each bore in turn about ¾ inch (19 mm) below the top of the bore. If an 0.010 inch (0.254 mm) feeler gauge can be slid between the piston and the cylinder wall on the thrust side of the bore then remedial action must be taken. Oversize pistons are available in the following sizes:

   + 0.010 inch (0.254 mm)   + 0.020 inch (0.508 mm)

3 These are accurately machined to just below these measurements so as to provide correct running clearances in bores bored out to the exact oversize dimensions.

4 If the bores are slightly worn but not so badly worn as to justify reboring them, special oil control rings can be fitted to the existing pistons which will restore compression and stop the engine burning oil. Several different types are available and the manufacturers instructions concerning their fitting must be followed closely.

31 Pistons and piston rings - examination and renovation

1 If the old pistons are to be refitted carefully remove the piston rings and then thoroughly clean them. Take particular care to clean out the piston ring grooves. Do not scratch the aluminium in any way. If new rings are to be fitted to the old pistons, then the top ring should be stepped so to clear the ridge left above the previous top ring. If a normal but oversize new ring is fitted it will hit the ridge and break, because the new ring will now have worn in the same way as the old, which will have worn in unison with the ridge.

2 Before fitting the rings on the pistons each should be inserted approximately 3 inches (76 mm) down the cylinder bore and the gap measured with a feeler gauge as shown in Fig.1.16. This should be between the limits given in the specifications at the beginning of this Chapter. It is essential that the gap is measured at the bottom of the ring travel, for if it is measured at the top of a worn bore and gives a perfect fit, it could easily seize at the bottom. If the ring gap is too small rub down the ends of the ring with a very fine file until the gap, is correct when fitted. To keep the rings square in the bore for measurement, line each one up in turn with an old piston in the bore upside down, and use

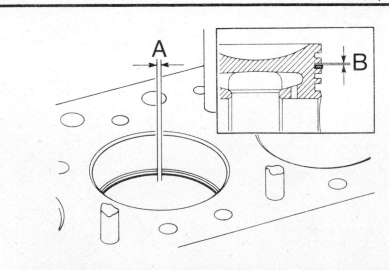

FIG.1.16 MEASUREMENT OF PISTON RING END GAP AND CLEARANCE

A End gap
B Ring to ring groove clearance

the piston to push the ring down about 3 inches (76 mm). Remove the piston and measure the piston ring gap.

3   When fitting new pistons and rings to a rebored engine the ring gap can be measured at the top of the bore as the bore will now not taper. It is not necessary to measure the side clearance in the piston ring grooves with rings fitted, as the groove dimensions are accurately machined during manufacture. When fitting new oil control rings to the pistons it may be necessary to have the grooves widened by machining to accept the new under rings. In this instance the manufacturer will make this quite clear and will supply the address to which the pistons must be sent for machining.

4   When new pistons are fitted; take great care to fit the exact size best suited to the particular bore of your engine. BLMC go one stage further than merely specifying one size piston for all standard bores. Because of very slight differences in cylinder machining during production it is necessary to select just the right piston for the bore. A range of different sizes are available either from the piston manufacturer or from the local BLMC stores.

5   Examination of the cylinder block face will show adjacent to each bore a small diamond shaped box with a number stamped in the metal. Careful examination of the piston crown will show a matching diamond and number. These are the standard piston sizes and will be the same for all bores. If the standard pistons are to be refitted or standard low compression pistons changed to standard high compression pistons, then it is essential that only pistons with the same number in the diamond are used. With larger pistons, the amount of oversize is stamped in an elipse on the piston crown.

6   On engines with tapered second and third compression rings, the top narrow side of the ring is marked with a 'T'. Always fit this side uppermost and carefully examine all rings for this mark before fitting.

32 Camshaft and camshaft bearings - examination and renovation

1   Carefully examine the camshaft bearings for wear. If the bearings are obviously worn or pitted or the metal underlay just showing through, then they must be renewed. This is an operation for your local BLMC garage or local engineering works as it demands the use of specialised equipment. The bearings are removed using a special drift after which the new bearings are pressed in, care being taken that the oil driving in the bearings line up with those in the block. With another special tool the bearings are

then reamed in position.

2   The camshaft itself should show no sign of wear, but, if very slight scoring marks on the cams are noticed, the score marks can be removed by gentle rubbing down with very fine emery cloth or an oil stove. The greatest care must be taken to keep the cam profiles smooth.

33 Valves and seats - examination and renovation

1   Examine the heads of the valves for pitting or burning, especially the heads of the exhaust valves. The valve seatings should be examined at the same time. If the pitting on the valves is very slight the marks can be removed by grinding the seats and valves together with coarse, and then fine valve grinding paste. Where bad pitting has occured to the valve seats it will be necessary to recut them and fit new valves. If the valve seats are so worn that they cannot be recut, then it will be necessary to fit new valve seat inserts. These latter two jobs should be entrusted to a BLMC garage or engineering works. In practice it is very seldom that the seats are so badly worn that they require renewal. Normally, it is the valve that is too badly worn, and you can easily purchase a new set of valves and match them to the seats by valve grinding.

2   Valve grinding is easily carried out:

Place the cylinder head upside down on a bench with a block of wood at each end to give clearance for the valve stems. Alternatively place the head at 45° to a wall with the combustion chambers facing away from the wall.

3   Smear a trace of coarse carborundum paste on the seat face and apply a suction grinding tool to the valve head as shown in Fig.1.17. With a semi-rotary action, grind the valve head to its seat, lifting the valve occasionally to redistribute the grinding paste. When a dull matt even surface finish is produced on both the valve seat and the valve, then wipe off the paste and repeat the process with fine carborundum paste, lifting and turning the valve to redistribute the paste as before. A light spring placed under the valve head will greatly ease this operation. When a smooth unbroken ring of light grey matt finish is produced, on both valve and valve seat faces, the grinding operation is complete.

4   Scrape away all carbon from the valve head and the valve stem. Carefully clean away every trace of grinding compound, taking great care to leave none in the ports or in the valve guides. Clean the valves and valve seats with a paraffin soaked rag then wipe with clean rag. (If an air line is available blow clean all parts).

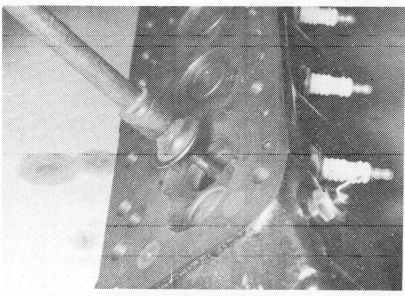

FIG.1.17 VALVE GRINDING

34 Timing gear and chain - examination and renovation

1 Examine the teeth on both the crankshaft gear wheel and the camshaft gear wheel for wear. Each tooth forms an inverted 'V' with the gear wheel periphery and if worn, the side of each tooth under tension will be slightly concave in shape when compared with the other side of the tooth ie one side of the inverted 'V' will be concave when compared with the other. If any sign of wear is present the gear wheels must be renewed.

2 Examine the links of the chain for side slackness and renew the chain if any slackness is noticeable when compared with a new chain. It is a sensible precaution to renew the chain every 30,000 miles (48,000 Km) and at a lesser mileage if the engine is stripped down for a major overhaul. The actual rollers on a very badly worn chain may be slightly grooved.

35 Rockers and rocker shaft - examination and renovation

1 Remove the threaded plug with a screwdriver from the end of the rocker shaft and thoroughly clean out the shaft. As it acts as the oil passages for the valve gear, clean out these passages and make sure they are quite clear. Check the shaft for straightness by rolling it on a flat surface. It is most unlikely that it will deviate from normal, but, if it does, you must purchase a new shaft. The surface of the shaft should be free from any worn ridges caused by the rocker arms. If any wear is present, renew the rocker shaft. Wear is likely to have occurred only if the rocker shaft oil holes have become blocked.

2 Check the rocker arms for wear of the rocker bushes, at the rocker arm face which bears on the valve stem, and of the adjusting ball ended screws. Wear in the rocker arm bush can be checked by gripping the rocker arm tip and holding the rocker arm in place on the shaft, noting if there is any lateral rocker arm shake. If any shake is present, and the arm is very loose on the shaft, remedial action must be taken. It is recommended that if a forged type of rocker arm is fitted it be taken to your local BLMC garage or engineering works to have the old bush drawn out and a new bush fitted. The correct placement of the bush shown in Fig. 1.18.

If a pressed steel rocker arm is fitted rebushing must not be undertaken but a new rocker arm obtained.

3 Check the tip of the rocker arm where it bears on the valve head, for cracking or serious wear on the case hardening. If none is present the rocker arm may be refitted, check the pushrods for straightness by rolling them on a flat surface. If bent they must be renewed.

36 Tappets - examination and renovation

Examine the bearing surface of the tappets which run on the camshaft. Any indentation in this surface or any cracks indicate serious wear and the tappets must be renewed. Thoroughly clean them out, removing all traces of sludge. It is most unlikely that the sides of the tappets will prove worn, but if they are a loose fit in their bores and can be readily rocked, they should be discarded and new tappets fitted. It is unusual to find worn tappets and any wear present is likely to occur only because of high mileages.

37 Flywheel starter ring gear - examination and renovation

1 If the teeth on the flywheel starter ring gear are badly worn, or if some are missing, then it will be necessary to remove the ring. This is achieved by splitting the old ring using a cold chisel. Care must be taken not to damage the flywheel during this process.

2 To fit a new ring gear, it will be necessary to heat it gently and evenly with an oxy-acetylene flame until a temperature of approximately 350° C is reached. (This is indicated by a grey/brown surface colour). With the ring gear at this temperature, fit

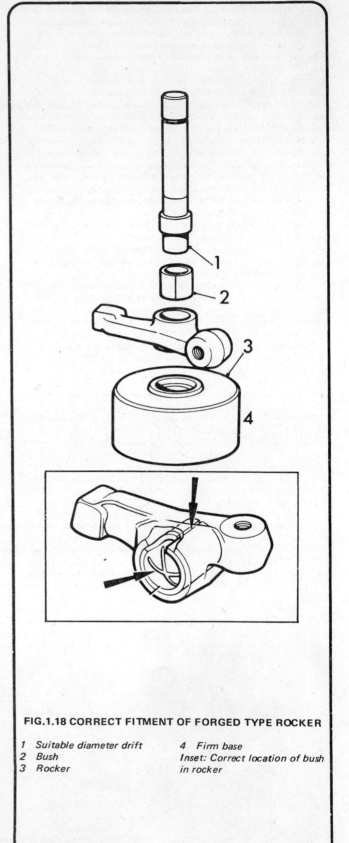

FIG.1.18 CORRECT FITMENT OF FORGED TYPE ROCKER

1 Suitable diameter drift	4 Firm base
2 Bush	Inset: Correct location of bush
3 Rocker	in rocker

it to the flywheel with the front of the teeth facing the clutch fitting end of the flywheel. The ring gear should be either pressed or lightly tapped onto its register and left to cool naturally when the contraction of the metal on cooling will ensure that it is a secure and permanent fit. Great care must be taken not to overheat the ring gear, as if this happens the temperature of the ring gear will be lost.

3 An alternative method is to use a high temperature oven to heat the ring.

4 Because of the need of oxy-acetylene equipment or a special oven it is not practical for refitment to take place at home. Take the flywheel and new starter ring to an engineering works willing to do the job.

38 Oil pump - examination and renovation

1 Thoroughly clean all the component parts in petrol and wipe dry with a clean non fluffy rag.

2 Fit the rotors into the pump body making sure the chamfered edge of the outer ring enters the pump body first.

3 Using a straight edge and feeler gauges check the end float of the inner rotor and outer ring. This should not exceed 0.005 inch (0.127 mm) Fig.1.19.

4 Using feeler gauges check the outer ring to pump body diametrical clearance which should not exceed 0.010 inch (0.254 mm).

5 Again using feeler gauges check the rotor lobe clearances which must not exceed 0.006 inch (0.152 mm).

6 If any of the readings taken in paragraphs 3,4 and 5 are in excess of the maximum limits quoted a new pump must be obtained.

39 Cylinder head and bore - decarbonisation

1 This operation can be carried out with the engine either in or out of the car. With the cylinder head off, carefully remove with a wire brush and blunt, plastic scraper all traces of carbon deposits from the combustion spaces and the ports. The valve stems and valve guides should also be freed from any carbon deposits. Wash the combustion spaces and posts down with petrol and scrape the cylinder head surface free of any foreign matter with the side of a steel rule or similar article. Take care not to scratch the surfaces.

2 Clean the pistons and top of the cylinder bores. If the pistons are still in the cylinder bores then it is essential that great care is taken to ensure that no carbon gets into the bores for this will scratch the cylinder walls or cause damage to the piston and rings. To stop it happening first turn the crankshaft so that two of the pistons are at TDC. Place a clean non-fluffy rag into the other two bores or seal them off with paper and masking tape. The waterways and pushrod holes should be covered with a small piece of masking tape to prevent particles of carbon entering the cooling system and damaging the water pump, or entering the lubrication system and causing damage to a bearing surface.

3 There are two schools of thought as to how much carbon ought to be removed from the piston union. One is that a ring of carbon should be left around the edge of the piston and on the cylinder bore wall as an aid to keep oil consumption low. Although this is probably true for engines with worn bores, on fresh engines however the tendency is to remove all traces of carbon

4 If all traces of carbon are to be removed, press a little grease into the gap between the cylinder walls and the two pistons which are to be worked upon. With a blunt scraper carefully scrape away all carbon from the piston crown, taking care not to scratch the aluminium. Also scrape away the carbon from the surrounding lip of the cylinder wall. When all carbon has been removed, scrape away the grease which will now be contaminated with carbon particles, taking care not to press any into the bores. To assist prevention of carbon build up the piston crown can be polished with a metal polish such as Brasso. Remove the rags or masking tape from the other two cylinders and turn the crankshaft so that the two pistons which were at the bottom are now at the top. Place non-fluffy rag into the other two bores or seal them off with paper and masking tape. Do not forget the waterways and oilways as well. Proceed as previously described.

5 If a ring of carbon is going to be left round the piston then this can be helped by inserting an old piston ring into the top of the bore to rest on the piston and ensure that carbon is not accidently removed. Check that there are no particles of carbon in the cylinder bores. Decarbonising is now complete.

40 Valve guides - examination and renovation

Examine the valve guides internally for wear. If the valves are a very loose fit in the guides and there is the slightest suspicion of lateral rocking, then new guides will have to be fitted, their correct location being shown in Fig.1.20. Try to compare them internally by visual inspection with a new guide as well.

41 Engine - reassembly - general

1 To ensure maximum life with minimum trouble from a rebuilt engine, not only must every part be correctly assembled but everything must be spotlessly clean, all the oilways must be clear, locking washers and spring washers must always be fitted where indicated and all bearings and other working surfaces must be thoroughly lubricated during assembly. Before assembly begins renew any bolts or studs the threads of which are in any way damaged, and whenever possible use new spring washers.

2 Apart from your normal tools, a supply of non-fluffy rag, an oil can filled with engine oil (an empty washing up liquid plastic bottle thoroughly cleaned and washed out will do), a supply of new spring washers, a set of new gaskets and a torque wrench should be collected together.

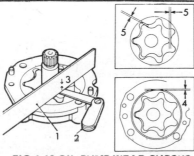
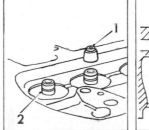
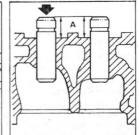

FIG.1.19 OIL PUMP WEAR CHECKS

1 Straight edge
2 Feeler gauge
3 Checking end-float of inner rotor and outer ring
4 Checking outer ring to pump body diametrical clearance
5 Checking rotor lobe clearances

FIG.1.20 LOCATION OF VALVE GUIDES

1 Oil seal (inlet valve only)
2 Valve guide
Dimension A = 0.540 in (13.72 mm)

42 Camshaft - replacement

1 Lightly lubricate the tappets and fit them into the same bores from which they were removed (photo).
2 Wipe the camshaft bearings and generously lubricate them with engine oil (photo).
3 Temporarily refit the camshaft gear wheel and locating plate and secure with the retaining nut. Using feeler gauges check the end float which should not exceed 0.003 to 0.007 inch (0.07 to 0.18 mm). If this maximum limit is exceeded obtain a new locating plate.
4 Remove the camshaft gear wheel retaining nut, gear wheel and locating plate.
5 Insert the camshaft into the crankcase gently, taking care not to damage the camshaft bearings with the sharp edges of the cams. Take care, the camshaft lobe edges are sharp! (photo).

43 Crankshaft - replacement

1 Ensure that the crankcase and that all oil ways are clear. A thin twist drill is useful for cleaning oilways out. If possible, blow them out with compressed air. Inject engine oil into the crankshaft oilways, now.
2 Replace the crankshaft rear main bearing oil deflector and secure with the three bolts and spring washers (photo).
3 Carefully clean away all traces of the protective grease with which new bearings are coated.
4 Fit the upper halves of the main bearing shells to their location in the crankcase. Note the tag which engages into the locating grooves (photo).
5 With the three upper bearing shells securely in place. wipe the lower bearing cap housings and fit the three lower shell bearings to their caps.
6 Wipe the recesses either side of the centre main bearing which locate the upper halves of the thrust washer.
7 Generously lubricate the crankshaft journals and the upper and lower main bearing shells. Apply a little grease to either side of the centre main bearing so as to retain the upper halves of the thrust washers.
8 Refit the upper thrust washers (the halves without tabs) to either side of the centre main bearing with the oil grooves outwards from the bearing (photo).
9 Carefully lower the crankshaft into position making sure it is the correct way round (photo).
10 During removal of the crankshaft gear wheel it should have been noted that there are shims behind the gear wheel. Replace the shims and then the Woodruff key (photo).
11 Apply a little non hardening sealer to the rear of the crankcase to which the rear main bearing cap fits (photo).
12 Replace the rear main bearing cap and lightly tighten the two securing bolts (photo).
13 Smear a little grease onto the thrust washer locations on either side of the centre main bearing cap and refit the lower halves of the thrust washers (the halves with tabs), with the lubrication grooves facing outwards, (photo). Refit the centre and front main bearing caps and lightly tighten the securing bolts.
14 Test the crankshaft for freedom of rotation. Should it be very stiff to turn or possess high spots a most careful inspection must be made, with a micrometer to trace the cause of the trouble. It is very seldom that any trouble of this nature will be experienced when fitting the crankshaft.
15 Tighten the main bearing bolts using a torque wrench set to 60 lb ft (8.3 Kg fm) (photo). Recheck the crankshaft for freedom of rotation.

44 Piston and connecting rod - reassembly

If the same pistons are being used, then they must be mated to the same connecting rod with the same gudgeon pin. If new pistons are being fitted it does matter which connecting rod they

are used with, but the gudgeon pins are not to be interchanged. As the gudgeon pin is a press fit a special BLMC tool 18G 1150 with adaptors 18G 1150A is required to fit the gudgeon pin as shown in Fig.1.11 and should be used as follows:
1 Unscrew the large nut and withdraw the centre screw from the body a few inches. Well lubricate the screw thread and correctly locate the piston support adaptor.
2 Carefully slide the parallel sleeve with the groove end last onto the centre screw, up as far as the shoulder. Lubricate the gudgeon pin and its bores in the connecting rod and piston with a graphited oil.
3 Fit the connecting rod and piston, side marked 'Front' or 'V' to the tool with the connecting rod entered on the sleeve up to the groove. Fit the gudgeon pin into the piston bore up to the connecting rod. Next fit the remover/replacer bush flange end towards the gudgeon pin.
4 Screw the stop nut onto the centre screw and adjust the nut to give a 0.032 inch (0.8 mm) end play, 'B' as shown in Fig.1.11). Lock the nut securely with the lock screw. Ensure that the curved face of the adaptor is clean and slide the piston on the tool so that it fits into the curved face of the adaptor with the piston rings over the adaptor cut-away.
5 Screw the large nut up the thrust race. Adjust the torque wrench to a setting of 16 lb ft (2.2 Kg fm) if of the 'click' type which will represent the minimum load for an acceptable fit. Use the torque wrench previously set on the large nut, and a ring spanner on the lock screw. Pull the gudgeon pin into the piston until the flange of the remover/replacer bush is 0.032 inch (0.8 mm) from the piston skirt. It is critically important that the flange is NOT allowed to contact the piston. Finally withdraw the BLMC service tool.
6 Should the torque wrench not 'click' or reach 16 lb ft (2.2 kg fm) throughout the pull, the fit of the gudgeon pin in the connecting rod is not within limits and the parts must be renewed.
7 Ensure that the piston pivots freely on the gudgeon pin and is free to slide sideways. Should stiffness exist wash the assembly in paraffin, lubricate the gudgeon pin with graphited oil and recheck. Again if stiffness exists dismantle the assembly and check for signs of ingrained dirt or damage.

45 Piston ring - replacement

1 Check that the piston ring grooves and oilways are thoroughly clean and unblocked. Piston rings must always be fitted over the head of the piston and never from the bottom (Fig.1.21).
2 Refitment is the exacting opposite procedure to removal, see section 20.
3 Set all ring gaps 90° to each other.
4 An alternative method is to fit the rings by holding them slightly open with the thumbs and both your index fingers. This method requires a steady hand and great care for it is easy to open the ring too much and break it.
5 The special oil control ring requires a special fitting procedure. First fit the bottom rail of the oil control ring to the piston and position it below the bottom groove. Refit the oil control expander into the bottom groove and move the bottom oil control ring rail up into the bottom groove. Fit the top oil control rail into the bottom groove.
6 Inspect the ends of the expander are butting out overlapping as shown in the inset in Fig.1.21.

46 Piston - replacement

Fit pistons, complete with connecting rods, to the cylinder bores as follows:
1 Wipe the cylinder bores clean with clean non-fluffy rag.
2 The pistons, complete with connecting rods, must be fitted to their bores from above. As each piston is inserted into the bore ensure that it is the correct piston/connecting rod assembly for that particular bore and that the front of the piston is towards the front of the bore assuming that the connecting rod is fitted

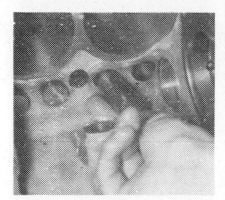
42.1. Oil the tappets well ......

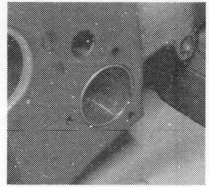
42.2. .... and the camshaft bearings

42.5. Go slowly and straight

43.2. Use a ring spanner

43.4. SPOTLESSLY CLEAN

43.8. Note the grease to retain them

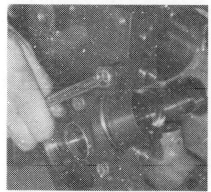
43.9. The crankshaft must be spotless and the bearings oiled

43.10. Do not forget the shims

43.11. A little bit of gasket cement

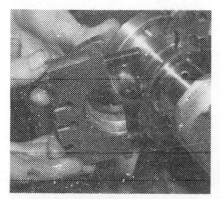
43.12. The bolts must be clear

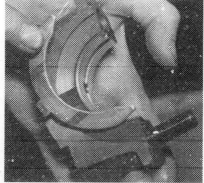
43.13. Note the tab locations

43.15. You must use a torque wrench

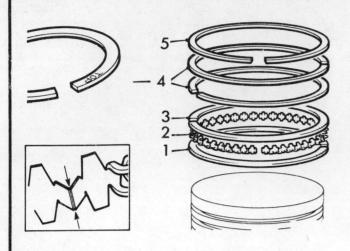

FIG.1.21 PISTON RINGS

1 Bottom rail of oil control ring
2 Expander of oil control ring
3 Top rail of oil control ring
4 Second and third taper rings
5 Top chromium plated ring
Inset: Expander ends correctly butted together

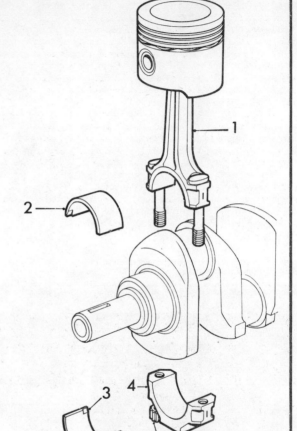

FIG.1.22 PISTON AND CONNECTING ROD ASSEMBLY

1 Connecting rod
2 Big end bearing shell (upper)
3 Big end bearing shell (lower)
4 Big end cap
5 Multi-sided nuts

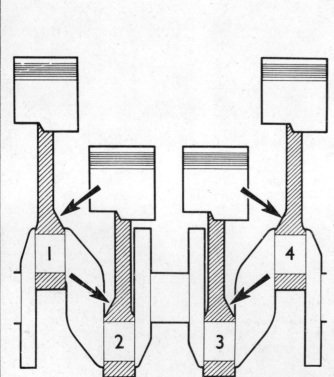

FIG.1.23 THE CORRECT POSITIONS OF THE OFFSETS ON THE CONNECTING ROD BIG ENDS

correctly ie, towards the front of the engine. Lubricate the piston well with clean engine oi. See Fig.1.23.

3 Check that the piston ring gaps are 90° to each other (photo).

4 The piston will slide into the bore only as far as the oil control ring and then it will be necessary to compress the piston rings into a clamp. The piston ring compressor should be fitted to the piston before it is inserted into the bore. (photo). If a proper piston ring clamp is not available then a suitable jubilee clip will do. Guide the piston into the bore until it reaches the ring compressor (photo). Gently tap the piston into the cylinder bore with a wooden or plastic hammer (photo).

47 Connecting rod to crankshaft - reassembly

1 Wipe the connecting rod half of the big end bearing location and the underside of the shell bearing clean, (as for the main bearing shells) and fit the shell bearing in position with its locating torque engaged with the corresponding groove in the connecting rod. Always fit new shells.

2 Generously lubricate the crankpin journals with engine oil and turn the crankshaft so that the crankpin is in the most advantageous position for the connecting rod to be drawn onto it.

3 Fit the bearing shell to the connecting rod cap in the same way as with the connecting rod itself (photo).

4 Generously lubricate the shell bearing and offer up the connecting rod bearing cap to the connecting rod (photo). Fit the connecting rod cap retaining nuts. It will be observed that these are special twelve sided nuts (photo).

5 Tighten the retaining nuts to the specified torque (photo).

48 Oil pump and coupling - replacement

1 Fit the coupling to the oil pump splined drive (photo).

2 Make sure the mating face of the oil pump is clean and fit a new gasket. Make sure it is fitted the correct way round (photo).

3 Wipe the location of the oil pump at the rear of the cylinder block and offer the oil pump up into position. Make sure that it is fitted correctly with the cutaway towards the bottom of the rear of the cylinder block.

4 Refit the four oil pump securing bolts and two shaped locking washers and tighten these bolts to a torque wrench setting of 9 lb ft (1.2 Kg fm) (photo).

5 Using a pair of pliers bend over the locking tabs (photo).

49 Oil pressure relief valve and switch - replacement

1 Assemble the valve components in the order of: valve, spring and domed nut with new washer.

2 Carefully insert the assembly into its location at the rear of the cylinder block. Tighten the domed nut fully (photo).

3 Locate the oil pressure switch in its drilling in the side of the cylinder block just above the oil pressure relief valve and tighten firmly using an open ended spanner (photo).

50 Engine front plate, timing gears, tensioner and cover - replacement

1 Wipe the mating faces of the front plate and cylinder block and smear the new gasket with a little grease. Attach the gasket to the rear of the front plate and offer up into position (photo).

2 Refit the two special screws located to the bottom of the crankshaft and tighten with an Allen key (photo).

3 Replace the two front plate to cylinder block securing bolts and spring washers (photo).

4 Refit the camshaft retainer to the front plate with the thrust face towards the camshaft (photo). The hole should be to the bottom of the cylinder block. Secure in position with the three

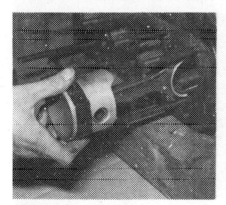
46.4A. Support the block on a piece of wood

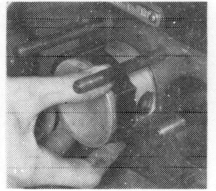
46.4B. Use a proper ring compressor

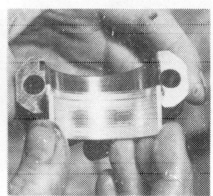
47.3. Oil the shells

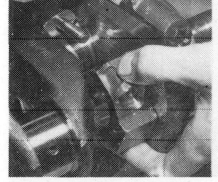
47.7A. Place the connecting rods squarely

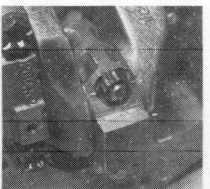
47.4B. Note the special nuts

47.5. Again a torque wrench should be used

48.1. Clean hands are necessary all the time

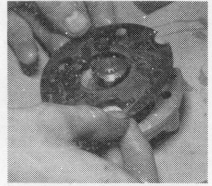

48.2. Note the cutout on the gasket

48.3. Position properly first time

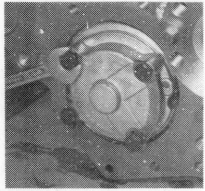

48.4. Tighten diagonally

48.5. Lock the tabs once for each bolt

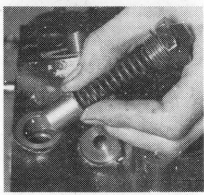

49.2. The plunger must be wiped clean

49.3A. Clean the thread first

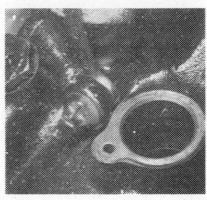

49.3B. Use an open-ender

50.1. Place the gasket first

50.2. ALWAYS USE AN ALLEN KEY

50.3. Tighten both bolts

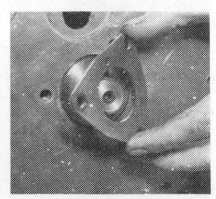

50.4. Position correctly

bolts and spring washers.

5 Check that the packing washers are in place on the crankshaft nose. If new gear wheels are being fitted it may be necessary to fit additional washers as described in paragraph 7. These washers ensure that the crankshaft gear wheel lines up correctly with the camshaft gear wheel.

6 Replace the woodruff key in its slot in the camshaft. If the edges of this key or the one fitted to the crankshaft are burred they must be cleaned with a fine file.

7 Lay the camshaft and crankshaft gearwheels on a clean surface so that the two timing marks - dot of camshaft gear wheel and a shaped protrusion on the hub of the crankshaft gear wheel are adjacent to each other. Slip the timing chain over the gearwheels and pull them apart into mesh with the chain so that the timing marks, although further apart, are still adjacent to each other. Check the gear alignment as shown in Fig.1.24.

8 Rotate the crankshaft so that the woodruff key is at T D C.

9 Rotate the camshaft so that when viewed from the front the woodruff key is at one o'clock position.

10 Fit the timing chain and gearwheel assembly onto the camshaft and crankshaft keeping the timing marks adjacent (photo).

11 If the camshaft and crankshaft have been positioned accurately it will be found that the keyways on the gearwheels will match the position of the keys, although it may be necessary to rotate the camshaft a fraction to ensure accurate lining up of the camshaft gearwheel.

12 Press the gearwheels into position on the crankshaft and camshaft as far as they will go. NOTE: If new gearwheels are being fitted they should be checked for alignment before finally fitting to the engine. Place the gearwheels in position without the timing chain and place the straight edge of a steel rule from the side of the camshaft gear teeth to the crankshaft gearwheel and measure the gap between the steel rule and the crankshaft gearwheel. Add or subtract shims to this thickness located on the crankshaft nose (see Fig.1.25).

13 Refit the camshaft gearwheel retaining lockwasher and nut and tighten this nut fully (photo).

14 Using a chisel bend over the lockwasher on one flat (photo).

50.10. Push on by hand as far as it will go   50.13. Use an appropriate socket   50.14. One lip will do

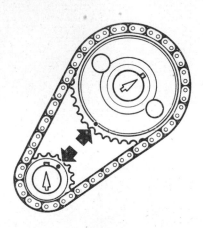

FIG.1.24 TIMING GEAR MARKS

FIG.1.25 ALIGNMENT OF TIMING GEARS

1 Camshaft gear
2 Crankshaft gear
3 Key
4 Gap between gear and

straight edge
5 Straight edge
6 Shims (located behind crankshaft gear)

15 If a tensioner is fitted, assemble the pivot screw, washer, tensioner and second washer and fit to the front of the cylinder block.

16 Fit the crankshaft oil thrower onto the crankshaft nose. The thrower should be fitted with the letter F facing towards the front of the engine (photo).

17 Wipe the cover mating face and the front end plate and smear a little grease onto the end plate. Fit a new gasket and align up all the holes (photo).

18 If oil leaked from the seal in the front cover this should be levered out using a screwdriver and a new one fitted. The lip when fitted faces inwards.

19 Generously oil the chain, gearwheels, and cover oil seal.

20 Offer up the front cover taking care not to dislodge the gasket and retain in position with the bolts and spring washers. Bolts of different sizes are used and they must go back in their original fitted position as was noted during dismantling. Do not tighten yet (photo).

21 Using the pulley centralise the cover and tighten as many bolts as possible (photo).

22 Remove the pulley again and tighten the three lower bolts (photo).

23 With the pulley back on the crankshaft nose again refit the pulley retaining bolt and lockwasher (photo).

25 Using a chisel bend up the lockwasher to one flat. (photo).

51 Engine backplate - refitting

1 Wipe the rear face of the cylinder block and smear a little grease onto a new gasket. Carefully fit the gasket to the cylinder block (photo).

2 Place the oil pump cover in position on the rear face of the cylinder block (photo).

3 Carefully refit the backplate, locating the dowel at the top of the cylinder block in the centre hole at the top of the backplate and the second dowel at the bottom left hand side of the cylinder block (photo).

4 Refit the backplate to the cylinder block securing bolts and spring washers and tighten fully (photo).

52 Oil strainer and sump - refitting

1 The gauze strainer and suction pipe should be thoroughly cleaned in petrol and allowed to dry. (Preferably blow dry with a compressed air line).

2 Insert the suction pipe into its bore and partially tighten the union nut (photo).

3 Refit the two bolts and spring washers securing the strainer bracket to the centre and rear main bearing end caps (photo).

4 Tighten the suction pipe union nut fully (photo).

5 After the sump has been thoroughly cleaned, scrape all traces of the old sump gasket from the sump flange, and fit new main bearing cap oil seals. Should the oil seal material stand out more than 1/16 inch (1.587 mm) above the sump flange it must be cut back to this figure (photo).

6 Thoroughly clean and scrape the crankshaft to sump flange. Apply grease to the crankcase to sump flange and carefully fit new gasket halves to the flange (ohm).

7 Carefully fit the sump to the underside of the crankcase (photo).

8 Refit the sump retaining bolts, shaped washers and spring washers (photo).

9 Tighten the sump bolts to a torque wrench setting of 6 lb ft (0.8 Kg fm) (photo).

53 Flywheel and clutch - refitting

1 Clean the mating faces of the crankshaft and flywheel and fit the flywheel to the dowel in the end of the crankshaft flange (photo).

2 Replace the six flywheel securing bolts and circular thrust washer and tighten these bolts to a torque wrench setting of 40 lb ft (5.5 Kg fm). It will be necessary to lock the flywheel using a screwdriver through the sump bracket and the end engaged in the starter ring teeth (photo).

3 Bend up the lockwasher tabs (photo).

4 Refit the clutch disc and pressure plate assembly and lightly secure in position with the six bolts and spring washers (photo).

5 If a spare first motion shaft is available use this to line up the clutch disc with the crankshaft spigot bearing. As an alternative use a suitable piece of wood as a dowel

6 Firmly tighten the clutch securing bolts in a diagonal manner. The flywheel may be locked using the screwdriver as described in paragraph 2 (photo).

54 Water and fuel pump - refitting

1 Make sure the mating faces of the water pump and cylinder block are free of old gasket or jointing compound.

2 Smear a little grease onto the water pump and place on a new gasket.

3 Fit the water pump to the cylinder block mating it to the dowels in the cylinder block face (photo).

4 Refit and tighten the four securing bolts and spring washers (photo).

5 Clean the mating faces of the crankcase and fuel pump and fit a new set of gaskets to the spacer. Slide the spacer and gaskets over the studs (photo).

6 Refit the fuel pump and secure with the two nuts and spring washers (photo).

55 Valve and valve spring - reassembly

Refit the valves and valve springs to the cylinder head.

1 Rest the cylinder head on its side, or if the manifold studs are still fitted with the gasket surface downwards.

2 Fit each valve and valve spring in turn, wiping down and lubricating each valve stem as it is inserted into the same valve guide from which it was removed (photo).

3 As each inlet valve is inserted slip on the oil seal and push it down over the valve guide (photo).

4 Move the cylinder head towards the edge of the work bench if it is facing downwards and slide it partially over the edge of the bench so as to fit the bottom half of the valve spring compressor to the valve head.

5 Slip the valve spring over the valve stem and down onto its seating (photo).

6 Refit the spring cap to the top of the valve spring (photo).

7 With the base of the valve spring compressor on the valve head compress the valve spring until the cotters can be slipped into place in the spring cap. Gently release the compressor. Check that the cotters are correctly located in the spring cap (photo).

8 Repeat for all eight valve assemblies

56 Rocker shaft - reassembly

To reassemble the rocker shaft fit the split pin, flat washer, and spring washer at the rear end of the shaft and then slide on the rocker arms, rocker shaft pedestals, and spacing springs in the same order in which they were removed (Fig.1.26).

With the front pedestal in position screw in the rocker shaft locating screw and slip the locating plate into position. Finally fit to the front of the shaft, the spring washer, plain washer, and

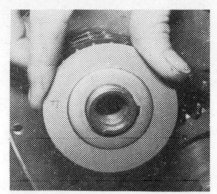
50.16. Note the position of F

50.17. Use a new gasket

50.20. Place on but do not tighten

50.21. Centre the oil seal properly

50.22. Now tighten

50.23. Clean the threads

50.24. Have someone hold the engine

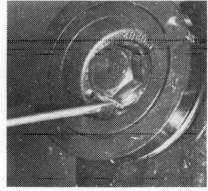
50.25. Lock one lip

51.1. This is a complex gasket

51.2. The end plate will hold it

51.3. Use the dowels to locate

51.4. Tighten progressively

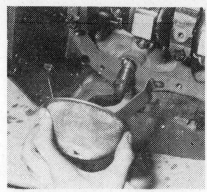
52.2. Again support the block to gain easy access

52.3. You must use a socket here

52.4. Do not cross the threads

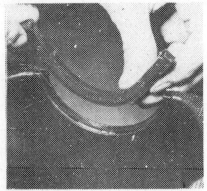
52.5. Make sure its the right length

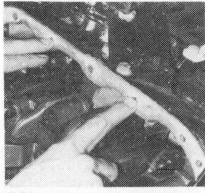
52.6. It will hold with a slight touch of grease

52.7. Check the mating faces of the sump

52.9. It helps to use a socket

53.1. Use the dowel to locate

53.2. Hold the flywheel as shown

53.3. You must lock the bolts

53.4. Clean hands are essential here

53.6. Tighten the clutch cover bolts progressively

54.3. Note the new gasket fitted

54.4. Tighten progressively

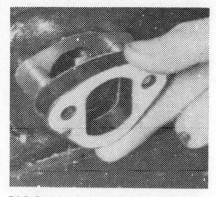
54.5. Position the gaskets in their correct sequence

54.6. Again use a socket here

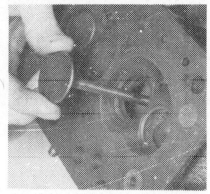
55.2. Note the smoothness of the valve seat

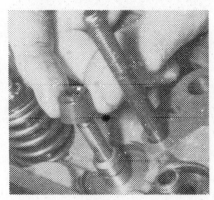
55.3. Inlet valves only!

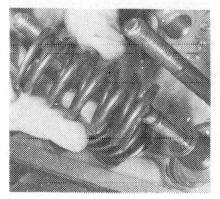
55.5. Hold the valve with the other hand

55.6. Note the clean fingers

55.7. Compress the valve spring fully

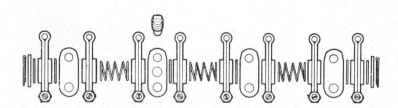

FIG.1.26 ROCKER GEAR — ROCKER ARM AND SPRING FITMENT ORDER

split pin, in that order.

57 Cylinder head - replacement

1   After checking that both the cylinder block and cylinder head mating faces are perfectly clean, generously lubricate each cylinder with engine oil (photo).

Always use a new cylinder head gasket. The old gasket will be compressed and incapable of giving a good seal. It is also easier at this stage to refit the small hose from the water pump to the cylinder head.

2   Never smear grease on gasket cement either side of the gasket, for pressure leaks may blow through it.

3   The cylinder head gasket is marked FRONT and TOP and should be fitted in position according to the markings. The copper side will be uppermost.

4   Carefully lower the gasket into position ensuring that the stud threads do not damage the side of the holes through which they pass (photo).

5   The cylinder head may now be lowered over the studs until it rests on the cylinder head gasket (photo).

6   With the cylinder head in position fit the pushrods in the same order in which they were removed. Ensure that they locate properly in the stems of the tappets (photo).

7   Refit the two tappet covers with new cork gaskets and tighten the two securing bolts and washers.

8   The rocker shaft assembly can now be lowered over its eight locating studs. Take care that the rocker arms are the right way round (photo). Lubricate the ball joints, and insert the rocker arm ball joints into the pushrod cups. NOTE: Failure to place he ball joints in the cups can result in the ball joints seating on the edge of a pushrod or outside it when the head and rocker assembly is pulled down tight (photo).

9   Fit the lock plate to the second pedestal (photo).

10 Fit the four rocker pedestal nuts and washers, and then the four cylinder head stud nuts and washers which also hold down the rocker pedestals. Pull the nuts down evenly, but without tightening them right up.

11 Fit the remaining nuts and washers to the cylinder head studs.

12 When all are in position tighten the rocker pedestal nuts and the cylinder head nuts to the specified torques. The correct order is shown in Fig. 1.5 (photo).

13 Finally tighten the water pump by pass hose clip (photo).

58 Rocker arm/valve - adjustment

1   The valve adjustments should be made with the engine cold. The importance of correct rocker arm/valve stem clearances cannot be overstressed as they vitally affect the performance.

2   If the clearances are set too wide, the efficiency of the engine is reduced as the valves open late and close earlier than was intended. If the clearances are set too close there is a danger that the stem and pushrods upon expantion when hot will not allow the valves to close properly which will cause burning of the valve head and possible warping.

3   If the engine is in the car, to get at the rockers, it is merely necessary to remove the two holding down dome shaped nuts from the recore cover, and then to lift the rocker cover and gasket away (photo).

4   It is important that the clearance is set when the tappet of the valve being adjusted is on the heel of the cam (ie opposite the peak). This can be done by carrying out the adjustments in the following order, which also avoids turning the crankshaft more than necessary.

Valve fully open	Check and adjust
Valve number 8	Valve number 1
Valve number 6	Valve number 3
Valve number 4	Valve number 5
Valve number 7	Valve number 2
Valve number 1	Valve number 8
Valve number 3	Valve number 6
Valve number 5	Valve number 4
Valve number 2	Valve number 7

5   The correct valve clearance is given in the Specifications at the beginning of this chapter. It is obtained by slackening the hexagonal locknut with a spanner while holding the ball pin against rotation with a screwdriver as shown in Fig.1.27. Then still pressing down with the screwdriver, insert feeler gauge of the required thickness between the valve stem and head and the rocker arm and adjust the ball pin until the feeler gauge will just move in and out without nipping (photo). Then, still holding the ball pin in the correct position, tighten the locknut.

6   An alternative method is to set the gaps with the engine running at idle speed. Although this method may be faster, more practice is needed and it is no more reliable.

7   Refit the rocker cover and gasket, and secure with the dome nuts and washers (photo).

59 Distributor and distributor drive - replacement

It is important to set the distributor drive correctly otherwise the ignition timing will be incorrect. It is easy to set the distributor drive in apparently the right position, but in fact exactly 180° out, by ommitting to select the correct cylinder which must not only be at T D C but must also be on the firing stroke with both valves closed. The distributor drive should therefore not be fitted until the cylinder head is in position and the valves can be observed. Alternatively if the timing chain cover has not been replaced, the distributor drive can be replaced when the marks on the timing wheels are adjacent to each other.

1   Rotate the crankshaft so that No 1 piston is at T D C, and on its firing stroke (the marks in the timing gears will be adjacent

57.1. Oil the bores well (the gasket is already on here!)

57.4. Press down lightly

57.5. Lower gently and square

57.6. Check the sequence of the pushrods

57.8A. Set the rocker shaft square

57.8B. Check each pushrod individually

57.9. You must not leave this out

57.12. Tighten the head and rockers together

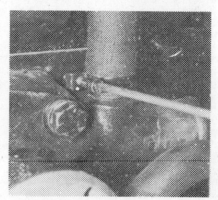

57.13. Now is the best time

58.3. Put the gasket on the cover

58.5. A sliding fit only

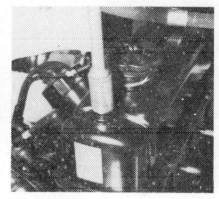

58.7. Not too tight!

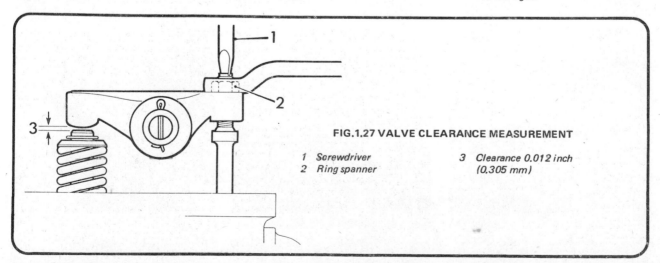

FIG.1.27 VALVE CLEARANCE MEASUREMENT

1 Screwdriver
2 Ring spanner

3 Clearance 0.012 inch
   (0.305 mm)

to each other). When No 1 piston is at T D C the inlet valve on No 4 cylinder is just opening and the exhaust valve closing.

2   When the marks '1/4' on the flywheel are at T D C or when the dimple on the crankshaft pulley wheel is in line with the T D C pointer on the timing gear cover, then Nos 1 and 4 pistons are at T D C.

3   Screw the tappet cover bolt into the lead of the distributor drive (any 5/16 inch U N F bolt).

4   Insert the distributor drive into its housing so that when fully home the smaller half of the offset distributor drive head is in the eleven o'clock position. To allow for rotation of the distributor drive as its skew gear meshes with the skew gear on the camshaft the drive should be inserted with the slot vertical and the smaller offset towards the front of the engine (photo). As the drive is pushed right home the skew gears will turn the drive shaft anti-clockwise to the eleven o'clock position (photos).

5   Remove the tappet cover bolt from the drive shaft.

6   Replace the distributor housing and lock it in position with the single bolt and lockwasher (photo).

7   The distributor can now be replaced and the two securing bolts and spring washers which hold the distributor clamping plate to the distributor housing tightened (photo). If the clamp bolt on the clamping plate was not previously loosened and the distributor body was not turned in the clamping plate, then the ignition timing will be as previously set. If the clamping bolt has been loosened, then it will be necessary to retime the ignition as described in Chapter 4.

8   Tighten the two distributor clamping plate securing bolts firmly (photo).

60 Final assembly

1   Refit the rocker cover, using a new cork gasket and secure in position with the two domed nuts.

2   Fit the two tappet cover plates, using new gaskets and tighten the tappet chest bolts to a torque wrench setting of 2 lb ft (0.3 Kg fm). Do not exceed this figure or the covers will distort and leak oil.

3   Fit a new manifold gasket over the studs taking care not to rip it as it passes over the stud threads (photo).

4   Replace the manifold and secure in position with the six nuts, spring and large plain washers (photo).

5   Insert the thermostat into its housing making sure the word 'FRONT' marked on the flange is towards the front of the engine (photo).

6   Fit a new gasket taking care not to rip the gasket as it passes over the threads of the three studs. Then refit the thermostat housing cover and secure with the three nuts and spring washers (photo).

7   If the dip stick guide tube was removed this should next be inserted into its drilling in the side of the crankcase (photo).

8   Fit a new oil filter canister (see Section 24) (photo).

9   It should be noted that in all cases it is best to reassemble the engine as far as possible before refitting it to the car. This means that the dynamo (or alternator), fan belt and other minor attachments should be replaced at this stage.

61 Engine - replacement

Although the engine or engine and gearbox can be replaced by one man and a suitable hoist, it is easier if two are present, one to lower the unit into the engine compartment, and the other to guide the unit into position and to ensure it does not foul anything. Generally replacement is the reverse sequence to removal (see Sections 5 and 6). In addition however;

1   Ensure all the loose leads, cables etc, are tucked out of the way. It is easy to trap one and cause much additional work after the engine is replaced.

2   Carefully lower the unit into position (photo). Then refit the

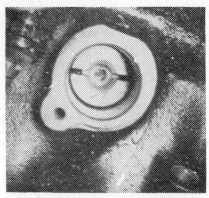
59.4A. It will move to 11 o'clock

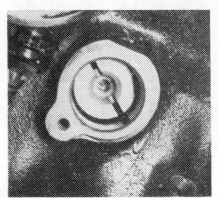
59.4B. 11 o'clock

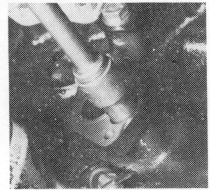
59.6. Use a socket here

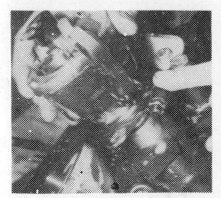
59.7. Slide squarely and gently

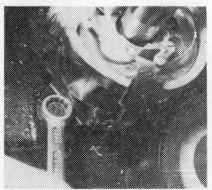
59.8. Lock

60.3. Do not bend the manifold gasket

60.4. Do not forget the spring washers

60.5. Handle the thermostat with care

60.6. Note the gasket

60.7. Its easier if the distributor cap is removed

60.8. Grease the sealing face lightly

61.2. Check that no wires are in the way

the following:

a) Mounting nuts, bolts and washers.
b) Propeller shaft coupling.
c) Reconnect the clutch pipe to the slave cylinder and bleed the system (see Chapter 5).
d) Speedometer cable.
e) Gear change lever and surround.
f) Carpets
g) Oil pressure switch cable
h) Water temperature indicator sender unit cable.
i) Wire to coil, distributor and dynamo/alternator.
j) Carburettor controls and air cleaner.
k) Exhaust manifold to down pipe.
l) Earth and starter motor cables.
m) Radiator and hoses.
n) Heater hoses.
0) Engine closed circuit breather holes.
p) Vacuum advance and retard pipe (if fitted).
q) Battery (if removed).
r) Fuel lines to carburettor and pump.
s) Bonnet.

3   Finally check that the drain taps are closed and refill the cooling system with water and the engine with Castrol GTX

---

62 Engine - initial start up after overhaul or major repair

Make sure that the battery is fully charged and that all lubri-

cants, coolants and fuel are replenished.

If the fuel system has been dismantled, it will require several revolutions of the engine on the starter motor to pump petrol up to the carburettor. An initial 'prime' of about 1/3 cupfull of petrol down the air intake of the carburettor will help the engine to fire quickly, thus relieving the load on the battery. Do not overdo this however, as flooding may result.

As soon as the engine fires and runs, keep it going at a fast tickover only (no faster) and bring it up to normal working temperatures.

As the engine warms up, there will be odd smells and some smoke from parts getting hot and burning off oil deposits. Look for leaks of water or oil which will be obvious if serious. Check also the clamp connection of the exhaust pipe to the manifold as these do not always 'find' their exact gas tight position until the warmth and vibration have acted on them, and it is almost certain that they will need tightening further. This should be done, of course, with the engine stopped.

When the engine running temperature has been reached, adjust the idling speed as described in Chapter 3.

Stop the engine and wait a few minutes to see if any lubricant or coolant drips out.

Road test the car to check that the timing is correct and giving the necessary smoothness and power. Do not race the engine - if new bearings and/or pistons and rings have been fitted, it should be treated as a new engine and run in at reduced revolutions for 500 miles (800 Km).

Fault diagnosis appears on the next page, page 50.

Symptom	Reason/s	Remedy
Engine will not turn over when starter switch is operated.	Flat battery Bad battery connections Bad connections at solenoid switch and/or starter motor	Check that battery is fully charged and that all connections are clean and tight.
	Starter motor jammed	Rock car back and forth with a gear engaged. If ineffective remove starter (not automatic).
	Defective solenoid Starter motor defective	Remove and check solenoid. Remove starter and overhaul.
Engine turns over normally but fails to fire and run	No spark at plugs	Check ignition system according to procedures given in Chapter 4.
	No fuel reaching engine	Check fuel system according to procedures given in Chapter 3.
	Too much fuel reaching the engine (flooding)	Check fuel system if necessary as described in Chapter 3.
Engine starts but runs unevenly and misfires	Ignition and/or fuel system faults	Check the ignition and fuel systems as though the engine had failed to start.
	Incorrect valve clearances Burnt out valves	Check and reset clearances. Remove cylinder head and examine and overhaul as necessary.
Lack of power	Ignition and/or fuel system faults	Check the ignition and fuel systems for correct ignition timing and carburettor settings.
	Incorrect valve clearances Burnt out valves	Check and reset the clearances. Remove cylinder head and examine and overhaul as necessary.
	Worn out piston or cylinder bores	Remove cylinder head and examine pistons and cylinder bores. Overhaul as necessary.
Excessive oil consumption	Oil leaks from crankshaft oil seal, rocker cover gasket, drain plug gasket, sump plug washer	Identify source of leak and repair as appropriate.
	Worn piston rings or cylinder bores resulting in oil being burnt by engine Smoky exhaust is an indication	Fit new rings or rebore cylinders and fit new pistons, depending on degree of wear.
	Worn valve guides and/or defective valve stem seals	Remove cylinder head and recondition valve guides and valves and seals as necessary.
Excessive mechanical noise from engine	Wrong valve to rocker clearances Worn crankshaft bearings Worn cylinders (piston slap)	Adjust valve clearances. Inspect and overhaul where necessary.
Unusual vibration	Misfiring on one or more cylinders Loose mounting bolts	Check ignition system. Check tightness of bolts and condition of flexible mountings.

NOTE: When investigating starting and uneven running faults do not be tempted into snap diagnosis. Start from the beginning of the check procedure and follow it through. It will take less time in the long run. Poor performance from an engine in terms of power and economy is not normally diagnosed quickly. In any event the ignition and fuel systems must be checked first before assuming any further investigation needs to be made.

Chapter 2 Cooling system

Contents

Specifications

Thermostat type	Pressurised system with expansion tank wax
Thermostat settings: Standard	82° C (180° F)
Hot climate	74° C (165° F)
Cold climate	88° C (190° F)
Blow off pressure of expansion tank cap	15 lb f/in^2 (1.05 Kg/cm^2)
Fan belt tension	0.5 in (13 mm) deflection on longest run
Water pump	Centrifugal type
Bearing spindle diameter	0.6262 to 0.0267 in (15.901 to 15.918 mm)
Impeller bore	0.6244 to 0.6252 in (15.860 to 15.880 mm)
Pulley hub bore	0.6239 to 0.6247 in (15.847 to 15.867 mm)
Bearing assembly diameter	1.1813 to 1.1818 in (30.005 to 30.017 mm)
Body bore	1.1807 to 1.1811 in (29.99 to 30.00 mm)
Cooling system capacity (with heater)	7.5 pints (4.3 litres)
Torque wrench settings	lb ft Kg fm
Water pump retaining bolts	17 2.35
Water outlet elbow	8 1.11
Water pump pulley set screws	18 2.49
Thermal transmitter	16 2.21

1 General description

The engine cooling water is circulated by a thermo-siphon, water pump assisted system, and the coolant is pressurised. This is primarily to prevent premature boiling in adverse conditions and to allow the engine to operate at its most efficient running temperature; this being just under the boiling point of water. The overflow pipe from the radiator is connected to an expansion chamber which makes topping up virtually unnecessary. The coolant expands when hot, and instead of being forced down an overflow pipe and lost, it flows into the expansion chamber. As the engine cools the coolant contracts and because of the pressure differential flows back into the radiator.

The cap on the expansion chamber is set to a pressure of 15 lb/in^2 (1.05 Kg/cm^2) which increases the boiling point of the coolant to 230°F. If the water temperature exceeds this figure and the water boils, the pressure in the system forces the internal valve of the cap off its seat thus exposing the expansion tank overflow pipe down which the steam from the boiling water escapes and so relieves the pressure. It is therefore, important to check that the expansion chamber cap is in good condition and that the spring behind the sealing washers has not weakened. Check that the rubber seal has not perished and its seating in the neck is clean to ensure a good seal. A special tool which enables a cap to be pressure tested is available at some garages.

The cooling system comprises the radiator, top and bottom hoses, heater hoses (if a heater/demister is fitted), the impeller water pump (mounted on the front of the engine it carries the fan blades and is driven by the fan belt), the thermostat and drain plugs.

The system functions as follows: Cold water from the radiator circulates up the lower radiator hose to the water pump where it is pushed round the water passages in the cylinder block, helping to keep the cylinder bores and pistons cool.

The water then travels up into the cylinder head and circulates round the combustion spaces and valve seats absorbing more heat. Then, when the engine is at its normal operating temperature, the water travels out of the cylinder head, past the now open thermostat into the upper radiator and so into the radiator. The Water passes along the radiator from one side to the other where it is rapidly cooled by the rush of cold air through the horizontal radiator core. The water now cool reaches the bottom hose when the cycle is repeated.

Then the engine is cold the thermostat (a valve which opens and closes according to water temperature) maintains the circulation of the same water in the engine by returning it via the bypass hose to the cylinder block. Only when the correct minimum operating temperature has been reached, as shown in the specifications, does the thermostat begin to open allowing water to return to the radiator.

2 Cooling system - draining

With the car on level ground drain the system as follows:
1 With the cooling system cold unscrew and remove the radiator filler plug. DO NOT REMOVE THE PLUG WHILST THE ENGINE IS HOT.
2 If anti-freeze is being used in the cooling system it should be collected in a bowl located under the bottom hose. Do not carry out the instruction in paragraph 5.
3 Release the expansion tank pressure cap.
4 Undo and remove the cylinder block drain plug. This is located to the rear of the left hand side of the cylinder block.
5 Slacken the hose clip and carefully ease the bottom hose at its connection to the radiator.
6 When the coolant has finished running out of the cylinder block drain hole probe the orifice with a short piece of wire to dislodge any particles of rust or sediment which may be causing a blockage preventing complete draining.

3 Cooling system - flushing

1 Even with proper use, the cooling system will gradually lose its efficiency as the radiator becomes choked with rust scale, deposits from water and other sediment. To clear the system out, remove the radiator filler plug cylinder block plug and bottom hose and leave a hose running in the radiator filler plug hole for fifteen minutes.
2 Reconnect the bottom hose, refit the cylinder block plug and refill the cooling system as described in Section 4, adding a proprietary cleansing compound. Run the engine for fifteen minutes. All sediment and sludge should now have been loosened and may be removed by draining the system and then refilling again.
3 In very bad cases the radiator should be reverse flushed. This can be done with the radiator in position, the cylinder block plug is left in position and a hose placed in the bottom hose union of the radiator. Water under pressure is forced through the orifice and out of the filler plug hole.
4 The hose is then removed and placed in the filler plug hole and the radiator washed out in the usual manner.

4 Cooling system - filling

1 Fit the cylinder block drain plug and if the bottom hose has been removed it should be reconnected.
2 Fill the system slowly to ensure that no air locks develop. Check that the valve to the heater unit is open, otherwise an air lock may form in the heater. The best type of water to use in the cooling system is rain water.
3 Fill up the radiator to the level of the filler plug and top up the level of coolant in the expansion tank to the level indicated. Refit the radiator filler plug and expansion tank cap.
4 Start the engine and run at a fast idle speed for 30 seconds.
5 Stop the engine and top up the radiator through the filler plug and refit the plug.
6 Run the engine until it has reached its normal operating temperature. Stop the engine and allow to cool.
7 Top up the expansion tank to the level marked.

5 Radiator - removal, and refitting

1 Drain the cooling system as described in Section 2.
2 Slacken the clip securing the expansion tank hose to the radiator. Carefully ease the hose from the union pipe on the radiator (Fig.2.1).
3 Slacken the clips securing the radiator top and bottom hoses to the radiator inlet and outlet pipes and carefully ease the two hoses from these pipes.
4 Undo and remove the screws with spring and plain washers securing the two top radiator mounting brackets to the front

panel. Lift away these two brackets (Fig.2.2).
5 The radiator may now be lifted up from its lower mounting and away from the front of the car.
6 Refitting the radiator is the reverse sequence to removal. Refill the cooling system as described in Section 4. Carefully check to ensure that all hose joints are water tight.

6 Radiator - inspection and cleaning

1 With the radiator out of the car, any leaks can be soldered up or repaired with a compound such as Cataloy. Clean out the inside of the radiator by flushing as described in Section 3.
2 When the radiator is out of the car, it is advantageous to turn it upside down for reverse flushing. Clean the exterior of the radiator by hosing down the radiator matrix with a strong jet of water to clean away road dirt, dead flies etc.
3 Inspect the radiator hoses for cracks, internal or external perishing and damage caused by overtightening of the hose clips. Replace the hoses as necessary. Examine the radiator hose clips and renew them if they are rusted or distorted. The drain plugs or washers should be renewed if leaking.

7 Thermostat - removal, testing and replacement

To remove the thermostat, partially drain the cooling system (usually 4 pints, 2.27 litres is enough), loosen the upper radiator hose at the thermostat end and ease it off the elbow. Unscrew the three nuts and lift away the washers from the thermostat housing. Lift away the thermostat elbow from the studs followed by the paper joint and finally the thermostat itself (Fig.2.3).

Test the thermostat for correct functioning by suspending it together with a thermometer on a string in a container of cold water. Heat the water and note the temperature at which the thermostat begins to open. This should be 82°C (180°F) for a standard thermostat. It is advantageous in winter to fit a thermostat that does not open until 88°C (190°F). Discard the thermostat if it opens too early. Continue heating the water until the thermostat is fully open. Then let it cool down naturally. If the thermostat does not fully open in boiling water, or does not close down as the water cools, then it must be discarded and a new one fitted. If the thermostat is stuck open when cold this will be apparent when removing it from the housing.

Refitting the thermostat is the reverse procedure to removal. Always ensure that the cylinder head and thermostat housing elbow faces are clean and flat. If the thermostat elbow is badly corroded and eaten away fit a new elbow. A new paper joint must always be used.

If a new winter thermostat is fitted, provided the summer one is functioning correctly it can be placed on one side and refitted in the spring. Thermostats should last for two to three years at least between renewal.

8 Water pump - removal and refitting

1 For safety reasons disconnect the battery.
2 Refer to Section 5 and remove the radiator.
3 Refer to Chapter 10 and remove the dynamo or alternator (if fitted).
4 Undo and remove the four bolts and spring washers securing the fan blades to the pulley hub. Lift away the circular metal plate, fan blades and pulley (Fig.2.4).
5 Slacken the clip securing the bottom hose to the water pump and carefully ease off the hose.
6 Slacken the clip that secures the bypass hose to the cylinder head.
7 Undo and remove the four bolts and spring washers which hold the pump to the front of the cylinder block. NOTE these bolts are of different lengths and must be refitted in their original positions.
8 Lift away the pump, disengaging it from the by-pass hose and

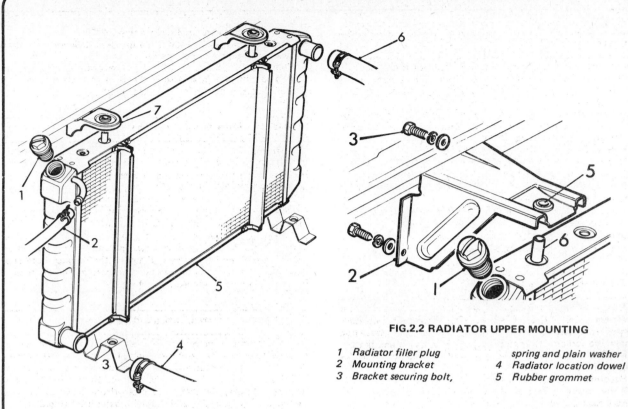

FIG.2.1 RADIATOR ASSEMBLY

1   Filler plug
2   Hose to expansion tank
3   Lower mounting bracket
(attached to body)
4   Bottom radiator hose
5   Radiator
6   Top radiator hose
7   Upper mounting bracket

FIG.2.2 RADIATOR UPPER MOUNTING

1   Radiator filler plug
2   Mounting bracket
3   Bracket securing bolt,
        spring and plain washer
4   Radiator location dowel
5   Rubber grommet

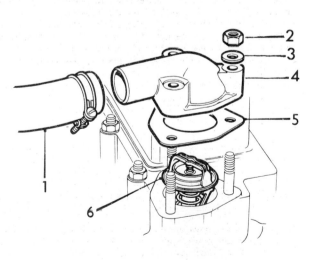

FIG.2.3 THERMOSTAT HOUSING

1   Radiator top hose
2   Nut
3   Plain washer
4   Thermostat housing
5   Gasket
6   Thermostat

FIG.2.4 WATER PUMP ATTACHMENTS

1   Fan securing bolts
2   Packing bolts
3   Fan
4   Pulley
5   Water pump retaining bolts
6   Radiator bottom hose
7   Inset. By pass hose

recover the paper gasket.

9 Refitting is the reverse sequence to removal but not in addition:

a) Clean the mating fares of the water pump body and cylinder block to ensure a good water tight joint.

b) Always use a new paper gasket.

c) The small by-pass hose should be renewed because it is very difficult to replace with the water pump in position.

d) Adjust the fan belt tension as described in Section 11.

9 Water pump - dismantling and overhaul

If the water pump starts to leak, shows signs of excessive movement of the spindle: or is noisy during operation the pump can be dismantled and overhauled. However, a better alternative will be to fit a service exchange reconditioned pump. Before commencing any dismantling, check on availability of spare parts.

1 Using a suitable universal puller or a press carefully press the bearing spindle out of the pulley hub (Fig.2.5).

2 Support the water pump body and carefully tap out the bearings assembly complete with impeller and seal.

3 Next press out the bearing spindle from the impeller and finally remove the water seal from the bearing spindle. Dismantling is new complete.

4 Thoroughly inspect all parts for wear or damage. Replace any faulty parts.

5 To reassemble first press the bearing assembly into the pump body until the dimensions in Fig.2.6 are reached.

6 Support the bearing spindle and press the pulley hub onto the spindle until dimension B (Fig.2.6) is reached.

7 Fit the water seal into the pump body, suitably supporting the bearing spindle. Smear the impeller face, which abuts with the water seal, with silicone grease, then press the impeller onto the spindle to obtain the dimension 'C' in Fig. 2.6.

8 Should it be observed during reassembly that the interference fit of either the hub or impeller on the bearing spindle has been lost the hub and/or impeller must be renewed.

10 Fan belt - removal and replacement

If the fan belt is worn or has over stretched it should be renewed. The most usual reason for replacement is that the belt has broken in service. It is therefore recommended that a spare belt is always carried in the car. Replacement is a reversal of the remove sequence, but if replacement is due to leakage:

1 Loosen the dynamo (or alternator if fitted) pivot and slotted link bolts and move the dynamo (or alternator) towards the engine.

2 Carefully fit the belt over the crankshaft, water pump and dynamo (or alternator) pulleys.

3 Adjust the belt as described in Section 11 and tighten the dynamo (or alternator) mounting bolts. NOTE: after fitting a new belt it will require adjustment 250 miles (400 Km) later.

11 Fan belt - adjustment

It is important to keep the fan belt correctly adjusted and should be checked every 6000 miles (9600 Km) or 6 months. If the belt is loose it will slip, wear rapidly and cause the dynamo (or alternator) and water pump to malfunction. If the belt is too tight the dynamo (or alternator) and water pump bearings will wear rapidly and cause premature failure.

The fan belt tension is correct when there is ½ inch (13 mm) of lateral movement at the mid point position between the dynamo (or alternator) pulley and the crankshaft pulley (Fig.2.7).

To adjust the fan belt, slacken the dynamo securing bolts and move the dynamo (or alternator) in or out until the correct tension is obtained. It is easier if the dynamo (or alternator) bolts are only slackened a little so it requires some effort to move the unit. In this way the tension of the belt can be arrived at more quickly than by making frequent adjustments. If difficulty is experienced in moving the unit away from the engine a tyre lever placed behind the unit and resting against the block gives good control so that it can be held in position whilst the securing bolts are tightened. Be careful of the alternator cover its fragile.

12 Expansion tank

The radiator coolant expansion tank is mounted on the left hand inner wing panel and does not require any maintenance. It is important that the expansion tank pressure filler cap is not removed whilst the engine is hot.

Should it be found necessary to remove the expansion tank, disconnect the radiator to expansion tank hose connection at the radiator union having first slackened the clip. Remove the bracket screws and carefully lift away the tank and its hose (Fig.2.8).

Refitting is the reverse sequence to removal. Add either water or anti freeze solution until it is up the level mark.

13 Temperature gauge thermal transmitter

The thermal transmitter is placed in the cylinder head just below the thermostat and is held in position by a special gland nut to ensure a water tight joint. It is connected to the gauge located on the instrument panel by a cable on the main ignition feed circuit and a special bi-metal voltage stabilizer.

To remove the thermal transmitter, partially drain the cooling system (usually 4 pints (2.27 litres) is enough). Unscrew the transmitter gland nut from the side of the cylinder head. Withdraw the thermal transmitter. Refitting is the reverse procedure to removal.

For information on the gauge refer to Chapter 10.

14 Anti-freeze mixture

1 In anticipation of freezing conditions, it is essential that some of the water is drained and an adequate amount of ethylene glycol anti freeze, (Castrol Anti-Freeze) is added to the cooling system.

2 If Castrol anti freeze is not available, any anti freeze which conforms with specification BS 3151 and BS 3152 can be used. Never use an anti freeze with an alcohol base as evaporation is too high.

3 Castrol anti freeze with an anti-corrosion additive can be left in the cooling system for up to two years, but after six months it is advisable to have the specific gravity of the coolant checked at your local garage and thereafter, every three months.

4 Listed below are the amounts of anti freeze which should be added to ensure adequate protection down to the temperature given:

Amount of anti freeze	Protection to:
33 1/3% mixture	
2½ pints (1.5 litres)	- 19°C (- 2°F)
50% mixture	
3¾ pints (2 litres)	- 36°C (- 33°F)

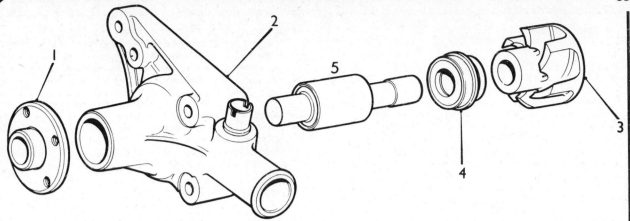

FIG.2.5 WATER PUMP COMPONENTS

1 Pulley hub   3 Impeller   4 Seal   5 Spindle and bearings
2 Water pump body

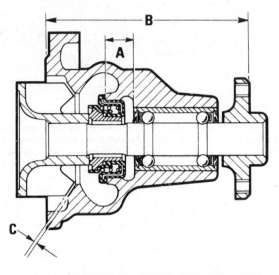

FIG.2.6 WATER PUMP REASSEMBLY DIMENSIONS

A 0.533 to 0.543 inch (13.54 to 13.79 mm)
B 3.712 to 3.732 inch (94.31 to 94.8 mm)
C 0.20 to 0.30 inch (0.508 to 0.762 mm)

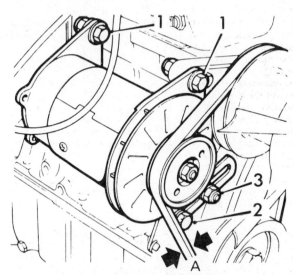

FIG.2.7 FAN BELT ADJUSTMENT

1 Upper mounting   3 Adjustment link securing nut
2 Lower mounting   A 0,5 inch (13 mm)

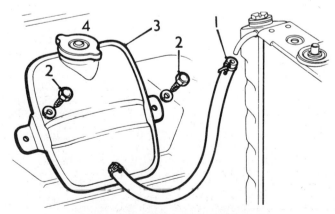

FIG.2.8 EXPANSION TANK ASSEMBLY

1 Hose to radiator   3 Expansion tank
2 Mounting bolt and spring   4 Pressure cap
   washer

Cause	Trouble	Remedy
Heat generated in cylinder not being successfully diposed of by radiator	Insufficient water in cooling system	Top up radiator.
	Fan belt slipping (Accompanied by a shrieking noise on rapid engine acceleration)	Tighten fan belt to recommended tension or replace if worn.
	Radiator core blocked or radiator grill restricted	Reverse flush radiator, remove obstructions.
	Bottom water hose collapsed, impeding flow	Remove and fit new hose.
	Thermostat not opening properly	Remove and fit new thermostat.
	Ignition advance and retard incorrectly set (Accompanied by loss of pwer and perhaps, misfiring)	Check and reset igntion timing.
	Carburettor incorrectly adjusted (mixture too weak)	Tune carburettor.
	Exhaust system partially blocked	Check exhaust pipe for constrictive dents and blockages.
	Oil level in sump too low	Top up sump to full mark on dipstick.
	Blown cylinder head gasket (Water/steam being forced down the radiator overflow pipe under pressure)	Remove cylinder head, fit new gasket.
	Engine not yet run-in	Run-in slowly and carefully.
	Brakes binding	Check and adjust brakes if necessary.
Too much heat being dispersed by radiator	Thermostat jammed open	Remove and renew thermostat.
	Incorrect grade of thermostat fitted allowing premature opening of valve	Remove and replace with new thermostat which opens at a higher temperature.
	Thermostat missing	Check and fit correct thermostat.
Leaks in system	Loose clips on water hoses	Check and tighten clips if necessary.
	Top or bottom water hoses perished and leaking	Check and replace any faulty hoses.
	Radiator core leaking	Remove radiator and repair.
	Thermostat gasket leaking	Inspect and renew gasket.
	Pressure cap spring worn or seal ineffective	Renew pressure cap.
	Blown cylinder head gasket (Pressure in system forcing water/steam down overflow pipe)	Remove cylinder head and fit new gasket.
	Cylinder wall or head cracked	Dismantle engine, dispatch to engineering works for repair.

Chapter 3 Carburation

Contents

Specifications

Air cleaner	Paper element with warm/cold air intake positions
Carburettor	S U HS4 - Horizontal
Piston spring	Red
Jet size	0.090 in (2.29 mm)
Standard needle	A A Q
Fuel pump	S U mechanical AUF 707
Suction (minimum)	6 inches (152 mm) Hg
Pressure (minimum)	3 lb/in^2 (0.21 Kg/cm^2)
Fuel tank	Flat tank under rear floor. Vented by breather pipes
Capacity	11.5 gallons (52 litres)

Torque wrench setting

	lb ft	Kg fm
Manifold to cylinder head	15	2.07

---

1 General description

The fuel system comprises a fuel tank at the rear of the car, a mechanical fuel pump located on the left hand side of the crankcase and a single horizontally mounted S U carburettor. A renewable paper element air cleaner is fitted. Operation of the individual components is described elsewhere in this chapter.

2 Fuel pump - general description

The mechanically operated fuel pump is located on the left hand side of the crankcase and is operated by a separate lobe on the camshaft. As the camshaft rotates the rocker lever is actuated, one end of which is connected to the diaphragm operating rod. When the rocker arm is moved by the cam lobe the diaphragm via the rocker arm moves downwards causing fuel to be drawn in through the filter, past the inlet valve flap and into the diaphragm chamber. As the cam lobe moves round, the diaphragm moves upwards under the action of the spring, and fuel flows via the large outlet valve to the carburettor float chamber.

When the float chamber has the requiste amount of fuel in it, the needle valve in the top of the float chamber shuts off the fuel supply, causing pressure in the fuel delivery line to hold the diaphragm down against the action of the diaphragm spring until the needle valve in the float chamber opens to admit more fuel.

3 Fuel pump - removal and replacement

1 Remove the fuel inlet and outlet connections from the fuel pump and plug the ends of the pipes to stop loss of fuel or dirt ingress.

2 Unscrew and remove the two pump mounting flange nuts and washers. Carefully slide the pump off the two studs followed by the insulating block assembly and gaskets.

3 Refitting is the reverse sequence to removal. Inspect the gaskets on either side of the insulating block and if damaged obtain and fit new ones.

4 Fuel pump - dismantling, inspection and reassembly

1 Thoroughly clean the outside of the pump in paraffin and dry. To ensure correct reassembly mark the cover and upper and lower body flanges (Fig.3.1).

2 Remove the three cover retaining screws, lift away the cover followed by the sealing ring and fuel filter (photo).

3 Remove the three remaining screws holding the upper body to the lower body. Separate the two halves taking care not to damage the diaphragm (photos).

4 As the combined inlet and outlet valve is a press fit into the body, very carefully remove the valve taking care not to damage the very fine edge of the inlet valve (photo).

5 Lift away the insert from the outlet cover.

6 With the diaphragm and rocker held down against the action of the diaphragm spring tap out the rocker lever pivot pin using a parallel pin punch. Lift out the rocker lever and spring (photos).

7 Lift out the diaphragm and spring having first well lubricated the lower seal to avoid damage as the spindle stirrup is drawn through. Unless the seal is damaged, it is best left in position as a special extractor is required for removal (photo).

8 Carefully wash the filter gauge in petrol and clean all traces of sediment from the upper body. Inspect the diaphragm for signs of distortion, cracking or perishing and fit a new one if suspect.

9 Inspect the fine edge and lips of the combined inlet and outlet valve and check that it is a firm fit in the upper body. Finally inspect the outlet cover for signs of corrosion, pitting or distortion and obtain a new part if necessary.

10 To reassemble first check that there are no sharp edges on the diaphragm spindle and stirrup and well lubricate the oil seals. Insert the stirrup and spindle into the spring and then through the oil seal and position the stirrup ready for rocker lever engagement.

11 Fit the combined inlet/outlet valve ensuring that the groove registers in the housing correctly. Check that the fine edge of the inlet valve contacts its seating correctly and evenly.

12 Match up the screw holes in the lower body and holes in the diaphragm and depress the rocker lever until the diaphragm lies flat, fit the upper body and hold in place by the three short screws, but do not tighten fully yet, (photo).

13 Refit the filter, outlet cover insert, new sealing washer and outlet cover suitably positioned by aligning up the previously made marks. Replace the three long screws and then tighten all screws firmly in a diagonal pattern.

14 Insert the rocker lever and spring into the lower body and retain in position using the rocker lever pivot pin.

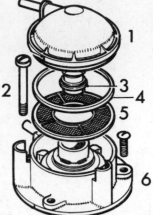

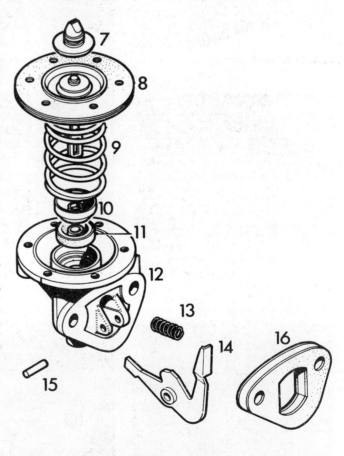

5 Fuel pump - testing

If the pump is suspect or has been overhauled it may be dry tested by holding a finger over the inlet union and operating the rocker lever through three complete strokes. When the finger is released a suction noise should be heard. Next hold a finger over the outlet nozzle and press the rocker arm fully. The pressure generated should hold for a minimum of fifteen seconds.

FIG.3.1 FUEL PUMP COMPONENT PARTS

1 Cover	9 Spring
2 Cover retaining screws	10 Lower body seal cup
3 Cover insert	11 Lower body seal
4 Sealing ring	12 Lower body
5 Filter	13 Rocker lever spring
6 Upper body	14 Rocker lever
7 Combined inlet and out-	15 Rocker pivot pin
let valve	16 Insulator block
8 Diaphragm	'x' Alignment marks

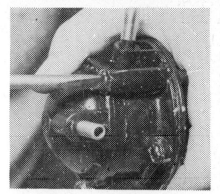
4.2A. Hold the pump firmly

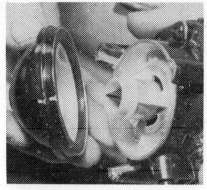
4.2B. Ease off the top cover

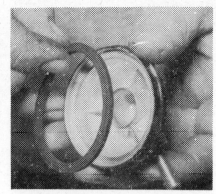
4.2C. Pick out the seal with your finger

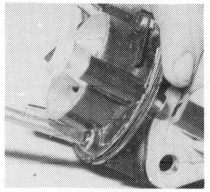
4.3A. Undo evenly all round

4.3B. Pull the two halves apart

4.4. Be careful at this stage

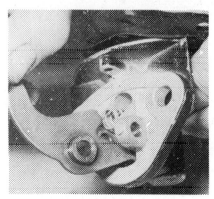
4.6A. Watch the little spring

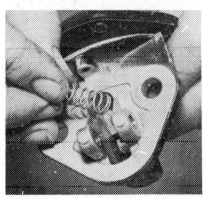
4.6B. Pull out the little spring now

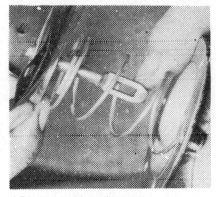
4.7A. Hold this spring whilst extracting the diaphragm

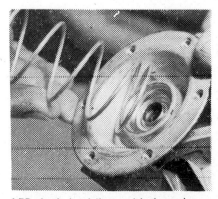
4.7B. Again be delicate with the spring

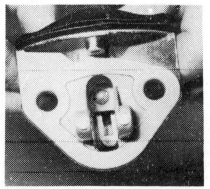
4.10. Press firmly but accurately with both hands

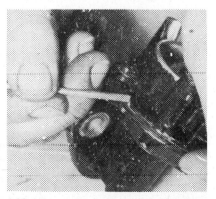
4.12. Line up the covers with the marks

6 S U Carburettor - description

1 The variable choke S U carburettor, shown in component form, (Fig.3.2) is a relatively simple instrument. It differs from most other carburettors in that instead of having a number of various sized fixed jets for different conditions, only one variable jet is fitted to deal with all possible conditions.

2 Air passing rapidly through the carburettor draws petrol from the jet so forming the petrol/air mixture. The amount of petrol drawn from the jet depends on the position of the tapered carburettor needle, which moves up and down the jet orifice according to the engine load and throttle opening, thus effectively altering the size of jet so that exactly the right amount of fuel is metered for the prevailing road conditions.

3 The position of the tapered needle in the jet is determined by engine vacuum. The shank of the needle is held at its top end in a piston which slides up and down the dashpot in response to the degree of manifold vacuum.

4 With the throttle fully open, the full effect of inlet manifold vacuum is felt by the piston which has an air bleed into the choke tube on the outside of the throttle. This causes the piston to rise fully, bringing the needle with it. With the accelerator partially closed, only slight inlet manifold vacuum is felt by the piston (although, of course, on the engine side of the throttle the vacuum is greater), and the piston only rises a little, blocking most of the jet orifice with the metering needle.

5 To prevent the piston fluttering and giving a richer mixture when the accelerator pedal is suddenly depressed, an oil damper and light spring are fitted inside the dashpot.

6 The only portion of the piston assembly to come into contact with the piston chamber or dashpot is the actual piston rod. All the other parts of the piston assembly, including the lower choke portion, have sufficient clearance to prevent any direct metal to metal contact which is essential if the carburettor is to function correctly.

7 The correct level of the petrol in the carburettor is determined by the level of the float chamber. When the level is correct the float rises and, by means of a lever resting on top of it, closes the needle valve in the cover of the float chamber. This closes off the supply of fuel from the pump. When the level in the float chamber drops as fuel is used in the carburettor, the float drops. As it does, the float needle is unseated so allowing more fuel to enter the float chamber and restore the correct level.

7 S U carburettor - removal and replacement

1 Unscrew the wing nut securing the air cleaner assembly and lift away the wing nut, fibre washer and air cleaner assembly.

2 Ease the fuel feed pipe from the union on the float chamber cover. Plug the end to prevent dirt ingress (Fig.3.3).

3 Slacken the clip and ease off the engine breather pipe from the union on the carburettor body.

4 Slacken the locknut and undo the nut locking the accelerator cable to the control arm on the side of the carburettor body. Detach the accelerator cable.

5 Slacken the bolt securing the choke control cable to the operating likage and detach the choke cable.

6 Undo and remove the four nuts and washers securing the carburettor body to the manifold studs. Lift away the carburettor complete with abutment bracket and linkage.

7 Recover the insulator block and gaskets.

8 Refitting the carburettor is the reverse sequence to removal. Always fit new gaskets to the inlet manifold flange and one each side of the insulator block. Refer to Section and adjust the choke control cable and to section for details of the throttle cable adjustment.

8 S U carburettor - dismantling and reassembly

1 Unscrew the piston damper and lift away from the chamber and piston assembly. Recover the fibre washer

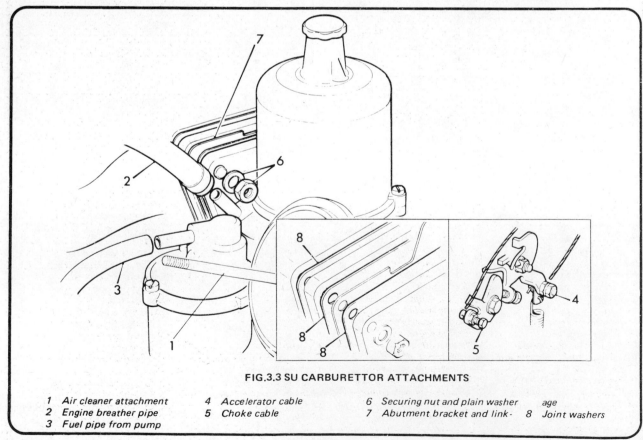

FIG.3.3 SU CARBURETTOR ATTACHMENTS

1	Air cleaner attachment	4	Accelerator cable	6	Securing nut and plain washer		age
2	Engine breather pipe	5	Choke cable	7	Abutment bracket and link-	8	Joint washers
3	Fuel pipe from pump						

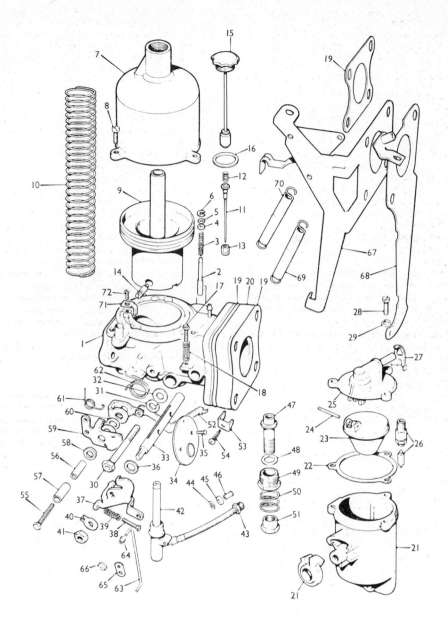

FIG.3.2 SU CARBURETTOR COMPONENT PARTS

1 Body	20 Insulator block	39 Spring	57 Pivot bolt tube—outer
2 Piston lifting pin	21 Float-chamber and spacer	40 Lock washer—throttle	58 Distance washer
3 Spring for pin	22 Joint washer—chamber	spindle nut	59 Cam lever
4 Sealing washer	23 Float	41 Nut—throttle spindle	60 Washer
5 Plain washer	24 Hinge pin—float	42 Jet assembly	61 Spring—cam lever
6 Circlip	25 Lid—float-chamber	43 Sleeve nut—jet flexible pipe	62 Spring—pick-up lever
7 Piston chamber	26 Needle and seat	44 Washer	63 Throttle lever rod
8 Screw—piston chamber	27 Baffle plate	45 Gland	64 Bush
9 Piston	28 Screw—float-chamber lid	46 Ferrule	65 Anchor tag
10 Spring	29 Spring washer	47 Jet bearing	66 Lock washer—throttle
11 Needle	30 Bolt—securing float-chamber	48 Sealing washer	lever rod
12 Spring—needle	31 Spring washer	49 Jet locating nut	67 Progressive throttle link-
13 Support guide—needle	32 Plain washer	50 Spring	age bracket
14 Locking screw—needle sup-	33 Throttle spindle	51 Jet adjustment nut	68 Throttle cable abutment
port guide	34 Throttle disc assembly	52 Pick-up lever	bracket
15 Piston chamber	35 Screw—securing disc assembly	53 Link—pick-up lever	69 Throttle return spring
16 Sealing washer—damper	36 Washer—throttle spindle	54 Screw—securing lever to jet	70 Tension spring
17 Throttle adjustment screw	37 Throttle return lever	55 Pivot bolt	71 Guide—suction chamber piston
18 Spring for screw	38 Fast-idle screw	56 Pivot bolt tube—inner	72 Screw—securing guide
19 Joint washers			

2 Using a screwdriver or small file, scratch identification marks on the suction chamber and carburettor body so that they may be fitted together again in their original position. Remove the three suction chamber retaining screws and lift the suction chamber from the carburettor body leaving the suction chamber in situ.

3 Lift the piston spring from the piston, noting which way round it is fitted, and remove the piston. Invert it and allow the oil in the damper bore to drain out. Place the piston in a safe place so that the needle will not be touched or the piston roll onto the floor. It is recommended that the piston be placed on the neck of a narrow jar with the needle inside so acting as a stand.

4 Mark the position of the float chamber lid relative to the body, and unscrew the three screws holding the float chamber lid to the float chamber body. Remove the lid and withdraw the pin thereby releasing the float and float lever. Using a spanner or socket remove the needle valve assembly.

5 Release the pick-up lever return spring from its retaining lug.

6 Support the plastic moulded base of the jet and remove the screw retaining the jet pick-up link and link bracket.

7 Carefully unscrew the flexible jet tube sleeve nut from the float chamber and lift away the jet assembly from the underside of the carburettor body. Note the gland, washer and ferrule at the end of the jet tube.

8 Undo and remove the jet adjustment nut and spring. Also unscrew the jet locknut and lift away together with the brass washer and jet bearing.

9 Unscrew and remove the lever pivot bolt and spacer. Detach the lever assembly and return the springs noting the pivot bolt tubes, skid washer and the locations of the cam and pick-up lever springs.

10 Close the throttle and lightly mark the relative position of the throttle disc and carburettor flange.

11 Unscrew the disc retaining screws, open the throttle and ease the disc from its slot in the throttle spindle.

12 Bend back the tabs of the lock washer securing the spindle nut. Undo and remove the nut and detach the lever arm, washer and throttle spindle.

13 Should it be necessary to remove the piston lifting pin, push it upwards and remove the securing clip. Lift away the pin and spring.

14 Reassembly is a straight reversal of the dismantling sequence.

9 S U carburettor - examination and repair

The S U carburettor is most reliable but even so it may develop one of several faults which may not be readily apparent unless a careful inspection is carried out. The common faults the carburettor is prone to are:

1 Piston sticking
2 Float needle sticking
3 Float chamber flooding
4 Water and dirt in the carburettor

In addition the following parts are susceptible to wear after high mileages and as they vitally affect the economy of the engine they should be checked and renewed where necessary, every 24,000 miles (38,600 km):

a) The carburettor needle: If this has been incorrectly fitted at some time so that it is not centrally located in the jet orifice, then the metering needle will have a tiny ridge worn on it. If a ridge can be seen then the needle must be renewed. S U carburettor needles are made to very fine tolerances and, should a ridge be apparent, no attempt should be made to rub the needle down with fine emery paper. If it is wished to clean the needle, it can be polished lightly with metal polish.

b) The carburettor jet: If the needle is worn it is likely that the rim of the jet will be damaged where the needle has been striking it. It should be renewed, otherwise fuel consumption will suffer. The jet can also be badly worn or ridged on the outside from where it has been sliding up and down between the jet bearing every time the choke has been pulled out. Removal and renewal is the only answer.

c) Check the edges of the throttle and choke tube for wear. Renew if worn.

d) The washers fitted to the base of the jet and under the float chamber lid may leak after a time and can cause a great deal of fuel wastage. It is wisest to renew them automatically when the carburettor is stripped down.

e) After high mileages the float chamber needle and seat are bound to be ridged. They are not an expensive item to replace and must be renewed as a set. They should never be renewed seaparately.

10 S U carburettor - piston sticking

1 The hardened piston rod which slides in the centre guide tube in the middle of the dashpot is the only part of the piston assembly (which comprises the jet needle, suction disc, and piston choke) which should make contact with the dashpot. The piston rim and the choke periphery are machined to very fine tolerances so that they will not touch the dashpot or the choke tube walls.

2 After high mileages wear in the centre guide tube may allow the piston to touch the dashpot wall. This condition is known as sticking.

3 If piston sticking is suspected and it is wished to test for this condition, rotate the piston about the centre guide tube at the same time as sliding it up and down inside the dashpot wall then that portion of the wall must be polished with a metal polish until clearance exists. In extreme cases, fine emery cloth can be used.

The greatest care should be taken to remove only the minimum amount of metal to provide the clearance, as too large a gap will cause air leakage and upset the function of the carburettor. Clean down the walls of the dashpot and the piston rim and ensure that there is no oil on them. A trace of oil may be judiciously applied to the piston rod.

4 If the piston is sticking, under no circumstances try to clear it by trying to alter the tension of the light return spring.

11 S U carburettor - float needle sticking

1 If the float needle sticks, the carburettor will soon run dry and the engine will stop, despite there being fuel in the tank.

The easiest way to check a suspected sticking float needle is to remove the inlet pipe at the carburettor and turn the engine over on the starter motor by pressing on the solenoid rubber button (manual gearbox) or operating the ignition/starter switch (Automatic Transmission). In the latter case remove the white lead on the ignition coil so that the engine does not start. If fuel spirts from the end of the pipe (direct it towards the ground, into a wad of cloth or into a jar) then the fault is almost certain to be a sticking float needle.

2 Remove the float chamber, dismantle the valve and clean the housing and float chamber out thoroughly.

12 S U carburettor - float chamber flooding

If fuel emerges from the small breather hole in the cover of the float chamber this is known as flooding. It is caused by the float chamber needle not seating properly in its housing: normally this is because a piece of foreign matter is jammed between the needle and needle housing. Alternatively the float may have developed a leak or be maladjusted so that it is holding open the float chamber needle valve even though the chamber is full of petrol. Remove the float chamber cover, clean the needle assembly, check the setting of the float as described later in this chapter and shake the float to verify if any petrol has leaked into it.

13 S U carburettor - water or dirt in the carburettor

1 Because of the size of the jet orifice, water or dirt in the carburettor is normally cleaned. If dirt in the carburettor is

suspected, lift the piston assembly and flood the float chamber. The normal level of the fuel should be about 1/16 inch (1.588mm) below the top of the jet, so that on flooding the carburettor the fuel should flow out of the jet hole.

2 If little or no petrol appears, start the engine (the jet is never completely blocked) and with the throttle butterfly fully open blank off the air intake. This will cause a partial vacuum in the choke tube and help suck out any foreign matter from the jet tube. Release the throttle as soon as the engine speed alters considerably. Repeat this procedure several times, stop the engine and then check the carburettor as described in the first paragraph of this section.

3 If this failed to do the trick then there is no alternative but to remove and blow out the jet.

---

14 S U carburettor - jet centering

---

1 This operation is always necessary if the carburettor has been dismantled: but to check if this is necessary on a carburettor in service, first screw up the jet adjusting nut as far as it will go without facing it, and lift the piston and then let it fall under its own weight. It should fall onto the bridge making a soft metallic click. Now repeat the above procedure but this time with the adjusting nut screwed right down. If the soft metallic click is not audible in either of the two tests proceed as follows:

2 Disconnect the jet link from the bottom of the jet, and the nylon flexible tube from the underside of the float chamber. Gently slide the jet and the nylon tube from the underside of the carburettor body. Next unscrew the jet adjusting nut and lift away the nut and the locking spring. Refit the adjusting nut without the locking spring and screw it up as far as possible without forcing. Replace the jet and tube but there is no need to reconnect the tube.

3 Slacken the jet locking nut so that it may be rotated with the fingers only. Unscrew the piston damper and lift away the damper. Gently press the piston down onto the bridge and tighten the locknut. Lift the piston using the lifting pin and check that it is able to fall freely under its own weight. Now lower the adjusting nut and check once again. If this time there is a difference in the two metallic clicks, repeat the centering procedure until the sound is the same for both tests.

4 Gently remove the jet and unscrew the adjusting nut. Refit the locking spring and jet adjusting nut. Top up the damper with oil, if necessary, and replace the damper. Connect the nylon flexible tube to the underside of the float chamber and finally reconnect the jet link.

---

15 S U carburettor - float chamber fuel level adjustment

---

1 It is essential that the fuel level in the float chamber is always correct as otherwise excessive fuel consumption may occur. Carburettors fitted to later models have non-adjustable floats.

2 (Early models only) with the carburettor fitted to the engine and the float chamber full of petrol remove the piston dashpot assembly.

3 Check that the level of fuel in the jet is about 1/16 inch (1.588 mm) below the top of the jet. If it is above or below this level it may be adjusted by removing the needle and seat from the underside of the float chamber lid and either add or remove washers so raising or lowering the relative position of the needle valve.

---

16 S U carburettor - needle replacement

---

1 Should it be necessary to fit a new needle, first remove the piston and suction chamber assembly, marking the chamber for correct reassembly in its original position (Fig.3.4).

2 Slacken the needle clamping screw and withdraw the needle, guide and spring from the underside of the piston.

3 To refit the needle assembly fit the spring and guide to the needle and insert the assembly into the piston making sure that the guide is fitted flush with the face of the piston and the flat on the guide positioned adjacent to the needle guide locking screw. Screw in the guide locking screw.

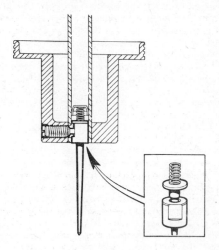

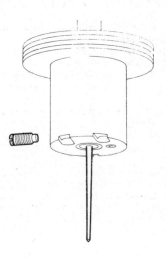

FIG.3.4 NEEDLE LOCATION IN PISTON

---

17 S U carburettor - adjustment and tuning

---

1 To adjust and tune the S U carburettor proceed as follows: Check the colour of the exhaust at idling speed with the choke fully in. If the exhaust tends to be black and the tail pipe interior is also black, it is a fair indication that the mixture is too rich. If the exhaust is colourless and the deposit in the exhaust pipe is very light grey it is likely that the mixture is too weak. This condition may also be accompanied by intermittent misfiring, while too rich a mixture will be accompanied by 'hunting'. Ideally the exhaust should be colourless with a medium grey pipe deposit.

2 The exhaust pipe deposit should only be checked after a good run of at least 20 miles. Idling in city traffic and stop/start motoring is bound to produce excessive dark exhaust pipe deposits.

3 Once the engine has reached its normal operating temperature, detach the carburettor air cleaner.

4 Only two adjustments are provided on the S U Carburettor. Idling speed is governed by the throttle adjusting screw and the mixture strength by the jet adjusting nut. The S U carburettor is correctly adjusted for the whole of its engine revolution range when the idling mixture strength is correct (Fig. 3.5).

5 To adjust the mixture set the engine to run at about 1000 rpm by screwing in the throttle adjusting screw.

6 Check the mixture strength by lifting the piston of the carburettor approximately 1/32 inch (0.79 mm) with the piston lifting pin so as to disturb the air flow as little as possible. If:

a) The speed of the engine increases appreciably the mixture is too rich.

b) The engine speed immediately decreases, the mixture is too weak.

c) The engine speed increases very slightly, the mixture is correct.

To enrich the mixture, rotate the adjusting nut which is at the bottom of the underside of the carburettor, in a clockwise direction, ie downwards. Only turn the adjusting nut a flat at a time and check the mixture strength between each turn. It is likely that there will be a slight increase or decrease in rpm after the mixture adjustment has been made so the throttle idling screw should be turned so that the engine idles at 650 rpm.

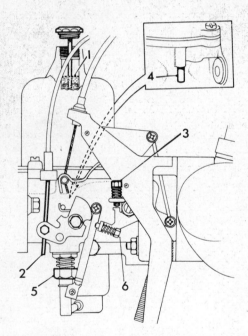

FIG. 3.5 CARBURETTOR ADJUSTMENT POINTS

1	Oil dashpot	4	Piston lifting pin
2	Throttle cable	5	Jet adjustment nut
3	Throttle adjustment screw	6	Fast idle screw

18 Throttle cable - removal and refitting

1 Using two thin open ended spanners unscrew the cable trunnion screw (Fig. 3.6).

2 Press in the plastic retainers located on the underside of the abutment bracket and carefully ease the cable through the bracket.

3 Detach the inner cable from the accelerator pedal and withdraw the cable into the engine compartment.

4 Refitting is the reverse sequence to removal but it is now necessary to adjust the effective length of the inner cable.

5 Pull down on the inner cable until all free movement of the throttle pedal is eliminated.

6 Feed the cable through the trunnion. Hold the throttle lever down against its stop and tighten the trunnion nut.

19 Choke cable - removal and refitting

1 Using two thin open ended spanners slacken the cable trunnion screw (Fig. 3.7).

2 Working behind the switch panel unscrew the large nut and shakeproof washer securing the control to the switch panel.

3 Carefully draw the cable through the body grommet and switch panel.

4 Refitting is the reverse sequence to removal but it is now necessary to adjust the effective length of the inner cable.

5 Set the position of the trunnion to give a free movement on the cable of 0.0625 inch (1.6 mm) before the cam lever begins to move (Fig. 3.8).

6 Pull out the control approximately 0.5 inch (13 mm) until the linkage is just about to move the jet.

7 Start the engine and adjust the carburettor fast idle screw to give an engine speed of 1000 to 1100 rpm.

8 Push the control knot fully in and check that there is a small gap between the end of the fast idle screw and the cam.

20 Throttle pedal - removal and refitting

1 Refer to Fig. 3.9 and detach the throttle cable from the end of the pedal.

2 Undo and remove the two nuts and spring washers securing the pedal bracket to the bulkhead panel. Lift the pedal assembly from the mounting studs.

3 Refitting the throttle pedal is the reverse sequence to removal.

21 Fuel tank - removal and refitting

1 Disconnect the battery.

2 Chock the front wheels, raise the rear of the car and support on axle stands located under the rear axle.

3 Unscrew the fuel tank drain plug and drain the contents of the fuel tank into a container of suitable capacity (Fig. 3.10).

4 Detach the cable terminal from the fuel tank sender unit.

5 Using a pair of pliers open the clips securing the hoses and vent pipes and ease off the pipes.

6 Release the vent pipe adjacent to the filler cap.

7 Undo and remove the four bolts, spring and shaped washers securing the tank to the brackets welded to the underside of the body. Lift away the fuel tank.

8 Refitting the fuel tank is the reverse sequence to removal.

22 Fuel tank - cleaning

With time it is likely that sediment will collect in the bottom of the fuel tank. Condensation, resulting in rust and other impurities is sometimes found in the fuel tank of a car more than three or four years old.

With the tank removed it should be vigorously flushed out and turned upside down, and if facilities are available, steam cleaned.

23 Fuel tank sender unit - removal and refitting

1 Disconnect the battery.

2 Disconnect the fuel gauge sender unit cable (Fig. 3.10).

3 Detach the main fuel pipe from the sender unit by squeezing the ears of the clip with a pair of pliers and pulling off the cable.

4 Using two crossed screwdrivers, remove the fuel gauge tank unit by turning through approximately 30°, and lift away from the tank. Take great care not to bend the float wire.

5 If the sender unit is suspect, check the circuit, gauge and sender unit as described in Chapter 10

6 Refitting is the reverse sequence to removal. Always fit a new sealing washer located between the fuel gauge tank unit and the tank itself.

FIG.3.6 THROTTLE CABLE ATTACHMENT

1 Cable trunnion
2 Outer cable retainer
3 Inner cable connection to
throttle pedal
4 Throttle return spring

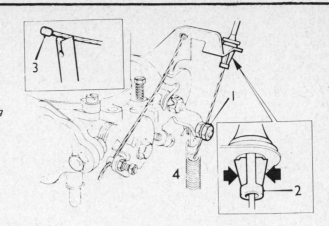

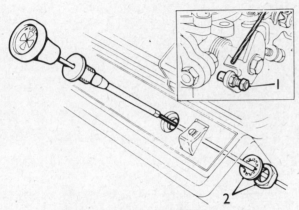

FIG. 3.7 CHOKE CABLE REMOVAL

1 Trunnion screw
2 Cable securing nut and
shakeproof washer

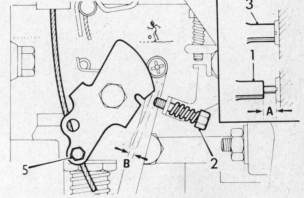

FIG. 3.8 CHOKE CABLE ADJUSTMENT

1 Choke control knob (out)
2 Fast idle screw
3 Choke control knob (in)
5 Cable trunnion screw
A = 0.5 inch (13 mm)
B = 0.0625 inch (1.6 mm)

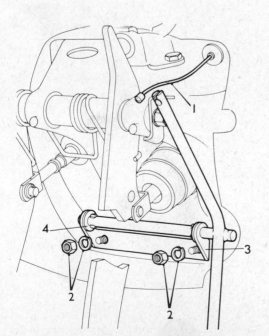

FIG. 3.9 THROTTLE PEDAL FIXING

1 Throttle cable
2 Throttle pedal bracket securing nut and spring
washer
3 Throttle pedal bracket
4 Clip

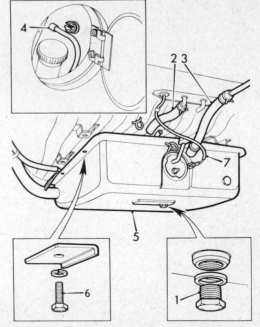

FIG. 3.10 FUEL TANK LOCATION

1 Drain plug and washer
2 Vent pipe
3 Main pipe to fuel pump
4 Vent pipe
5 Fuel tank
6 Securing bolt and spring washer
7 Sender unit electric cable

Unsatisfactory engine performance and excessive fuel consumption are not necessarily the fault of the fuel system or carburettor. In fact they more commonly occur as a result of ignition faults. Before acting on the fuel system it is necessary to check the ignition system first. Even though a fault may lie in the fuel system it will be difficult to trace unless the ignition is correct.

The table below therefore, assumes that the ignition system is in order.

Symptom	Reason/s	Remedy
Smell of petrol when engine is stopped	Leaking fuel lines or unions Leaking fuel tank	Repair or renew as necessary. Fill fuel tank to capacity and examine carefully at seams, unions and filler pipe connections. Repair as necessary.
Smell of petrol when engine is idling	Leaking fuel line unions between pump and carburettor Overflow of fuel from float chamber due to wrong level setting or ineffective needle valve or punctured float	Check line and unions and tighten or repair. Check fuel level setting and condition of float and needle valve and renew if necessary.
Excessive fuel consumption for reasons not covered by leaks or float chamber faults	Worn needle Sticking needle	Renew needles. Check correct movement of needle body.
Difficult starting, uneven running, lack of power, cutting out	One or more blockages Float chamber fuel level too low or needle sticking Fuel pump not delivering sufficient fuel Intake manifold gaskets leaking, or manifold fractured	Dismantle and clean out float chamber and body. Dismantle and check fuel level and needle. Check pump delivery and clean or repair as required. Check tightness of mounting nuts and inspect manifold.

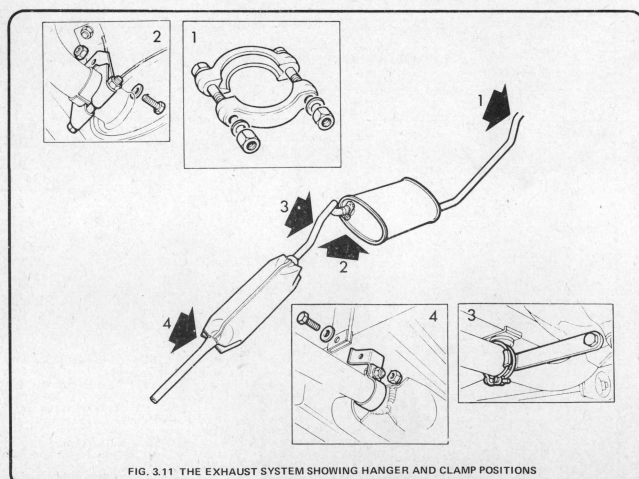

FIG. 3.11 THE EXHAUST SYSTEM SHOWING HANGER AND CLAMP POSITIONS

Chapter 4 Ignition system

Contents

Specifications

Spark plugs	Champion N - 9Y
Size	14 mm
Gap	0.024 to 0.026 inch (0.625 to 0.660 mm)
Firing order	1 3 4 2
Ignition coil	Lucas LA 12
Primary resistance at 20°C (68°F)	3.2 to 3.4 ohms
Consumption:	
Ignition on	3 to 4 amps
at 2000 rpm	1 amp
Distributor	Lucas 23D4 (High compression) 25D4 (Low compression)
Serial number: HC	41372
LC	41234
Direction of rotor rotation	anti clockwise
Dwell angle	60° ± 3°
Contact breaker gap	0.014 to 0.016 in (0.35 to 0.40 mm)
Condenser capacity	0.18 to 0.24 m fd

Centrifugal advance

	HC	LC
Deceleration check (crankshaft degrees and rpm) ... ... with vacuum disconnected	18° to 22° at 4000 rpm	26° to 30° at 4800 rpm
	11° to 15° at 2800 rpm	20° to 24° at 3600 rpm
	4° to 8° at 1600 rpm	10° to 14° at 2200 rpm
	0° to 3° at 800 rpm	2° to 6° at 1200 rpm
No advance below	300 rpm	500 rpm

Vacuum advance: Starts	4 in (101.6 mm) Hg
Finishes	12 in (304.8 mm) Hg

Torque wrench settings

	lb ft	Kg fm
Distributor flange retaining screws	8 to 10	1.1 to 1.4
Spark plug	14	1.9

1 General description

In order that the engine may run it is necessary for an electrical spark to ignite the fuel/air mixture in the combustion chamber at exactly the right moment in relation to engine speed and load. The ignition system is based on supplying low tension voltage from the battery to the ignition coil, where it is converted into high tension voltage. The high tension voltage is powerful enough to jump the spark plug gap in the cylinders many times a second under high compression pressure, providing that the ignition system is in good working order and that all adjustments are correct.

The ignition system comprises two individual circuits known as the low tension and high tension circuit.

The low tension circuit (primary circuit) comprises the battery, lead to control box, lead to the ignition switch, to the low tension or primary coil windings (terminal SW) and the lead from the low tension coil windings (terminal CB) to the contact breaker points and condenser in the distributor.

The high tension (secondary circuit) comprises the high tension or secondary coil winding, the heavily insulated ignition lead from the centre of the coil to the centre of the distributor cap, the rotor arm, the spark plug leads and the spark plugs.

The complete ignition system operation is as follows: Low tension voltage from the battery is charged within the ignition coil to high tension voltage by the opening and closing of the contact breaker points in the low tension circuit. High tension voltage is then fed via the carbon brush in the centre of the distributor cap to the rotor arm of the distributor. The rotor arm revolves inside the distributor cap and each time it comes into line with one of the four metal segments in the cap, these being connected to the spark plug leads, the opening and closing of the contact breaker points causes the high tension voltage to build up, jump the gap from the rotor arm to the appropriate metal segment and so, via the spark plug lead, to the spark plug where it finally jumps the gap between the two spark plug electrodes, one being connected to the earth system.

The ignition timing is advanced and retarded automatically to ensure the spark occurs at just the right instant for the particular load at the prevailing engine speed.

The ignition advance is controlled by a mechanical and vacuum (LC engines only) operated system. The mechanical governor mechanism comprises two lead weights which move out under centrifugal force from the central distributor shaft as the engine speed uses. As they move outwards they rotate the cams relative to the distributor shaft, and so advance the spark. The weights are held in position by two springs, and it is the tension of the springs which is largely responsible for correct spark advancement.

When fitted the vacuum control comprises a diaphragm, one side of which is connected via a small bore tube to the carburettor, and the other side to the contact breaker plate. Depression in the induction manifold and carburettor, which varies with engine speed and throttle opening, causes the diaphragm to move, so moving the contact breaker plate and advancing or retarding the spark. A fine degree of control is achieved by a spring in the vacuum assembly.

2 Contact breaker points - adjustment

1 To adjust the contact breaker points so that the correct gap is obtained, first release the two clips securing the distributor cap to the distributor body, and lift away the cap. Clean the inside and outside the cap with a dry cloth. It is unlikely that the four segments will be badly burned or scored, but if they are the cap must be renewed. If only a small deposit is on the segments it may be scraped away using a small screwdriver.

2 Push in the carbon brush, located in the top of the cap, several times to ensure that it moves freely. The brush should protrude at least ¼ inch (6.35 mm).

3 Gently prise the contact breaker points open to examine the condition of their faces. If they are rough, pitted or dirty it will be necessary to remove them for replacement points to be fitted (Fig.4.1).

4 Presuming the points are satisfactory, or that they have been cleaned and replaced, measure the gap between the points by turning the engine over until the contact breaker arm is on the peak of one of the four cam lobes. A 0.014 to 0.016 in (0.36 to 0.30 mm) feeler gauge should now just fit between the points.

5 If the gap varies from this amount, slacken the contact plate securing screw and adjust the contact gap by inserting a screwdriver in the notched hole at the end of the plate, turning clockwise to decrease, and anticlockwise to increase, the gap. Tighten the securing screw and recheck the gap again.

6 Replace the rotor arm and distributor cap and clip the spring blade retainers into position.

3 Contact breaker points - removal and replacement

1 If the contact breaker points are burned, pitted or badly worn, they must be removed and replaced.

2 To remove the points, unscrew the terminal nut and remove it together with the top insulating bush and both leads from the stud. Lift off the contact breaker arm and remove the large fibre washer from the terminal pin.

3 The adjustable contact breaker plate is removed by unscrewing one holding down screw and removing it, complete with spring and flat washer.

4 Later type contact breaker points: Undo the nut securing the terminals to the contact breaker point assembly (photo).

5 Lift the terminals from the threaded stud on the base plate assembly (photo).

6 Undo and remove the bolt and plain washer securing the contact breaker point assembly to the base plate assembly (photo).

7 Lift away the contact breaker point assembly (photo).

8 To replace the points, first position the adjustable table contact breaker plate, and secure it with its screw, spring and flat washer. Fit the fibre washer to the terminal pin and fit the contact breaker arm over it. Insert the flanged nylon bush with the condenser lead immediately under its head, and the low ten-

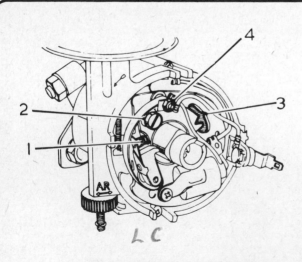

FIG.4.1 CONTACT BREAKER POINTS

1 Contact breaker points
2 Contact plate securing screw
3 Screwdriver slot
4 Moving contact spring and
   terminals securing nut

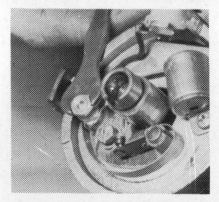

3.4. Try to use the correct 'distributor' spanner

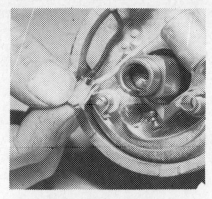

3.5. Release carefully

3.6. Use the right sized screwdriver — not too small!

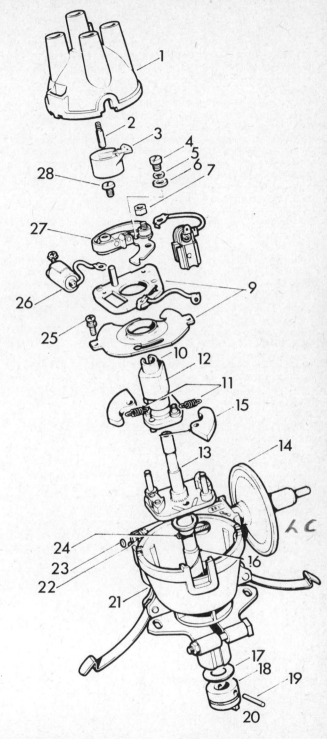

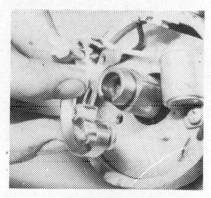

3.7. Use the thumb and two fingers

FIG. 4.2 25D4 DISTRIBUTOR COMPONENT PARTS

The 23D4 distributor is similar, but no vacuum unit is fitted

1 Distributor cap	10 Note relative position of slot and offset dog (20)	17 Thrust washer	24 Vacuum unit flexible coupling
2 Carbon brush and spring		18 Drive dog	
3 Rotor arm	11 Springs	19 Pin	25 Baseplate assembly securing bolt
4 Screw	12 Cam	20 Offset on dog (see also 10)	
5 Washer (spring)	13 Centre spindle (upper)	21 Body	26 Condenser
6 Washer (plain)	14 Vacuum unit	22 Knurled unit flexible coupling	27 Contact breaker point assembly
7 Nut	15 Centrifugal weight	23 Circlip	28 Cam retaining screw
8 Terminal block	16 Centre spindle (lower)		
9 Baseplate assembly			

sion lead under that, over the terminal pin. Fit the steel washer and screw on the securing nut.

9 Later type contact breaker points. Place the contact breaker points assembly on the baseplate assembly and lightly secure with the bolt and plain washer.

10 Refit the terminals to the threaded stud and secure with the nut. The points are now reassembled and the gap should be set as detailed in the previous section.

4 Condenser - removal, testing and replacement

1 The purpose of the condenser (capacitor) is to ensure that when the contact breaker points open there is no sparking across them which would waste voltage and cause wear.

2 The condenser is fitted in parallel with the contact breaker points. If it develops a short circuit, it will cause ignition failure, as the points will be prevented from interrupting the low tension circuit.

3 If the engine becomes very difficult to start, or begins to miss often several miles running, and the breaker points show signs of excessive burning, then the condition of the condenser must be suspect. A further test can be made by separating the points by hand with the ignition switched on. If this is accompanied by a flash it is indicative that the condenser has failed.

4 Without special test equipment, the only sure way to diagnose condenser trouble is to replace a suspected unit with a new one and note if there is any improvement.

5 To remove the condenser from the distributor, remove the distributor cap and the rotor arm. Unscrew the contact breaker arm terminal nut, remove the nut, and flanged nylon bush. Undo and remove the condenser securing screw and lift away the condenser.

6 Replacement of the condenser is simply a reversal of the removal process. Take particular care that the condenser lead does not short circuit against any portion of the breaker plate.

5 Distributor - lubrication

1 It is important that the distributor cam is lubricated with petroleum jelly or grease at the specified mileages and that the breaker arm, governor weights and cam spindle are lubricated with oil once every 6000 miles (10,000 km).

2 Great care should be taken not to use too much lubricant as any excess that might find its way onto the contact breaker points could cause burning and misfiring.

3 To gain access to the cam spindle, lift away the rotor arm. Drop no more than two drops of engine oil onto the screw head. This will run down the spindle when the engine is hot and lubricate the bearings. No more than ONE drop of oil should be applied to the pivot post.

6 Distributor - removal and replacement

1 For safety reasons disconnect the battery.

2 Release the clips securing the distributor cap to the body and lift away the distributor cap.

3 Slowly turn the crankshaft until the groove in the crankshaft pulley lines up with the static ignition point on the timing indicator, and at the same time the rotor arm is pointing to the distributor cap segment which is connected to No 1 spark plug (Fig.4.3).

4 Disconnect the low tension lead from the terminal on the side of the distributor.

5 Detach the vacuum pipe from the distributor vacuum advance unit (not 1.3 HC engine).

6 Undo and remove the two screws, spring and plain washers securing the distributor clamp plate to the cylinder block. The distributor may now be lifted up together with the clamp plate still attached.

7 If it is not wished to disturb the ignition timing, then under

no circumstances should the clamp pinch bolt, which secures the distributor in its relative position in the clamp, be loosened. Providing the distributor is removed without the clamp being loosened from the distributor, and the engine is not turned, the ignition timing will not be lost.

8 Replacement is a reversal of the above sequence. If the engine has been turned, it will be necessary to retime the ignition. This will also be necessary if the clamp pinch bolt has been loosened. Tighten the flange retaining screws to a torque wrench setting of 8 to 10 lb ft (1.1 to 1.4 Kg fm).

7 Distributor - dismantling

1 With the distributor removed from the car and on the bench, if the distributor cap is still in position, ease back the clips and lift it away. Lift off the rotor arm. If it is very tight lever it off gently with a screwdriver (photo).

2 Remove the contact breaker points as described in Section 3.

3 Remove the condenser securing screw from the contact plate by releasing its securing screw (photo).

4 Release the vacuum unit flexible link (1.3 LC engine only) from its mounting pin on the moving contact plate.

5 Unscrew and remove the two screws and washers which hold the contact breaker plate and base plate to the distributor body. Note the earth lead which is secured by one of the two screws. Remember to replace this lead on reassembly.

6 Lift away the contact breaker plate and base plate. Hold the contact breaker plate and turn the base plate in a clockwise direction to separate the two halves (photo).

7 Note the position of the slot in the rotor arm drive in relation to the offset drive dog at the opposite end of the distributor. It is essential that this is reassembled correctly as otherwise the timing may be 180° out (photo).

8 Unscrew the cam spindle retaining screw which is located in the centre of the rotor arm drive shaft cam. Lift away the screw (photo).

9 Detach the two return springs from their posts, and separate the cam plate. Lift away the two control weights.

10 To remove the vacuum unit (1.3 LC model only), spring off the small circlip securing the advance adjustment knurled nut which should then be unscrewed. With the micrometer adjusting nut removed, release the spring and the micrometer adjusting nut lock spring clip. This is the clip that is responsible for the 'clicks' when the micrometer adjuster nut is turned and it is small and easily lost, as is the circlip, so put them in a safe place. Do not forget to replace the lock spring clip on reassembly.

11 It is necessary to remove the distributor drive shaft or spindle only if it is thought to be excessively worn. With a thin parallel pin punch drive out the retaining pin from the driving torque collar on the bottom end of the distributor drive shaft. The shaft can then be removed. Recover the thrust washers.

12 The distributor is now ready for inspection.

8 Distributor - inspection and repair

1 Thoroughly wash all mechanical parts in petrol and wipe dry using a clean non-fluffy rag.

2 Check the contact breaker points as described in Section 3. Check the distributor cap for signs of tracking, indicated by a thin black line between the segments. Replace the cap if evident.

3 If the metal portion of the rotor arm is badly burned or loose, renew the arm. If slightly burnt, clean the arm with a fine file. Check that the carbon brush moves freely in the centre of the distributor cover.

4 Examine the fit of the contact breaker plate on the base plate and also check the breaker arm pivot for looseness, or wear, and obtain new as necessary.

5 Examine the centrifugal weights and pivot pins for wear, and renew the weights or cam assembly if a degree of wear is found.

6 Examine the shaft and the fit of the cam assembly on the shaft. If the clearance is excessive compare the items with new

7.1. Be firm but not careless

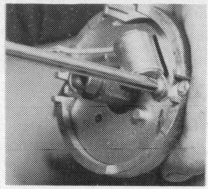

7.3. Only use a phillips screwdriver

7.6.   Do not burr the screw

7.7.   Avoid fiddling with the balance springs

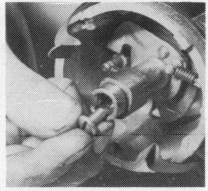

7.8. The screw can be held with a little grease to a screwdriver lip

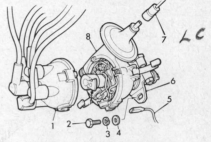

FIG.4.3. DISTRIBUTOR ATTACHMENT POINTS

1 Distributor cap	5 LT lead
2 Bolt	6 Clamp
3 Spring washer	7 Vacuum pipe
4 Plain washer	8 Distributor body

units and renew either, or both, if they show excessive wear.

7 If the shaft is a loose fit in the distributor bush and can be seen to be worn, it will be necessary to fit a new shaft and bush. Renewal of the bush consists of drifting out the old bush and fitting a new one. NOTE: Before inserting a new bush it should be stood in engine oil for 24 hours or two hours in hot oil at 100ºC (212ºF).

8 If possible examine the length of the centrifugal weight springs and compare them with new springs. If they have stretched they should be renewed.

9 Distributor - reassembly

1 Reassembly is a straight reversal of the dismantling process. Note in addition:

2 Lubricate the centrifugal weights and other parts of the mechanical advance mechanism, the distributor shaft, and the portion of the shaft on which the cam bears with Castrol GTX oil during reassembly. Do not oil excessively but ensure that these parts are adequately lubricated.

3 On reassembling the cam driving pins with the centrifugal weights check that they are in the correct position so that when viewed from above, the rotor arm should be at the 6 o'clock position, and the small offset on the driving dog must be on the right.

4 Check the action of the weights in the fully advanced and fully retarded positions and ensure they are not binding.

5 Tighten the micrometer adjusting nut to the middle position of the timing scale (1.3 engine only).

10 Ignition - timing

1 If the clamp plate pinch bolt has been loosened on the distributor and the static timing lost, or if for any other reason it is wished to set the ignition timing proceed as follows:

2 Refer to Section 2 and check the contact breaker points. Reset as necessary.

3 If necessary, assemble the clamp plate to the distributor - but do not tighten the pinch bolt fully.

4 Remove the rocker cover from the engine. Then, using a suitable spanner or socket on the crankshaft pulley bolt, turn the crankshaft until the cut-out in the pulley is in the correct position, relative to the timing cover pointer, to give 9º BTDC (see Fig. 4.4). Both valves for number one cylinder should now be closed. This means that the two valve springs will be uncompressed and thus there will be noticeable play between the two rocker arms and the valves. If this is not the case, continue to rotate the crankshaft in a clockwise direction until you have both the correct timing setting and both valves for number 1 cylinder closed. Should you accidentally go slightly past the correct setting do not turn the engine backwards to regain it.

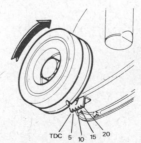

FIG.4.4 ALIGNMENT OF TIMING MARKS ON CRANK-SHAFT PULLEY AND POINTER ON FRONT COVER

TDC   5   10   15   20

Instead, continue to turn the crankshaft in a clockwise direction until the correct setting is again reached. **The crankshaft must not be turned again until ignition timing is completed.**

5 Now is the time to refit the distributor (where necessary). If a vernier adjuster is fitted, set this to its central position. Rotate

the clamp about the distributor body until the lamp and body are approximately in the relative position shown in Fig. 4.3. Offer up the distributor to the engine and align the clamp plate holes over the holes in the block. Rotate the distributor shaft, via the rotor arm, until the distributor dog engages and the distributor clamp goes fully home against the cylinder block. If the distributor cap were fitted the rotor arm should be pointing to the segment which leads to number 1 cylinder spark plug. If necessary, the distributor body can be rotated slightly to align the segment and rotor.

6 Remove the rotor arm. Bearing in mind that the distributor shaft turns anti-clockwise, the heel of the contact breaker should now be just in front of the distributor cam lobe which will open the points. Rotate the distributor body to achieve this, if necessary. In this position the contact breaker points should be closed - if they are not rotate the distributor body slightly anti-clockwise until they are.

7 Grip the top of the distributor shaft and turn it lightly in a clockwise direction to take up any play in the advance/retard mechanism. While doing this carefully rotate the distributor body in a clockwise direction until the contact breaker points *just* begin to open. Tighten the distributor clamp pinch bolt. If it is found difficult to determine exactly when the points begin to open, use the following method. Disconnect the low-tension lead from the distributor. Reconnect the lead with a low wattage bulb fitted in series and switch on the ignition. When the light goes out the points have just opened.

8 Ignition timing is now complete. Refit the distributor cap and leads, then replace the rocker cover. If necessary, fine adjustment can be made to the ignition timing using the vernier adjuster (where fitted). The handbook supplied with your car will tell you how this is accomplished.

9 If it was found not possible to align the rotor arm correctly, one of two things is wrong. Either the distributor driveshaft has been incorrectly fitted, in which case it must be removed and replaced, as described in Chapter 1, or the distributor has been dismantled and the distributor cam spindle refitted 180º out. To rectify, it will be necessary to partially dismantle the distributor, lift the cam spindle pins from the centrifugal weight holes and turn the cam spindle through 180º. Refit the pins into the weights and reassemble.

11 Spark plugs and leads

1 The correct functioning of the spark plugs is vital for the proper running and efficient operation of the engine.

2 At intervals of 6000 miles (10,000 Km) the plugs should be removed, examined, cleaned, and if worn excessively, renewed. The condition of the spark plug will also tell much about the general condition of the engine.

3 If the insulator nose of the spark plug is clean and white, with no deposits, this is indicative of a weak mixture, or too hot a plug (a hot plug transfers heat away from the electrode slowly — a cold plug transfers heat away quickly).

4 If the insulator nose is covered with hard black looking deposits, then this is indicative that the mixture is too rich. Should the plug be black and oily, then it is likely that the engine is fairly worn, as well as the mixture being too rich.

5 If the insulator nose is covered with light tan to greyish brown deposits, then the mixture is correct, and it is likely that the engine is in good condition.

6 If there are any traces of long brown tapering stains on the outside of the white portion of the plug, then the plug will have to be renewed, as this shows that there is a faulty joint between the plug body and the insulator, and compression is being allowed to leak away.

7 Plugs should be cleaned by a sand blasting machine, which will free them from carbon more than by cleaning by hand. The machine will test the condition of the plugs under compression. Any plug that fails to spark at the recommended pressure should be renewed.

8 The spark plugs gap is of considerable importance, as, if it is too large or too small the size of the spark and its efficiency will be seriously impaired. The spark plug gap should be set to 0.025 inch (0.6425 mm).

9 To set it, measure the gap with a feeler gauge, and then bend open, or close, the outer plug electrode until the correct gap is achieved. The centre electrode should never be bent as this may crack the insulation and cause plug failure, if nothing worse (Fig.4.5).

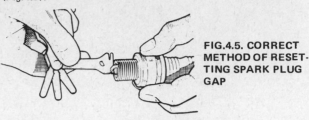

FIG.4.5. CORRECT METHOD OF RESETTING SPARK PLUG GAP

10 When replacing the plugs, remember to use new washers and replace the leads from the distributor cap in the correct firing order which is 1 3 4 2, No 1 cylinder being the one nearest the fan.

11 The plug leads require no maintenance other than being kept clean and wiped over regularly. At intervals of 6000 miles (10,000 Km), however, pull each lead off the plug in turn and remove them from the distributor cap. Water can seep down these joints giving rise to a white corrosive deposit which must be carefully removed from the end of each cable.

12 Ignition system - fault symptoms

There are two general symptoms of ignition faults. Either the engine will not fire, or the engine is difficult to start and misfires. If it is a regular misfire, ie the engine is only running on two or three cylinders, the fault is almost sure to be in the high tension, circuit. If the misfiring is intermittent, the fault could be in either the high or low tension circuits. If the engine stops suddenly, or will not start at all, it is likely that the fault is in the low tension circuit. Loss of power and overheating, apart from faulty carburettor settings, are normally due to faults in the distributor, or incorrect igniton timing.

13 Fault diagnosis - engine fails to start

1 If the engine fails to start and it was running normally when it was last used, first check that there is fuel in the petrol tank. If the engine turns over normally on the starter motor and the battery is evidently well charged, then the fault may be in either the high or low tension circuits. First check the HT circuit. NOTE: If the battery is shown to be fully charged, the ignition comes on, and the starter motor fails to turn the engine, CHECK THE TIGHTNESS OF THE LEADS ON THE BATTERY TERMINALS and also the secureness of the earth lead to its CONNECTION TO THE BODY. It is quite common for the leads to have worked loose, even if they look and feel secure. If one of the battery terminal posts gets very hot when trying to operate the starter motor this is a sure indication of a faulty connection to that terminal.

2 One of the commonist reasons for bad starting is wet or damp spark plugs leads and distributor. Remove the distributor cap. If the condensation is visible, internally dry the cap with a rag and also wipe over the leads. Replace the cap.

3 If the engine still fails to start, check that current is reaching the plugs by disconnecting each plug lead in turn at the spark plug end, and holding the end of the cable about 3/16 inch (4.726 mm) away from the cylinder block. Spin the engine on the starter motor by pressing the rubber button on the starter motor solenoid switch (under the bonnet) for manual gearbox models. For automatic transmission models a second person should operate the ignition/starter switch.

Measuring plug gap. A feeler gauge of the correct size (see ignition system specifications) should have a slight 'drag' when slid between the electrodes. Adjust gap if necessary

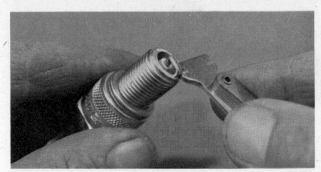

Adjusting plug gap. The plug gap is adjusted by bending the earth electrode inwards, or outwards, as necessary until the correct clearance is obtained. Note the use of the correct tool

Normal. Grey-brown deposits lightly coated core nose. Gap increasing by around 0.001 in (0.025 mm) per 1000 miles (1600 km). Plugs ideally suited to engine and engine in good condition

Carbon fouling. Dry, black, sooty deposits. Will cause weak spark and eventually misfire. Fault: over-rich fuel mixture. Check: carburettor mixture settings, float level and jet sizes; choke operation and cleanliness of air filter. Plugs can be re-used after cleaning

Oil fouling. Wet, oily deposits. Will cause weak spark and eventually misfire. Fault: worn bores/piston rings or valve guides; sometimes occurs (temporarily) during running-in period. Plugs can be re-used after thorough cleaning

Overheating. Electrodes have glazed appearance, core nose very white - few deposits. Fault: plug overheating. Check: plug value, ignition timing, fuel octane rating (too low) and fuel mixture (too weak). Discard plugs and cure fault immediately

Electrode damage. Electrodes burned away; core nose has burned, glazed appearance. Fault: initial pre-ignition. Check: as for 'Overheating' but may be more severe. Discard plugs and remedy fault before piston or valve damage occurs

Split core nose (may appear initially as a crack). Damage is self-evident, but cracks will only show after cleaning. Fault: pre-ignition or wrong gap-setting technique. Check: ignition timing, cooling system, fuel octane rating (too low) and fuel mixture (too weak). Discard plugs, rectify fault immediately

4 Sparking between the end of the cable and the block should by fairly strong with a regular blue spark (hold the lead with rubber to avoid electric shocks). If current is reaching the spark plugs, then remove them and clean and regap them to 0.024 to 0.026 inch (0.625 to 0.660 mm). The engine should now start.

5 Spin the engine as before, when a rapid succession of blue sparks between the end of the lead and the block indicate that the coil is in order, and that either the distributor cap is cracked: the carbon brush is stuck or worn: the rotor arm is faulty: or the contact points are burnt, pitted or dirty. If the points are in bad shape, clean and reset them as described in Section 3.

6 If there are no sparks from the end of the lead from the coil, then check the connections of the lead to the coil and distributor cap, and if they are in order, check out the low tension circuit starting with the battery.

7 Switch on the ignition and turn the crankshaft so that the contact breaker points have fully opened. Then with either a 20 volt voltmeter or bulb and length of wire, check that current from the battery is reaching the starter solenoid switch. No reading indicates that there is a fault in the cable to the switch or in the connections at the switch or at the battery terminals. Alternatively, the battery earth lead may not be properly earthed to the body.

8 If in order, check that current is reaching terminal A (the one with the brown lead) in the control box, by connecting the voltmeter between A and an earth point. If there is no reading, this indicates a faulty cable or loose connection between the solenoid switch and the A terminal. Remedy and the car will start.

9 Check with the voltmeter between the control box terminal A1 and earth. No reading means a fault in the control box. Fit a new control box and start the car.

10 If in order, then check that current is reaching the ignition switch by connecting the voltmeter to the ignition switch input terminal (the one connected to the brown cable) and earth. No reading indicates a break in the wire or a faulty connection at the switch or A1 terminals.

11 If the correct reading (approx 12 volts) is obtained check the output terminal on the ignition switch (the one with the white cable). No reading means that the ignition switch is broken. Replace with a new unit and start the car.

12 If current is reaching the ignition switch output terminal, then check the A3 terminal on the fuse unit with the voltmeter. No reading indicates a break in the wire or loose connections between the ignition and the A3 terminal. Even if the A3 -A4 fuse is broken, current should still be reaching the coil as it does not pass through the fuse. Remedy and the car should now start.

13 Check the switch terminal on the coil (it is marked + and the lead from the switch is connected to it). No reading indicates loose connections or a broken wire from the A3 terminal in the fuse unit. If this proves to be at fault, remedy and restart the car.

14 Check the contact breaker terminal on the coil (it is marked — and the lead to the distributor is connected to it). If no reading is recorded on the voltmeter then the coil is broken and must be replaced. The car should start when a new coil has been fitted.

15 If a reading is obtained at the terminal then check the wire from the coil for loose connections etc. The final check on the loose tension circuit is across the contact breaker points. No reading indicates a broken condenser, which when replaced will enable the car to finally start.

14 Fault diagnosis - engine misfires

1 If the engine misfires regularly, run it at a fast idling speed, and short out each of the spark plugs in turn by placing an insulated screwdriver across the plug terminal to the cylinder block.

2 No difference in engine running will be noticed when the plug in the defective cylinder is short circuited. Short circuiting the working plugs will accentuate the misfire.

3 Remove the plug lead from the end of the defective plug and hold it about 3/16 inch (4.76 mm) away from the block. Restart the engine. If sparking is fairly strong and regular the fault must lie in the spark plug.

4 The plug may be loose, the insulation may be cracked or the electrodes may have burnt away giving too wide a gap for the spark to jump across. Worse still, the earth electrode may have broken off. Either renew the plug, or clean it, reset the gap and then test it.

5 If there is no spark at the end of the plug lead, or if it is weak and intermittent, check the ignition lead from the distributor to the plug. If the insulation is cracked or damaged, renew the lead. Check the connections at the distributor cap.

6 If there is still no spark, examine the distributor cap carefully for signs of tracking. This can be recognised by a very thin black line running between two or more segments, or between a segment and some other part of the distributor. These lines are paths which now conduct electricity across the cap thus letting it run to earth. The only answer is to fit a new distributor cap.

7 Apart from the ignition timing being incorrect, other causes of misfiring have already been dealt with under the Section dealing with failure of the engine to start.

8 If the ignition timing is too far retarded, it should be noted that the engine will tend to overheat, and this will be a quite noticeable drop in power. If the engine is overheating and power is down, and the ignition is correct, then the carburettor should be checked, as it is likely that this is where the fault lies. See Chapter 3 for details.

Chapter 5 Clutch

Contents

Specifications

Borg and Beck or Laycock diaphragm spring

Drive plate diameter	6.5 inch (165 mm)	
Number of damper springs...	4	
Damper spring colour	2 pale blue/red	
	2 pale blue/black	
Facing materials (identification colour)...	H26 wound yard	green/red
	WR7 wound yarn	white
	RYZ wound yarn	blue
	DSW8 wound asbestos	red
Master cylinder bore	0.625 inch (15.8750 mm)	
Slave cylinder bore	1.0 inch (25.4 mm)	

1. General description

A 6½ inch diameter diaphragm spring clutch operated hydraulically by a master cylinder and slave cylinder is fitted.

The clutch comprises a steel cover which is bolted and dowelled to the rear face of the flywheel and contains the pressure plate and clutch disc or driven plate.

The pressure plate, diaphragm spring, and release plate are all attached to the clutch assembly cover.

The clutch disc is free to slide along the splined first motion shaft and is held in position between the flywheel and pressure plate by the pressure of the diaphragm spring.

Friction lining material is riveted to the clutch disc which has a spring cushioned hub to absorb transmission shocks and to help ensure a smooth take off.

The clutch is actuated hydraulically. The pendant clutch pedal is connected to the clutch master cylinder and hydraulic fluid reservoir by a short pushrod. The master cylinder and hydraulic reservoir are mounted on the engine side of the bulkhead in front of the driver.

Depressing the clutch pedal moves the piston in the master cylinder forwards, so forcing hydraulic fluid through the clutch hydraulic pipe to the slave cylinder.

The piston in the slave cylinder moves forward on the entry of the fluid and actuates the clutch release arm by means of a short pushrod. The opposite end of the release arm is forked and is located behind the release bearing.

As this pivoted clutch release arm moves backwards it bears against the release bearing pushing it forwards to bear against the release plate, so moving the centre of the diaphragm spring inwards. The spring is sandwiched between two annular rings which act as fulcrum points. As the centre of the spring is pushed out, so moving the pressure plate backwards and disengaging the pressure plate from the clutch disc.

When the clutch pedal is released, the diaphragm spring forces the pressure plate into contact with the high friction linings on the clutch disc and at the same time pushes the clutch disc a fraction of an inch forwards on its splines so engaging the clutch disc with the flywheel. The clutch disc is now firmly sandwiched between the pressure plate and the flywheel so the drive is taken up.

As the friction linings on the clutch disc wear the pressure plate automatically moves closer to the disc to compensate. There is therefore no need to adjust the clutch regularly.

2. Clutch system - bleeding

1   Gather together a clean jar, a length of rubber tubing which fits tightly over the bleed nipple on the slave cylinder, a tin of hydraulic brake fluid and someone to help.
2   Check that the master cylinder is full. If it is not, fill it and cover the bottom two inches of the jar with hydraulic fluid.
3   Remove the rubber dust cap from the bleed nipple (if fitted) on the slave cylinder, and with a suitable spanner open the bleed nipple approximately three quarters of a turn.

4   Place one end of the tube securely over the nipple and insert the other end in the jam jar so that the tube orifice is below the level of the fluid (Fig.5.1).

5   The assistant should now depress the pedal and hold it down at the end of its stroke. Close the bleed screw and allow the pedal to return to its normal position.

6   Continue this series of operations until clear hydraulic fluid without any traces of air bubbles emerge from the end of the turbing. Make sure that the reservoir is checked frequently to ensure that the hydraulic fluid does not drop too far thus letting air into the system.

7   When no more air bubbles appear, tighten the bleed nipple on the downstroke.

8   Replace the rubber dust cap (if fitted) over the bleed nipple. Allow the hydraulic fluid in the jar to stand for at least 24 hours before re-using it to allow all the minute air bubbles to escape.

3. Clutch pedal - removal and replacement

1   Refer to Chapter 12 and remove the parcel shelf.

2   Straighten the ears and extract the split pin that retains the master cylinder operating rod yoke to pedal clevis pin. Lift away the plain washer and withdraw the clevis pin (Fig.5.2).

3   Straighten the ears and extract the split pin from the clutch pedal end of the pedal pivot shaft. Lift away the plain washer.

4   Carefully release the pedal return spring from the pedal and slide the pedal from the end of the shaft.

5   Inspect the pedal bush for signs of wear which evident either the old bush should be drifted out and a new one fitted or a new pedal assembly obtained.

6   Refitting is the reverse sequence to removal. Lubricate the pedal bush and shaft and also the spring coils to prevent squealing.

4. Clutch - removal and refitting

1   Remove the gearbox as described in Chapter 6, Section 2.

2   With a scriber or file mark the relative position of the clutch cover and flywheel to ensure correct refitting if the original parts are to be used (Fig.5.3).

3   Remove the clutch assembly by unscrewing the six bolts holding the cover to the rear face of the flywheel. Unscrew the bolts diagonally half a turn at a time to prevent distortion of the cover flange and to prevent the cover flange binding on the dowels and suddenly flying off.

4   With the bolts and spring washers removed, lift the clutch assembly off the locating dowels. The driven plate or clutch disc will fall out at this stage. Carefully make a note of which way round it is fitted.

5   It is important that no oil or grease gets on the clutch disc friction linings, or the pressure plate and flywheel faces. It is advisable to handle the parts with clean hands and to wipe down the pressure plate and flywheel faces with a clean dry rag before inspection or refitting commences.

6   To refit the clutch place the clutch disc against the flywheel with the clutch spring housing facing outwards away from the flywheel. Fitment the wrong way round result in non-operation of the clutch.

7   Replace the clutch cover assembly loosely on the dowels, replace the six bolts and spring washers and tighten them finger tight so that the clutch disc is gripped but can still be moved.

8   The clutch disc must now be centralised so that when the engine and gearbox are mated, the gearbox input shaft splines will pass through the splines in the centre of the hub.

9   Centralisation can be carried out quite easily by inserting a round bar or long screwdriver through the hole in the centre of the clutch, so that the end of the bar rests in the small hole in the end of the crankshaft containing the input shaft bearing bush. Moving the bar sideways or up and down will move the clutch disc in whichever direction is necessary to achieve centralisation.

10 Centralisation is easily judged by removing the bar and viewing the driven plate hub in relation to the hole in the centre of the diaphragm spring. When the hub appears exactly in the centre of the release bearing hole all is correct. Alternatively if an old input shaft can be used instant fitment will result.

11 Tighten the clutch bolts firmly in a diagonal sequence to ensure that the cover plate is pulled down evenly, and without distortion of the flange.

12 Mate the engine and gearbox, bleed the slave cylinder if the pipe was disconnected and check the clutch for correct operation.

5. Clutch - inspection

1   In the normal course of events clutch dismantling and reassembly is the term used for simply fitting a new clutch pressure plate and friction disc. Under no circumstances should the diaphragm spring clutch unit be dismantled. If a fault develops in the pressure plate assembly an exchange replacement unit must besfitted.

2   If a new clutch disc is being fitted it is false economy not to renew the release bearing at the same time. This will preclude having to replace it at a later date when wear on the clutch linings is very small.

3   Examine the clutch disc friction linings for wear or loose rivets and the disc for rim distortion, cracks and worn splines.

4   It is always best to renew the clutch driven plate as an assembly to preclude further trouble but, if it is wished to merely renew the linings, the rivets should be drilled out, and not knocked out with a centre punch. The manufacturers do not advise that the linings only are renewed and personal experience dictates that it is far more satisfactory to renew the driven plate complete than to try to economise by fitting only new friction linings.

5   Check the machined faces of the flywheel and the pressure plate. If either is badly grooved it should be machined until smooth, or replaced with a new item. If the pressure plate is cracked or split it must be renewed.

6   Examine the hub splines for wear and also make sure that the centre hub is not loose.

6. Clutch flexible hose - removal and replacement

1   Wipe the slave cylinder end of the translucent hose to prevent dirt ingress. Obtain a clean and dry glass jam jar and have it ready to catch hydraulic fluid during the next operation.

2   Carefully detach the hose from the metal pipe at the slave cylinder end and place in the jam jar. Allow all the hydraulic fluid to drain out (Fig.5.4).

3   Detach the hose from the metal pipe at the master cylinder end.

4   Undo and remove the self tapping screw securing the pipe bracket to the bulkhead. Do not refit the original pipe.

5   To fit the new pipe dip the ends in brake fluid to act as a lubrication and push the ends onto the metal pipes.

6   It will be necessary to bleed the clutch hydraulic system as described in Section 2 of this Chapter.

7. Clutch master cylinder - removal and refitting

1   Drain the fluid from the clutch master cylinder reservoir by attaching a rubber tube to the slave cylinder bleed nipple; undo the nipple by approximately three quarters of a turn and then pump the fluid out into a suitable container by means of operating the clutch pedal. Note that the pedal must be held against the floor at the completion of each stroke and the bleed nipple tightened before the pedal is allowed to return. When the pedal has returned to its normal position loosen the bleed nipple and repeat the process, until the clutch master cylinder is empty.

2   Place a rag under the master cylinder to catch any hydraulic fluid that may be split. Unscrew the union nut from the end of the metal pipe where it enters the clutch master cylinder and gently pull the pipe clear.

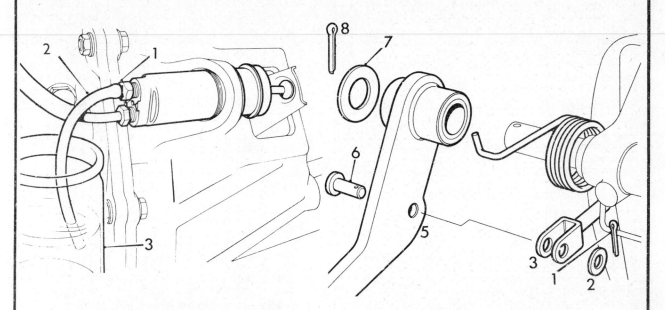

FIG.5.1. BLEEDING CLUTCH HYDRAULIC SYSTEM

1 Bleed nipple
2 Bleed tube
3 Glass jar

FIG.5.2. CLUTCH PEDAL MOUNTING

1 Split pin   5 Clutch pedal
2 Plain washer   6 Clevis pin
3 Pushrod   7 Plain washer
4 Spring   8 Split pin

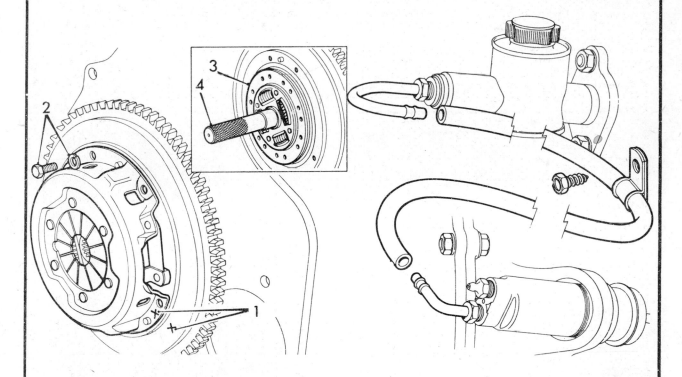

FIG.5.3. CLUTCH MOUNTED ON FLYWHEEL

1 Alignment marks   3 Clutch drive plate
2 Securing bolt and spring 4 Mandrel
  washer

FIG.5.4. CLUTCH FLEXIBLE HOSE AND ATTACHMENT

3 Straighten the ears and extract the split pin from the operating fork clevis pin on the pedal (Fig.5.5).

4 Unscrew and remove the two nuts and spring washers securing the master cylinder and lift away. Take care not to allow any hydraulic fluid to come into contact with the paintwork as it acts as a solvent.

5 Refitting the master cylinder is the reverse sequence to removal. Bleed the system as described in Section 2 of this chapter.

8. Clutch master cylinder - dismantling, examination and reassembly

1 Ease back the rubber dirt cover from the pushrod end, (Fig.5.6).

2 Using a pair of circlip pliers release the circlip retaining the pushrod assembly. Lift away the pushrod complete with rubber boost and plain washer.

3 By shaking hard, the piston with its seal, dished washer, second seal, and spring retainer may be removed from the cylinder bore.

4 Lift away the long spring noting which way round it is fitted.

5 If they prove stubborn carefully use a foot pump air jet on the hydraulic pipe connection and this should move the internal parts, but do take care as they will fly out. We recommend placing a pad over the pushrod end to catch the parts.

6 Carefully ease the secondary cup seal from the piston noticing which way round it is fitted.

7 Thoroughly clean the parts in brake fluid or methylated spirits. After drying the items inspect the seals for signs of distortion, swelling, splitting or hardening although it is recommended new rubber parts are always fitted after dismantling as a matter of course.

8 Inspect the bore and piston for signs of deep scoring which, if evident, means a new cylinder should be fitted. Make sure the by-pass parts are clear by poking gently with a piece of thin wire.

9 As the parts are refitted to the cylinder bore make sure that they are thoroughly wetted with clean hydraulic fluid.

10 Refit the secondary cup seal onto the piston making sure it is the correct way round.

11 Insert the spring with its retainer into the master cylinder bore.

12 Next refit the main cup seal with its flat end facing towards the open end of the bore.

13 Replace the wavy washer and carefully insert the piston into the bore. The small end of the piston should be towards the wavy washer. Make sure that the lip of the seal does not roll over as it enters the bore.

14 Smear a little rubber grease onto the ball end of the pushrod and refit the pushrod assembly. Slide down the plain washer and secure in position with the circlip.

15 Pack the rubber dust cover with rubber grease and place over the end of the master cylinder.

9. Clutch slave cylinder - removal and replacement

1 Wipe the top of the master cylinder reservoir and unscrew the cap. Place a piece of polythene sheet over the top of the reservoir and replace the cap. This will stop hydraulic fluid syphoning out during subsequent operations.

2 Wipe the area around the hydraulic pipe on the slave cylinder and disconnect the metal pipe from the slave cylinder.

3 Turn the slave cylinder until the flat on the shoulder faces the clutch housing.

4 Using a piece of metal bar or a large screwdriver carefully draw the clutch release lever rearwards until it is possible to lift out the slave cylinder. It will be found helpful to push the operating rod into the slave cylinder and then disengage it from the release lever, so assisting in lifting out the slave cylinder.

5 Refitting the slave cylinder is the reverse sequence to removal. It is very important that the bleed nipple is uppermost as it will be impossible to bleed fully.

6 Bleed the clutch hydraulic system as described in Section 2.

10. Clutch slave cylinder - dismantling, examination and reassembly

1 Clean the outside of the slave cylinder before dismantling.

2 Refer to Fig.5.7 and pull off the rubber dust cover and by shaking hard, the piston, seal, filler and spring should come out of the cylinder bore.

3 If they prove stubborn carefully use a foot pump air jet on the hydraulic hose connection and this should remove the internal parts, but do take care as they will fly out. We recommend placing a pad over the dust cover end to catch the parts.

4 Wash all the internal parts with either brake fluid or methylated spirits and dry using a non-fluffy rag.

5 Inspect the bore and piston for signs of deep scoring which, if evident, means a new cylinder should be fitted.

6 Carefully examine the rubber components for signs of swelling, distortion, splitting, hardening or other wear although it is recommended new rubber parts are always fitted after dismantling.

7 All parts should be reassembled suitably wetted with clean hydraulic fluid.

8 Refit the spring, large end first into the cylinder bore.

9 Replace the cup filler into the bore.

10 Fit a new cup seal and replace the piston making sure that both are fitted the correct way round.

11 Apply a little rubber grease to both ends of the pushrod and also pack the dust cover.

12 Fit the dust cover over the end of the slave cylinder engaging the lips over the groove in the body.

13 Fit the pushrod to the slave cylinder by pushing through the hole in the dust cover.

11. Clutch release bearing assembly - removal, overhaul and refitting

1 To gain access it is necessary to remove the gearbox as described in Chapter 6/2

2 Detach the operating lever from the release bearing and slide off the bearing assembly (Fig.5.8).

3 If the bearing is worn or shows signs of overheating it may be removed using a large bench vice or a press and suitable packing.

4 When refitting a new bearing always apply the load to the inner race.

5 Fit the release bearing onto the gearbox first motion shaft front end cover.

6 Engage the pivots of the operating lever into the groove in the release bearing and at the same time engage the lever retaining spring clip with the fulcrum pin in the gearbox housing.

7 Press the operating lever filler into position.

8 Replacement of the gearbox is now the reverse sequence to removal.

12. Faulty diagnosis and remedy

There are four main faults to which the clutch and release mechanism are prone. They may occur by themselves or in conjunction with any of the other faults. They are clutch squeal, slip, spin and judder.

13. Clutch squeal

1 If on taking up the drive or when changing gear, the clutch squeals, this is sure indication of a badly worn clutch release bearing.

2 As well as regular wear due to normal use, wear of the clutch release bearing is much accentuated if the clutch is ridden or held down for long periods in gear, with the engine running.

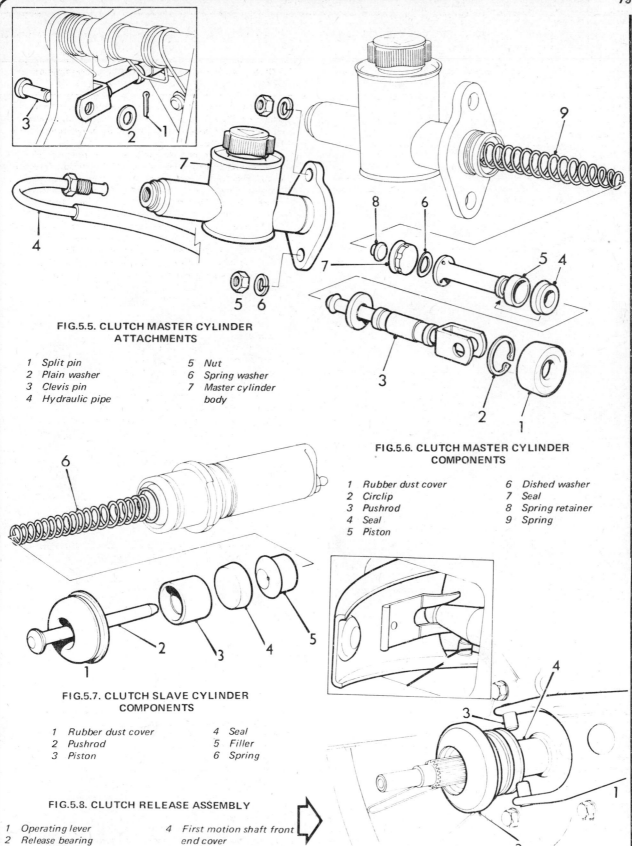

FIG.5.5. CLUTCH MASTER CYLINDER ATTACHMENTS

1 Split pin	5 Nut
2 Plain washer	6 Spring washer
3 Clevis pin	7 Master cylinder
4 Hydraulic pipe	body

FIG.5.6. CLUTCH MASTER CYLINDER COMPONENTS

1 Rubber dust cover	6 Dished washer
2 Circlip	7 Seal
3 Pushrod	8 Spring retainer
4 Seal	9 Spring
5 Piston	

FIG.5.7. CLUTCH SLAVE CYLINDER COMPONENTS

1 Rubber dust cover	4 Seal
2 Pushrod	5 Filler
3 Piston	6 Spring

FIG.5.8. CLUTCH RELEASE ASSEMBLY

1 Operating lever	4 First motion shaft front
2 Release bearing	end cover
3 Operating lever dowels	

To minimise wear of this component the car should always be taken out of gear at traffic lights and for similar hold ups.

3 The clutch release bearing is not an expensive item, but difficult to get at.

14. Clutch slip

1 Clutch slip is a self evident condition which occurs when the clutch friction plate is badly worn, oil or grease have got onto the flywheel or pressure plate faces, or the pressure plate itself is faulty.

2 The reason for clutch slip is that due to one of the faults above, there is either insufficient pressure from the pressure plate, or insufficient friction from the friction plate to ensure solid drive.

3 If small amounts of oil get onto the clutch, they will be burnt off under the heat of the clutch engagement, and in the process, gradually darken the linings. Excessive oil on the clutch will burn off leaving a carbon deposit which can cause quite bad slip, or fierceness, spin and judder.

4 If clutch slip is suspected, and confirmation of this condition is required, there are several tests which can be made.

5 With the engine in second or third gear and pulling lightly, sudden depression of the accelerator pedal may cause the engine to increase its speed without any increase in road speed. Easing off on the accelerator will then give a definite drop in engine speed without the car slowing.

6 In extreme cases of clutch slip the engine will race under normal acceleration conditions.

7 If slip is due to oil or grease on the linings a temporary cure can sometimes be effected by squirting carbon tetrachloride into the clutch. The permanent cure is, of course, to renew the clutch driven plate and trace and rectify the oil leak.

15. Clutch spin

1 Clutch spin is a condition which occurs when there is a leak

in the clutch hydraulic actuating mechanism; there is an obstruction in the clutch either on the first motion shaft or in the operating lever itself; or the oil may have partially burnt off the clutch lining and have left a resinous deposit which is causing the clutch disc to stick to the pressure plate or flywheel.

2 The reason for clutch spin is that due to any, or a combination of, the faults just listed, the clutch pressure plate is not completely freeing from the centre plate even with the clutch pedal fully depressed.

3 If clutch spin is suspected, the condition can be confirmed by extreme difficulty in engaging first gear from rest, difficulty in changing gear, and very sudden take up of the clutch drive at the full depressed end of the clutch pedal travel as the clutch is released.

4 Check the clutch master cylinder and slave cylinder and the connecting hydraulic pipe for leaks. Fluid in one of the rubber dust covers fitted over the end of either the master or slave cylinder is a sure sign of a leaking piston seal.

5 If these points are checked and found to be in order then the fault lies internally in the clutch, and it will be necessary to remove the clutch for examination.

16. Clutch judder

1 Clutch judder is a self evident condition which occurs when the gearbox or engine mountings are loose or too flexible; when there is oil on the face of the clutch friction plate; or when the clutch pressure plate has been incorrectly adjusted.

2 The reason for clutch judder is that due to one of the faults just listed, the clutch pressure plate is not freeing smoothly from the friction disc, and is snatching.

3 Clutch judder normally occurs when the clutch pedal is released in first or reverse gears, and the whole car shudders as it moves backwards or forwards.

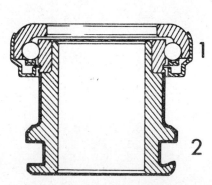

FIG.5.9. CROSS SECTION THROUGH CLUTCH RELEASE BEARING

1 Bearing assembly
2 Bearing carrier

Chapter 6 Gearbox and automatic transmission

Contents

Manual gearbox
4 forward speeds, 1 reverse. Synchromesh fitted to forward speeds

Gearbox ratios
Fourth (Top)	1.000:1
Third	1.433:1
Second	2.112:1
First	3.412:1
Reverse	3.753:1

Overall ratios
Fourth (Top)	4.111:1
Third	5.891:1
Second	8.682:1
First	14.026:1
Reverse	15.428:1
Road speed per 1000 rpm in top gear	15.9 mph (25.6 kph)
2nd and 3rd gear end-float on bushes	0.002 to 0.006 in (0.050 to 0.152 mm)
End-float of bushes on shaft	0.004 to 0.006 in (0.101 to 0.152 mm)

Washer sizes available:
colour code: Plain	0.152 to 0.154 in (3.860 to 3.911 mm)
Green	0.156 to 0.158 in (3.962 to 4.013 mm)
Blue	0.161 to 0.163 in (4.089 to 4.140 mm)
Orange	0.165 to 0.167 in (4.191 to 4.241 mm)

Laygear needle roller retaining rings:
Fitted depth - inner	0.840 to 0.850 in (21.336 to 21.590 mm)
outer	0.010 to 0.015 in (0.254 to 0.381 mm)

Centre bearing to circlip end float ... ... 0.000 to 0.002 in (0.000 to 0.050 mm)
Washer sizes available:
Colour code: Plain	0.119 to 0.121 in (3.022 to 3.073 mm)
Green	0.122 to 0.124 in (3.123 to 3.173 mm)
Blue	0.125 to 0.127 in (3.198 to 3.248 mm)
Orange	0.128 to 0.130 in (3.273 to 3.323 mm)

Reverse idler gear bush - fitted depth, Flush to 0.010 in (0.254 mm) below gear face

Automatic transmission ... ...
Borg-Warner model 35

Shift speeds	['D' selected with accelerator in kick down position]
Up shift	
1 - 2	36 - 43 mph (58 - 69 kph)
2 - 3	61 - 67 mph (98 - 108 kph)
Down shift	
3 - 2	56 - 63 mph (90 - 101 kph)
2 - 1 or 3 - 1	29 - 38 mph (47 - 61 kph)

Ratios:

First	2.39 : 1
Second..	1.45 : 1
Third	1 : 1
Reverse	2.09 : 1

Capacities

Manual gearbox	1½ pints (0.85 litres)
Automatic transmission:	
Oil pan only	5 pints (3 litres)
With torque convertor	9.5 pints (5.4 litres)
With torque convertor and oil cooler	11 pints (6.2 litres)

Torque wrench settings

	lb ft	Kg fm
Manual gearbox		
Flywheel housing retaining bolts	28 to 30	3.9 to 4.1
Rear extension to gearbox bolts	18 to 20	2.4 to 2.7
Drive flange nut	90 to 100	12.4 to 13.8
Automatic transmission:		
Drive flange nut	55 to 60	7.6 to 8.3
Drive plate to crankshaft	50	6.9
Convertor to drive plate bolts	25 to 30	3.4 to 4.1
Oil pan to gearbox bolts	9 to 12	1.2 to 1.6
Drain plug..	8 to 10	1.1 to 1.4
Starter inhibitor switch locknut	4 to 6	0.5 to 0.8

1. General description

The manual gearbox contains 4 forward and 1 reverse gear. Synchromesh is fitted to all forward gears.

The gear change lever is mounted on the extension housing and operates the selector mechanism in the gearbox by a long shaft. When the gear change lever is moved sideways the shaft is rotated so that the pins in the gearbox end of the shaft locate in the appropriate selector fork. Forward or rearward movement of the gear change lever moves the selector fork which in turn, moves the synchromesh unit outer sleeve until the gear is firmly engaged. When reverse gear is selected, a pin on the selector shaft engages with a lever and this in turn moves the reverse idler gear into mesh with the laygear reverse gear and mainshaft. The direction of rotation of the mainshaft is thereby reversed.

The gearbox input shaft is splined and it is onto these splines that the clutch driven plate is located. The gearbox end of the input shaft is in constant mesh with the laygear cluster, and the gears formed on the laygear are in constant mesh with the gears on the mainshaft with the exception of the reverse gear. The gears on the mainshaft are able to rotate freely which means that when the neutral position is selected the mainshaft does not rotate.

When the gear change lever moves the synchromesh unit outer sleeve via the selector fork, the synchromesh cup first moves and friction caused by the conical surfaces meeting takes up initial rotational movement until the mainshaft and gear are both rotating at the same speed. This condition achieved, the sleeve is able to slide over the dog teeth of the selected gear and thereby giving a firm drive. The synchromesh unit inner hub is splined to the mainshaft and because the outer sleeve is splined to the inner hub engine torque is passed to the mainshaft and propeller shaft.

2. Gearbox - removal and replacement

1   The gearbox can be removed with the engine as described in Chapter 1/5 and 1/7. Alternatively, another method is to separate the gearbox from the engine and to lower the gearbox and remove from under the car, leaving the engine in posiiton. Use this method if only clutch and/or gearbox repairs are to be made.
2   Disconnect the battery, raise the car and put on axle stands if a ramp is not available. The higher the car is off the ground the better.
3   Undo the gearbox drain plug and drain out the oil. When all

oil has drained out replace the drain plug.
4   Undo and remove the two nuts and plain washers that secure the exhaust manifold to downpipe clamp.
5   Refer to Chapter 3/7 and remove the carburettor.
6   Wipe the top of the clutch master cylinder and unscrew the cap. Place a piece of thin polythene sheet over the filler neck and refit the cap. This is to stop clutch hydraulic fluid syphoning out during subsequent operations.
7   Undo the union nut that secures the clutch hydraulic pipe to the end of the slave cylinder. Unscrew the hydraulic pipe clip securing screw and tie back the hydraulic pipe.
8   Unscrew and remove the self tapping screws securing each carpet finisher to the door sill. Lift away the finisher and carpeting so exposing the gear change lever rubber moulding retaining plate.
9   Undo and remove the self tapping screws securing the gear change lever rubber moulding retaining plate to the floor panel. Lift away the plate. Then slide the rubber moulding and foam sleeve up the gear change lever. Note that sealer is used under the rubber moulding flange.
10 Turn the gear change lever retaining cup in an anticlockwise direction so releasing the bayonet fixing. Ease the gear change lever up, at the same time being prepared to depress the plunger and spring in the fulcrum ball. Recover the plunger and spring from the fulcrum ball.
11 With a scriber or file mark the gearbox and propeller shaft drive flanges to ensure correct refitting. Then undo and remove the four locknuts and bolts that secure the gearbox and propeller shaft drive flange. Using string or wire tie the propeller shaft to the torsion bar.
12 Undo and remove the bolt and spring washer that secures the speedometer drive cable retaining clip on the side of the gearbox extension. Lift away the clip and carefully withdraw the speedometer cable.
13 Make a note of the electric cable connections to the starter motor, detach the cables and undo and remove the two bolts and spring washers securing the starter motor. Carefully lift away the starter motor.
14 Undo and remove the nut and spring washer from the exhaust clamp bolt. Withdraw the bolt and disconnect the clamp from the steady bracket. Then undo and remove the nut, spring washer and bolt from the exhaust steady bracket.
15 Using a hoist or jack support the weight of the engine and gearbox. If a jack is being used place it under the rear of the sump with a piece of wood between jack and sump.
16 Undo and remove the two bolts, plain and spring washers that

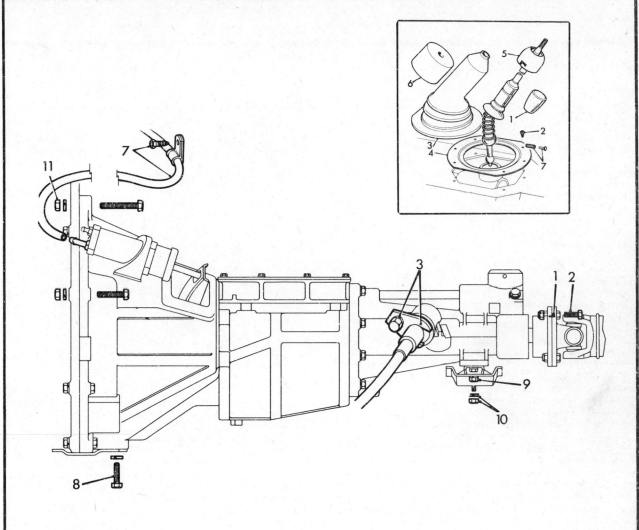

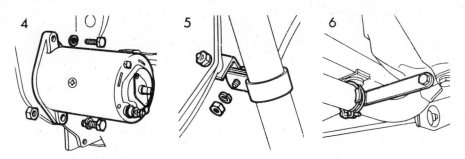

FIG.6.1. GEARBOX REMOVAL. SUMMARY OF ITEMS TO BE DISCONNECTED

1	Drive and propeller shaft flange marks	3	Speedometer cable	6	Exhaust pipe underbody bracket	9	Rear mounting to body
2	Flange securing bolt and locknut	4	Starter motor	7	Clutch hydraulic pipe bracket	10	Rear mounting to gearbox
		5	Exhaust pipe bracket at engine backplate	8	Sump plate	11	Bellhousing securing nuts and bolts

INSET: GEAR CHANGE LEVER ASSEMBLY

1	Knob	3	Rubber moulding	5	Cup	7	Plunger and spring
2	Screw	4	Moulding retaining plate	6	Foam sleeve		

secure the sump connecting plate to the underside of the gearbox bellhousing.

17 Undo and remove the two bolts, flat and spring washers that secure the gearbox rear crossmember to the underside of the body frame.

18 Undo and remove the nut and spring washer that secures the rear crossmember to the rear mounting.

19 Undo and remove the seven bolts and spring washers securing the flywheel housing to the mounting plate.

20 Disconnect the power unit braided earthing strap.

21 Make sure the weight of the gearbox is not allowed to be taken solely on the first motion shaft as it bends easily.

22 Lower the rear of the engine until there is sufficient clearance between the top of the bellhousing and underside of body and carefully draw the gearbox rearwards. Lift away the gearbox from the underside of the car.

23 Refitting the gearbox is the reverse sequence to removal. Do not forget to refill the gearbox if the oil has been previously drained. It will be necessary to bleed the clutch hydraulic system as described in Chapter 5/2

3. Gearbox - dismantling

1 Before commencing work, clean the exterior of the gearbox thoroughly using a solvent such as paraffin or 'Gunk'. After the solvent has been applied and allowed to stand for a time, a vigorous jet of water will wash off the solvent together with all oil and dirt. Finally wipe down the exterior of the unit with a dry non-fluffy rag.

2 NOTE: All numbers in brackets refer to Fig.6.2. unless stated otherwise.

3 Detach the operating lever from the release bearing and slide off the bearing assembly.

4 Undo and remove the five bolts securing the clutch bell housing to ghe gearbox casing. Note that the lowermost boit has a plain copper washer whereas the remaining bolts have spring washers.

5 Lift away the bellhousing. Recover the paper gasket from the front of the gearbox casing.

6 Withdraw the oil seal carrier from the bellhousing and ease off the rubber 'O' ring. If there were signs of oil leaks from the front of the gearbox into the clutch bellhousing the oil seal should be removed using a screwdriver and a new one obtained. Note that the lip faces outwards

7 Undo and remove the nine bolts and spring washers secuirng the top cover to the main casing. Lift away the cover and paper gasket. The main casing has been modified on later cars: the top extension and main casing are one casting. If the gearbox is of the earlier type comprising two parts temporarily replace two of the bolts to hold the two parts together.

8 Note which way up the interlock spool is fitted and lift it from the top of the main casing.

9 Undo and remove the one bolt and spring washer securing the reverse lift plate (26) to the rear extension. Lift away the lift plate.

10 Using a screwdriver carefully remove the rear extension end cover (13).

11 With a mole wrench hold the drive flange (81) and using a socket wrench undo and remove the locking nut (83) and plain washer (82).

12 Tap the drive flange (81) from the end of the mainshaft (78).

13 Lift out the speedometer drive pinion and housing assembly (21–24 - from the rear extension.

14 Make a special note of the location of the selector shaft pegs and interlock spool (37) so that there will be no mistakes on reassembly.

15 Using a suitable diameter parallel pin punch carefully remove the roll pin (38) from the bell housing end of the selector shaft (39).

16 Undo and remove the eight bolts and spring washers securing the rear extension (12) to the gearbox casing (92).

17 Draw the rear extension rearwards whilst at the same time

FIG.6.2. GEARBOX COMPONENTS

1 Oil filler level plug	36 Reverse operating lever	55 Gear bush
2 'O' ring	37 Interlock spool	56 2nd speed gear
3 'O' ring	38 Selector shaft roll pin	57 Thrust washer
4 Gearbox top extension	39 Gear selector shaft	58 Synchromesh cup
5 Joint gaskets	40 Interlock spool plate	59 Ball
6 Top cover	41 3rd/4th speed selector forks	60 Spring
7 Top cover bolt	42 1st/2nd speed selector forks	61 1st/2nd speed operating sleeve
8 Joint gasket	43 Selector fork shaft	62 Mainshaft reverse gear
9 Plug	44 Synchromesh cup	63 Synchromesh cup
10 Detent plunger	45 Ball	64 Split collar
11 Detent spring	46 Spring	65 1st speed gear
12 Rear extension	47 3rd/4th speed synchro hub	66 Thrust washer
13 End cover	48 3rd/4th speed operating sleeve	67 Mainshaft centre bearing
14 Dust cover	49 Synchromesh cup	68 Snap - ring
15 Knob	50 Mainshaft circlip	69 Selective washer
16 Upper gear-change lever	51 3rd speed gear thrust washer	70 Circlip
17 Lower gear-change lever	52 3rd speed gear	71 Speedometer wheel
18 Lower gear-change lever distance	53 Gear bush	72 Circlip
piece	54 Selective washer	73 Snap - ring
19 Seat		
20 Gear lever yoke		74 Ball bearing
21 Speedometer pinion		75 Oil flinger
22 'O' ring		76 1st motion shaft
23 Housing		77 Needle roller bearing
24 Seal		78 Mainshaft
25 Retaining clip		79 Washer
26 Reverse lift plate		80 Ball bearing
27 Oil seal		81 Drive flange
28 Reverse light switch		82 Washer
29 Magnet		83 Self-locking nut
30 Reverse idler spindle		84 Front thrust washer
set screw		85 Bearing outer retaining ring
31 Reverse idler spindle		86 Laygear gear cluster
32 Reverse idler gear bush		87 Bearing inner retaining ring
33 Reverse idler gear		88 Needle rollers
34 Reverse idler distance		89 Rear thrust washer
35 Reverse operating lever pin		90 Layshaft
		91 Layshaft dowel
		92 Gearbox case

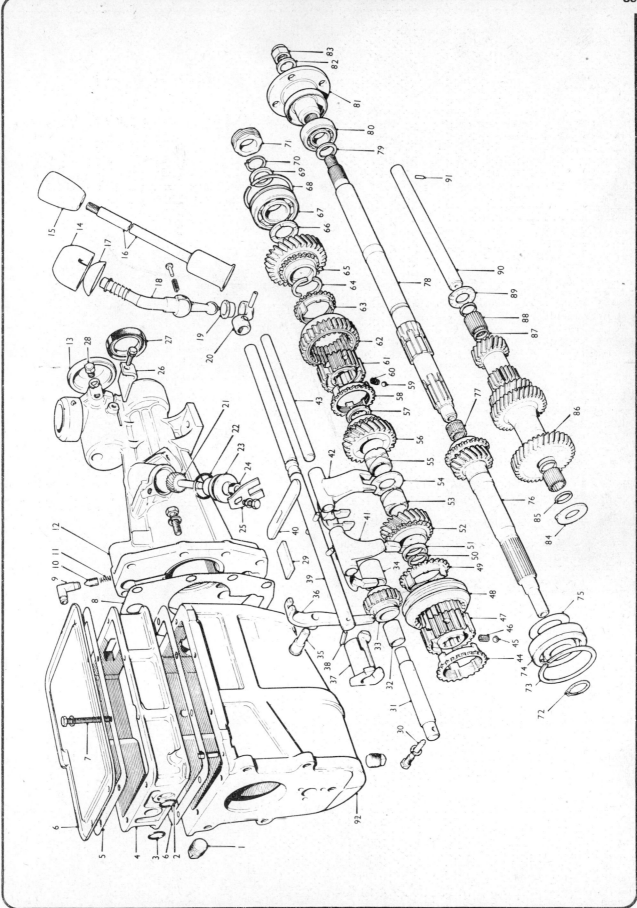

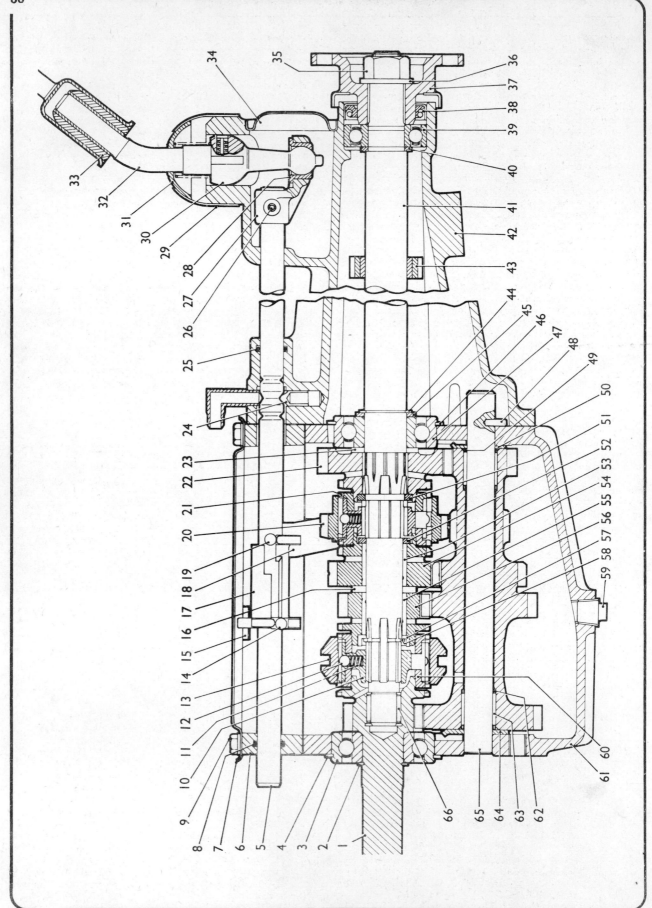

feeding the interlock spool (37) from the selector shaft (39).

18 With the rear extension (12) and selector shaft (39) away from the gearbox casing lift out the interlock spool (37).

19 Recover the paper gasket (8) from the rear face of the gearbox casing (92).

20 If oil was leaking from the end of the rear extension or the bearing (80) requires renewal the oil seal must be removed and discarded. It must never be refitted but always renewed. Ease it out with a screwdriver noting which way round the lip is fitted.

21 To remove the bearing obtain a long metal drift and tap it out working from the inside of the rear extension. Note which way round the bearing is fitted as indicated by the lettering.

22 Slide the washer from over the end of the mainshaft.

23 Make a special note of the location of the speedometer drive gear (71) on the mainshaft, if necessary by taking a measurement.

24 Using a tapered but blunt drift drive the speedometer drive gear from the mainshaft. Beware because it is very tight and it can break.

25 Using a suitable diameter drift tap out the selector fork shaft (43) towards the front of the gearbox casing.

26 Note the location of the two forward gear selector forks (41, 42) and lift these from the synchromesh sleeves (48,62).

27 Using a suitable diameter drift tap out the layshaft (90), working from the front of the gearbox casing. This is because there is a layshaft restraining pin (91) at the rear to stop it rotating.

28 Invert the gearbox and this will allow the laygear cluster (86) to drop into the bottom of the casing.

29 Using a small drift placed on the bearing outer track tap out the gearbox input shaft (76). If necessary recover the caged needle roller bearing (77) from the end of the mainshaft.

30 The mainshaft may now be drifted rearwards slightly sufficiently to move the bearing and locating circlip (67). Using a screwdriver between the circlip (68) and gearbox casing ease the bearing out of its bore and from its locating shoulder on the mainshaft. Lift away the bearing from the end of the mainshaft

31 The complete mainshaft may now be lifted away through the top of the gearbox main casing.

32 Unscrew the dowel bolt (30) that locks the reverse idler shaft (31) to the gearbox casing. Lift away the bolt and spring washer.

33 Using a small drift tap the reverse idler shaft rearwards noting the hole in the shaft into which the dowel bolt locates.

34 Note which way round the reverse idler is fitted and lift it from the casing.

35 Lift out the laygear cluster noting which way round it is fitted.

36 Recover the two thrust washers noting that the tags locate in grooves in the gearbox casing.

4. Gearbox - examination

1 The gearbox has been stripped, presumably, because wear or malfunction; possibly excessive noise, ineffective synchromesh, or failure to stay in a selected gear. The cause of most gearbox

ailments is failure of the ball bearings on the input or mainshaft and wear on the synchro rings, both the bore surfaces and dogs. The nose of the mainshaft which runs in the needle roller bearing in the input shaft is also subject to wear. This can prove very expensive as the mainshaft would need replacement and this represents about 20% of the total cost of a new gearbox.

2 Examine the teeth of all gears for signs of uneven or excessive wear and, of course, chipping. If a gear on the mainshaft requires replacement check that the corresponding laygear is not equally damaged. If it is the whole laygear may need replacing also.

3 All gears should be a good running fit on the shaft with no signs of rocking. The hubs should not be a sloppy fit on the splines.

4 Selector forks should be examined for signs of wear or ridging on the faces which are in contact with the operating sleeve.

5 Check for wear on the selector rod and interlock spool.

6 The ball bearings may not be obviously worn but if one has gone to the trouble of dismantling the gearbox it would be short sighted not to renew them. The same applies to the four synchronizer rings although for these the mainshaft has to be completely dismantled for the new ones to be fitted.

7 The input shaft bearing retainer is fitted with an oil seal and this should be removed if there are any signs that oil has leaked past it into the clutch housing or, of course, if it is obviously damaged. The rear extension has an oil seal at the rear as well as a ball bearing race. If either have worn or oil has leaked past the seal the parts should be renewed.

8 Before finally deciding to dismantle the mainshaft and replace parts it is advisable to make enquiries regarding the availability of parts and their cost. It may still be worth considering an exchange gearbox even at this stage. You should reassemble it before exchange!

5. Input shaft - dismantling and reassembly

1 Place the input shaft in a vice, splined end upwards and, with a pair of circlip pliers, remove the circlip which retains the ball bearing in place. Lift away the spacer.

2 With the bearing resting on the top of open jaws of the vice and splined end upwards, tap the shaft through the bearing with a soft faced hammer. Note that the offset circlip groove in the outer track of the bearing is towards the front of the input shaft.

3 Lift away the oil flinger.

4 Remove the old caged needle roller bearing from the centre of the rear of the input shaft if it is still in place.

5 Remove the circlip from the old bearing outer track and transfer it to the new bearing.

6 Replace the oil flinger and with the aid of a block of wood and vice lap the bearing into place. Make sure it is the right way round.

7 Finally refit the spacer and bearing retaining circlip.

FIG.6.3. THE MANUAL GEARBOX — CROSS SECTION

1 1st motion shaft	18 Reverse operating lever	35 Self-locking nut	51 Split collar
2 Circlip	19 Selector shaft roll pin	36 Flange washer	52 Thrust washer
3 Front ball bearing	20 Mainshaft reverse gear	37 Flange and stoneguard	53 Gear bush
4 Snap - ring	21 Synchromesh cup	38 Seal	54 3rd speed gear
5 Gear selector shaft	22 1st speed gear	39 End ball bearing	55 Gear brush
6 Hearbox top extension	23 Thrust washer	40 Thrust washer	56 2nd speed gear
7 Top cover	24 Detent plunger	41 Mainshaft	57 Thrust washer
8 Selector shaft 'O' ring	25 Selector shaft 'O' ring	42 Gearbox rear extension	58 Circlip
9 Top cover bolt	26 Yoke pin	43 Speedometer wheel	59 Drain plug
10 3rd/4th speed synchro hub	27 Gear lever yoke	44 Circlip	60 Synchromesh cup
11 Spring	28 Seat	45 Selective washer	61 Gearbox case
12 Ball	29 Dust cover	46 Snap - ring	62 Bearing inner retaining ring
13 3rd/4th speed operating sleeve	30 Lower gear-change lever	47 Cenre ball bearing	63 Needle rollers
14 Selector shaft pin	31 Dust cover seal	48 Layshaft dowel	64 Front thrust washer
15 Interlock spool plate	32 Upper gear-change lever	49 Bearing outer retaining ring	65 Layshaft
16 Selective washer	33 Bush	50 Rear thrust washer	66 Needle roller bearing
17 Interlock spool	34 End cover		

6. Mainshaft - dismantling and reassembly

1   The component parts of the mainshaft are shown in Fig.6.4.

2   Lift the 3rd and 4th gear synchromesh hub and operating sleeve assembly from the end of the mainshaft.

3   Remove the 3rd gear synchromesh cup.

4   Using a small screwdriver ease the 3rd gear retaining circlip from its groove in the mainshaft. Lift away the circlip.

5   Lift away the 4rd gear thrust washer.

6   Slide the 3rd gear and bush from the mainshaft followed by the thrust washer. Note this is a selective thrust washer.

7   Slide the 2nd gear and bush from the mainshaft followed by the grooved washer. Note which way round it is fitted.

8   Detach the 2nd gear synchromesh cup from inside the 2nd and 1st gear synchromesh hub and lift away.

9   Slide the 2nd and 1st gear synchromesh hub and reverse gear sleeve assembly from the mainshaft. Recover the 1st gear synchromesh cup.

10 Using a small electricians screwdriver lift out the two split collars from their groove in the mainshaft.

11 Slide the 1st gear mainshaft washer from the mainshaft and follow this with the 1st gear and its bush.

12 The mainshaft is now completely dismantled.

13 Before reassembling refer to Fig.6.5. and measure the end float of the 2nd and 3rd gears on their respective bushes. The end float should be within the limits quoted in the specifications. Obtain a new bush if necessary to achieve the correct end float.

14 Temporarily refit the 2nd gear washer, oil grooved face away from the mainshaft shoulder, to the mainshaft. Assemble to the mainshift the 3rd gear bush, selective washer, 2nd gear bush, 3rd gear thrust washer with its oil grooved face to the bush, and fit the 3rd gear mainshaft circlip. Measure the end float of the bushes

on the mainshaft which should be within the limits quoted in the specifications. Obtain a new selective washer to obtain the correct end float. Remove the parts from the mainshaft.

15 To reassemble first slide the bush into the 1st gear hub (photo).

16 Insert the washer into the coned end of the 1st gear (photo).

17 Slide the 1st gear onto the mainshaft followed by the larger washer (photo).

18 Fit the two halves of the split collar into the groove in the mainshaft and push the 1st gear hard up against the collar (photo).

19 Fit the synchromesh cup onto the cone of the 1st gear (photo).

20 Slide the 1st and 2nd gear synchromesh hub and reverse gear sleeve on the mainshaft and engage it with the synchromesh cup (photo).

21 Fit the 2nd gear synchromesh cup to the synchromesh hub (photo).

22 Fit the 2nd gear washer onto the end of the mainshaft splines so that the oil grooved face is towards the front of the mainshaft (photo).

23 Slide the 2nd gear bush onto the mainshaft (photo).

24 Fit the 2nd gear onto the bush on the mainshaft and engage the taper with the internal taper of the synchromesh cup (photo).

25 Fit the 2nd and 3rd gear selective washer (photo).

26 Slide the 3rd gear bush onto the mainshaft (photo).

27 Fit the 3rd gear onto the bush on the mainshaft, the cone facing the front of the mainshaft (photo).

28 Slide the 3rd gear thrust washer onto the mainshaft splines (photo).

29 Ease the 3rd gear retaining circlip into its groove in the mainshaft. Make quite sure it is fully seated (photo).

30 Fit the 3rd gear synchromesh cup onto the cone of the 3rd gear (photo).

31 Finally slide the 3rd and 4th gear synchromesh hub and operating sleeve assembly and engage it with the synchromesh cup (photo).

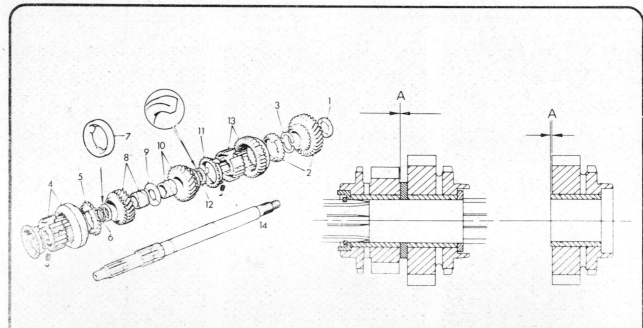

FIG 6.4. MAINSHAFT ASSEMBLY   **FIG.6.5. MAINSHAFT GEAR END FLOAT**

1	Thrust washer	7	3rd speed gear thrust washer
2	1st speed gear and synchro cup	8	3rd speed gear and bush
3	Split collar	9	Selective washer
4	3rd and 4th speed synchro unit	10	2nd speed gear and bush
5	Synchro cup	11	Synchromesh cup
6	Mainshaft circlip	12	Thrust washer
		13	1st/2nd speed synchro
		14	Mainshaft

$A = 0.002$ to 0.006 in (0.050 to 0.152 mm)

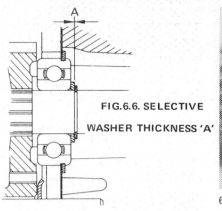

FIG.6.6. SELECTIVE WASHER THICKNESS 'A'

6.15. Face the bush the correct way

6.16. Check the flat of the washer facing out

6.17. Don't forget the larger washer next

6.18. Now the split collar

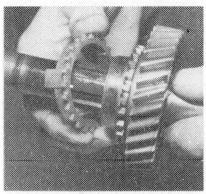

6.19. The synchro cup must be in unworn condition (1st)

6.20. Align the 'large' splines

6.21. Now the next synchro cup (2nd)

6.22. Oil groove to the front of the mainshaft

6.23. Note the clean hands

6.24. Now 2nd gear wheel

6.25. A selective washer - 2nd and 3rd gear

6.26. The 3rd gear bush

6.27. Note the direction of the cone

6.28. 3rd gear thrust washer

6.29. Make sure it seats fully

6.30. Another synchro cup (3rd)

6.31. Meet the splines and mesh with the synchro cup

7. Gearbox - reassembly

1   Place the magnet in the base of the gearbox. On later produced gearboxes the magnet is cast into the gearbox casing (photo).

2   Position the laygear needle bearing roller bearing inner retainers into the laygear bore. Apply Castrol LM Grease to the ends of the laygear and replace the needle rollers. Return in position with the outer retainers (photo).

3   Make up a piece of tube the same diameter as the layshaft and the length of the laygear plus thrust washers and slide the tube into the laygear. This will retain the needle rollers in position. Apply grease to the thrust washers and fit to the ends of the laygear. The tags must face outwards (photo).

4   Carefully lower the laygear into the bottom of the gearbox casing (photo).

5   Fit the reverse gear operating lever to the operating lever pivot. Hold the reverse idler in its approximate fitted position and slide in the idler shaft, drilled end first (photo).

6   Carefully line up the drilled hole in the idler shaft and gear-box casing and replace the dowel bolt and spring washer (photo).

7   The assembled mainshaft may now be fitted into the gearbox casing (photo).

8   Ease the mainshaft bearing up the mainshaft, circlip offset on the outer track towards the rear (photo).

9   Place a metal lever in the position shown in this photo so supporting the mainshaft spigot (photo).

10 Using a suitable diameter tube carefully drift the mainshaft bearing into position in the rear casing (photo).

11 Fit the 4th gear synchromesh cup onto the end of the input shaft.

12 Lubricate the needle roller bearing and fit into the end of the input shaft (photo).

13 Fit the input to the front of the gearbox casing, taking care to engage the synchromesh cup with the synchromesh hub (photo).

14 Tap the input bearing until the circlip is hard up against the front gearbox casing. Check that the mainshaft bearing outer track circlip is hard up against the rear casing. Refit the washer and circlip.

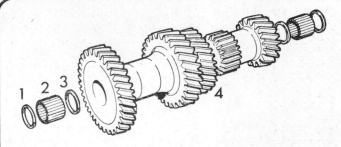

FIG 6.7. LAYGEAR BEARING ASSEMBLIES

1   Bearing outer retaining ring   3   Bearing inner retaining ring
2   Needle rollers   4   Laygear

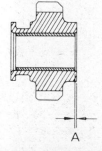

FIG.6.8. CORRECT REVERSE IDLER BUSH LOCATION

A = 0.000 to 0.010 in. (0.000 to 0.254 mm)

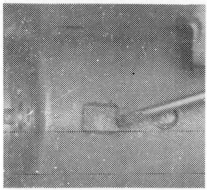
7.1. The screwdriver blade points to the magnet

7.2. Use grease to hold the rollers

7.3. The tag must face outwards

7.4. Note the spotless inside casing

7.5. Drilled end first

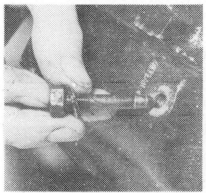
7.6. This the dowel bolt. Note the shaped end

7.7. Support the casing on a block of wood

7.8. Note the position of the large circlip

7.9. How to support the mainshaft spigot

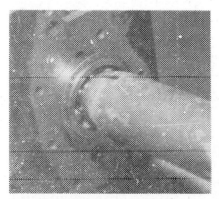
7.10. Drift in the bearing as shown

7.12. Hold the rollers in the cage with grease

7.13. Engage the synchro hub properly

15 Invert the gearbox. Fit the pin into the drilled hole in the layshaft and carefully insert the layshaft from the rear of the main casing. This will push out the previously inserted tube. The pin must be to the rear of the main casing (photo).

16 Line up the layshaft pin with the groove in the rear face and push the layshaft fully home (photo).

17 Fit the 3rd and 4th gear selector fork to the synchromesh sleeve (photo).

18 Fit the 1st and 2nd gear selector fork to the synchromesh sleeve (photo).

19 Slide the selector fork shaft from the front through the two selector forks and into the rear of the main casing (photo).

20 Fit a new gasket to the rear face of the main casing and retain in position with a little grease (photo).

21 Place the speedometer drive gear onto the mainshaft and using a tube drive the gear into its previously noted position (photo).

22 Slide the washer up the mainshaft to the speedometer drive gear (photo).

23 Place the rear extension bearing into its bore, letters facing outwards (photo).

24 Tap the bearing into position using a suitable diameter socket (photo).

25 Fit a new rear extension oil seal and tap into position with the previously used socket. The lip must face inwards (photo).

26 Slide the interlock spool onto the selector shaft making sure it is the correct way round as shown. This is to give an idea of the final fitted position. Remove the interlock spool again (photo).

27 Place the interlock spool on the selector forks with the flanges correctly engaged (photo).

28 Offer up the gearbox rear extension to the rear of the main casing, at the same time feeding the selector shaft through the interlock spool. It will be necessary to rotate the selector shaft to obtain correct engagement (photo).

29 Secure the rear extension with the eight bolts and spring washers (photo).

30 Refit the spring pin into the end of the selector shaft ensuring the ends are equidistant from the shaft (photo).

31 This photo shows the interlock spool and selector shaft correctly aligned with the pegs engaged (photo).

32 Insert the speedometer driven gear and housing into the rear extension (photo).

33 Fit the drive flange onto the mainshaft splines (photo).

34 Hold the drive flange and tighten the retaining nut and washer fully (photo).

35 Replace the reverse lift plate and secure with the bolt and spring washer (photo).

36 Refit the rear extension end cover and tap into position with the end of the lip flush with the end of the casting (photo).

37 Replace the interlock spool plate in the same position as was noted before removal (photo).

38 Fit a new gasket to the top of the gearbox casing and replace the top cover (photo).

39 Secure the top cover with the nine bolts and spring washers which should be progressively tightened in a diagonal manner (photo).

40 Fit a new 'O' ring to the input shaft retainer and refit the retainer (photo).

41 Fit a new gearbox casing front face gasket and retain in position with a little grease (photo).

42 Move the gearbox to the end of the bench and offer up the clutch bell housing (photo).

43 Replace the five bolts securing the bell housing to the main casing. Note four bolts have spring washers and the fifth (lowermost) has a copper washer (photo).

44 Slide the clutch release bearing assembly onto its guide at the same time engaging the release lever (photo).

45 If the gearbox was removed in unit with the engine it may now be reattached. Secure in position with the retaining nuts, bolts and spring washers (photo).

46 Refill the gearbox with 1½ pints (0.85 litres) Castrol Hypoy B (photo).

7.15. Note the pin next to his thumb

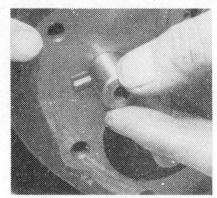
7.16. The pin in its groove

7.17. 3rd and 4th selector fork

7.18. 1st and 2nd selector fork

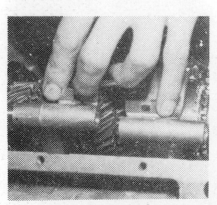
7.19. Slide the shaft through to capture both selectors

7.20. Use grease to hold - not gasket cement

7.21. Drift up to mark previously made

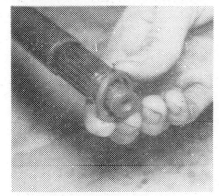

7.22. Now another washer

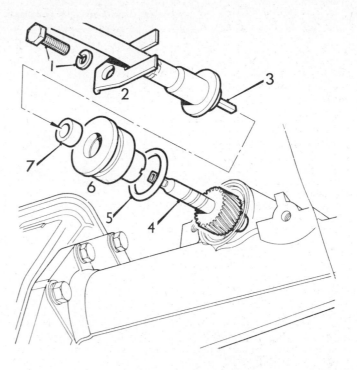

FIG.6.9. SPEEDOMETER DRIVE ASSEMBLY

1	Bolt and spring washer	4	Speedometer pinion
2	Retaining clip	5	'O' ring
3	Inner cable	6	Housing
		7	Seal

7.23. Face upwards for the bearing coding

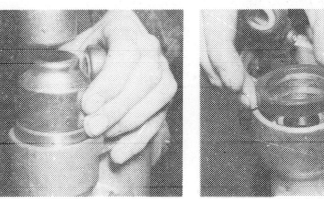

7.24. Drift it in like this

7.25. Lip face inwards - tap gently

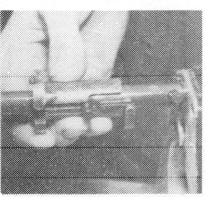

7.26. The right way round - just an example

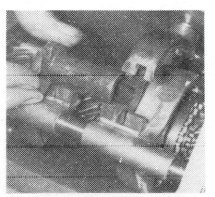

7.27. The actual fitment of the interlock spool

7.28. Rotate the selector shaft if necessary

7.29. Always fit the washer

7.30. Keep the offsets of the pin equal

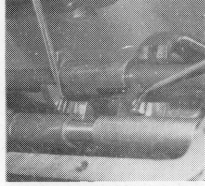

7.31. Pegs engaged - screwdrivers show correct alignment

7.32. The finger sits on the rubber O ring

7.33. Offer up the flange

7.34. Use a socket to tighten the flange nut

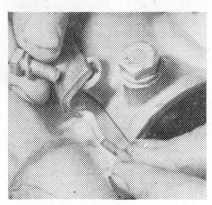

7.35. This is important - don't leave it out

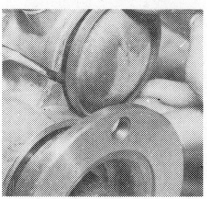

7.36. The lip must be flush

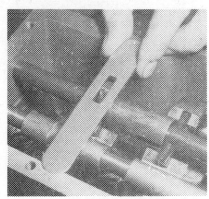

7.37. It must go back in the same place

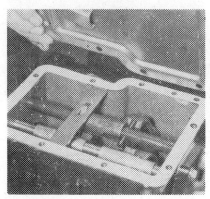

7.38. Always a new gasket

7.39. Tighten evenly and progressively

7.40. You must use a new O ring

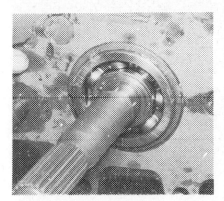

7.41. A new gasket is fitted

7.42. Offer up the extension as shown

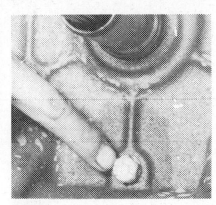

7.43. This is the copper washer one!

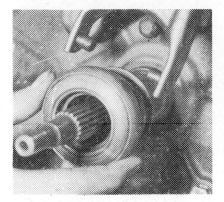

7.44. Engage the release lever

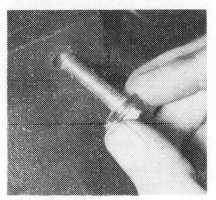

7.45. Securing the gearbox to the engine

7.46. Use a funnel if possible - flexitops will work

8. Manual gearbox - fault diagnosis

Symptom	Reason/s	Remedy
WEAK OR INEFFECTIVE SYNCHROMESH General wear	Synchronising cones worn, split or damaged	Dismantle and overhaul gearbox. Fit new gear wheels and synchronising cones
	Synchromesh dogs worn, or damaged	Dismantle and overhaul gearbox. Fit new synchromesh unit.
JUMPS OUT OF GEAR General wear or damage	Broken gearchange fork rod spring Gearbox coupling dogs badly worn Selector fork rod groove badly worn	Dismantle and replace spring. Dismantle gearbox. Fit new coupling dogs. Fit new selector fork rod.
EXCESSIVE NOISE Lack of maintenance	Incorrect grade of oil in gearbox or oil level too low Bush or needle roller bearings worn or damaged Gearteeth excessively worn or damaged Laygear thrust washers worn allowing excessive end play	Drain, refill, or top up gearbox with correct grade of oil. Dismantle and overhaul gearbox. Renew bearings. Dismantle and overhaul gearbox. Renew gear wheels. Dismantle and overhaul gearbox. Renew thrust washers.
EXCESSIVE DIFFICULTY IN ENGAGING GEAR Clutch not fully disengaging	Clutch fault	Refer to Chapter 5.

9. Automatic transmission - general description

Borg-Warner automatic transmission is fitted.

The automatic transmission system comprises two main components: a three-element hydrokinetic torque converter coupling capable of torque multiplication at an infinitely variable ratio between 2:1 and 1:1 and a torque speed responsive and hydraulically operated epicyclic gearbox comprising a planetary gear set providing three forward ratios and reverse ratio.

Due to the complexity of the automatic transmission unit, if performance is not up to standard, or overhaul is necessary, it is imperative that this is undertaken by BLMC main agents who will have special equipment for accurate fault diagnosis and rectification.

The content of the following sections is therefore solely general and servicing information.

10. Automatic transmission - fluid level

It is important that the transmission fluid is manufactured to the correct specification, use Castrol TQF. The capacity of the unit is approximately 9½ pints (5.4 litres) - with oil cooler 11 pints (6.2 litres), when dry, but for a drain and refill, which is not actually necessary except during repairs, the capacity will be approximately 5 pints (3 litres) as the converter cannot be completely drained. The location of the dipstick is shown in Fig. 6.12. Full information on checking the oil level will be found in the Routine maintenance section at the beginning of this manual.

11. Automatic transmission - removal and replacement

1 Any suspected faults must be referred to the main agent before unit removal as with this tupe of transmission its fault must be confirmed using special equipment before it is removed from the car.
2 As the automatic transmission is relatively heavy it is best if the car is raised from the ground on ramps but it is possible to remove the unit if the car is placed on high axle stands.
3 Disconnect the battery.
4 Disconnect the downshift cable from the throttle linkage at the side of the carburettor.
5 Remove the dipstick from its guide tube.

6 Detach the exhaust downpipe from the manifold. Release the support clip from the support bracket.
7 Undo the bolt securing the engine earth cable to the torque converter.
8 Place a clean container of 8 pints (4.55 litres) capacity under the sump drain plug, remove the drain plug and allow to drain Replace the drain plug.
9 Release the spire nut securing the manual selector rod to the gearbox lever. Draw the selector rod from the lever.
10 Make a note of the electric cable connections to the starter inhibitor and reverse lamp switch. Detach the cable terminals.
11 Undo the dipstick filler tube union nut whilst the adaptor is held to stop if moving.
12 If an oil cooler is fitted wipe the area around the two union nuts and undo the nuts. Plug the ends to stop dirt ingress.
13 With a scriber or file mark the propeller shaft and gearbox flanges so that they may be refitted in their original positions.
14 Undo and remove the four locknuts and bolts that secure the two flanges together.
15 Lift the front end of the propeller shaft away from the rear of the gearbox and tie to the torsion bar with spring or wire.
16 Undo and remove the speedometer cable clamp bolt and spring washer on the gearbox extension. Lift away the clamp and withdraw the inner cable.
17 Using a hoist take the weight of the complete power unit or alternatively a hydraulic jack to take the weight under the torque converter housing.
18 Undo and remove the two bolts, spring and plain washers that secure the rear mounting cross member to the underside of the body.
19 Carefully lower the gearbox so as to give access to the top,
20 Using a second jack support the weight of the gearbox.
21 Undo and remove the six bolts and spring washers that secure the gearbox to the torque converter housing.
22 Very carefully draw the gearbox rearwards until it is clear of the torque converter and then lift away from the underside of the car. It is very important that the weight of the gearbox is not allowed to hang on the input shaft.
23 Refitting is the reverse sequence to removal but in addition:
24 Carefully align the converter and front pump driving dogs and slots in the horizontal plane.
25 Carefully align and then locate the input shaft and drive dogs.
26 Tighten the six gearbox securing bolts to a torque wrench setting of 8 to 13 lb ft (1.1 to 1.8 kg cm).
27 Refill the gearbox with Castrol TQF and check the fluid level as described in Section 9.

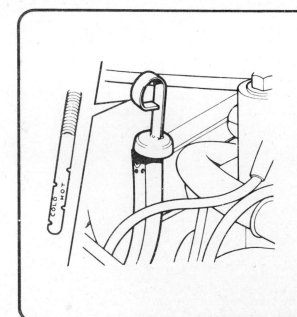

FIG.6.12. LOCATION OF AUTOMATIC TRANSMISSION DIPSTICK AND FILLER TUBE

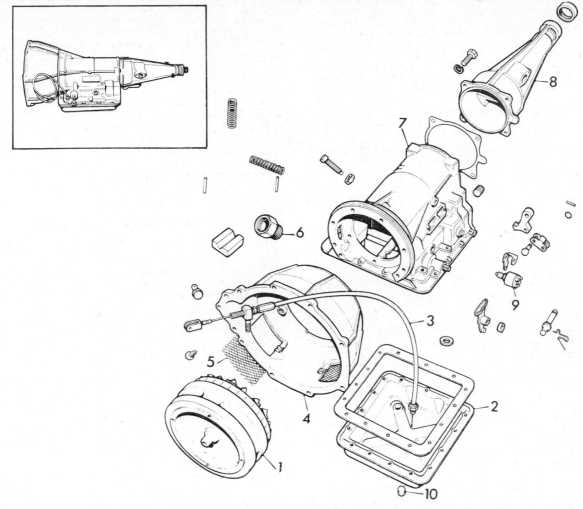

FIG.6.10. MAIN COMPONENTS OF EXTERNAL CASING WITH TORQUE CONVERTER
Inset: Borg Warner model 35 (assembled)

1 Torque converter	4 Converter housing	7 Case assembly	9 Inhibitor switch
2 Oil pan	5 Stone guard	8 Rear extension	10 Sump drain plug
3 Downshift cable	6 Dipstick tube adaptor	housing	

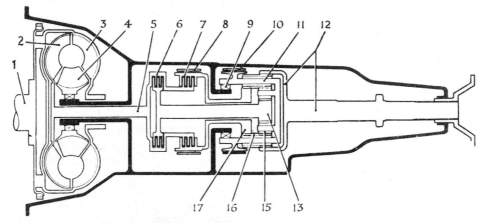

FIG.6.11. MAIN MECHANICAL COMPONENTS IN SECTION

1 Engine crankshaft	6 Front clutch	11 Plant pinion carrier	14 Parking pawl teeth
2 Turbine	7 Rear clutch	12 Ring gear and output	15 Short planet pinion
3 Impeller	8 Front brake band	shaft	16 Long planet pinion
4 Stator	9 Unidirectional clutch	13 Forward sun gear	17 Reverse sun gear
5 Input shaft	10 Rear brake band	and shaft	

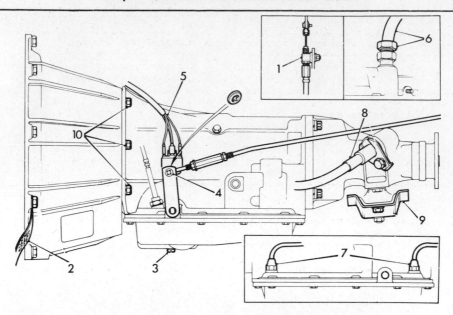

**FIG.6.13. AUTOMATIC TRANSMISSION GEARBOX REMOVAL.
SUMMARY OF ITEMS TO BE DISCONNECTED**

1 Downshift cable	4 Manual selector rod	6 Dipstick tube	9 Rear mounting
2 Earth cable	5 Starter inhibitor and	7 Oil cooler pipes	10 Bolts and spring
3 Drain plug	reverse light switch	8 Speedometer cable	washers

12. Torque converter - removal and replacement

1 Refer to Section 1 and remove the gearbox.
2 Undo and remove the starter motor electric cable terminal secuirng nut and washers. Detach the cable. Pre engaged starter motor, detach the cable terminals from the solenoid.
8 Undo and remove the two starter motor securing nut and spring washer and bolt and spring washer. Lift away the starter motor.
4 Undo and remove the two bolts and spring washers securing the engine sump connecting plate to the torque converter housing.
5 Support the weight of the engine and then undo and remove the bolts and spring washers that secure the torque converter housing to the gearbox mounting plate.
6 Lower the rear of the engine until it is possible to lift away the torque converter housing.
7 With a scriber mark the relative positions of the drive plate and torque converter if these are to be refitted. This will ensure

they are replaced in their original positions.
8 Working through the aperture in the mounting plate, turn the converter, unlock the tab washers and then progressively slacken the four bolts.
9 Support the torque converter and completely remove the bolts and lock washers. Lift away the torque converter. Be perpared to mop up oil that will issue from the torque converter as it cannot be drained completely.
10 Refitting the torque converter is the reverse sequence to removal but in addition:
11 Position the torque converter onto the drive plate aligning up the previously made marks if original parts are being refitted. Refit the four bolts with new tab washers and tighten in a progressive manner to a final torque wrench setting of 25 to 30 lb ft (3.4 to 4.1 Kg fm). Bend over the lock tabs.
12 Check that the dowel is in position and then place the converter housing in position on the mounting plate aligning the dowel hole. Refit the bolts and spring washers and tighten in a progressive manner to a torque wrench setting of 8 to 13 lb ft. (1.1 to 1.8 Kg fm).

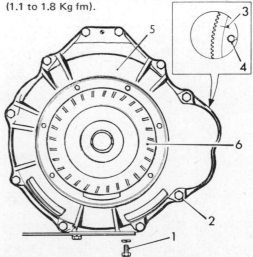

FIG.6.14. TORQUE CONVERTER REMOVAL

1 Sump connecting plate securing bolt	3 Alignment marks
2 Housing retaining bolts	4 Securing plate
	5 Housing
	6 Torque converter

13. Starter inhibitor/reverse light switch - check and adjustment

1   Firmly chock all wheels and apply the handbrake.

2   Make a note of the electrical cable connections to the switch and then detach the terminals. Starter terminals (narrow) white/red. Reverse terminals (wide) green/green and brown.

3   Connect a test lamp and battery across the starter terminals (Fig.6.15) - these are the narrow ones - and select positions P R N D 2 1 in order. The test light should only come on in the P and N positions.

3   Connect the test lamp and battery across the reverse light terminals - these are the wide ones - and select ' 1 2 D N R P' in order. The test light should only come on in the R position.

4   If adjustment is necessary leave the test light connected to the reverse terminals. If the light is out slacken the switch locknut using a cranked spanner. Do not grip the switch body.

5   Unscrew the switch slowly until the test light comes on. Screw the switch in until the light just goes out and mark the relative positions of the switch and case.

6   Connect the test light to the starter terminals and the light should be off. Slowly screw in the switch until the test light comes on (approximately three quarters of a turn) and mark the position of the switch relative to the previous made mark on the case. Remove the test light.

7   Turn the switch until it is mid way between the two marks and retighten the locknut.

8   Reconnect the cables to the switch.

9   Check that the starter motor only operates in the P and N position of the selector and that the reverse light only comes on in the R position.

10   If the switch is to be renewed always apply a little liquid sealer to the threads of the new switch to stop any possibility of oil leaks from this point.

14. Downshift cable - adjustment

Before the cable is adjusted it is necessary to confirm that it is the cable that is malajusted and not some other fault. Generally if difficulty is experienced in obtaining 2:1 downshift in the 'kick-down' position at just below 31 mph it is an indication that the outer cable is too short. If there is a bumpy or delayed shift at low throttle opening it is an indication the outer cable is too long.

During production of the car the adjustment is set by a crimped stop on the carburettor end of the inner cable and it is unusual for this setting to change except at high mileages when the inner cable can stretch. To adjust proceed as follows:—

1   Apply the handbrake firmly and chock the front wheels.

2   Run the engine until it reaches normal operating temperature. Adjust the engine idle speed to approximately 700—750 rpm with the selector in the 'D' position.

3   Stop the engine and with an open spanner slacken the locknut (4), Fig.6.16, and adjust the outer cable control to the stop (2), should the stop have been moved or be loose it will be necessary to remove the transmission sump pan.

4   Reset the engine idle to normal speed with the selector in the 'N' position. Stop the engine.

5   Wipe the area around the drain plug and sump. Place a clean container of at least 8 pints capacity under the pan drain plug. Undo the plug and allow the oil to drain into the container.

6   Undo and remove the fifteen sump pan retaining bolts and spring washers. Take care not to damage the joint between the transmission casing and sump pan.

7   Refer to Fig.6.16 and check that the position of the downshift cam is in the idling position as shown in the illustration.

8   Adjust the length of the outer cable so as to remove all the slack from the inner cable.

9   Again refer to Fig.6.16 and check the position of the downshift cam with the throttle pedal in the 'kickdown' position as shown in the illustration.

10   Refit the sump pan joint, sump pan and retaining bolts with spring washers. Tighten the bolts in a diagonal pattern.

11   Refill the transmission with correct grade transmission fluid.

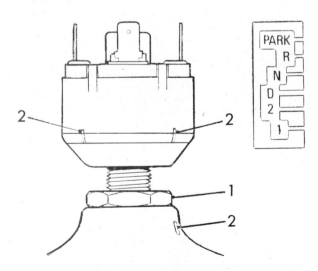

FIG.6.15. STARTER INHIBITOR/REVERSE LIGHT SWITCH

1 Locknut
2 Pencil mark

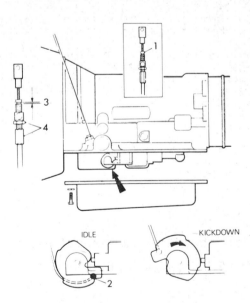

FIG.6.16. DOWNSHIFT CABLE ADJUSTMENT

1 Nipple		3 Clearance
2 Cable located in cam		4 Adjuster/locknut

15. Selector linkage - adjustment

1 Apply the handbrake firmly.

2 Move the selector handle to the 'N' position and adjust its position slightly to ensure that it is under the control of the control valve detent.

3 Move the selector handle to the 'P' position and release the handbrake. Rock the car to and fro and the pawl should hold the vehicle. If either of the two above conditions do not exist the selector rod must be reset.

4 Refer to Fig.6.17 and disconnect the selector rod from the manual lever.

5 Move the manual lever fully forwards as far as it will go and then move it back by three detents (clicks) to the neutral position.

6 Hold the selector in the 'N' position and the end of the selector rod should enter the hole in the manual lever.

7 If necessary adjust the length of the selector rod with the

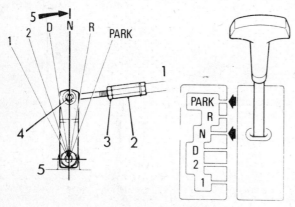

FIG.6.17. SELECTOR LINKAGE ADJUSTMENT

1 *Selector rod*	4 *Spire nut*
2 *Turnbuckle*	5 *Manual lever*
3 *Locknut*	

turnbuckle until the selector rod end will enter the hole.

8 Reconnect the selector rod and tighten the turnbuckle locknuts.

9 Carefully move the selector handle into all positions to make sure that the control valve detent is not over-ridden.

16. Automatic transmission - fault diagnosis

Stall test procedure

The function of a stall test is to determine that the torque converter and gearbox are operating satisfactorily.

1 Check the condition of the engine. An engine which is not developing full power will affect the stall test readings.

2 Allow the engine and transmission to reach correct working temperatures.

3 Connect a tachometer to the vehicle.

4 Check the wheels and apply the handbrake and footbrake.

5 Select L or R and depress the throttle to the 'kickdown' position. Note the reading on the tachometer which should be 1800 rpm. If the reading is below 1000 rpm suspect the converter for stator slip. If the reading is down to 1200 rpm the engine is not developing full power. If the reading is in excess of 2000 rpm, suspect the gearbox for brake band or clutch slip.

NOTE: Do not carry out a stall test for a longer period than 10 seconds, otherwise the transmission will overheat.

Converter diagnosis

Inability to start on steep gradients, combined with poor acceleration from rest and low stall speed (1000 rpm), indicates that the converter stator uni-directional clutch is slipping. This condition permits the stator to rotate in an opposite direction to the impeller and turbine, and torque multiplication cannot occur.

Poor acceleration in third gear above 30 mph and reduced maximum speed, indicates that the stator uni-directional clutch has seized. The stator will not rotate with the turbine and impeller and the 'fluid flywheel' phase cannot occur. This condition will also be indicated by excessive overheating of the transmission although the stall speed will be correct.

Chapter 7 Propeller shaft

Contents

Specifications

Split, in two halves (front and rear) tubular with centre bearing

Diameter: Front ... ...   3 inch (76.2 mm)
  Rear ... ...   2 inch (50.8 mm)

Universal joints ... ...   Hardy Spicer with roller bearings, spiders fitted by peened yokes

Torque wrench settings

	lb ft	Kg fm
Centre bearing mounting bolts..	22	3.0
Flange retaining bolt nuts	28	3.8

1. General description

Drive is transmitted from the gearbox to the rear axle by means of a finely balanced Hardy Spicer tubular propeller shaft split into two halves and supported at the centre by a rubber mounted bearing.

Fitted to the front, centre and rear of the propeller shaft assembly are universal joints which allow for vertical movement of the rear axle and slight movement of the complete power unit on its rubber mountings. Each universal joint comprises a four legged centre spider, four needle roller bearings and two yokes.

Fore and aft movement of the rear axle is absorbed by a sliding spline at the rear of the propeller shaft assembly. This is splined and mates with a sleeve and yoke assembly. When assembled a dust cap, steel washer, and cork washer seal the end of the sleeve and sliding joint.

The yoke flange of the front universal joint is fitted to the gearbox mainshaft flange with four bolts, spring washers and nuts, and the yoke flange on the rear universal joint is secured to the pinion flange on the rear axle in the same way.

The propeller shaft is a relatively simple component and to overhaul and repair is fairly easy.

2. Propeller shaft - front - removal and replacement

1 Jack up the rear of the car and support on firmly based axle stands. Alternatively position the rear of the car on a ramp. Chock the front wheels.
2 The propeller shaft is carefully balanced to fine limits and it is important that it is replaced in its exact same position prior to its removal. Scratch marks on the gearbox, differential pinion and propeller shaft drive flanges for correct re-alignment when refitting.
3 Support the weight of the front propeller shaft. Undo and remove the four gearbox end flange nuts and bolts (Fig,7.2).
4 Support the weight of the rear propeller shaft. Undo and remove the four axle end flange nuts and bolts.
5 Undo and remove the two bolts, spring and plain washers that retain the centre bearing mounting to the body brackets (Fig.7.3).
6 Lift away the propeller shaft assembly from the underside of the car.
7 To separate the two halves of the propeller shaft assembly, first bend back the locking washer tab and undo and remove the retaining bolt. Lift away the 'C' washer and tab washer (Fig.7.4).
8 Draw the front propeller shaft away from the rear propeller shaft universal joint splines.
9 Reconnection and refitting the two propeller shaft halves is the reverse sequence to removal but the following additional points should be noted:
a) Ensure that the mating marks scratched on the propeller shaft, gearbox and differential pinion flange are lined up.
b) Tighten the centre bearing mounting bolts to a torque wrench setting of 22 lb ft (3.0 Kg fm).
c) Tighten the front and rear flange retaining nuts to a torque wrench setting of 28 lb ft (3.8 Kg fm).

3. Propeller shaft - rear - removal and replacement

The sequence for removing the rear propeller shaft is the same as for removing the front propeller shaft in that the complete assembly must be removed first and then the two halves parted. See Section 2.

4. Universal joints - inspection

1 Wear in the needle roller bearings is characterised by vibration in the transmission, 'clonks' on taking up the drive, and in extreme cases of lack of lubrication, metallic squeaking, and ultimately grating and shrieking sounds as the bearings break up.
2 It is easy to check if the needle roller bearings are worn with the propeller shaft in position, by trying to turn the shaft with one hand, the other hand holding the rear axle flange when the rear universal is being checked, and the front half coupling when the front universal joint is being checked. Any movement between the propeller shaft and the front, centre or rear half couplings is indicative of considerable wear.

3 Check also by trying to lift the shaft and noticing any movement in the splines.

4 If there is any measurable wear in the universal joints it will be necessary to purchase a service exchange propeller shaft. No repair is available at present for universal joints of this type. Propeller shafts may be available in halves.

5. Centre bearing - removal and replacement

1 Refer to Section 2 and remove the propeller shaft assembly. Separate the two halves.

2 Using a universal puller and suitable thrust block (a suitable size bolt will do) draw the centre bearing from the end of the front propeller shaft.

3 To fit a new bearing simply drift it into position using a piece of suitable diameter metal tube.

4 Reconnect and refit the propeller shaft assembly, this being the reverse sequence to removal.

6. Sliding joint - dismantling, overhaul and reassembly

1 Refer to Section 2 and remove the propeller shaft assembly.

2 Unscrew and dust cap from the sleeve and then slide the sleeve from the shaft. Take off the steel washer and the cork washer.

3 With the sleeve separated from the shaft assembly the splines can be inspected. If worn it will be necessary to purchase a new sleeve assembly.

4 To reassemble, fit the dust cap, steel washer, and a new cork gasket over the splined part of the propeller shaft.

5 Grease the splines and then line up the arrow on the sleeve assembly with the arrow on the splined portion of the propeller shaft, and push the sleeve over the splines. Fit the washers to the sleeve and screw up the dust cap.

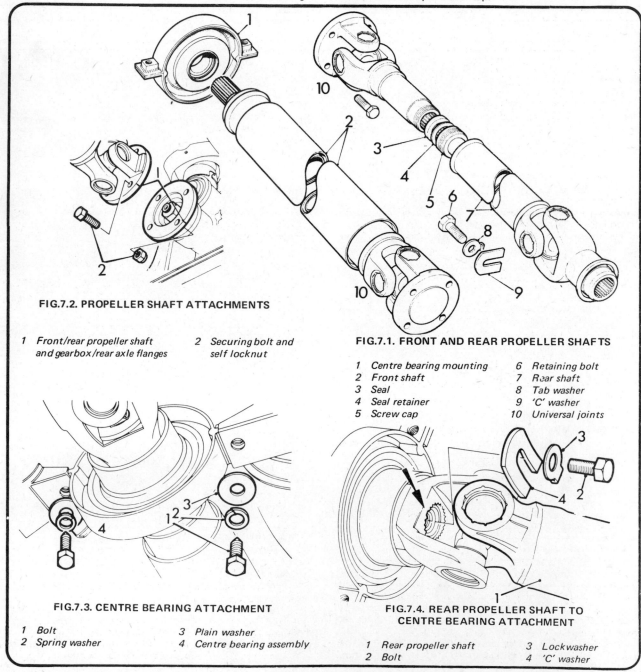

FIG.7.2. PROPELLER SHAFT ATTACHMENTS

1 Front/rear propeller shaft and gearbox/rear axle flanges	2 Securing bolt and self locknut

FIG.7.1. FRONT AND REAR PROPELLER SHAFTS

1 Centre bearing mounting	6 Retaining bolt
2 Front shaft	7 Rear shaft
3 Seal	8 Tab washer
4 Seal retainer	9 'C' washer
5 Screw cap	10 Universal joints

FIG.7.3. CENTRE BEARING ATTACHMENT

1 Bolt	3 Plain washer
2 Spring washer	4 Centre bearing assembly

FIG.7.4. REAR PROPELLER SHAFT TO CENTRE BEARING ATTACHMENT

1 Rear propeller shaft	3 Lockwasher
2 Bolt	4 'C' washer

Chapter 8 Rear axle

Contents

Specifications

Hypoid - Semi-floating
Ratio	4.11 : 1 (9/37)
Distance of bearing from threaded end of axle shaft	2.84 inch (69.94 mm)

Differential bearing shims	0.003 in. (0.076 mm)
	0.005 in. (0.127 mm)
	0.010 in. (0.254 mm)
	0.020 in. (0.508 mm)
Differential case - maximum stretch	0.008 in. (0.20 mm)
Differential pinion gears thrust washer range	Eight in increments of 0.002 in. (0.05 mm)
Thrust washer range	0.027 in. (0.685 mm) to 0.043 in. (1.092 mm)
Crownwheel run-out (max)..	0.003 in. (0.076 mm)
Crownwheel optimum setting...	0.005 in. (0.127 mm)
Pinion bearing pre-load...	15 to 18 lb ft (0.17 to 0.21 Kg fm)

Pinion lead washer sizes:
Standard ... ...?	0.077 in. (1.956 mm)
Alternatives	0.075 in. (1.905 mm) to 0.096 in. (2.438 mm) in a range of 21 increments
Pinion bearing shims	0.003 in. (0.76 mm)
	0.005 in. (0.127 mm)
	0.010 in. (0.254 mm)
	0.030 in. (0.762 mm)
Lubricating capacity	1.25 pints (0.71 litres)

Torque wrench settings	lb ft	Kg fm
Backplate securing nuts	18	2.5
Axle shaft nut..	85	11.7
Differential case to axle retaining nuts	20	2.7
Pinion bearing pre-load	15 to 18	0.17 to 0.21
Drive flange nut	90	12.4
Axle to spring 'U' bolt nuts	14	1.9
Propeller shaft flange retaining nuts	28	3.8

1. General description

The rear axle is semi-floating and is held in place by semi-elliptic springs. These springs provide the necessary lateral and longitudinal location of the axle. The rear axle incorporates a hypoid crownwheel and pinion, and a two pinion differential. All repairs can be carried out to the component parts of the rear axle without removing the axle casing from the car.

The crown wheel and pinion together with the differential gears are mounted in the differential unit which is bolted to the front face of the banjo type axle casing.

Adjustments are provided for the crown wheel and pinion backlash; pinion depth of mesh; pinion shaft bearing pre-load; and backlash between the differential gears. All these adjustments may be made by varying the thickness of the various shims and thrust washers.

The axle or half shafts are easily withdrawn and are splined at their inner ends to fit into the splines in the differential wheels. The inner wheel bearing races are mounted on the outer ends of the axle casing and are secured by nuts and lockwashers. The rear bearing outer races are located in the hubs.

2. Rear axle - removal and replacement

1 Chock the front wheels, jack up the rear of the car and place on firmly based axle stands located under the body and forward of the rear axle.

2 With a scriber or file mark the pinion and propeller shaft drive flange so that they may be refitted in thin original positions (Fig.8.2).

3 Undo and remove the four nuts and bolts that secure the rear propeller shaft flange to the pinion flange. Lower the propeller shaft.

4 Remove the rear wheels.

5 Wipe the top of the brake master cylinder reservoir, unscrew the cap and place a piece of thin polythene sheet over the top of the reservoir. Refit the cap. This will prevent hydraulic fluid syphoning out during subsequent operations.

6 Wipe the area around the union nut on the brake feed pipe at the axle bracket. Unscrew the union nut.

7 Undo and remove the locknut and washer from the flexible hose.

8 Detach the flexible hose from its support bracket.

9 Extract the split pins chocking the brake lever clevis pins. Lift away the plain washers and withdraw the clevis pins.

10 Undo and remove the nut and spring washer that secures the compensating lever pin to the axle case support bracket. Lift away the compensating lever assembly.

11 Undo and remove the bolt and spring washer that secures the handbrake cable clip to the axle casing.

12 Using axle stands or other suitable means support the weight of the rear axle.

13 Undo and remove the eight 'U' bolt locknuts.

14 Detach the shock absorber mounting brackets and move back to one side. If necessary tie back with string or wire.

15 Detach the lower mounting plates and rubber pads.

16 Lift away the 'U' bolts and rubber bump stops.

17 The rear axle may now be lifted over the rear springs and drawn away from one side of the car. Make a special note of the location of the spring packing wedge, upper locating plates and rubber pad.

18 Refitting the rear axle is the reverse sequence to removal. In addition:

a) Make sure that the spring packing wedges are refitted in their original positions.

b) Inspect the rubber mounting pads and if they show signs of deterioration fit new.

c) Tighten the 'U' bolt nuts to a torque wrench setting of 14 lbft. (1.9 Kg fm).

d) It will be necessary to bleed the brake hydraulic system. See Chapter 9.

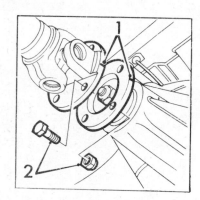
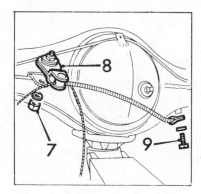
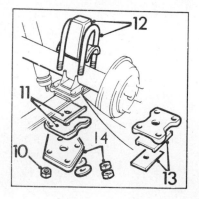
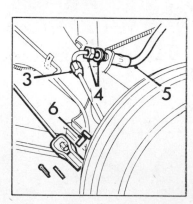

FIG.8.2. REAR AXLE ATTACHMENT POINTS FOR AXLE REMOVAL

1 Propeller shaft and pinion drive flange mating marks	hose locknut & washer	spring washer	rubber pad
2 Bolt & self-locking nut	5 Brake hydraulic flexible hose	8 Compensator	12 'U' bolts and rubber bump stops
3 Brake hydraulic pipe union nut	6 Handbrake cable clevis pin, plain washer & split pin	9 Cable mounting bracket bolt and spring washer	13 Spring packing wedge, upper locating plate, rubber pad
4 Brake hydraulic flexible	7 Compensating lever nut &	10 'U' bolt locknuts	
		11 Shock absorber mounting	

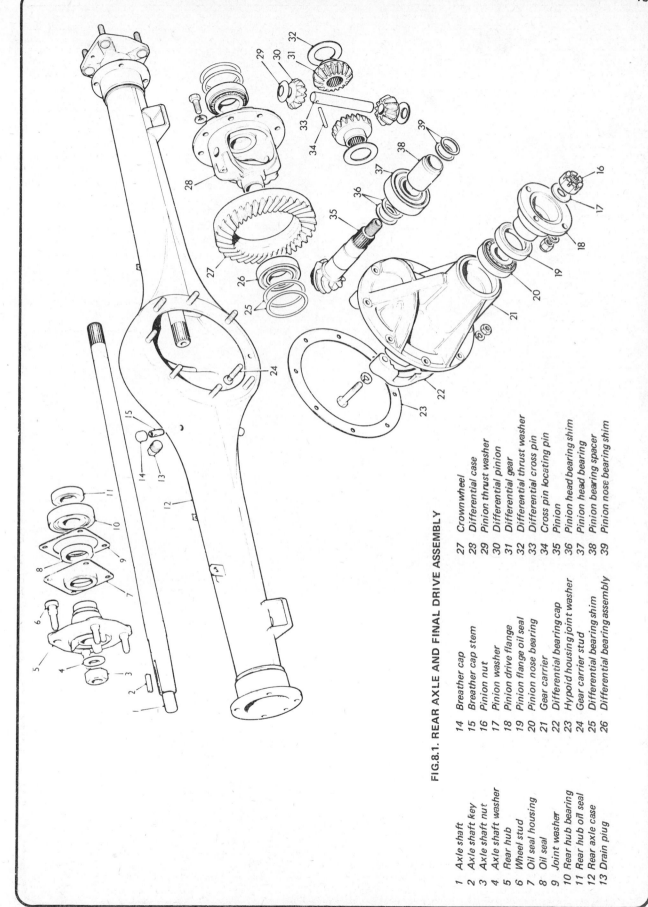

FIG.8.1. REAR AXLE AND FINAL DRIVE ASSEMBLY

1 Axle shaft
2 Axle shaft key
3 Axle shaft nut
4 Axle shaft washer
5 Rear hub
6 Wheel stud
7 Oil seal housing
8 Oil seal
9 Joint washer
10 Rear hub bearing
11 Rear hub oil seal
12 Rear axle case
13 Drain plug

14 Breather cap
15 Breather cap stem
16 Pinion nut
17 Pinion washer
18 Pinion drive flange
19 Pinion flange oil seal
20 Pinion nose bearing
21 Gear carrier
22 Differential bearing cap
23 Hypoid housing joint washer
24 Gear carrier stud
25 Differential bearing shim
26 Differential bearing assembly

27 Crownwheel
28 Differential case
29 Pinion thrust washer
30 Differential pinion
31 Differential gear
32 Differential thrust washer
33 Differential cross pin
34 Cross pin locating pin
35 Pinion
36 Pinion head bearing shim
37 Pinion head bearing
38 Pinion bearing spacer
39 Pinion nose bearing shim

3. Axle shaft, bearing and oil seal - removal and replacement

1   Chock the front wheels, jack up the rear of the car and place on firmly based axle stands. Remove the rear wheels.
2   Undo and remove the axle shaft nut and plain washer.
3   Undo and remove the two screws that secure the brake drum to the hub flange. Lift away the brake drum (Fig.8.3).
4   Should it be tight to remove, back off the brake adjusters and using a soft faced hammer tap outwards on the circumference of the brake drum.
5   Using a universal puller and a suitable thrust block over the end of the axle shaft draw off the rear hub from the axle shaft.
6   Extract the split pin from the handbrake lever clevis pin at the rear of the brake backplate. Lift away the plain washer and withdraw the clevis pin so separating the handbrake cable yoke from the handbrake lever.
7   Wipe the top of the brake master cylinder reservoir, unscrew the cap and place a piece of thin polythene sheet over the top of the reservoir. Refit the cap. This will prevent hydraulic fluid syphoning out during subsequent operations.
8   Wipe the area of the brake pipe union/s at the rear of the wheel cylinder and unscrew the union/s from the wheel cylinder.
9   Undo and remove the four nuts, spring washers and bolts that secure the brake backplate to the axle casing.
10 Make a note of the fitted position of the dry lip relative to the brake slave cylinder and remove the oil catcher.
11 The brake backplate assembly may now be lifted away.
12 Remove the rear hub oil seal and housing assembly. If the oil seal showed signs of leaking it should be renewed. To remove the old seal carefully ease it out using a screwdriver. Once removed an oil seal must never be refitted.
13 Place a clean container under the end of the axle banjo to catch any oil that will issue from the end.
14 Using a screwdriver or pair of pliers remove the axle shaft key and put in a safe place where it will not be lost.
15 Using either an impact slide hammer or, if not available, mole

grips on the end of the axle shaft (with the nut refitted), draw the axle shaft from the casing.
16 The inner oil seal may be removed by using a piece of metal bar shaped in the form of a hook. Pull on the seal and draw it from inside the axle casing.
17 If required the bearing may be removed from the axle shaft by placing the bearing on the top of the jaws of the vice and driving the axle shaft through using a soft faced hammer on the end of the axle shaft nut.
18 Refitting the oil seal, bearing and axle shaft is the reverse sequence to removal. In addition:
a)   Pack the bearing with a lithium based grease. Lubricate the new oil seal with a little Castrol GTX.
b)   When refitting the oil seal the lip must face inwards.
c)   (Using a suitable diameter tube drift the bearing onto the axle shaft until the distance of the bearing to the threaded end of the axle shaft is 2.84 inches (69.94 mm).
d)   Always use a new rear hub joint washer.
e)   The backplate securing nuts should be tightened to a torque wrench setting of 18 lb ft (2.5 Kg fm).
f)   To ensure positive locking of the axle shaft nut always apply a little Loctite CV to the axle shaft thread.
g)   Tighten the axle shaft nut to a torque wrench setting of 85 lb ft (11.7 Kg fm).
h)   Top up the rear axle oil level.
i)   Bleed the brake hydraulic system as described in Chapter 9.

4. Pinion oil seal - removal and replacement

1   Chock the front wheels, jack up the rear of the car and support on firmly based axle stands.
2   With a scriber or file mark the propeller shaft and pinion flanges so that they may be refitted correctly in their original positions.
3   Undo and remove the four nuts, bolts and spring washers that

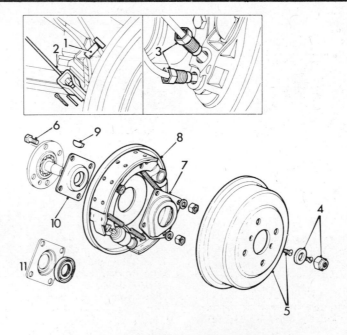

FIG.8.3. HUB AND AXLE SHAFT REMOVAL

1 Clevis pin, plain washer and split pin	unions	retaining screw	8 Brake backplate assembly
2 Handbrake cable	4 Axle shaft nut and plain washer	6 Brake backplate securing screw	9 Axle shaft key
3 Brake hydraulic pipe	5 Brake drum and	7 Oil catcher	10 Oil seal housing
			11 Oil seal

secure the pinion flange to the propeller shaft flange. Lower the propeller shaft to the floor.

4   Apply the handbrake really firmly. Using a pair of pliers extract the flange nut locking split pin.

5   With a socket wrench undo the flange nut. Lift away the nut and plain washer. See Fig.8.1.

6   Place a container under the pinion end of the rear axle to catch any oil that seeps out.

7   Using a universal puller and suitable thrust block draw the pinion flange from the pinion.

8   The old oil seal may now be prised out using a screwdriver or thin piece of metal bar with a small hook on one end.

9   Refitting the new oil seal is the reverse sequence to removal. In addition:

a)   Soak the new oil seal in Castrol GTX for 1 hour prior to fitting.

b)   Fit the new seal with the lip facing inwards using a tubular drift.

c)   Tighten the driving flange nut to a torque wrench setting of 90 lb ft (12.4 Kg fm). Lock with a new split pin.

d)   Top up the rear axle oil level as necessary.

5. Differential assembly - removal and replacement

1   If it is wished to overhaul the differential carrier assembly or to exchange it for a factory reconditioned unit first remove the axle shafts as described in Section 2.

2   Mark the propeller shaft and pinion flanges to ensure their replacment in the same relative position.

3   Undo and remove the four nuts and bolts from the flanges, separate the two parts and lower the propeller shaft to the ground.

4   Place a container under the differential unit assembly to catch oil that will drain out during subsequent operations.

5   Undo and remove the eight nuts and spring washers that secure the differential unit assembly to the axle casing (Fig.8.4).

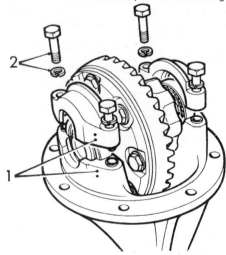

FIG.8.4. DIFFERENTIAL BEARING CAP REMOVAL

1   Bearing cap identification
marks

2   Bearing cap securing bolt
and spring washer

6   Draw the assembly forwards from over the studs on the axle casing. Lift away from under the car. Recover the paper joint washer.

7   Refitting the differential assembly is the reverse sequence to removal. The following additional points should be noted:

a)   Always use a new joint washer and make sure the mating faces are clean.

b)   Tighten the differential retaining nuts to a torque wrench setting of 20 lb ft (2.7 Kg fm).

c)   Refill the axle with 1.2 pints (0.71 litre) of Castrol Hypoy B.

6. Differential unit - dismantling, inspection, reassembly and adjustment

Make sure before attempting to dismantle the differential that it is both necessary and economic. A special tool is needed and whilst not too difficult some critical measurements have to be taken. It may well be cheaper to exchange the rear axle as a complete unit at the outset.

1   Obtain a special tool called an axle stretcher before commencing to dismantle the unit. It has a BLMC part number of 18G 131C with adaptor plates 18G 131E.

2   Hodl the differential unit vertically in a vice and then using a scriber mark the bearing caps and adjacent side of the differential carrier so that the bearing caps are refitted to their original positions.

3   Undo and remove the four bolts and spring washers securing the end caps.

4   Assemble the axle housing stretcher adaptor plates on the differential unit casing. Next fit the stretcher to the adaptor plates.

5   The differential unit case should now be stretched by tightening the nut three or four flats until the differential carrier can be levered out and the bearing shims and caps removed. IMPORTANT: To avoid damage to the case do not attempt to spread any more than is necessary. To assist each flat on the nut is numbered to give a check on the amount turned. The maximum stretch is 0.008 inch (0.20 mm). When removing the differential carrier do not lever against the spreader.

6   If the differential gear carrier bearing cups are to be renewed they should be removed using a universal 3 leg puller and a suitable thrust block.

7   Mark the relative positions of the crownwheel and differential carrier to ensure correct refitting.

8   Undo and remove the bolts securing the crownwheel to the differential carrier.

9   Separate the crownwheel from the differential carrier.

10 Using a parallel pin punch carefully drive out the differential pinion pin locking peg.

11 With a suitable soft metal drift remove the differential pinion pin.

12 Rotate the differential gear wheels until the differential pinions are opposite the openings in the differential gear case: remove the differential pinions and their selective thrust washers. Keep the pinions and respective thrust washers together.

13 Remove the differential gear wheels and their thrust washers.

14 Transfer the differential unit casing from its position in the vice and hold the drive flange firmly in the jaws.

15 Extract the drive flange nut split pin and remove the drive flange nut and washer.

16 Using a universal puller and suitable thrust block remove the drive flange from the pinion.

17 Drive out the pinion using a hard wood block and hammer.

18 Remove the pinion bearing shims and spacer.

19 If the pinion bearings are to be renewed the inner bearing should be drawn off the pinion using a universal puller with long legs.

20 Lift the pinion lead washer away from behind the pinion head.

21 Using a tapered soft metal drift carefully drift out the pinion outer bearing cup, bearing and oil seal. Also remove the pinion inner bearing cup.

22 Dismantling is now complete. Thoroughly wash all parts in petrol or paraffin and wipe dry using a clean non-fluffy rag.

23 Lightly lubricate the bearings and reassemble. Test for signs of roughness by rotating the inner and outer tracks. Check the rollers for signs of pitting, wear or excessive looseness in their cage. Inspect the thrust washers for signs of excessive wear. Check for signs of wear on the differential pinion shaft and pinion gears. Any parts that show signs of wear should be renewed.

24 The crownwheel and pinion must only be replaced as a matched pair. The pair number is etched on the outer face of the crownwheel and the forward face of the pinion.

25 If it is found that only one of the differential bearings is worn, both differential bearings must be renewed. Likewise if one pinion bearing is worn, both pinion bearings must be renewed.

26 To reassemble first fit the differential bearing cones to the gear carrier using a piece of tube of suitable diameter.

27 Place the thrust washers behind the two differential gears and then fit them to their bores in the gear carrier. Make sure the gears rotate easily.

28 Place the two pinion gears in mesh with the two differential gears, leaving out the thrust washers and rotate the gear cluster until the pinion pin hole in the carrier is lined up with the pinions. Insert the pinion pin.

29 Press each pinion in turn firmly into mesh with the differential gears. Measure the required thrust washer thickness using feeler gauge so that no backlash exists.

30 Remove the pinion gears, keeping them in their respective positions and select a thrust washer whose thickness is the same as that determined by the feeler gauges. Eight thrust washers are available in 0.002 in (0.05 mm) micrometers from 0.027 to 0.041 inch (0.685 to 1.03 mm).

31 Lubricate the thrust washers, pinions and pinion pin and reassemble into the differential carrier. Check that there is no backlash. When this condition exists the gears will be stiff to rotate by hand.

32 Lock the pinion pin using the locking peg. Secure the peg by peening the metal of the differential carrier.

33 Carefully clean the crownwheel and gear carrier mating faces and fit the crownwheel. Any burrs can be removed with a fine oilstone If the original parts are being used line up the previously made marks.

34 Secure the crownwheel with the eight bolts to be tightened in a diagonal and progressive manner.

35 Fit the carrier bearing cups to the bearings and place the assembly in the case. Leave out the shims at this stage.

36 Replace the bearing caps in their original positions and tighten the retaining bolts. Using either a dial indicator gauge or feeler gauges check the run-out of the crownwheel and carrier. This must not exceed 0.003 inch (0.076 mm).

37 If a reading in excess is obtained check for dirt on the crownwheel or carrier mating faces or under the bearing caps.

38 Remove the bearing caps again.

39 If the pinion bearing cups were removed for the fitting of new bearings, these should next be replaced. For this use a tube of suitable diameter and carefully drift them into position. Make sure they are fitted the correct way round with the tapers facing outwards.

40 Fit the spacer behind the pinion head and using a tube of suitable diameter refit the inner bearing again using a piece of metal tube of similar diameter.

41 Lubricate the bearing and fit the pinion to the casing. Slide on the bearing spacer chamfered end towards the drive flange followed by the shims that were previously removed.

42 Lubricate the outer bearing and then fit to the end of the pinion.

43 Fit the drive flange and nut. Tighten the nut to a torque wrench setting of 90 lb ft (12.4 Kg fm). Rotate the pinion several times before the nut is fully tightened so that the bearings settle to their running positions.

44 If available use a full scale and determine the bearing preload by wrapping string around the pinion flange and locking the other end onto the full scale. The reading should be between 15 to 18 lb in. (0.17 to 0.21 Kg fm). Should the reading be in excess of this amount the shim thickness should be increased and conversely if the reading is too low decrease the shim thickness.

45 Remove the pinion nut, pinion and outer bearing and fit the required thickness shim to the pinion. Four shims are available in sizes from 0.003 to 0.030 inch (0.076 to 0.76 mm). For assistance 0.001 inch (0.254 mm) thickness shim equals approximately 4 lb in. (0.046 Kg fm) pre-load.

46 Soak a new oil seal in Castrol GTX for 1 hour and then fit to the differential case. Replace the drive flange, washer and nut and tighten the nut to a torque wrench setting of 90 lb ft (12.4 Kg fm).

47 Lock the nut using a new split pin.

48 Place the bearing cups on the differential bearings and fit the differential carrier into the case. Replace the shims in their original positions.

49 Refit the bearing caps in their original positions and tighten the bearing cap bolts with spring washers in a progressive and diagonal manner.

50 Remove the axle spreader.

51 Using a dial indicator gauge or feeler gauges and determine the total backlash which should be between 0.004 to 0.006 inch (0.10 to 0.15 mm).

52 Should adjustment be necessary remove the shims behind the differential bearings once the caps have been removed and fit different thickness shims. It should be noted that a movement of 0.002 in (0.05 mm) shim thickness from one differential bearing to the other will vary the backlash by approximately 0.002 in (0.05 mm).

53 When the backlash is correct the final drive unit may now be refitted.

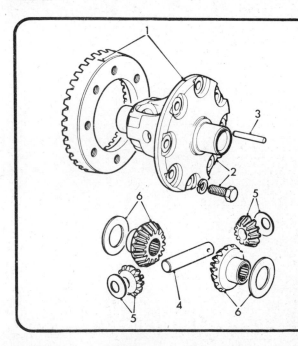

FIG.8.5. DIFFERENTIAL UNIT COMPONENTS

1 Crownwheel and differential carrier mating marks
2 Crownwheel securing bolt and spring washer
3 Locking peg
4 Differential pinion pin
5 Differential pinion and thrust washer
6 Differential gear wheel and thrust washer

Chapter 9   Braking system

Contents

Specifications

Front - drum (standard)

Drum diameter	8 in (203.2 mm)
Lining dimensions	8 x 1.75 x 0.1875 in (203.2 x 44.45 x 4.76 mm)
Total sweft area	88 in^2 (567.74 cm^2)
Lining material (non servo)	DON 202
Wheel cylinder diameter	0.750 in (17.78 mm)
Minimum lining thickness	1/16 in (1.6 mm)

Disc -(optional)

Disc diameter	9.785 in (248.5 mm)
Disc runout	0.006 in (0.152 mm)
Total pad area	17.4 in^2 (286.77 cm^2)
Total swept area	182.8 in^2 (267.1 cm^2)
Pad lining material (non servo)	DON 227
(with servo)	F 2430
Minimum pad thickness...	1/16 in (1.6 mm)

Rear - drum

Drum diameter	8 in (203.2 mm)
Lining dimensions	8 x 1.5 x 0.1875 in (203.2 x 38.1 x 4.76 mm)
Total swept area	76 in^2 (490.2 cm^2)
Lining material	DON 202
Wheel cylinder diameter	0.70 in (17.78 mm)

Master cylinder

Diameter (non servo)	0.70 in (17.78 mm)
(with servo)	0.75 in (19.05 mm)

Servo unit - (optional) ... ...   Girling Super Vac

Torque wrench settings

	lb ft	Kg fm
Bleed screw	4 to 6	0.5 to 0.8
Master cylinder retaining nuts	15.5 to 19.5	1.7 to 2.1
Caliper retaining bolts	50	6.9
Wheel cylinder retaining bolts	4 to 5	0.55 to 0.7
Backplate securing nuts and bolts	35 to 42	4.8 to 5.8
Brake drum retaining screws	26 to 28	3.5 to 3.8
Brake disc securing bolts	38 to 45	5.25 to 6.22

1. General description

The standard models are fitted with drum brakes to both the front and rear wheels but front disc brakes may be fitted as a factory option.

Both types of brakes are operated by hydraulic pressure created in the master cylinder when the brake pedal is depressed. This pressure is transferred to the respective wheel or caliper cylinders by a system of metal and flexible pipes and hoses.

The metal pipe to the rear brakes is connected to a flexible hose located on the right hand rear suspension. A short metal pipe connects the hose to the bottom union connection on the rear right hand wheel cylinder. The upper part of the right hand wheel cylinder is connected to the lower part of the left hand wheel cylinder by a metal pipe which is attached to the rear axle casing.

The drum brakes are of the internally expanding type whereby the shoes and linings are moved outwards into contact with the rotating brake drum. The rear brake units are fitted with one wheel cylinder and front brakes units have two wheel cylinders enabling two leading shoe operations. This term means that the leading edge of the shoe is moved into contact with the rotating drum by the wheel cylinder and by a self servo or wrapping action the brake shoe tends to pull on further thereby giving braking assistance.

The handbrake operates on the rear brakes only using a system of links and cables.

The front disc brakes, fitted are of the conventional fixed caliper design. Each half of the caliper contains a piston which operates in a bore both being interconnected so that under hydraulic pressure these pistons move towards each other. By this action they clamp the rotating disc between two friction pads so slowing rotational movement of the disc. Special seals are fitted between the piston and bore and these seals are able to distort slightly when the piston moves to apply the brake. When the hydraulic pressure is released the seals return to their natural shape and draw the pistons back slightly so giving a running clearance between the pads and disc. As the pads wear the piston is able to slide through the seal so allowing wear to be taken up.

The front disc brakes, are self adjusting but the drum brakes have to be manually adjusted at regular intervals.

Also offered as an optional extra is a brake servo unit which is fitted between the brake pedal and master cylinder to add to the pressure on the master cylinder pushrod when the brake pedal is being depressed.

2. Drum brake - adjustment

FRONT

1 Chock the rear wheels, apply the handbrake, jack up the front of the car and support on firmly based stands.
2 Refer to Fig.9.1. and locate the two adjusters on each backplate.
3 Remove dirt from the area of the adjusters and lightly lubricate with penetrating oil.
4 Turn the top adjuster in a clockwise direction when looking on the backplate from the centre of the car, until the brake shoe makes firm contact with the drum. Back off the adjuster until the drum rotates without signs of binding.
5 A slight rubbing noise will probably be due to dust in the drum.
6 Repeat operations 4 and 5 for the lower adjuster.
7 The second foot brake may now be adjusted in a similar manner to the first.

REAR

1 Chock the front wheels, release the handbrake completely, jack up the rear of the car and place on firmly based stands.
2 Refer to Fig.9.2. and locate the one adjuster on each backplate.

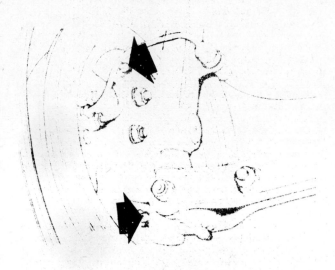

FIG.9.1. FRONT DRUM BRAKE ADJUSTERS

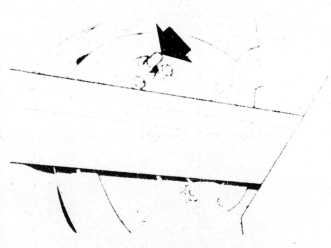

FIG.9.2. REAR DRUM BRAKE ADJUSTER

3   Remove the dirt from the area of the adjusters and lightly lubricate with penetrating oil.

4   Make sure that the handbrake cables are not in tension so causing the brakes to be partially applied.

5   Turn the adjuster in a clockwise direction, when looking on the backplate from the centre of the car, until the brake shoe makes firm contact with the drum. Back off the adjuster until the drum rotates without signs of binding.

6   A slight rubbing noise will probably be due to dust in the drum.

7   Repeat operations 5 and 6 for the second rear brake.

3. Bleeding the hydraulic system

Whenever the brake hydraulic system has been overhauled, a part renewed, or the level in the reservoir becomes too low, air will have entered the system necessitating its bleeding. During the operation, the level of hydraulic fluid in the reservoir should not be allowed to fall below half full, otherwise air will be drawn in again.

1   Obtain a clean and dry glass jar, plastic tubing fifteen inches long and of suitable diameter to fit tightly over the bleed screw, and a supply of Castrol Girling Brake Fluid.

2   Check that on each rear brake backplate the wheel cylinder is free to slide within its locating slot. Ensure that all connections are tight and all bleed screws closed. Chock the wheels and release the handbrake.

3   Fill the master cylinder reservoir and the bottom inch of the jar with hydraulic fluid. Take extreme care that no fluid is allowed to come into contact with the paintwork. It will damage the finish

4   Remove the rubber dust cap (if fitted) from the end of the bleed screw on the front drum brake wheel cylinder/disc brake caliper which is furthest away from the master cylinder. Insert the other end of the bleed tube in the jar containing one inch of hydraulic fluid.

5   Use a suitable open ended spanner and unscrew the bleed screw about half a turn.

6   An assistant should now pump the brake pedal by first depressing it one full stroke followed by three short but rapid strokes and allowing the pedal to return of its own accord. Check the fluid level in the reservoir. Carefully watch the flow of fluid into the glass jar and, when air bubbles cease to emerge with the fluid, during the next down stroke, tighten the bleed screw.

Remove the plastic bleed tube and tighten the bleed screw. Replace the rubber dust cap.

7   Repeat operations in paragraphs 4 to 6 for the second front brake.

8   The rear brakes should be bled in the same manner as the front, except that each brake pedal stroke should be slow with a pause of three or four seconds between each stroke.

9   Sometimes it may be found that the bleeding operation for one or more cylinders is taking a considerable time. This is probably due to air being drawn past the bleed screw threads when the screw is loose. To counteract this condition, at the end of each downward stroke, tighten the bleed screw to stop air being drawn past the threads.

10 If after the bleed operation has been completed, the brake pedal operation still feels spongy, there is still air in the system, or the master cylinder is faulty.

11 Check and top up the reservoir fluid level with fresh hydraulic fluid. Never re-use old brake fluid.

4. Front drum brake shoes - inspection, removal and refitting

Refitting new brake linings or shoes is not considered economic, or possible, without the use of special equipment. However, if the services of a local garage or workshop having brake re-lining equipment are available, then there is no reason why the original shoes should not be successfully relined. Ensure that the correct specification linings are fitted.

1   Chock the rear wheels, apply the handbrake, jack up the front of the car and place on firmly based axle stands. Remove the wheel.

2   Back off the brake shoe adjusters by turning in an anti-clockwise direction, when viewed from the centre of the car.

3   Undo and remove the two brake drum retaining screws and carefully pull off the brake drum. If it is tight it may be tapped outwards using a soft faced hammer (Fig.9.3).

4   The brake linings should be renewed if they are so worn that the rivet leads are flush with the surface of the lining. If bonded linings are fitted, they must be renewed when the lining material has worn down to 1/16 inch (1.6 mm), at its thinnest point.

5   Using a pair of pliers, release the steady springs and pins from the shoes by rotating through 90°. Lift away the steady spring and pin from each brake shoe web (Fig.9.4).

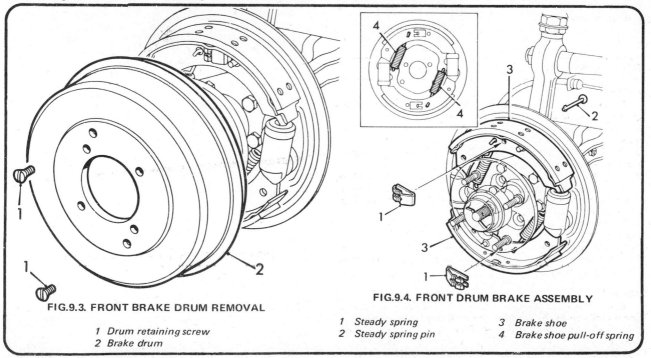

FIG.9.3. FRONT BRAKE DRUM REMOVAL

1   Drum retaining screw
2   Brake drum

FIG.9.4. FRONT DRUM BRAKE ASSEMBLY

1 Steady spring	3 Brake shoe
2 Steady spring pin	4 Brake shoe pull-off spring

6   Carefully remove the top brake shoe from its engagement with the wheel cylinders and unhook it from the spring. Lift away the shoe, and detach the spring from the backplate.

7   Repeat the operation in the previous paragraph for the lower brake shoe and spring.

8   If the shoes are to be left off for a while, do not depress the pedal otherwise the pistons will be ejected from the cylinders causing unnecessary work. Retain the pistons with strong elastic bands.

9   Thoroughly clean all traces of dust from the shoes, backplate and drum using a stiff brush. Do not use compressed air as it blows up dust which should not be inhaled. Brake dust can cause judder or squeal. It is important to clean it out.

10   Check that each piston is free in its cylinder, that the rubber dust covers are undamaged and in position, and that there are no hydraulic fluid leaks.

11   Lubricate the adjusters with a little penetrating oil.

12   Prior to reassembly, smear a trace of Castrol PH Brake Grease to the steady platforms, both ends of the brake shoes, and adjuster cams. Do not allow any grease to come into contact with the linings or rubber parts. Refit the shoes in the reverse sequence to removal. The two pull off springs should preferably be renewed every time new shoes are fitted, and must be refitted in their original web holes. Position them between the web and backplate.

13   Back off the adjusters and replace the brake drum. Secure with the two retaining screws which should be tightened to a torque wrench setting of 26 to 28 lb ft (3.5 to 3.8 Kg fm).

14   Refit the road wheel and adjust the front brakes as described in Section 2. Lower the car to the ground and road test.

5. Rear drum brake shoes - inspection, removal and refitting

1   Refer to the introduction at the beginning of Section 4, and then undertake the operations up to paragraph 7 inclusive, but apply to the rear wheels.

2   Using a pair of pliers release the steady pins, springs and cup washers from the shoes. Lift away the steady pin spring and cap washer from each brake shoe web (Fig.9.5).

3   Remove the trailing shoe from its adjuster link and wheel cylinder.

4   Lift away the brake shoes complete with return springs, easing the leading shoe from its adjuster link and wheel cylinder.

5   Note the location of the springs and into which holes in the brake shoe web they locate. Detach the springs from the brake shoes.

6   Remove the retaining spring and support plate from the leading shoe.

7   Now read Section 4 paragraphs 8 to 11 inclusive.

8   Prior to reassembly, smear a trace of Castrol PH Brake Grease to the steady platforms, both ends of the brake shoes and the adjuster links. Do not allow any grease to come into contact with the linings or rubber parts.

9   Check that the adjuster links are correctly positioned in the housing with the angle of the link registering against the adjuster wedge.

10   The two pull off springs should preferably be renewed every time new shoes are fitted and must be refitted in their original web holes.

11   Refitting is now the reverse sequence to removal. In addition:
a)   Make sure that the support plate on the leading shoe is correctly fitted with the retaining spring.
b)   The pull off springs should be located as shown in Fig.9.5.

12   Back off the adjuster and replace the brake drum. Secure with the two retaining screws which should be tightened to a torque wrench setting of 26 to 28 lb ft (3.5 to 3.8 Kg fm).

13   Refit the road wheel and adjust the brakes as described in Section 2. Check correct adjustment of the handbrake and finally road test.

6. Rear brake shoe adjuster - removal and refitting

1   Should it be necessary to remove the brake adjuster first remove the road wheel, brake drum and brake shoes as described in Section 5.

2   Undo and remove the two adjuster retaining nuts and spring washers. The adjuster can now be lifted away from the backplate (Fig.9.6).

3   Check that the wedge can be screwed both in and out to its fullest extent without showing signs of tightness.

4   Lift away the two adjuster links and thoroughly clean the adjuster assembly. Inspect the adjuster body and the two links for signs of excessive wear, and obtain new parts as necessary.

5   Lightly smear the adjuster links with Castrol PH Grease and reassemble. Double check correct operation by holding the two links between the fingers and rotating the adjuster screw whereupon the links should move out together.

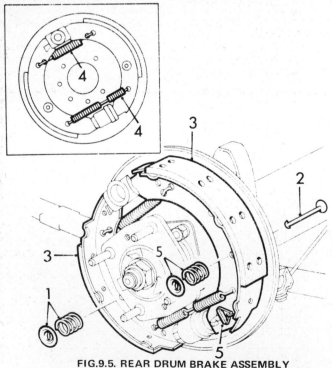

FIG.9.5. REAR DRUM BRAKE ASSEMBLY

1 Cup washer and spring	4 Brake shoe pull-off spring
2 Steady pin	5 Shoe retaining spring and
3 Brake shoe	support plate

FIG.9.6. REAR BRAKE SHOE ADJUSTER

1   Body
2   Adjuster link
3   Wedge

7. Front drum backplate - removal and refitting

1   Chock the rear wheels, apply the handbrake, jack up the front of the car and place on firmly based stands. Remove the road wheels.

2   Undo and remove the two screws securing the brake drum to the hub. Turn the brake adjusters in an anticlockwise direction to back off the brake adjustment and remove the brake drum. If it is tight it may be tapped outwards using a soft faced hammer.

3   Using a wide blade screwdriver ease off the hub grease cap.

4   Straighten the hub nut retainer locking split pin ears and extract the split pin. Remove the nut retainer and then undo and remove the nut and splined washer.

5   Withdraw the complete front hub assembly from the spindle.

6   Wipe the top of the brake master cylinder reservoir and unscrew. Place a piece of thin polythene sheet over the reservoir and refit the cap. This will stop hydraulic fluid syphoning out during subsequent operations.

7   Using an open ended spanner disconnect the flexible brake pipe at the swivel pin bracket.

8   Undo and remove the four nuts, bolts and spring washers securing the brake backplate to the swivel pin. Lift away the backplate assembly.

9   Refitting the backplate assembly is the reverse sequence to removal but the following additional points should be noted:

a)   Tighten the backplate securing nuts and bolts to a torque wrench setting of 35 to 42 lb ft (4.8 to 5.8 Kg fm).

b)   Tighten the brake drum retaining screws to a torque wrench setting of 26 to 28 lb ft (3.5 to 3.8 Kg fm).

c)   The hub bearing end float must be adjusted as described in Chapter 11.

d)   Bleed the brake hydraulic system as described in Section 3.

e)   Adjust the brakes as described in Section 2.

8. Rear drum backplate - removal and refitting

For full information refer to Chapter 8, Section 3 which describes removal of the axle shaft and hub assembly.

9. Front disc brake caliper pad - removal and refitting

1   Chock the rear wheels, apply the handbrake, jack up the front

of the car and support on firmly based axle stands. Remove the road wheel.

2   Extract the two pad retaining pin spring clips and withdraw the two retaining pins (Fig.9.7).

3   Lift away the brake pads and anti-rattle shims noting which way round the shims are fitted.

4   Inspect the thickness of the lining material and, if it is less than 1/16 inch (1.6 mm) the pads must be renewed. If one of the pads is slightly more worn than the other, it is permissible to change these round.

5   If new pads are being fitted always replace with high quality branded pads of similar specification to those given at the start of this chapter.

6   To refit the pads, it is first necessary to extract a little brake fluid from the system. To do this, fit a plastic bleed tube to the bleed screw and immerse the free end in 1 inch of hydraulic fluid in a jar. Slacken off the bleed screw one complete turn and press back the pistons into their bores. Tighten the bleed screw and remove the bleed tube.

7   Wipe the exposed end of the pistons and in the recesses of the caliper free of dust or road dirt.

8   Refitting the pads is now the reverse sequence to removal. In addition:

a)   The anti-squeal shims are fitted with the arrows pointing upwards.

b)   If it is suspected that air has entered the system during the operation described in paragraph 6 the system must be bled as described in Section 3.

9   Wipe the top of the hydraulic fluid reservoir and remove the cap. Top up and depress the brake pedal several times to settle the pads. Recheck the hydraulic fluid level.

10. Front brake disc - removal and refitting

1   Chock the rear wheels, apply the handbrake, jack up the front of the car and support on firmly based axle stands. Remove the road wheel

2   Refer to Section 17 of this chapter and remove the caliper assembly.

3   Using a wide blade screwdriver ease off the hub grease cap (Fig.9.8).

4   Straighten the hub nut retainer locking split pin ears and extract the split pin. Remove the nut retainer and then undo and remove the nut and splined washer.

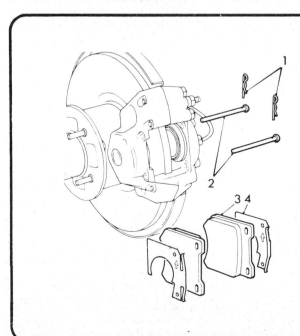

**FIG.9.7. FRONT DISC BRAKE PAD
REMOVAL**

1   Spring clip   3   Pad
2   Retaining pin   4   Anti-squeak shim

5 Withdraw the complete front hub assembly from the spindle.

6 To separate the disc from the hub first mark the relative psoition of the hub and disc. Undo and remove the four bolts securing the hub to the disc and separate the two parts.

7 Should the disc surfaces be grooved and a new disc not obtainable, it is permissible to have the two faces ground by an engineering works (but only so far). Score marks are not serious provided that they are concentric but not excessively deep. It is however far better to fit a disc rather than to re-grind the original one.

8 To refit the disc to the hub make sure that the mating faces are very clean and then line up the previously made alignment marks if the original parts are to be used. Secure with the four bolts which should be tightened in a progressive and diagonal manner to a final torque wrench setting of 38 to 45 lb ft (5.25 to 6.22 Kg fm).

9 Refitting is now the reverse sequence to removal but the following additional points should be noted:

a) Before refitting the caliper check the disc run-out at a 4.75 inch (120.7 mm) radius of the disc. The run-out must not exceed 0.006 inch (0.152 mm). If necessary remove the disc and check for dirt on the mating faces. Should these be clean re-position the disc on the hub.

b) The hub bearing end float must be adjusted as described in Chapter 11.

11. Master cylinder - removal and refitting

STANDARD FITMENT (NON-SERVO)

1 Apply the handbrake and chock the front wheels. Drain the fluid from the master cylinder reservoir and master cylinder by attaching a plastic bleed tube to one of the front brake bleed screws. Undo the screw one turn and then pump the fluid out into a clean glass container by means of the brake pedal. Hold the brake pedal against the floor at the end of each stroke and tighten the bleed nipple. When the pedal has returned to its normal position, loosen the bleed nipple and repeat the process until the master cylinder reservoir is empty.

2 Wipe the area around the hydraulic pipe union on the master cylinder. Undo the union nut and lift out the hydraulic pipe.

3 Undo and remove the nuts and spring washers securing the master cylinder to the pedal bracket.

4 Straighten the ears on the split pin retaining the pushrod to brake pedal clevis pin, extract the split pin, lift away the plain washer and withdraw the clevis pin.

5 Lift away the master cylinder taking care not to allow any hydraulic fluid to drip onto the paintwork.

6 To refit the master cylinder position the pushrod in line with the top hole in the brake pedal. Insert the clevis pin, replace the plain washer and lock with a new split pin. It is important that the master cylinder pushrod is connected to the TOP HOLE of the two holes in the brake pedal lever.

7 Replace the two nuts and spring washers that secure the master cylinder to the pedal bracket. Tighten to a torque wrench setting of 15.5 to 19.5 lb ft (1.7 to 2.1 Kg fm).

8 Reconnect the hydraulic pipe to the master cylinder union. Slide down the union nut and very carefully start the threads as it is easy to cross thread. Tighten the union fully.

9 Refer to Section 3 and bleed the brake hydraulic system.

SERVO FITMENT

1 Drain the hydraulic fluid from the reservoir and master cylinder as described in paragraph 1 in the previous sub-section.

2 Wipe the area around the hydraulic pipe union on the master cylinder. Undo the union nut and lift out the hydraulic pipe

3 Undo and remove the two nuts and spring washers that secure the master cylinder to the servo unit.

4 Lift away the master cylinder taking care not to allow any hydraulic fluid to drip onto the paintwork.

5 Refitting is the reverse sequence to removal. Refer to paragraphs 8 and 9 of the previous sub-section for additional information.

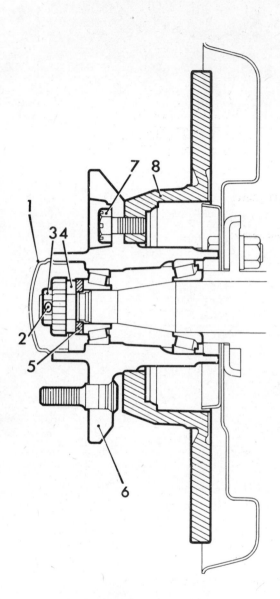

FIG.9.8. FRONT BRAKE DISC

1 Grease cap	5 Splined washer
2 Split pin	6 Hub
3 Nut retainer	7 Disc securing bolt
4 Nut	8 Disc

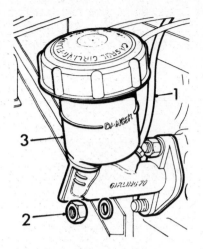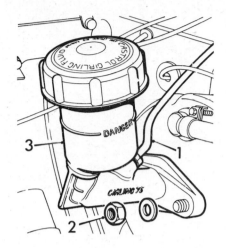

FIG.9.9. BRAKE MASTER CYLINDER FIXING: NON-SERVO, LEFT: SERVO, RIGHT

1 Hydraulic pipe
2 Securing nut and spring washer
3 Master cylinder

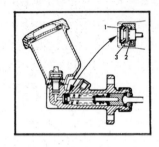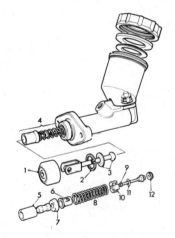

FIG.9.10. BRAKE MASTER CYLINDER COMPONENT PARTS

1	*Rubber boot*	*4*	*Piston assembly*	*7*	*Piston seal*	*10 Valve spacer*
2	*Circlip*	*5*	*Piston*	*8*	*Spring*	*11 Curved washer*
3	*Pushrod and dished washer*	*6*	*Thimble*	*9*	*Valve*	*12 Valve seal*

Inset: Section through hole master cylinder plus valve assembly
1 Seal
2 Dished washer
3 Valve spacer

12. Master cylinder - dismantling and reassembly

If a replacement master cylinder is to be fitted, it will be necessary to lubricate the seals before fitting to the car as they have a protective coating when originally assembled. Remove the blanking plug from the hydraulic pipe union seating. Ease back and remove the plunger dust cover. Inject clean hydraulic fluid into the master cylinder and operate the piston several times so the fluid will spread over all the internal working surfaces.

If the master cylinder is to be dismantled after removal, proceed as follows:

1 Standard. Ease back the dust cover from the end of the master cylinder body. Using a pair of pointed pliers contract and lift out the circlip. Withdraw the pushrod and dished washers (Fig.9.10).

2 Carefully withdraw the complete piston assembly from the master cylinder bore. If this is difficult apply a low air pressure jet to the hydraulic pipe outlet connection.

3 With a small screwdriver lift the thimble leaf and separate the piston from the thimble.

4 Using the fingers remove the piston seal from the piston.

5 Compress the spring and remove the valve stem through the elongated hole in the thimble.

6 Lift away the thimble from the spring.

7 Remove the valve spacer and curved washer from the valve stem.

8 Carefully remove the valve seal from the valve head.

9 Thoroughly wash all parts in Girling Cleaning Fluid or methylated spirits.

10 Examine the bore of the cylinder carefully for any signs of scores or ridges. If this is found to be smooth all over, new seals can be fitted. If there is any doubt of the condition of the bore, then a new master cylinder must be fitted.

11 If examination of the seals shows them to be apparently oversize or swollen, or very loose on the piston or valve suspect oil contamination in the system. Ordinary lubricating oil will swell these rubber seals, and if one is found to be swollen it is reasonable to assume that all seals in the braking system will need attention.

12 All components should be assembled wet by dipping in clean brake fluid.

13 Fit the valve seal to the valve head so that the smallest diameter is on the valve head.

14 Fit the curved washer to the shoulder of the valve stem so that the domed side is to the shoulder.

15 Fit the valve spacer with the legs of the spacer towards the curved washer.

16 Locate the spring centrally on the valve spacer and insert the thimble into the spring.

17 Carefully push the end of the thimble so as to compress the spring against the valve spacer and insert the valve stem through the elongated hole of the thimble. Locate the valve stem in the centre of the thimble.

18 Fit the seal to the piston with the flat surface of the seal against the piston.

19 Insert the small end of the piston into the thimble until the thimble leaf engages under the shoulder of the piston.

20 Carefully insert the piston assembly into the master cylinder bore making sure the seal is not rolled or nipped as it enters the bore.

21 Standard: Fit the pushrod with the dished washer into the cylinder bore and retain in position with the circlip. Make sure the circlip is fully seated into its locating groove. Smear the pushrod and master cylinder bore of the dust cover with Girling rubber grease and refit the dust cover.

22 The master cylinder is now ready for refitting to the car.

13. Front drum brake wheel cylinders - removal and refitting

If hydraulic fluid is leaking from the brake wheel cylinder, it will be necessary to dismantle it and replace the seal.

1 Remove the brake drum and brake shoes as described in Section 4.

2 Wipe the top of the brake master cylinder reservoir and unscrew the cap. Place a piece of thin polythene sheet over the top of the reservoir and replace the cap. This is to stop hydraulic fluid syphoning out.

3 Forward wheel cylinder. Using an open ended spanner, carefully unscrew the bridge pipe from the forward wheel cylinder (Fig.9.11).

4 Undo and remove the retaining bolts and lift away the forward wheel cylinder and its sealing gasket.

5 Rear wheel cylinder. Using an open ended spanner, carefully unscrew the bridge pipe from the rear wheel cylinder.

6 Disconnect the metal brake pipe from the flexible hose.

7 Disconnect the brake pipe from the rear wheel cylinder.

8 Undo and remove the retaining bolts and lift away the rear wheel cylinder and its sealing gasket.

9 Refitting the wheel cylinders is the reverse sequence to removal. In addition:

a) Always use new sealing gaskets located behind the wheel cylinders.

b) Tighten the wheel cylinder retaining bolts to a torque wrench setting of 4 to 5 lb ft (0.55 to 0.7 Kg fm).

c) Adjust the brakes as described in Section 2.

d) Bleed the hydraulic system as described in Section 3.

14. Rear drum brake wheel cylinder - removal and refitting

1 Refer to the introduction to Section 13.

2 Remove the brake drum and brake shoes as described in Section 5.

3 Wipe the top of the brake master cylinder reservoir and unscrew the cap. Place a piece of thin polythene sheet over the top of the reservoir and replace the cap. This is to stop hydraulic fluid syphoning out.

4 Using an open ended spanner, carefully unscrew the hydraulic pipe connection union to the rear of the wheel cylinder. Note that the feed pipe for the left hand and right hand wheel cylinder locates in the lower opening (Fig.9.12).

5 Again using an open ended spanner undo and remove the bridge feed pipe from the right hand wheel cylinder.

6 Extract the split pin and lift away the washer and clevis pin that connects the handbrake cable yoke to the wheel cylinder operating lever.

7 Ease off the rubber boot from the rear of the wheel cylinder.

8 Using a screwdriver carefully draw off the retaining plate and spring plate from the rear of the wheel cylinder.

9 The wheel cylinder may now be lifted away from the brake backplate. Detach the handbrake lever from the wheel cylinder.

10 To refit the wheel cylinder first smear the backplate where the wheel cylinder slides with a little Castrol PH Brake Grease. Refit the handbrake lever on the wheel cylinder ensuring that it is the correct way round. The spindles of the lever most engage in the recess on the cylinder arms.

11 Slide the spring plate between the wheel cylinder and backplate. The retaining plate may now be inserted between the spring plate and wheel cylinder taking care the pipes of the spring plate engage in the holes of the retaining plate.

12 Replace the rubber boot and reconnect the handbrake cable yoke to the handbrake lever. Insert the clevis pin, head upwards, and plain washer. Lock with a new split pin.

13 Refitting the brake shoes and drum is the reverse sequence to remove. Adjust the brakes as described in Section 2 and finally bleed the hydraulic system following the instructions in Section 3.

15. Front drum brake wheel cylinder - overhaul

1 Ease off the rubber dust cover protecting the open end of the cylinder bore (Fig.9.13).

2 Withdraw the piston from the wheel cylinder body followed by the spring. Note which way round the spring is fitted.

3 Using fingers carefully remove the piston seal from the piston noting which way round it is fitted. (Do not use a screwdriver as this could scratch the piston).

4 Inspect the inside of the cylinder for score marks caused by impurities in the hydraulic fluid. If any are found the cylinder will require renewal. Note, if the wheel cylinder is to be renewed always ensure that the replacement is exactly similar to the one removed.

5 If the cylinder is sound, thoroughly clean it out with fresh hydraulic fluid.

6 The old rubber seal will probably be swollen and visibly worn so it must be discarded. Smear the new rubber seal with hydraulic fluid and fit it to the piston so that the flat surface is towards the piston.

7 Fit the spring into the cylinder bore and carefully insert the piston and seal into the bore making sure the fine edge lip does not roll or become trapped.

8 Refit the dust cover engaging the lip with the groove in the outer surface of the wheel cylinder body.

16. Rear drum brake wheel cylinder - overhaul

1 Ease off the rubber dust cover protecting the open end of cylinder bore (Fig.9.14).

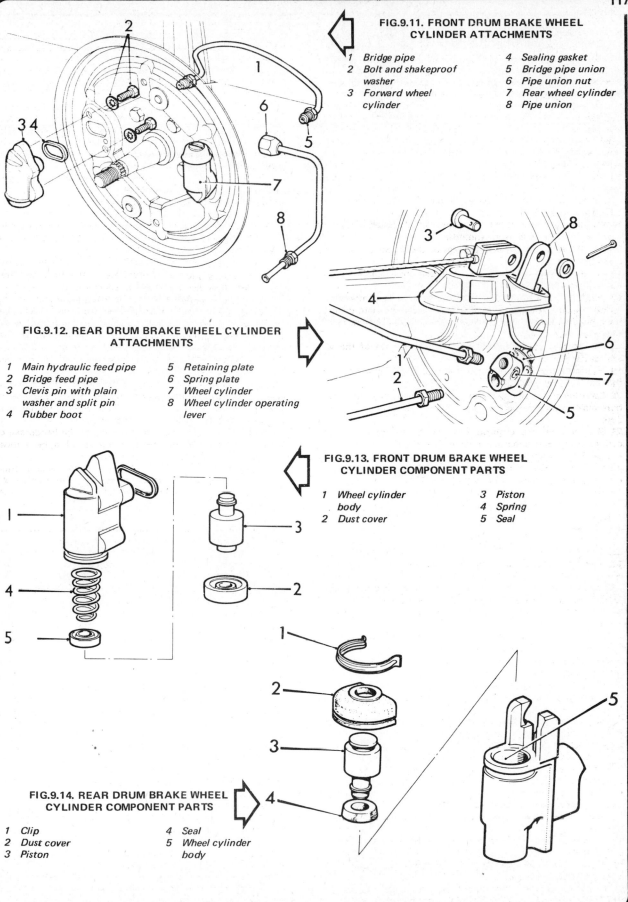

FIG.9.11. FRONT DRUM BRAKE WHEEL CYLINDER ATTACHMENTS

1	Bridge pipe	4	Sealing gasket
2	Bolt and shakeproof washer	5	Bridge pipe union
3	Forward wheel cylinder	6	Pipe union nut
		7	Rear wheel cylinder
		8	Pipe union

FIG.9.12. REAR DRUM BRAKE WHEEL CYLINDER ATTACHMENTS

1	Main hydraulic feed pipe	5	Retaining plate
2	Bridge feed pipe	6	Spring plate
3	Clevis pin with plain washer and split pin	7	Wheel cylinder
4	Rubber boot	8	Wheel cylinder operating lever

FIG.9.13. FRONT DRUM BRAKE WHEEL CYLINDER COMPONENT PARTS

1	Wheel cylinder body	3	Piston
2	Dust cover	4	Spring
		5	Seal

FIG.9.14. REAR DRUM BRAKE WHEEL CYLINDER COMPONENT PARTS

1	Clip	4	Seal
2	Dust cover	5	Wheel cylinder body
3	Piston		

2   Withdraw the piston from the wheel cylinder body.

3   Using fingers carefully remove the piston seal from the piston noting which way round it is fitted. (Do not use a screwdriver as this could scratch the piston).

4   Inspect the inside of the cylinder for score marks caused by impurities in the hydraulic fluid. If any are found the cylinder will require renewal. Note: If the wheel cylinder is to be renewed always ensure that the replacement is exactly similar to the one removed.

5   If the cylinder is sound, thoroughly clean it out with fresh hydraulic fluid.

6   The old rubber seal will probably be swollen and visibly worn so it must be discarded. Smear the new rubber seal with hydraulic fluid and fit it to the piston so that the small diameter is towards the piston.

7   Carefully insert the piston and seal into the bore making sure the fine edge lip does not roll or become trapped.

8   Refit the dust cover engaging the lip with the groove in the outer surface of the wheel cylinder body.

17. Front disc brake caliper - removal and refitting

1   Apply the handbrake, chock the rear wheels, jack up the front of the car and support on firmly based stands. Remove the road wheel.

2   Wipe the top of the master cylinder reservoir, unscrew the cap and place a piece of polythene sheet over the top. Refit the cap. This is to stop hydraulic fluid syphoning out during subsequent operations.

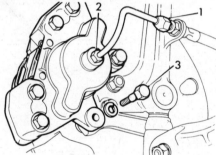

FIG.9.15. FRONT DISC BRAKE CALIPER ATTACHMENTS

1   Metal pipe union nut   3   Securing bolt and spring
2   Metal pipe union   washer

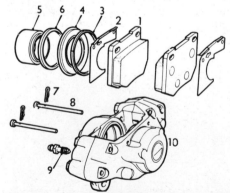

FIG.9.16. FRONT DISC BRAKE CALIPER COMPONENT PARTS

1   Pad   6   Sealing ring
2   Anti-squeak shim   7   Spring clip
3   Dust cover retaining ring   8   Retaining pin
4   Dust cover   9   Bleed screw
5   Piston   10   Caliper body

3   Wipe the area around the caliper flexible hose to metal pipe union and also metal pipe to caliper connection. Unscrew the union nuts, and lift away the metal pipe (Fig.9.15).

4   Undo and remove the two bolts and spring washers securing the caliper to the steering swivel. Lift the caliper from the disc.

5   Refitting the caliper is the reverse sequence to removal. In addition:

a)   The two caliper securing bolts should be tightened to a torque wrench setting of 50 lb ft (6.9 Kg fm).

b)   Bleed the brake hydraulic system as described in Section 3.

c)   Depress the brake pedal several times to reset the pads in their correct operating position.

18. Front disc brake caliper - overhaul

1   Extract the two pad retaining pin spring clips and withdraw the two retaining pins (Fig.9.16).

2   Lift away the brake pads and anti-squeak shims noting which way round the shims are fitted.

3   Temporarily reconnect the caliper to the hydraulic system and support its weight. Do not allow the caliper to hang on the flexible hose, but support its weight. Using a small G clamp hold the piston in the mounting half of the caliper. Carefully depress the footbrake pedal with the bleed nipple open so as to bleed the system, and then close the nipple. Depress the footbrake again and this will push the piston in the rim half of the caliper outwards. Release the dust cover retaining ring and the cover. Depress the footbrake again until the piston has been ejected sufficiently to continue removal by hand. It is advisable to have a container or tray available to catch any hydraulic fluid once the piston is removed.

4   Using a tapered wooden rod or an old plastic knitting needle, carefully extract the fluid seal from its bore in the caliper half.

5   Remove the G clamp from the mounting half piston. Temporarily refit the rim half piston and repeat the operations in paragraphs 3 and 4 of this Section.

6   Thoroughly clean the internal parts of the caliper using methylated spirits. Any other fluid cleaner will damage the internal seals between the two halves of the caliper. DO NOT SEPARATE THE TWO HALVES OF THE CALIPER.

7   Inspect the caliper bores and pistons for signs of scoring which if evident a new assembly should be fitted.

8   To reassemble the caliper, first wet a new fluid seal with Castrol Girling Brake Fluid and carefully insert it into its groove in the rim half of the caliper seating, ensuring that it is correctly fitted. Refit the dust cover into its special groove in the cylinder.

9   Release the bleed screw in the caliper one complete turn. Coat the side of the piston with hydraulic fluid and with it positioned squarely in the top of the cylinder bore, ease the piston in until approximately 5/16 inch (7.94 mm) is left protruding. Engage the outer lip of the dust cover in the piston groove and push the piston into the cylinder as far as it will go. Fit the dust cover retaining ring.

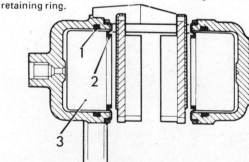

Inset: Correct fitted position of piston seal and dust cover

1   Piston seal
2   Dust cover
3   Piston

10 Repeat the operations in paragraphs 8 and 9 for the mounting half of the caliper.

11 Fit the pads and anti-squeak shims into the caliper and retain in position with the two pins and spring clips.

12 The caliper is now ready for refitting.

19. Handbrake cable - adjustment

1 Refer to Section 2 and adjust the rear brakes.

2 Chock the front wheels and completely release the handbrake. Pull on the handbrake four clicks of the ratchet.

3 Jack up the rear of the car and support on firmly based stands.

4 Check the cable adjustment by attempting to rotate the rear wheels. If this is possible the cable may be adjusted as described in the subsequent paragraphs.

5 Refer to Fig.9.17 and slacken the adjuster locknut.

6 Turn the adjustment nut clockwise whilst the outer cable is held with an open ended spanner until the correct adjustment is obtained. Retighten the locknut.

7 Release the handbrake and check that the rear wheels can be rotated freely.

8 Lower the rear of the car to the ground.

20. Handbrake cable - removal and refitting

1 Slacken the two adjustment nuts securing the cable to its support bracket (Fig.9.17).

2 Straighten the ears, extract the split pin locking the clevis pin retaining the inner cable yoke to the handbrake lever. Lift away the plain washer and withdraw the clevis pin.

3 Repeat the previous paragraph sequence for the clevis pin on both rear wheel cylinder operating levers.

4 Undo and remove the bolt and spring washer that secures the handbrake cable clip to the axle casing.

5 Undo and remove the trunnion retaining nut and spring washer.

6 Slacken the nut securing the compensating levers to the bracket.

7 Slacken the nut securing the cables to the compensating lever and remove the cables.

8 Refitting the cables is the reverse sequence to removal. It will be necessary to adjust the handbrake as described in Section 18 of this Chapter.

21. Handbrake lever assembly - removal and refitting

1 Draw back the floor covering from around the handbrake lever. Undo and remove the four self tapping screws retaining the handbrake lever gaiter to the floor panel (Fig.9.18).

2 Straighten the ears and extract the split pin retaining the handbrake cable to lever clevis pin. Lift away the plain washer and withdraw the clevis pin.

3 Slide the gaiter up the handbrake. Undo and remove the two nuts, spring washers and bolts that secure the handbrake lever assembly to its mounting bracket. Lift away the handbrake lever assembly.

4 Refitting the handbrake lever assembly is the reverse sequence to removal. Lubricate all pivots with Castrol GTX.

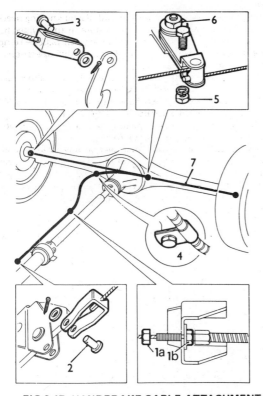

FIG.9.17. HANDBRAKE CABLE ATTACHMENT PIVOTS

1A Locknut
1B Adjustment nut
2 Clevis pin, plain washer and split pin
3 Clevis pin, plain washer and split pin
4 Handbrake cable clip
5 Retaining nut and spring washer
6 Trunnion retaining nut and spring washer
7 Rear cable

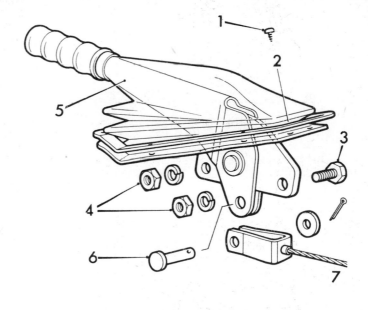

FIG.9.18. HANDBRAKE LEVER ATTACHMENTS

1 Self-tapping screw
2 Gaiter and metal plate
3 Mounting bolt
4 Nut and spring washer
5 Handbrake lever
6 Clevis pin with plain washer and split pin
7 Handbrake cable

22. Brake pedal assembly - removal and refitting

1 Refer to Chapter 12 and remove the complete instrument panel and the front parcel tray.
2 Refer to Chapter 3 and remove the throttle pedal.
3 Refer to Chapter 5 and remove the clutch master cylinder
4 Wipe the top of the brake master cylinder and remove the cap. Place a piece of thick polythene over the top of the reservoir and refit the cap. This is to prevent the hydraulic fluid syphoning out during subsequent operations.
5 Disconnect the brake master cylinder fluid pipe from the four way connector on the bulkhead.
6 Slacken the clip and detach the vacuum hose from the servo unit connector if a brake servo unit is fitted.
7 Make a note of the cable connections on the ignition coil. Detach the cables and remove the ignition coil.
8 Undo and remove the nuts, bolts, spring and plain washers securing the pedal housing assembly to the bulkhead (Fig.9.19).
9 Partially withdraw the pedal assembly and disconnect the electrical connections at the stop light switch.
10 Carefully pull the throttle and speedometer cable through the grommets in the pedal assembly.
11 The pedal and housing assembly may now be lifted away from inside the car.
12 Detach the return spring from the brake and clutch pedals (Fig.9.20).
13 Undo and remove the locknut and plain washer retaining the brake pedal pivot pin. Lift away the throttle pedal stop noting which way round it is fitted.
14 Withdraw the clutch pedal complete with pivot pin and finally remove the brake pedal.
15 Refitting the pedal assembly is the reverse sequence to removal. Lubricate all pivots with Castrol GTX.

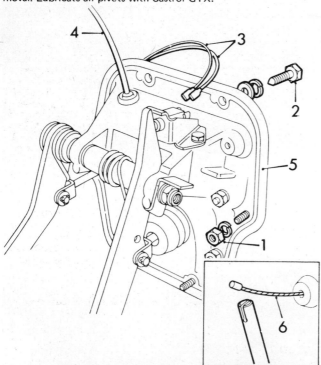

FIG.9.19. PEDAL MOUNTING BRACKET ATTACHMENTS

1 Bracket retaining nut and spring washer
2 Bracket retaining bolt with spring and plain washer
3 Stop light cables
4 Speedometer cable
5 Pedal mounting bracket
6 Inset: Throttle cable attachment to pedal

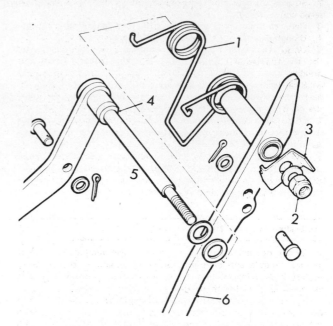

FIG.9.20. BRAKE AND CLUTCH PEDAL COMPONENTS

1 Return spring
2 Locknut and plain washer
3 Throttle pedal stop
4 Clutch pedal
5 Pivot pin
6 Brake pedal

23. Brake servo unit - description

A vacuum servo unit offered as an optional extra is fitted into the brake hydraulic circuit in series with the master cylinder, to provide 'power' assistance to the driver when the brake pedal is depressed.

The unit operates by vacuum obtained from the inlet manifold and comprises basically a booster diaphragm and a non-return valve.

The servo unit and hydraulic master cylinder are connected together so that the servo unit piston rod acts as the master cylinder pushrod. The drivers braking effort is transmitted through another pushrod to the servo unit piston and its built-in control system. The servo unit piston does not fit tightly into the cylinder but has a strong diaphragm to keep its edges in constant contact with the cylinder wall, so assuring an air under vacuum conditions created in the inlet manifold of the engine and, during periods when the brake pedal is not in use, the controls open a passage to the rear chamber so placing it under vacuum. When the brake pedal is depressed, the vacuum passage to the rear chamber is cut off and the chamber opened to atmospheric pressure. The consequent rush of air pushes the servo piston forward in the vacuum chamber and operates the main pushrod to the master cylinder. The controls are designed so that assistance is given under all conditions and, when the brakes are not required, vacuum in the rear chamber is established when the brake pedal is released. All air from the atmosphere entering the rear chamber is passed through a small air filter.

24. Brake servo unit - removal and replacement

1 Refer to Section 11 and remove the brake master cylinder.

2 Slacken the hose clip and detach the vacuum hose from the servo connector.

3 Refer to Chapter 12 and remove the front parcel tray.

4 Detach the throttle cable from the throttle pedal (Fig.9.21).

5 Undo and remove the two nuts and spring washers that secure the throttle pedal bracket. Lift away the throttle pedal and brakcet.

6 Straighten the ears of the split pin retaining the servo to brake pedal pushrod clevis pin. Extract the split pin, lift away the plain washer and withdraw the clevis pin.

7 Undo and remove the four nuts and spring washers that secure the servo unit to the mounting bracket. Lift away the servo unit.

8 Refitting the servo unit is the reverse sequence to removal. It is important that the servo operating rod is attached to the BOTTOM hole of the two holes in the brake pedal lever. Bleed the brake hydraulic system as described in Section 3.

---

25. Brake servo unit - service kit

Under normal operating conditions the vacuum servo unit is very reliable and does not require overhaul except possibly at very high mileages. In all cases it is better to obtain a service exchange unit, rather than repair the original.

However a service kit may be available and a fitment operation description is given but this will not repair any major fault. The kit should be used when the action of the unit becomes 'tired' rather than unreliable.

1 Having removed the servo unit pull back the dust cover (See Fig.9.22) and remove the end cap.

2 Withdraw the filter and then remove the seal and plate assembly from the front shell recess.

3 Remove the non-return valve and grommet.

4 Having obtained the service kit, replacement is a straightforward reversal of the removal sequence but using the new parts supplied.

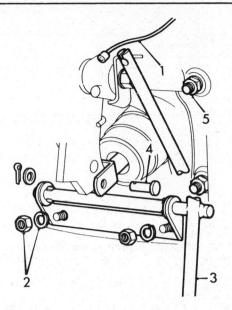

FIG.9.21. BRAKE SERVO UNIT ATTACHMENTS — CAR INTERIOR

1 Throttle cable	4 Clevis pin with plain washer and split pin
2 Throttle pedal bracket securing nut and spring washer	5 Servo unit securing nut and spring washer
3 Throttle pedal	

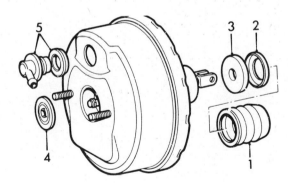

FIG.9.22. SERVO SERVICE KIT FITTING

1 Dust cover	4 Front seal
2 End cap	5 Non-return valve and grommet
3 Filter	

Turn to page 122 for Braking system fault diagnosis

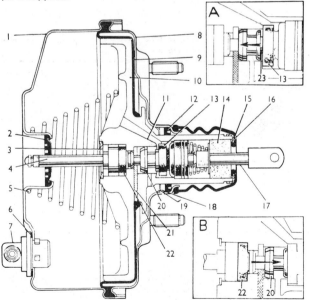

FIG.9.23. GIRLING SUPERVAC SERVO UNIT — IN SECTION

1 Front shell	7 Non-return valve	13 Control valve	18 Bearing
2 Seal and plate assembly	8 Rear shell	14 Filter	19 Retainer
3 Retainer (sprag washer)	9 Diaphragm	15 Dust cover	20 Control piston
4 Pushrod - hydraulic	10 Diaphragm plate	16 End cap	21 Valve retaining plate
5 Diaphragm return spring	11 Vacuum port	17 Valve operating rod assembly	22 Reaction disc
6 'O' ring	12 Seal		23 Atmospheric port

Insets: A Control valve closed, control piston moved forward - atmospheric port open.

B Pressure from diaphragm plate causes reaction disc to extrude, presses back control piston and closes atmospheric port

Symptom	Reason/s	Remedy
PEDAL TRAVELS ALMOST TO FLOORBOARDS BEFORE BRAKES OPERATE		
Leaks and air bubbles in hydraulic system	Brake fluid level too low	Top up master cylinder reservoir. Check for leaks.
	Wheel cylinder or caliper leaking	Dismantle wheel cylinder or caliper, clean fit new rubbers and bleed brakes.
	Master cylinder leaking (bubbles in master cylinder fluid)	Dismantle master cylinder, clean, and fit new rubbers. Bleed brakes.
	Brake flexible hose leaking	Examine and fit new hose if old hose leaking Bleed brakes.
	Brake line fractured	Replace with new brake pipe. Bleed brakes.
	Brake system unions loose	Check all unions in brake system and tighten as necessary. Bleed brakes.
Normal wear	Linings over 75% worn	Fit replacement shoes and brake linings.
	Drum brakes badly out of adjustment	Jack up car and adjust rear brakes.
BRAKE PEDAL FEELS SPRINGY		
Brake lining renewal	New linings not yet bedded-in	Use brakes gently until springy pedal feeling leaves.
	Brake drums or discs badly worn and weak or cracked	Fit new brake drums or discs.
	Master cylinder securing nuts loose	Tighten master cylinder securing nuts. Ensure spring washers are fitted.
BRAKE PEDAL FEELS SPONGY AND SOGGY		
Leaks or bubbles in hydraulic system	Wheel cylinder or caliper leaking	Dismantle wheel cylinder or caliper, clean, fit new rubbers, and bleed brakes.
	Master cylinder leaking (bubbles in master cylinder reservoir)	Dismantle master cylinder, clean, and fit new rubbers and bleed brakes. Replace cylinder if internal walls scored.
	Brake pipe line or flexible hose leaking	Fit new pipe line or hose.
	Unions in brake system loose	Examine for leaks, tighten as necessary.
BRAKES UNEVEN & PULLING TO ONE SIDE		
Oil or grease leaks	Linings and brake drums or discs contaminated with oil, grease, or hydraulic fluid	Ascertain and rectify source of leak, clean brake drums, fit new linings.
	Tyre pressures unequal	Check and inflate as necessary.
	Brake backplate caliper or disc loose	Tighten backplate caliper or disc securing nuts and bolts.
	Brake shoes or pads fitted incorrectly	Remove and fit shoes or pads correct way round.
	Different type of linings fitted at each wheel	Fit the linings specified all round.
	Anchorages for front or rear suspension loose	Tighten front and rear suspension pick-up points including spring locations.
	Brake drums or discs badly worn, cracked or distorted	Fit new brake drums or discs.
BRAKES TEND TO BIND, DRAG, OR LOCK-ON		
Incorrect adjustment	Brake shoes adjusted too tightly	Slacken off rear brake shoe adjusters two clicks.
	Handbrake cable over-tightened	Slacken off handbrake cable adjustment.
	Master cylinder pushrod out of adjustment giving too little brake pedal free movement	Reset to specifications.
Wear or dirt in hydraulic system or incorrect fluid	Reservoir vent hole in cap blocked with dirt	Clean and blow through hole.
	Master cylinder by-pass port restricted brakes seize in 'on' position	Dismantle, clean, and overhaul master cylinder. Bleed brakes.
	Wheel cylinder seizes in 'on' position	Dismantle, clean and overhaul wheel cylinder. Bleed brakes.
Mechanical wear	Drum brake shoe pull-off springs broken, stretched or loose	Examine springs and replace if worn or loose.
Incorrect brake assembly	Drum brake shoe pull-off springs fitted wrong way round, omitted, or wrong type used	Examine, and rectify as appropriate.

Chapter 10 Electrical system

Contents

Specifications

12 volt negative earth system

Battery: Lucas A9, A11, A13
Exide   ... ...   6 VTP 7-BR; 6 VTP 9-BR; 6 VTPZ 11-BR
Capacity at 20 hr rate/maximum fast charge time:

A9	40 amp : 1½ hours
A11	50 amp : 1½ hours
A13	60 amp : 1 hour
6 VTP 7-BR	30 amp : 1½ hours
6 VTP 9-BR	40 amp : 1½ hours
6 VTPZ 11-BR	50 amp : 1½ hours

Dynamo   ... ...   Lucas C 40 – 1, Two brush, two pole, current voltage control
Rotation ... ...   Clockwise
Field resistance ... ...   6 ohms at 20°C (68°F)
Maximum output at 13.5 volts ... ...   22 amps at 2250 rpm at load of 0.61 ohms
Brush tension ... ...   20 to 34 oz (567 to 964 gm)
Minimum brush length ... ...   0.25 inch (6.5 mm)
Pulley ratio 1.7:1

Control box   ... ...   Lucas RB106
Setting at 20°C (68°F) and dynamo at 3000 RPM ...   16.0 to 16.6 volts
Cut-in voltage ... ...   12.7 to 13.3 volts
Drop off voltage ... ...   8.5 to 11.0 volts
Points gap ... ...   0.018 inch (0.46 mm)

Alternator (optional)   ... ...   Lucas 16ACR
Output at 14 volts and 6000 RPM ... ...   34 amps
Maximum permissible rotor speed ... ...   12,500 rpm
Stator phases   3

Rotor poles	12
Rotor windings resistance (pink winding identification)	4.33 ohms ± 5% at 20°C (68°F)
Brush length (new)	0.5 inch (12.6 mm)
Brush spring tension	7 to 10 oz (198 to 283 gm) with brush face flush with brush box
Control unit	Integral with alternator
Starter motor - Standard	Lucas M35J
- Automatic	Lucas M35J (pre-engaged)
Brush spring tension...	28 oz (0.8 Kg)
Minimum brush length	3/8 inch (9.5 mm)
Lock torque	7 lb ft (0.97 Kg fm) with 350 to 375 amp load
Torque at 1000 rpm	4.4 lb ft (0.61 Kg fm) with 260 to 270 amp
Light running current	65 amp at 8000 to 10,000 rpm
Solenoid pre-engaged types:	
Closing coil resistance	0.21 to 0.25 ohms
Holding coil resistance	0.9 to 1.1 ohms
Wiper motor	Lucas 14W (two speed)
Armature end float	0.004 to 0.008 inch (0.1 to 0.21 mm)
Light running current: normal speed	1 to 5 amp
high speed	2.0 amp
Light running speed: normal speed	46 to 52 rpm
high speed	60 to 70 rpm

Replacement bulbs

	Watts	Part number
Headlamp	60/45	GLU 101
Sidelamp	6	GLB 989
Front flasher	21	GLB 382
Stop, tail lamp	6/21	GLB 380
Rear flasher	21	GLB 382
Number plate...	5	GLB 501
Interior	6	GLB 254
Panel and warning	2.2	37H 2139
Reverse lamp (when fitted)		BFS 272
Boot lamp (when fitted)		GLB 254
Automatic transmission selector (when fitted)...		88 - 625625

1. General description

The electrical system is of the 12 volt type and the major components comprise a 12 volt battery of which the negative terminal is earthed; a voltage regulator and cut-out; a Lucas dynamo or alternator which is fitted to the front right hand side of the engine and is driven from the pulley on the front of the crankshaft; and a starter motor which is mounted on the rear right hand side of the engine.

The battery supplies a steady amount of current for the ignition, lighting and other electrical circuits, and provides a reserve of electricity when the current consumed by the electrical equipment exceeds that being produced by the dynamo or alternator.

The dynamo is of the two brush type and works in conjunction with the voltage regulator and cut-out. It is cooled by a multi-bladed fan mounted behind the dynamo pulley, and blows air through cooling holes in the dynamo end brackets. The output of the dynamo is controlled by the voltage regulator which ensures a high output if the battery is in a low state of charge or the demand from the electrical is high, and a low output if the battery is fully charged and there is little demand from the electrical equipment.

Offered as a factory optional, is an alternator instead of a dynamo.

When fitting electrical accessories to cars with a negative earth system it is important, if they contain silicone diodes or transistors, that they are connected correctly, otherwise serious damage may result to the component concerned. Items such as radios, tape recorders, and electronic tachometers, all be checked for correct polarity.

It is important that the battery positive earth lead is always disconnected if the battery is to be boost charged or if anybody and most mechanical repairs are to be carried out. Serious damage can be caused to the more delicate instruments.

2. Battery - removal and replacement

1   The battery is in a carrier fitted on the right hand wing valance of the engine compartment. It should be removed once every three months for cleaning and testing. Disconnect the positive and then the negative leads from the battery terminals by slackening the clamp retaining nuts and bolts or by unscrewing the retaining screws if terminal caps are fitted instead of clamps.

2   Unscrew the clamp bar retaining nuts and lower the clamp bar to the side of the battery. Carefully lift the battery from its carrier. Hold the battery vertical to ensure that none of the electrolyte is spilled.

3   Replacement is a direct reversal of this procedure. NOTE. Replace the negative lead before the positive lead and smear the terminals with petroleum jelly (vaseline) to prevent corrosion. NEVER use an ordinary grease.

3. Battery - maintenance and inspection

1   Normal weekly battery maintenance consists of checking the electrolyte level of each cell to ensure that the separators are covered by ¼ inch of electrolyte. If the level has fallen, top up the battery using distilled water only. Do not overfill. If the battery is overfilled or any electrolyte spilled, immediately wipe away excess as electrolyte attacks and corrodes any metal it comes into contact with very rapidly.

2   If the battery of a special type, such as the Lucas Pacemaker or 'Auto-fill' type, full instructions as to how these should be checked will be given on the battery.

3   As well as keeping the terminals clean and covered with petroleum jelly, the top of the battery, and especially the top of the cells, should be kept clean and dry. This helps to prevent corrosion and ensures that the battery does not become partially discharged by leakage through dampness and dirt.

4 Once every three months remove the battery and inspect the battery securing nuts, battery clamp plate, tray and battery leads for corrosion (white fluffy deposits on the metal which are brittle to touch). If any corrosion is found, clean off the deposit with ammonia and paint over the clean metal with an anti-rust, anti-acid paint.

5 At the same time inspect the battery case for cracks. If found, clean and plug it with a proprietary compound. If leakage through the crack has been excessive then it will be necessary to refill the appropriate cell with fresh electrolyte as described later. Cracks are frequently caused at the top of the battery case by pouring in distilled water in the middle of winter AFTER instead of BEFORE a run. This gives the water no chance to mix with the electrolyte and so the former freezes and splits the battery case.

6 If the topping up becomes excessive and the case has been inspected for cracks that could cause leakage, but none are found, the battery is being overhcarged and the voltage regulator will have to be checked and reset.

7 With the battery on the bench at the three monthly interval check, measure the specific gravity with a hydrometer to determine the state of charge and condition of the electrolyte. There should be very little variation between the different cells and, if a variation in excess of 0.025 is present, it will be due to either:

a) Loss of electrolyte from the battery at some time caused by spillage or a leak, resulting in a drop in the specific gravity of the electrolyte when the deficiency was replaced with distilled water instead of fresh electrolyte.

b) An internal short circuit caused by buckling of the plates or similar malady pointing to the likelihood of total battery failure in the near future.

8 The specific gravity of the electrolyte for fully charged conditions at the electrolyte temperatures indicated, is listed in Table A. The specific gravity of a fully discharged battery at different temperatures of the electrolyte is given in Table B.

TABLE A

Specific gravity - battery fully charged

1.268 at 100°F or 38°C electrolyte temperature
1.272 at 90°F or 32°C   "   "
1.276 at 80°F or 27°C   "   "
1.280 at 70°F or 21°C   "   "
1.284 at 60°F or 16°C   "   "
1.288 at 50°F or 10°C   "   "
1.292 at 40°F or 4°C   "   "
1.296 at 30°F or -1.5°C "   "

TABLE B

Specific gravity - battery fully discharged

1.098 at 100°F or 38°C electrolyte temperature
1.102 at 90°F or 32°C   "   "
1.106 at 80°F or 27°C   "   "
1.110 at 70°F or 21°C   "   "
1.114 at 60°F or 16°C   "   "
1.118 at 50°F or 10°C   "   "
1.122 at 40°F or 4°C   "   "
1.126 at 30°F or -1.5°C "   "

4. Battery - electrolyte replenishment

1 If the battery is in a fully charged state and one of the cells maintains a specific gravity reading which is 0.025 or lower than the others and a check of each cell has been made with a voltage meter to check for short circuits (a four to seven second test should give a steady reading of between 1.2 and 1.8 volts), then it is likely that electrolyte has been lost from the cell with the low reading at some time.

2 Top up the cell with a solution of 1 part sulphuric acid to

2.5 parts of water. If the cell is already fully topped up draw some electrolyte out of it with a pipette. The total capacity of each cell is approximately 1/3 pint.

3 When mixing the sulphuric acid and water NEVER ADD WATER TO SULPHURIC ACID - always pour the acid slowly onto the water in a glass container. IF WATER IS ADDED TO SULPHURIC ACID IT WILL EXPLODE.

4 Continue to top up the cell with the freshly made electrolyte and then recharge the battery and check the hydrometer readings.

5. Battery - charging

1 It is a good idea to occasionally have the battery fully charged from an external source at a rate of 3.5 to 4 amps, particularly after heavy loading.

2 Continue to charge the battery at this rate until no further rise in specific gravity is noted over a four hour period.

3 Alternatively, a trickle charger, charging at the rate of 1.5 amps can be safely used overnight.

4 Special rapid 'boost' charges which are claimed to restore the power of the battery in 1 to 2 hours are most dangerous unless they are thermostatically controlled as they can cause serious damage to the battery plates through overheating.

5 While charging the battery note that the temperature of the electrolyte should never exceed 100°F.

6. Dynamo - maintenance

1 Routine maintenance consists of checking the tension of the fan belt, and lubricating the dynamo rear bearing once every 6,000 miles, (10,000 Km) or 6 month intervals.

2 To check the fan belt tension see Chapter 2, Section 11.

3 Lubrication of the dynamo consists of inserting three drops of engine oil in the small oil hole in the centre of the commutator end bracket, to lubricate the rear bearing. The front bearing is pre-packed with grease and requires no attention.

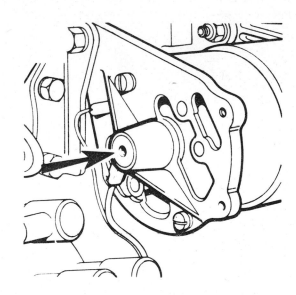

FIG.10.1. DYNAMO REAR BEARING LUBRICATION

7. Dynamo - testing in position

1 If, with the engine running, no charge comes from the dynamo, or the charge is very low, first check that the fan belt is in place and is not slipping. Then check that the leads from the control box to the dynamo are firmly attached and that one has not come loose from its terminal.

2 The lead from the 'D' terminal on the dynamo should be connected to the 'D' terminal of the control box, and similarly the 'F' terminals on both. Check that the leads are correctly fitted.

3 Make sure that none of the electrical equipment such as the lights or radio, is on, and then pull the leads off the dynamo terminals marked 'D' and 'F'. Join the terminals together with a short length of wire.

4 Attach to the centre of this length of wire the negative clip of a 0—20 volts voltmeter and run the other clip to earth on the dynamo body. Start the engine and allow it to idle at approximately 750 rpm. At this speed the dynamo should give a reading of about 15 volts on the voltmeter. There is no point in raising the engine speed above a fast idle as the reading will then be inaccurate.

5 If no reading is recorded then check the brushes and brush connections. If a very low reading of approximately 1 volt is observed then the field winding may be suspect.

6 If a reading of between 4 and 6 volts is recorded it is likely that the armature winding is at fault.

7 With the Lucas C40—1 windowless yoke dynamo, it must be removed and dismantled before the brushes and commutator can be attended to.

8 If the voltmeter shows a good reading, then with the temporary link still in position, connect both leads from the control box 'D' and 'F' on the dynamo ('D' to 'D' and 'F' to 'F'). Release the lead from the 'D' terminal at the control box end and clip one lead from the voltmeter to the end of the cable, and the other lead to a good earth. With the engine running at the same speed as previously, an identical voltage to that recorded at the dynamo should be noted on the voltmeter. If no voltage is recorded there is a break in the wire. If the voltage is the same as recorded at the dynamo then check the 'F' lead in a similar fashion. If both readings are the same as the dynamo then it will be necessary to test the control box

8. Dynamo - removal and replacement

1 Detach the two terminals from the rear of the dynamo.

2 Undo and remove the bolt from the adjustment link.

3 Slacken the two mounting bolts and nuts and push the dynamo towards the engine. Lift the fan belt from the pulley.

4 Remove the mounting nuts and bolts and lift away the dynamo.

5 Replacement is a reversal of the above procedure. Do not finally tighten the retaining bolts and adjustment link bolt until the fan belt has been tensioned correctly.

9. Dynamo - dismantling and inspection

Apart from dynamo brush replacement there is little that can be done to a dynamo by the D.i.Y man. It will certainly be less frustrating and probably cheaper in the end, to take a faulty dynamo to an auto electrician for repair. He has specialist testing and machining equipment. Certain parts may not be readily available for dynamo repair.

However, a description is given of dismantling a dynamo and what to look for.

1 Mount the dynamo in a vice and unscrew and remove the two through bolts from the commutator end bracket (Fig.10.3).

2 Mark the commutator end bracket and the dynamo casing so that the end bracket can be replaced in its original position. Pull the end bracket off the armature shaft. NOTE: Some versions of the dynamo may have a raised pip on the edge of the casing. If so, marking the end bracket and casing is unnecessary. A pip may also be found on the drive end bracket at the opposite end of the casing.

3 Lift the two brush springs and draw the brushes out of the brush holders.

4 Measure the brushes and if worn down to ½ inch or less, unscrew the screws holding the brush leads to the end bracket. Take off the brushes complete with leads.

5 If no locating pip can be found, mark the drive end bracket and the dynamo casing so that the drive end bracket can be replaced in its original position. Then pull the drive end bracket,

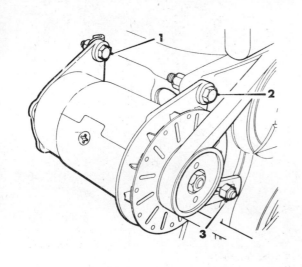
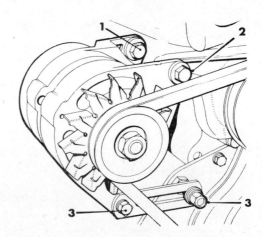

FIG.10.2. DYNAMO (LEFT) AND ALTERNATOR (RIGHT) MOUNTINGS

1 Securing nut and bolt (rear)
2 Securing nut and bolt (front)
3 Adjustment link fixings

complete with armature, out of the casing.

6 Check the condition of the ball bearing in the drive end by firmly holding the bracket and noting if there is visible side movement of the armature shaft in relation to the end bracket. If play is present, the armature assembly must be separated from the end bracket. If the bearing is sound there is no need to carry out the work described next.

7 Hold the armature in one hand (mount if carefully in a vice if preferred) and undo the nut holding the pulley wheel and fan in place. Pull off the pulley wheel, fan and distance piece.

8 Next remove the woodruff key from its slot in the armature shaft, also the bearing locating ring.

9 Place the drive end bracket across the open jaws of a vice with the armature downwards and gently tap the armature shaft from the bearing in the end plate with the aid of a suitable drift.

10 Carefully inspect the armature and check it for open or short circuited windings. An indication of an open circuited armature is shown by burnt commutator segments. If the armature has short circuited, the commutator segments will be very badly burnt, and the overheated armature windings badly discoloured. If open or short circuits are suspected then test by substituting the suspect armature for a new one.

11 Have the resistance of the field coils checked with an ohm meter between the field terminals and the body. The reading should be about 6 ohms. If the ohmmeter reading is infinity this indicates an open circuit in the field winding. If the ohmmeter reading is below 5 ohms this indicates that one of the field coils is faulty and must be replaced.

12 Field coil replacement is involved, as is the previous check, and this should be undertaken by an auto electrician.

13 Next check the condition of the commutator. If it is dirty and blackened, clean it with a petrol dampened rag. If the commutator is in good condition the surface will be smooth and quite free from pits or burnt areas, and the insulated segments clearly defined.

14 If after the commutator has been cleaned, pits and burnt spots are still present, wrap a strip of glass paper round the commutator taking great care to move the commutator a quarter of a turn every ten rubs until it is thoroughly clean.

15 In extreme cases of wear, the commutator should be cleaned and the segments undercut by an auto electrician.

16 Check the brush bearing in the commutator end bracket for wear by noting if the armature spindle rocks when placed in it. If worn it must be renewed. This again is best left to an auto electrician.

10. Dynamo - repair and reassembly

As has already been stated apart from brush replacement any repair work is best undertaken by an auto electrician.

Any disassembly undertaken at home is easily reassembled as an exact reverse sequence. It is essential to have all parts spotlessly clean.

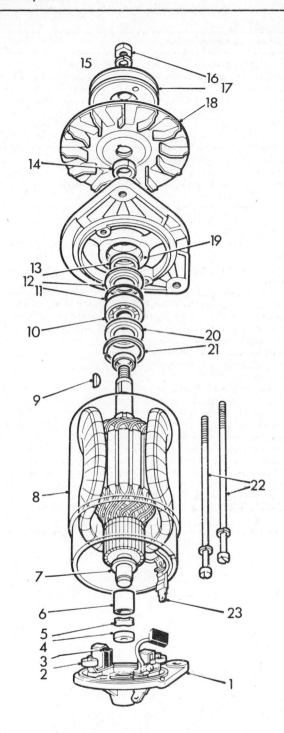

FIG.10.3. COMPONENT PARTS OF THE DYNAMO

1 Commutator end bracket	6 Porous bronze bush	12 Plate	18 Fan
2 Brush spring	7 Fibre thrust washer	13 Felt ring	19 Drive end bracket
3 Brush	8 Body	14 Pulley spacer	20 Plate
4 Felt ring	9 Key	15 Spring washer	21 Circlip
5 Felt ring retainer	10 Ball race	16 Pulley securing nut	22 Through bolts
	11 'O' ring	17 Pulley	23 Output terminal 'D'

11. Control box - general description

The control box comprises the voltage regulator and the cut-out. The voltage regulator controls the output from the dynamo depending on the state of the battery and the demands of the electrical equipment and ensures that the battery is not over-charged. The cut-out is really an automatic switch and connects the dynamo to the battery when the dynamo is turning fast enough to produce a charge. Similarly it disconnects the battery from the dynamo when the engine is idling or stationary so that the battery does not discharge through the dynamo.

12. Cut-out and regulator contacts - maintenance

1 Every 12,000 miles (20,000 km) check the cut-out and regulator contacts. If they are dirty, rough or burnt place a piece of fine glass paper (DO NOT USE EMERY PAPER OR CAR-BORUNDUM PAPER) between the cut-out contacts, close them manually and draw the glass paper through several times. Always disconnect the battery.
2 Clean the regulator contacts in exactly the same way, but use emery or carborundum paper and not glass paper. Carefully clean both sets of contacts from all traces of dust with a rag moistened in methylated spirits.

13. Voltage regulator - adjustment

1 If the battery is in sound condition, but is not holding its charge, or is being continually overcharged as indicated by the need to top up the electrolyte more than usual, and the dynamo is in good order, then the voltage regulator in the control box must be adjusted.
2 Check the regulator setting by removing and joining together the two cables from the control box terminals 'A' and 'A1'. Then connect the negative lead of a 20 volt voltmeter to the 'D' terminal on the dynamo and the positive lead to the 'E' terminal on the control box. Start the engine and increase its speed until the

voltmeter needle flicks and then steadies. This should occur at about 2000 rpm. If the voltage at which the needle steadies out-side the limits given in the specifications then remove the control box cover and turn the adjusting screw clockwise a quarter of a turn at a time to raise the setting and a similar amount, anticlockwise, to lower it.
3 It is vital that the adjustments be completed within 30 seconds of starting the engine as otherwise the heat from the shunt coil will affect the readings.

14. Cut-out - adjustment

1 Check the voltage required to operate the cut-out by connecting a voltmeter between the control box terminals 'D' and 'E'.
2 Remove the control box cover, start the engine and gradually increases its speed until the cut-out points close. This should occur when the reading is between 12.7 to 13.3 volts.
3 If the reading is outside these limits turn the cut-out adjust-ment screw a fraction at a time clockwise to raise the voltage, and anticlockwise to lower it. To adjust the drop off voltage bend the fixed contact blade carefully. The adjustment to the cut-out should be completed within 30 seconds of starting the engine as otherwise heat build up from the shunt coil will affect the readings.
4 If the cut-out fails to work, clean the contacts, and, if there is still no response, renew the cut-out and regulator unit.

15. Alternator - general description

The Lucas 16 ACR series alternator is offered as a factory fitted option.   The main advantage of the alternator lies in its ability to provide a high charge at slow revolutions. Driving slowly in heavy traffic with a dynamo invariably means no charge is reaching the battery. In similar conditions even with the wipers, heater, lights and perhaps radio switched on, an alternator will ensure a charge reaches the battery.
An important feature of the alternator is a built in output

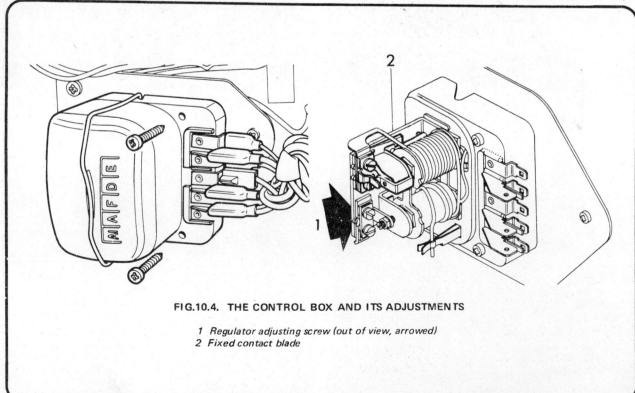

FIG.10.4. THE CONTROL BOX AND ITS ADJUSTMENTS

1 Regulator adjusting screw (out of view, arrowed)
2 Fixed contact blade

control regulator, based on 'thick film' hybrid integrated micro-circuit technique, which results in this alternator being a self contained generating and control unit.

The system provides for direct connection of a charge light, and eliminates the need for a field switching relay and warning light control unit, necessary with former systems.

The alternator is of the rotating field ventilated design and comprises principally, a laminated stator on which is wound a start connected 3 - phase output winding; a twelve pole rotor carrying the field windings - each end of the rotor shaft runs in ball race bearings which are lubricated for life; natural finish aluminium die cast end brackets, incorporating the mounting lugs; a rectifier pack for converting the AC output of the machine to DC for battery charging; and an output control regulator.

The rotor is belt driven from the engine through a pulley keyed to the rotor shaft. A pressed steel fan adjacent to the pulley draw scooling air through the machine. This fan forms an integral part of the alternator specification. It has been designed to provide adequate air flow with a minimum of noise, and to withstand the high stresses associated with maximum speed. Rotation is clockwise viewed on the drive end. Maximum continuous rotor speed is 12,500 rpm.

Rectification of alternator output is achieved by six silicone diodes housed in a rectifier pack and connected as a 3-phase full-wave budge. The rectifier pack is attached to the outer face of the slip ring end bracket and contains also three 'field' diodes, at normal operating speeds, rectified current from the stator output windings flows through these diodes to provide self-excitation of the rotor field, via brushes bearing on face type slip rings.

The slip rings are carried on a small diameter moulded drum attached to the rotor shaft outboard of the rotor shaft axle, while the outer ring has a mean diameter of ¾ inch. By keeping the mean diameter of the slip rings to a minimum, relative speeds between brushes and rings, and hence wear, are also minimal. The slip rings are connected to the rotor field winding by wires carried in grooves in the rotor shaft.

The brush gear is housed in a moulding screwed to the outside of the slip ring end bracket. This moulding thus encloses the slip ring and brush gear assembly, and, together with the shielded bearing, protects the assembly against the entry of dust and moisture.

The regulator is set during manufacture and requires no further attention. Briefly the 'thick film' regulator comprises resistors and conductors screen printed onto a 1 inch square alumina substrate. Mounted on the substrate are Lucas semi-conductors consisting of three transistors, a voltage reference diode and a field recirculation diode, and also two capacitors. The internal connections between these components and the substrate are made by Lucas patented connectors. The whole assembly is 1/16 inch thick, and is housed in a recess in an aluminium heat sink, which is attached to the slip ring end bracket. Complete hermetic sealing is achieved by a silicone rubber encapsulant to provide environmental protection.

Electrical connections to external circuits are brought out to Lucar connector blades, these being grouped to accept a moulded connector socket which ensures correct connections.

16. Alternator - routine maintenance

1   The equipment has been designed for the minimum amount of maintenance in service, the only items subject to wear being the brushes and bearings.
2   Brushes should be examined after 60,000 miles (100,000 km) and renewed if necessary. This is a job best left to an auto electrician.
3   The bearings are pre-packed with grease for life, and should not require any further attention.

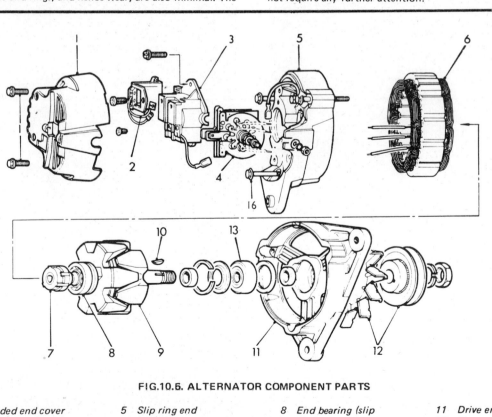

FIG.10.6. ALTERNATOR COMPONENT PARTS

1 Moulded end cover	5 Slip ring end bracket	8 End bearing (slip ring)	11 Drive end bracket
2 Connector	6 Stator windings	9 Pressure ring	12 Fan and pulley
3 Brushbox assembly	7 Slip ring moulding	10 Key	13 End bearing (drive end)
4 Rectifier pack			

17. Starter motor - general description

One of two types of starter motor have been fitted to the 1.3 Marina models, an inertia or pre-engaged type. The relay for the inertia starter motor is mounted next to the ignition coil whereas the pre-engaged type has the solenoid switch on the top of the motor.

The principle of operation of the inertia type starter motor is as follows: When the ignition switch is turned, current flows from the battery to the starter motor solenoid switch which causes it to become energized. Its internal plunger moves inwards and closes an internal switch so allowing full starting current to flow from the battery to the starter motor. This creates a powerful magnetic field to be induced into the field coils which causes the armature to rotate.

Mounted on helical splines is the drive pinion which, because of the sudden rotation of the armature, is thrown forwards along the armature shaft and so into engagement with the flywheel ring gear. The engine crankshaft will then be rotated until the engine starts to operate on its own and, at this point, the drive pinion is thrown out of mesh with the flywheel ring gear.

The pre-engaged starter motor operates by a slightly different method but still using end face commutator brushes instead of brushes located on the side of the commutator.

The method of engagement on the pre-engaged starter differs considerably in that the drive pinion is brought into mesh with the starter ring gear before the main starter current is applied.

When the ignition is switched on, current flows from the battery to the solenoid which is mounted on the top of the starter motor body. The plunger in the solenoid moves inwards so causing a centrally pivoted lever to move in such a manner that the forked end pushes the drive pinion into mesh with the starter ring gear. When the solenoid plunger reaches the end of its travel, it closes an internal contact and full starting current flows to the starter field coils. The armature is then able to rotate the crankshaft so starting the engine.

A special one way clutch is fitted to the starter drive pinion so that when the engine just fires and starts to operate on its own, it does not drive the starter motor.

18. Starter motor (M35J) - testing on engine

1 If the starter motor fails to operate, then check the condition of the battery by turning on the headlamps. If they glow brightly for several seconds and then gradually dim, the battery is in an uncharged condition.

2 If the headlamps glow brightly and it is obvious that the battery is in good condition then check the tightness of the battery wiring connections (and in particular the earth lead from the battery terminal to its connection on the body frame). Check the tightness of the connections at the relay switch and at the starter motor. Check the wiring with a voltmeter for breaks or shorts due to failure of insulation.

3 If the wiring is in order then check that the starter motor switch is operating. To do this, press the rubber covered button in the centre of the relay switch located next to the ignition coil. If it is working the starter motor will be heard to 'click' as it tries to rotate. Alternatively check it with a voltmeter.

4 If the battery is fully charged, the wiring in order, and the switch working but the starter motor fails to operate then it will have to be removed from the car for examination. Before this is done, however, ensure that the starter pinion has not jammed in mesh with the flywheel, check by turning the square end of the armature shaft with a spanner. This will free the pinion if it is stuck in engagement with the flywheel teeth.

19. Starter motor (M35J) - removal and replacement

1 Disconnect the positive and then the negative terminals from the battery. Also disconnect the starter motor cable from the terminal on the starter motor end cover (Fig.10.6).

2 Undo and remove the bolt and spring washer and the nut and spring washer that secure the starter motor to the engine back plate.

3 Lift the starter motor away by manipulating the drive gear out from the ring gear area and then from the engine compartment.

4 Refitting is the reverse sequence to removal. Make sure that the starter motor cable, when secured in position by its terminal retaining nut, does not touch any part of the body or power unit which could damage the insulation.

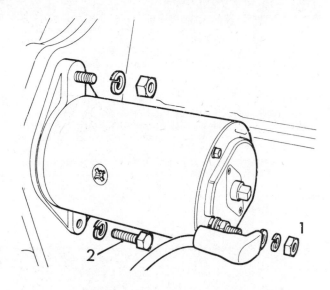

FIG.10.6. STARTER MOTOR REMOVAL

1 *Cable terminal securing nut, spring and plain washer*

2 *Securing bolt and spring washer*

20. Starter motor (M35J) - dismantling and reassembly

Such is the reliability of starter motors generally and the difficulty in undertaking an effective repair without special equipment any dismantling and overhaul work is best left to an auto electrician. However, the drive gear can be dismantled from this type of starter motor easily if this, solely, is at fault. An exploded component illustration, Fig.10.7. is given to show just how a starter motor would dismantle.

1 To dismantle the starter motor drive, first use a press or large valve spring compressor to push the retainer clear of the circlip which can then be removed. Lift away the retainer and main spring.

2 Slide off the remaining parts with a rotary action of the armature shaft.

3 It is most important that the drive gear is completely free from oil, grease and dirt. With the drive gear removed, clean all parts thoroughly in paraffin. Under no circumstances oil the drive components. Lubrication of the drive components could easily cause the pinion to stick.

4 Reassembly of the starter motor drive is the reverse sequence to dismantling. Use a press or the large valve spring compressor to compress the spring and retainer sufficiently to allow a new circlip to be fitted to its groove on the shaft.

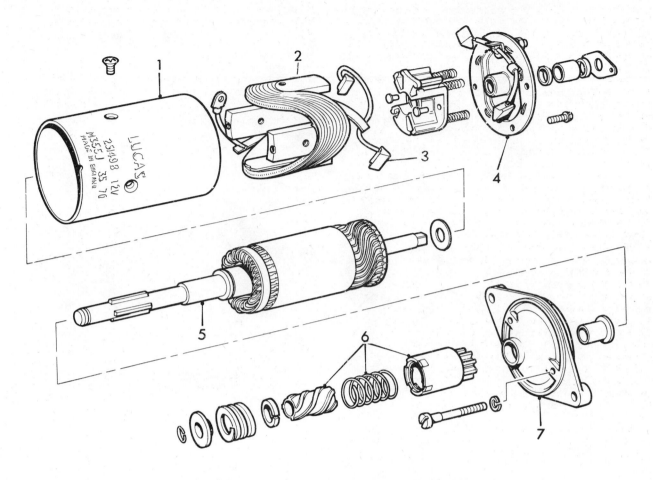

FIG.10.7. M35J INERTIA STARTER MOTOR COMPONENTS

| 1 Body | 3 Brushes | bracket | 6 Drive |
| 2 Field coils | 4 Commutator end | 5 Commutator | 7 Drive end bracket |

21. Starter motor (M35J pre-engaged) - testing on engine

The testing procedure is basically similar to the inertia engagement type as described in Section 18. However, note the following instructions before finally deciding to remove the starter motor.

Ensure that the pinion gear has not jammed in mesh with the flywheels due either to a broken solenoid spring or dirty pinion gear splines. To release the pinion, engage a low gear and, with the ignition switched off, rock the car backwards and forwards which should release the pinion from mesh with the ring gear. If the pinion still remains jammed the starter motor must be removed for further examination.

22. Starter motor (M35J pre-engaged) - removal and replacement

1 Disconnect the positive and then the negative terminals from the battery.
2 Make a note of the electrical connections at the rear of the solenoid and disconnect the top heavy duty cable. Also release the two Lucar terminals from the rear of the solenoid. There is no need to undo the lower heavy duty cable at the rear of the solenoid.
3 Undo and remove the bolt and spring washer, and nut and spring washer which hold the starter motor in place and lift away upwards.
4 Replacement is a straightforward reversal of the removal sequence. Check that the electrical cable connections are clean and firmly attached to their respective terminals.

23. Starter motor (M35J pre-engaged) - dismantling and re-assembly

See Section 20 concerning the difficulty in effective repairs on the inertia starter motor. The pre-engaged is of similar complexity and should be left totally in the hands of an auto electrician.

Again an exploded component illustration is given, Fig.10.8 to show how this type of starter motor would dismantle.

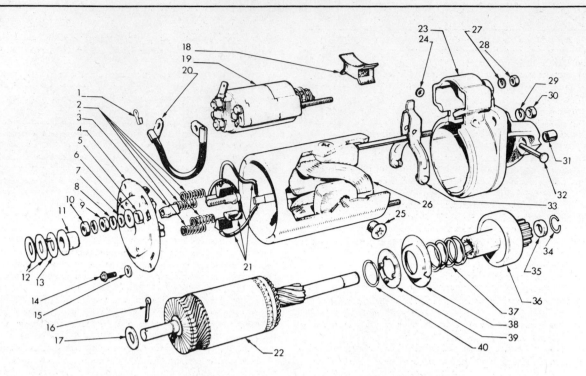

FIG.10.8. M35J (PRE-ENGAGED) STARTER MOTOR COMPONENTS

1	Hook	11	Bush	22	Armature	30	Nut
2	Brush springs	12	Washer	23	Starter drive cover and	31	Bush
3	Insulator	13	Tabbed washer		starter motor end	32	Lever swivel pin
4	End plate and brush	14	Bolt		plate	33	Actuating lever
	holder	15	Washer	24	Pin retaining ring	34	Circlip
5	Spacer	16	Split pin	25	Field coil retaining	35	Spacer
6	Washer	17	Washer		screw	36	Pinion
7	Washer	18	Grommet	26	Field coils	37	Spring
8	Lockwasher	19	Solenoid assembly	27	Washer	38	Clutch
9	Nut	20	Cable assembly	28	Nut	39	Clutch
10	Nut	21	Brush assembly	29	Lockwasher	40	Retaining ring

---

24. Starter motor solenoid (M35J) - removal and replacement

---

1   Disconnect the battery.

2   Carefully ease back the rubber covers to gain access to the terminals (Fig.10.9).

3   Make a note of the Lucas terminal connections and detach these connections.

4   Undo and remove the heavy duty cable terminal connection nuts and spring washers. Detach the two terminal connectors.

5   Undo and remove the two retaining screws and lift away the solenoid.

6   Refitting is the reverse sequence to removal.

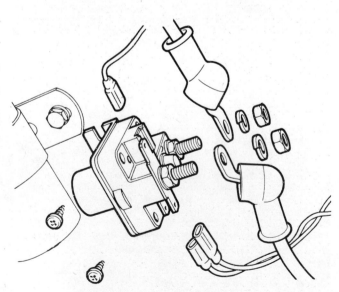

FIG.10.9. INERTIA STARTER MOTOR SOLENOID AND CONNECTIONS

25. Flasher unit and circuit - fault tracing and rectification

The flasher unit located as shown in Fig.10.10 is enclosed in a small metal container and is operated only when the ignition is on by the composite switch mounted on the right hand side of the steering column.

If the flasher unit fails to operate, or works either very slowly or rapidly, check out the flasher indicator circuit as described next, before assuming there is a fault in the unit itself.

1   Examine the direction indicator bulbs front and rear for broken filaments.

2   If the external flashers are working but the internal flasher warning lights on one or both sides have ceased to function, check the filaments and replace as necessary.

3   With the aid of the wiring diagram check all the flasher circuit connections if a flasher bulb is sound but does not work.

4   In the event of total indicator failure check fuse A3—A4.

5   With the ignition switched on, check that current is reaching the flasher unit by connecting a voltmeter between the 'plus' or 'B' terminal and earth. If this test is positive, connect the 'plus' of 'B' terminal and the 'L' terminal and operate the flasher switch. If the flasher bulb lights up the flasher unit itself is defective and must be replaced as it is not possible to dismantle and repair it.

6   To remove the flasher unit first disconnect the battery. Make a note of the electrical cable terminal positions and detach the two terminal connectors. The unit may now be pulled out from its holder.

7   Refitting the flasher unit is the reverse sequence to removal.

26. Windscreen wiper arms - removal and replacement

1   Before removing a wiper arm, turn the windscreen wiper switch on and off to ensure the arms are in their normal parked position with the blades parallel with the bottom of the windscreen.

2   To remove the arm, pivot the arm back and pull the wiper arm head off the splined drive, at the same time easing back the clip with a screwdriver.

3   When replacing an arm, place it so it is in the correct relative parked position and then press the arm head onto the splined drive until the retaining clip clicks into place.

27. Windscreen wiper mechanism - fault diagnosis and rectification

Should the windscreen wipers fail, or work very slowly then check the terminals for loose connections, and make sure the insulation of the external wiring is not broken or cracked. If this is in order, then check the current the motor is taking by connecting up an ammeter in the circuit and turning on the wiper switch. Consumption should be between 1 to 5 amps for normal speed or 2 amps for high speed.

If no current is passing, check the A3 - A4 fuse. If the fuse has blown, replace if after having checked the wiring to the motor and other electrical circuits serviced by this fuse for short circuits. Further information will be found in Section 48. If the fuse is in good condition, check the wiper switch.

Should the wiper take a very high current, check the wiper blades for freedom of movement. If this is satisfactory check the wiper motor and drive cable for signs of damage. Measure the end float which should be between 0.002 and 0.008 inch (0.051 to 0.203 mm). The end float is set by the thrust screw. Check that excessive friction in the cable connecting tubes, caused by too small a curvature, is not the cause of the high consumption.

If the motor takes a very low current, ensure that the battery is fully charged. Check the brush gear after removing the commutator yoke assembly, and ensure that the brushes are free to move. If necessary, renew the tension springs. If the brushes are very worn they should be replaced with new ones. The armature may be checked by substitution

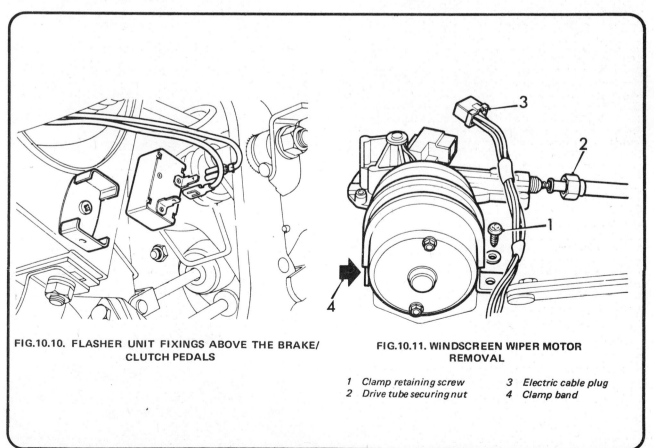

FIG.10.10. FLASHER UNIT FIXINGS ABOVE THE BRAKE/ CLUTCH PEDALS

FIG.10.11. WINDSCREEN WIPER MOTOR REMOVAL

1   Clamp retaining screw   3   Electric cable plug
2   Drive tube securing nut   4   Clamp band

28. Windscreen wiper motor - removal and replacement

1 Refer to Section 26 and remove the wiper arms and blades.
2 Undo and remove the screw and plain washer that secures the wiper motor clamp to the body valance. Release the clamp and rubber moulding by pressing the clamp band into the release slot.
3 Undo the wiper drive tube securing nut and slide the nut down the tube.
4 Next disconnect the electrical cable plug from the motor socket.
5 Lift the motor clear of the body valance whilst at the same time pulling the inner drive cable from the tube.
6 Refitting the wiper motor and inner cable is the reverse sequence to removal. Take care in feeding the inner cable through the outer tube and engaging the inner cable with each wiper wheelbox spindle. Lubricate the inner cable with Castrol LM Grease.

29. Windscreen wiper motor - dismantling, inspection and re-assembly

The only repair which can be effectively undertaken by the D.I.Y mechanic to a wiper motor is brush replacement. Anything more serious than this will mean either exchanging the complete motor or having a repair done by an auto electrician. Spare part availability is really the problem. Brush replacement is described here.
1 Refer to Fig.10.12. and remove the four gearbox cover retaining screws (2) and lift away the cover (1). Release the circlip (4) and flat washer (5) securing the connecting rod (3) to the crankpin on the shaft and gear (7). Lift away the connecting rod (3) followed by the second flat washer (5).
2 Release the circlip (4) and flat washer (5) securing the shaft and gear (6) to the gearbox body (9).
3 De-burr the gear shaft and lift away the gear (7) making a careful note of the location of the dished washer (8).
4 Scribe a mark on the yoke assembly (15) and gearbox (9) to ensure correct reassembly and unscrew the two yoke bolts (14) from the motor yoke assembly. Part the yoke assembly including armature from the gearbox body. As the yoke assembly has residual magentism ensure that the yoke is kept well away from metallic dust.
5 Unscrew the two screws securing the brush gear and the terminal and switch assembly and remove both the assemblies.
6 Inspect the brushes for excessive wear. If the main brushes are worn to a limit of 3/16 inch (4.763 mm) or the narrow section of the third brush is worn to the full width of the brush fit a new brush gear assembly. Ensure that the three brushes move freely in their boxes.
7 Reassembly at this stage is a straight reversal of the disassembly.

30. Wheelboxes and drive cable tubes - removal and replacement

1 Refer to Section 28 and remove the windscreen wiper motor.
2 Refer to Chapter 12, Section 32 and remove the instrument panel.
3 Refer to Chapter 12, Section 25 and remove the glovebox.
4 Refer to Section 26 and remove the windscreen wiper arms.
5 Undo and remove the nuts that secure the wheelboxes to the body. Lift away the shaped spacer from each wheelbox.
6 Slacken the two nuts that calmp the two wheelbox plates on the glovebox side. Carefully pull out the drive tube from the wheelbox.
7 Carefully remove the free drive tube and its grommet through the glovebox opening.
8 Lift away the two wheelbox units through the instrument panel opening.
9 Recover the spacer and washer from each wheelbox unit.
10 Refitting the wheelboxes and drive cable tubes is the reverse sequence to removal.

31. Horns - fault tracing and rectification

1 If a horn works badly or fails completely, first check that the wiring leading to it for short circuits and loose connections. Also check that the horn is firmly secured and that there is nothing lying on the horn body.
2 The horn is protected by the A1 - A2 fuse and if this has blown the circuit should be checked for short circuits. Further information will be found in Section 48.
3 The horn should never be dismantled, but it is possible to adjust it. This adjustment is to compensate for wear of the moving parts only and will not affect the tone. To adjust the horn proceed as follows:
a) There is a small adjustment screw on the broad rim of the horn nearly opposite the two terminals (see Fig.10.14). Do not confuse this with the large screw in the centre.
b) Turn the adjustment screw anticlockwise until the horn just fails to sound. Then turn the screw a quarter of a turn clockwise which is the optimum setting.
c) It is recommended that if the horn has to be reset in the car, the A1 - A2 fuse should be removed and replaced with a piece of wire, otherwise the fuse will continually blow due to the high current required for the horn in continual operation.
d) Should twin horns be fitted, the horn which is not being adjusted be disconnected while adjustment of the other takes place.

32. Headlight units - removal and replacement

1 Sealed beam or renewable bulb light units are fitted.
2 The method of gaining access to the light unit for replacement is identical for all types of light units and bulbs.
3 Undo and remove the four screws that secure the top of the front grille to the body panel.
4 Carefully lift the grille outwards and upwards so releasing it from its locating holes in the body.
5 Undo and remove the three securing screws and lift away the headlamp rim.
6 Sealed beam unit. Disconnect the plug from the rear of the light unit and lift away the light unit.
Spring clip bulb holder. Disconnect the plug from the bulb holder and release the spring clip from the reflector. Lift away the bulb.
Cap type bulb holder. Push and turn the cap anticlockwise. Lift off the cap and withdraw the bulb.
7 Refitting in all cases is the reverse sequence to removal. Where a bulb is fitted make sure that the locating clip or slot in the bulb correctly registers in the reflector.

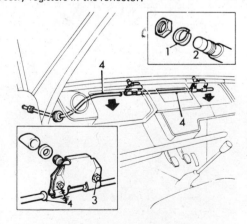

FIG.10.13. WINDSCREEN WIPER RACK AND WHEELBOX ASSEMBLY

1 Wheelbox securing nut   3 Wheelbox plates securing nut
2 Shaped spacer   4 Drive tube

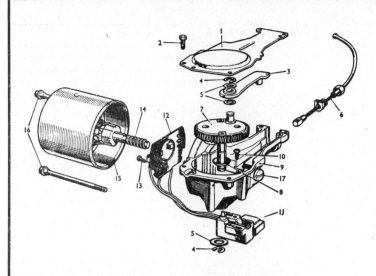

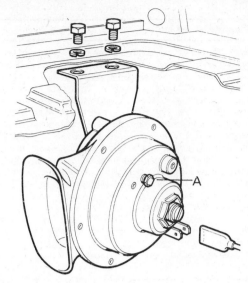

FIG.10.12. WINDSCREEN WIPER MOTOR COMPONENT PARTS

1	Gearbox cover	10	Screw for limit switch
2	Screw for cover	11	Limit switch assembly
3	Connecting rod	12	Brush gear
4	Circlip	13	Screw for brush gear
5	Plain washers	14	Armature
6	Cross-head	15	Yoke assembly
7	Shaft and gear	16	Yoke bolts
8	Dished washer	17	Armature thrust screw
9	Gearbox		

FIG.10.14. THE HORN

A Adjustment screw

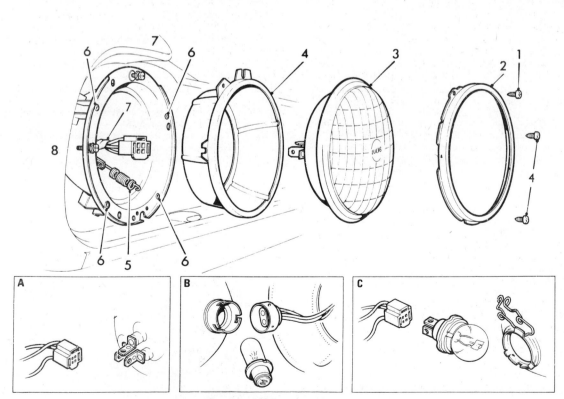

FIG.10.15. HEADLIGHT UNIT COMPONENT PARTS

1	Rim securing screws	4	Inner shell	7	Vertical adjustment screw
2	Rim	5	Inner shell tensioning spring	8	Horizontal adjustment screw
3	Light unit	6	Snap rivets	A	Sealed beam light unit connection
				B	Cap type bulb holder
				C	Spring clip bulb holder

33. Headlight beam - adjustment

The headlights may be adjusted for both vertical and horizontal beam positions by the two screws, these being shown in Fig.10.5. For vertical movement screw (7) should be used and horizontal movement screw (8).

They should be set so that on full or high beam, the beams are set slightly below parallel with a level road surface. Do not forget that the beam position is affected by how the car is normally loaded for night driving, and set the beams with the car loaded to this position.

Although this adjustment can be approximately set at home, it is recommended that this be left to a local garage who will have the necessary equipment to do the job more accurately.

34. Side and front flasher bulbs - removal and replacement

1 Undo and remove the two screws securing the lamp lens to the lamp body and lift away the lenses.
2 Either bulb is retained by a bayonet fixing, so to remove a bulb push in slightly and rotate in an anticlockwise direction.
3 Refitting is the reverse sequence to removal. Take care not to tighten the two lens retaining screw as the lenses can be easily cracked.

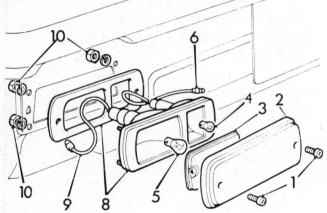

FIG.10.16. SIDE AND FRONT FLASHER ASSEMBLY

1 Lens securing screws	6 Sidelamp connection
2 Lens - plain	7 Light assembly body
3 Lens - coloured	8 Rubber seal
4 Sidelamp bulb	9 Flasher connection
5 Flasher bulb	10 Light assembly retaining nuts

35. Stop, tail and rear flasher bulbs - removal and replacement

1 Open the boot lid.
2 The bulb holders may now be drawn downwards and rearwards into the luggage compartment.
3 Two bulbs are used, the inner one being of the double filament type and are retained in position by a bayonet fixing. To remove a bulb, push in slightly and rotate in an anticlockwise direction.
4 The double filament bulb has offset pins on the bayonet fixing so it is not possible to fit it the wrong way round.
5 Refitting is the reverse sequence to removal.

36. Number plate light bulb - removal and replacement

1 The lenses may be removed by depressing and turning through 90°. Lift away the lenses.
2 Carefully pull on the bulb and it will be released from its holder. It will be noticed that capless bulbs are used.
3 Refitting is the reverse sequence to removal.

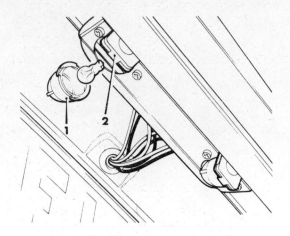

FIG.10.18. REAR NUMBER PLATE LIGHTS

1 Lens
2 Lens fixing clip

37. Panel illumination lamp bulb - removal and replacement

1 Disconnect the battery.
2 Refer to Chapter 12, and remove the instrument panel.
3 Pull out the bulb holder from the rear of the panel giving access to the bulb (Fig.10.19).
4 Carefully pull on the bulb and it will be released from its holder. It will be noticed that capless bulbs are used.
5 Refitting is the reverse sequence to removal.

38. Ignition, starter, steering lock switch - removal and replacement

1 Disconnect the battery.
2 Undo and remove the four screws that secure the switch cowls. Lift the cowls from over the switch stalks.
3 Detach the multi-pin plug for the electrical leads to the switch assembly at the harness socket (Fig.10.20).
4 Undo and remove the one screw that retains the switch assembly in the lock housing.
5 Slide the switch assembly from the lock housing.
6 Refitting is the reverse sequence to removal. Make sure that the locating peg on the switch correctly registers in the groove in the lock housing.

39. Headlamp dip/flasher, horn, direction indicator switch - removal and replacement

1 Disconnect the battery.
2 Refer to Chapter 11, Section 17 and remove the steering wheel.
3 Detach the multi pin plug for the electrical leads to the switch assembly at the harness socket located under the facia.
4 Slacken the switch clamp tightening screw located on the underside of the switch and ease the switch assembly from the steering column.
5 Refitting the switch assembly is the reverse sequence to removal. Make sure that the lug on the inner diameter of the switch locates in the slot in the outer steering column as shown in 'B', Fig.10.22 and also that the striker dog on the nylon switch centre is in line with and towards the switch stalk 'A'.

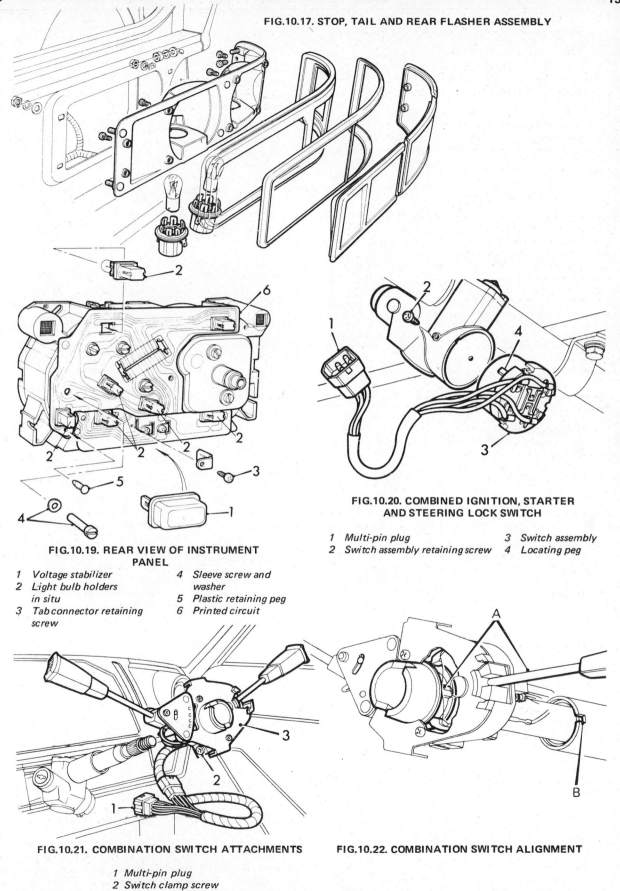

FIG.10.17. STOP, TAIL AND REAR FLASHER ASSEMBLY

FIG.10.19. REAR VIEW OF INSTRUMENT PANEL

1 Voltage stabilizer
2 Light bulb holders in situ
3 Tab connector retaining screw
4 Sleeve screw and washer
5 Plastic retaining peg
6 Printed circuit

FIG.10.20. COMBINED IGNITION, STARTER AND STEERING LOCK SWITCH

1 Multi-pin plug
2 Switch assembly retaining screw
3 Switch assembly
4 Locating peg

FIG.10.21. COMBINATION SWITCH ATTACHMENTS

1 Multi-pin plug
2 Switch clamp screw
3 Switch assembly

FIG.10.22. COMBINATION SWITCH ALIGNMENT

40. Lighting switch - removal and replacement

1   Disconnect the battery.
2   Withdraw the choke control as far as possible.
3   Undo and remove the two crosshead screws retaining the finisher and move the finisher up the choke control knob as far as possible.
4   Make a note of the two cable connections at the rear of the switch and detach the two terminals.
5   To remove the switch it is necessary to compress four little clips, two each side of the switch body and then draw the switch forwards from the panel. Although a 'V' shaped tool is desirable to do this it is possible for one person to compress the clips whilst a second person pulls the switch forwards.
6   Refitting the lighting switch is the reverse sequence to removal.

41. Heater fan switch - removal and replacement

1   Disconnect the battery.
2   Carefully pull off the two heater control knobs.
3   Undo and remove the three crosshead screws securing the finisher. Lift away the finisher.
4   Make a note of the two cable connections at the rear of the switch and detach the two terminals.
5   To remove the switch it is necessary to compress four little clips, two each side of the switch body and then draw the switch forwards from the panel. Although a 'U' shaped tool is desirable to do this it is possible for one person to compress the clips whilst a second person pulls the switch forwards.
6   Refitting this switch is the reverse sequence to removal.

42. Stop light switch - removal and replacement

1   Make a note of the two cable connections at the rear of the switch located on the top of the brake pedal mounting bracket. Detach the two terminals (Fig.10.24).
2   Undo and remove the two bolts and spring washers securing the switch mounting bracket to the brake pedal mounting bracket. Lift away the switch and bracket.
3   Straighten the ears of the switch locking split pin and withdraw the split pin.
4   The switch may now be unscrewed from its mounting bracket.
5   Refitting the stop light switch is the reverse sequence to removal. It is however, necessary to adjust the position of the switch when refitting to its mounting bracket.
6   Screw the switch into its mounting bracket until one complete thread of the switch housing is visible on the pedal side of the bracket. Lock with a new split pin.

43. Instrument panel printed circuit - removal and replacement

1   Refer to Chapter 12, Section 32 and remove the instrument panel.
2   Withdraw the voltage stabilizer from the rear of the instrument panel printed circuit (Fig.10.19).
3   Withdraw the warning light and panel light bulb holders from the speedometer and gauges.
4   Undo and remove the three screws securing the voltage stabilizer tag connectors to the rear of the instrument panel printed circuit. Lift away the tag connectors.
5   Undo and remove the four long sleeve screws and shaped washers that secure the gauge units to the rear of the instrument panel.
6   Very carefully ease out the five plastic pegs securing the printed circuit to the rear of the instrument panel. Lift away the printed circuit.
7   Refitting the printed circuit is the reverse sequence to removal.

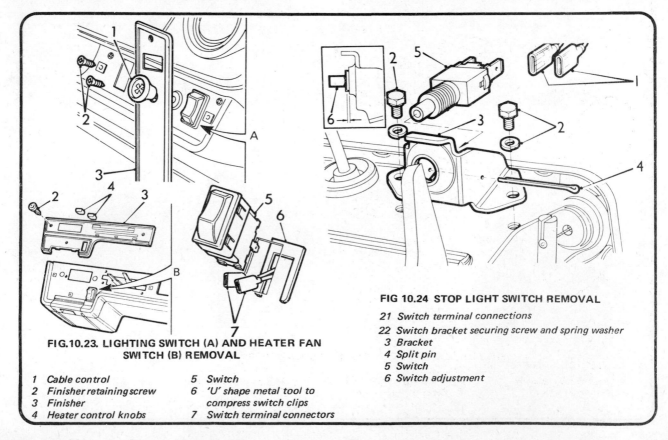

FIG.10.23. LIGHTING SWITCH (A) AND HEATER FAN SWITCH (B) REMOVAL

1   Cable control
2   Finisher retaining screw
3   Finisher
4   Heater control knobs
5   Switch
6   'U' shape metal tool to compress switch clips
7   Switch terminal connectors

FIG 10.24 STOP LIGHT SWITCH REMOVAL

21   Switch terminal connections
22   Switch bracket securing screw and spring washer
3   Bracket
4   Split pin
5   Switch
6   Switch adjustment

44. Gauge units - removal and replacement

1   This section is applicable for the removal of either the fuel gauge or temperature gauge.

2   Refer to Chapter 12, Section 32 and remove the instrument panel.

3   Undo and remove the four screws and washers that secure the instrument pack to the instrument panel.

4   Undo and remove the four long sleeve screws and shaped washers that secure the gauge units to the rear of the instrument panel.

5   Spring back the three clips that retain the instrument glass and panel.

6   Undo and remove the three screws that secure the instruments face plate.

7   Lift away the fuel gauge and/or temperature gauge.

8   Refitting the gauge units is the reverse sequence to removal.

45. Speedometer - removal and replacement

1   Refer to Chapter 12, Section 32 and remove the instrument panel.

2   Undo and remove the four screws and washers that secure the instrument pack to the instrument panel. Lift away the instrument pack.

3   Undo and remove the two screws that secure the speedometer in position.

4   Spring back the three clips that retain the instrument glass and bezel. Lift away the speedometer head.

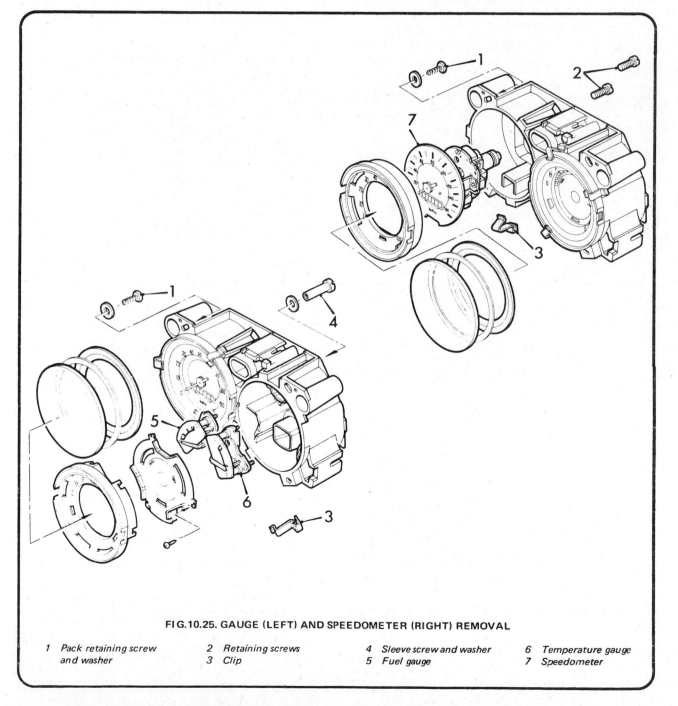

FIG.10.25. GAUGE (LEFT) AND SPEEDOMETER (RIGHT) REMOVAL

1	Pack retaining screw and washer	2	Retaining screws	4	Sleeve screw and washer	6	Temperature gauge
		3	Clip	5	Fuel gauge	7	Speedometer

46. Voltage stabilizer - removal and replacement

1   The voltage stabilizer is a push fit into the rear of the instrument panel printed circuit board (Fig.10.19).
2   Before removal, as a safety precaution disconnect the battery.
3   Carefully pull the voltage stabilizer from the rear of the printed circuit.
4   Refitting is the reverse sequence to removal. Note that the terminals of the stabilizer are offset, so it cannot be fitted the wrong way round.

47. Instrument operation - testing

The bi-metal resistance equipment for the fuel and thermal type temperature gauges comprises an indicator head and transmitter with the unit connected to a common voltage stabilizer. This item is fitted because the method of operation of the equipment is voltage sensitive, and a voltage stabilizer is necessary to ensure a constant voltage supply at all times.

Special test equipment is necessary when checking the operation of the stabilizer, but should it be found that both the fuel and temperature gauges are both reading inaccurately, it is worthwhile removing the stabilizer and tapping it firmly onto a hard surface. In many cases this will provide, at the very least, a temporary cure.

The gauges can be checked by applying 8 volts DC directly to their terminals. This can be done in situ by removing the voltage stabilizer, connecting 8 volts (+) to the voltage stabilizer 1 socket on the rear of the printed circuit panel (or to the fuel gauge lead on Van models) and 8 volt (-) to earth. The gauges should give a full scale deflection. If the leads to the thermal transmitter or fuel tank unit are disconnected the gauges should not give any reading when the ignition is switched on. If these leads are then earthed, both gauges should give a full scale deflection.

48. Fuses

The fuse box is located inside the car behind the facia panel just above the parcel shelf and is attached to the inner body panel on the steering wheel side of the car.
Fuse A1 - A2. This has a 35 amp rating and protects the equipment which operates independent of the ignition switch. These include, interior lamp, horn-push, headlamp flasher and luggage compartment lamp (if fitted). When fitting accessories which are required to operate independently of the ignition circuit connect to the terminal marked '2'.
Fuse A3 - A4. This has a 35 amp rating and protects the circuits which operate only when the ignition is switched on. These include, flashing direction indicators, windscreen wiper motor, brake stop warning lamps, reverse lamps (when fitted), and heated backlight (when fitted). When fitting accessories which are required to operate only when the ignition is switched on, connect to the terminal marked '4'.

A line fuse located in a cylindrical fuse holder adjacent to the instrument wiring connector near the fuse box protects the rear and number plate light bulbs.

A second line fuse located adjacent to the heater blower motor switch protects the heater blower motor. This fuse is accessible from behind the centre facia panel.

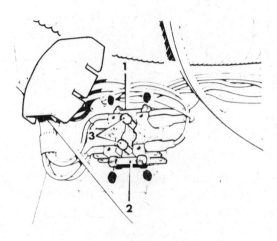

FIG.10.26. FUSE BOX

1   *Fuse A1 (left end) — A2 (right end)*
2   *Fuse A3 (left end) — A4 (right end)*
3   *Spare fuses*

49. Fault diagnosis

Symptoms	Reason/s	Remedy
STARTER MOTOR FAILS TO TURN ENGINE		
No electricity at starter motor	Battery discharged	Charge battery.
	Battery defective internally	Fit new battery.
	Battery terminal leads loose or earth lead not securely attached to body	Check and tighten leads.
	Loose or broken connections in starter motor circuit	Check all connections and check any that are loose.
	Starter motor switch or solenoid faulty	Test and replace faulty components with new.
Electricity at starter motor: faulty motor	Starter motor pinion jammed in mesh with ring gear	Disengage pinion by turning squared end of armature shaft.
	Starter brushes badly worn, sticking, or brush wires loose	Examine brushes, replace as necessary, tighten down brush wires.
	Commutator dirty, worn, or burnt	Clean commutator, recut if badly burnt.
	Starter motor armature faulty	Overhaul starter motor, fit new armature.
	Field coils earthed	Overhaul starter motor.

Symptom	Reason/s	Remedy
STARTER MOTOR TURNS ENGINE VERY SLOWLY		
Electrical defects	Battery in discharged condition	Charge battery.
	Starter brushes badly worn, sticking, or brush wires loose	Examine brushes, replace as necessary, tighten down brush wires.
	Loose wires in starter motor circuit	Check wiring and tighten as necessary.
STARTER MOTOR OPERATES WITHOUT TURNING ENGINE		
Dirt or oil on drive gear	Starter motor pinion sticking on the screwed sleeve	Remove starter motor, clean starter motor drive.
Mechanical damage	Pinion or ring gear teeth broken or worn	Fit new gear ring, and new pinion to starter motor drive.
STARTER MOTOR NOISY OR EXCESSIVELY ROUGH ENGAGEMENT		
Lack of attention or mechanical damage	Pinion or ring gear teeth broken or worn	Fit new ring gear, or new pinion to starter motor drive.
	Starter drive main spring broken	Dismantle and fit new main spring.
	Starter motor retaining bolts loose	Tighten starter motor securing bolts. Fit new spring washer if necessary.
BATTERY WILL NOT HOLD CHARGE FOR MORE THAN A FEW DAYS		
Wear or damage	Battery defective internally	Remove and fit new battery.
	Electrolyte level too low or electrolyte too weak due to leakage	Top up electrolyte level to just above plates.
	Plate separators no longer fully effective	Remove and fit new battery.
	Battery plates severely sulphated	Remove and fit new battery.
	Drive belt slipping	Check belt for wear, replace if necessary, and tighten.
	Battery terminal connections loose or corroded	Check terminals for tightness, and remove all corrosion.
	Dynamo not charging properly	Remove and overhaul dynamo.
	Short in lighting circuit causing continual battery drain	Trace and rectify.
	Regulator unit not working correctly	Check setting, clean, and replace if defective.
IGNITION LIGHT FAILS TO GO OUT, BATTERY RUNS FLAT IN A FEW DAYS		
Dynamo not charging	Drive belt loose and slipping, or broken	Check, replace, and tighten as necessary.
	Brushes worn, sticking, broken or dirty	Examine, clean, or replace brushes as necessary.
	Brush springs weak or broken	Examine and test. Replace as necessary.
	Commutator dirty, greasy, worn, or burnt	Clean commutator and undercut segment separators.
	Armature badly worn or armature shaft bent	Fit new or reconditioned armature.
	Contacts in light switch faulty	By-pass light switch to ascertain if fault is in switch and fit new switch as appropriate.
Or alternator not charging		Seek professional advice from BLMC garage.
WIPERS		
Wiper motor fails to work	Blown fuse	Check and replace fuse if necessary.
	Wire connections loose, disconnected, or broken	Check wiper wiring. Tighten loose connections.
	Brushes badly worn	Remove and fit new brushes.
	Armature worn or faulty	If electricity at wiper motor remove and overhaul and fit replacement armature.
	Field coils faulty	Purchase reconditioned wiper motor.
Wiper motor works very slow and takes excessive current	Commutator dirty, greasy, or burnt	Clean commutator thoroughly.
	Drive to wheelboxes too bent or unlubricated	Examine drive and straighten out severe curvature. Lubricate.
	Wheelbox spindle binding or damaged	Removal, **overhaul, or fit replacement**.
	Armature bearings dry or unaligned	Replace with new bearings correctly aligned.
	Armature badly worn or faulty	Remove, overhaul, or fit replacement armature.
Wiper motor works slowly and takes little current	Brushes badly worn	Remove and fit new brushes.
	Commutator dirty, greasy, or burnt	Clean commutator thoroughly.
	Armature badly worn or faulty	Remove and overhaul armature or fit replacement.
Wiper motor works but wiper blades remain static	Driving cable rack disengaged or faulty	Examine and if faulty, replace.
	Wheelbox gear and spindle damaged or worn	Examine and if faulty, replace.
	Wiper motor gearbox parts badly worn	Overhaul or fit new gearbox.

WIRING DIAGRAMS CODING — SEE PAGE 143 FOR DYNAMO EQUIPPED CARS AND PAGE 144 FOR THOSE WITH ALTERNATORS

1 Dynamo or alternator
2 Control box
3 Battery
4 Starter solenoid
5 Starter motor
6 Lighting switch
7 Dip switch
8 Headlamp high beam
9 Headlamp low beam
10 Main beam warning lamp
11 RH sidelamp
12 LH sidelamp
14 Panel lamps
15 Number plate lamps
16 Stop lamps
17 RH tail lamp
18 Stop lamp switch
19 Fuse unit
20 Interior light
21 Door switch
22 LH tail lamp
23 Horns
24 Horn - push
25 Flasher unit
26 Direction indicator switch
27 Direction indicator warning light
28 RH front flasher
29 LH front flasher
30 RH rear flasher
31 LH rear flasher
32 Heater switch
33 Heater motor
34 Fuel gauge

35 Fuel gauge tank unit
36 Wiper switch
37 Wiper motor
38 Ignition switch
39 Ignition coil
40 Distributor
42 Oil pressure switch
43 Oil pressure warning light
44 Ignition warning light
45 Headlamp flasher switch
46 Water temperature gauge
47 Water temperature transmitter
49 Reverse lamp switch (if fitted)
50 Reverse lamps (if fitted)
57 Cigar lighter (if fitted)
60 Radio (if fitted)
64 Voltage stabilizer
65 Boot light switch (if fitted)
66 Boot lamp (if fitted)
67 Line fuse
75 Automatic gearbox safety switch (if fitted)
76 Automatic gearbox quadrant lamp (if fitted)
77 Electric screen washer motor
78 Electric screen washer switch
95 Tachometer (if fitted)
115 Rear window demist switch (if fitted)
116 Rear window demist unit (if fitted)
150 Rear window demist warning light (if fitted)
158 Printed circuit instrument panel

CABLE COLOUR CODE

N	Brown	P	Purple	W	White
U	Blue	G	Green	Y	Yellow
R	Red	LG	Light Green	B	Black
		O	Orange		

When a cable has two colour code letters the first denotes the main colour and the second denotes the tracer colour

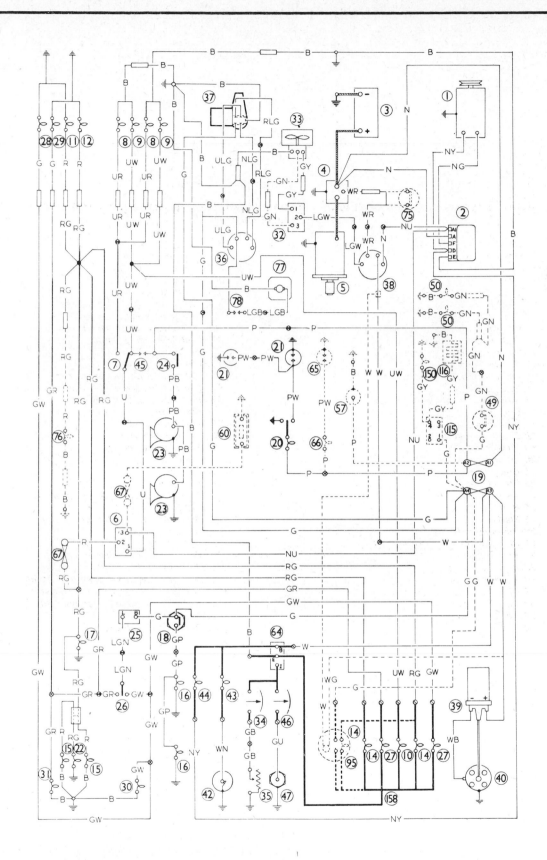

PLAN WIRING DIAGRAM FOR CARS FITTED WITH A DYNAMO (RHD) SEE PAGE 142 FOR CODING

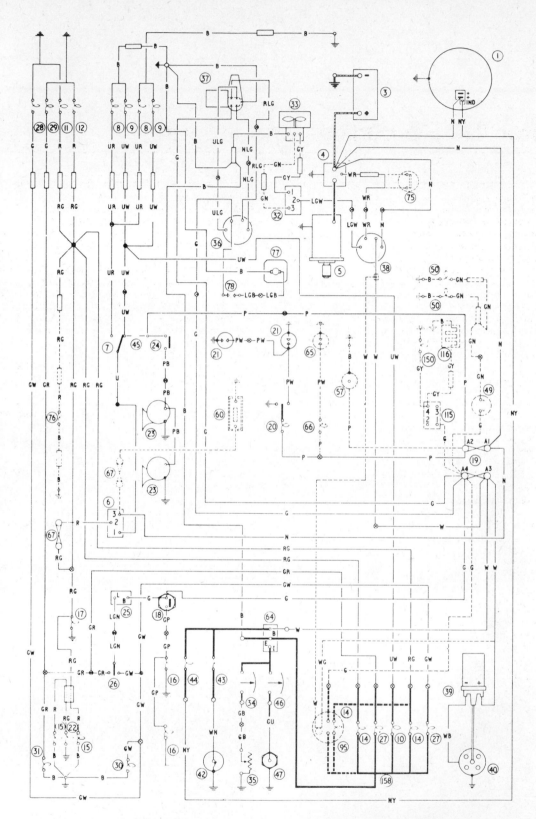

PLAN WIRING DIAGRAM FOR CARS FITTED WITH AN ALTERNATOR (RHD) SEE PAGE 142 FOR CODING

Chapter 11 Suspension and steering

Contents

Specifications

Front suspension ... ...   Independent by torsion bar with lever - type shock absorbers
King pin inclination ... ...   7½° Positive
Camber angle ... ...   0° 50' Positive
Castor angle ... ...   2° Positive; early produced cars 5°
Hub-bearing end-float ... ...   0.001 to 0.005 inch (0.025 to 0.0127 mm)
Swivel pin link lower bush finished diameter ... ...   0.688 ± 0.0005 inch (17.48 ± 0.013 mm)
Trim height: normal ... ...   25 3/8 ± ¼ inch (7.715 ± 0.064 mm)
          with new torsion bars ... ...   + 5/16 inch (7.94 mm)

Rear suspension   Semi-elliptic leaf spring with telescopic shock absorbers
Number of spring leaves   2
Width of leaves ... ...   2 inch (50.8 mm)
Gauge of leaves ... ...   0.3 to 0.164 inch (7.62 to 0.076 mm)
Working load ... ...   270 lb (122.7 Kg)

Steering ... ...   Rack and pinion
Steering wheel turns - lock to lock   4
Front wheel alignment ... ...   1/16 in (1.6 mm) toe-in
Pinion bearing pre-load ... ...   0.001 to 0.003 in (0.025 to 0.076 mm)
Oil capacity of rack and pinion ... ...   1/3 pint (190 cm³)
Rack travel ... ...   6.5 inch (16.5 cm)
Rack travel either side of centre ... ...   3.25 inch (8.25 cm)
Pinion rotations, full rack travel ... ...   3.98 turns
Pinion pre-load ... ...   0.001 to 0.003 inch (0.025 to 0.76 mm)
   shims available ... ...   0.002 inch (0.050 mm)
                                  0.005 inch (0.127 mm)
                                  0.010 inch (0.254 mm)
                                  0.060 inch (1.524 mm)
   cover gasket thickness ... ...   0.010 inch (0.254 mm)
Yoke clearance ... ...   0.002 to 0.005 inch (0.050 to 0.127 mm)
   shims available ... ...   0.002 inch (0.050 mm)
                                  0.005 inch (0.127 mm)
                                  0.010 inch (0.254 mm)
   cover gasket thickness ... ...   0.010 inch (0.254 mm)
Ball pin centre dimension (ball pins screwed to tie-rod equal
amount) ... ...   43.7 inch (1109.98 mm)

Wheels ... ...   4 stud pressed steel 13 inch x 4½
Tyre fitment:
   standard ... ...   5.20 x 13 cross ply
   optional ... ...   145 x 13 radial ply

Tyre pressures

	Front	Rear	Front	Rear
Crossply tyres	26 lb/sq in (1.8 Kg/cm^2)	28 lb/sq in (2.0 Kg/cm^2)	28 lb/sq in (2.0 Kg/cm^2)	30 lb/sq in (2.1 Kg/cm^2)
Radial tyres	24 lb/sq in (1.6 Kg/cm^2)	26 lb/sq in (1.8 Kg/cm^2)	26 lb/sq in (1.8 Kg/cm^2)	28 lb/sq in (2.0 Kg/cm^2)

Torque wrench settings

Front suspension

	lb ft	Kg fm
Ball pin retainer locknut	70 to 80	9.6 to 11.0
Eye bolt nut	50 to 54	6.9 to 7.4
Torsion bar reaction lever lock bolt	22	3.0
Reaction pad nut	35 to 40	4.8 to 5.5
Shock absorber retaining nuts	26 to 28	3.5 to 3.8
Tie-rod fork nut	48 to 55	6.6 to 7.6
Tie-rod to fork	22	3.0
Caliper bracket or mud flat bolts	35 to 42	4.8 to 5.8
Brake drum retaining screws	26 to 28	3.5 to 3.8

Rear suspension

Upper shackle pin nuts	28	3.9
Spring eye bolt nuts	40	5.5
Spring 'U' bolt nuts	14	1.9
Shock absorber to spring bracket	28	3.9
Shock absorber to body bracket	28	3.9

Steering

Rack clamp bracket nuts	20 to 22	2.77 to 3.04
Tie-rod ball pin nuts	20 to 24	2.77 to 3.3
Flexible joint pinch-bolt nut	6 to 8	0.4 to 0.5
Pinion end cover retaining bolts	12 to 15	1.6 to 2.0
Pinion pre-load	15 (lb in)	0.17
Rack yoke cover bolts	12 to 15	1.6 to 2.0
Tie-rod housing locknut	33 to 37	4.6 to 5.6
Tie-rod ball spheres pre-load	32 to 52 (lb in)	0.37 to 0.6
Steering - column mounting bolts	14 to 18	1.94 to 2.49
Flexible joint coupling bolts	20 to 22	2.77 to 3.04
Steering - column lock shear screw	14	1.94
Steering wheel nut	43 to 50	6.1 to 6.9
Tie-rod locknuts	35 to 40	4.8 to 5.5

1. General description

The component parts of the right hand side front suspension unit are shown in Fig.11.1. Although the left hand side front suspension is identical in principle some parts are handed and therefore not interchangeable.

Attached to the hub (Fig.11.2) is the road wheel as is also the brake drum or disc, these being retained by countersunk screws or bolts. The hub rotates on two opposed tapered roller bearings mounted on the swivel pin stub axle and is retained on the stub axle by a nut. Also attached to the swivel pin is the brake drum backplate or disc brake dust shield.

The shock absorber is attached to the body and its arm carries at the outer end, the ball joint for the swivel pin top attachment. Its arm therefore acts as an upper suspension withbone. The bottom end of the steering swivel screws into the lower link which is mounted between the outer end of the lower arms. This link is mounted on a pivot pin so that the suspension is able to move in a vertical manner. Horizontal movement of the suspension is controlled by a tie rod assembly. The inner ends of the lower arms are free to pivot about an eyebolt and the rear arm is spline attached to the torsion bar. The rear of the torsion bar is attached to the body so that both the body weight and road shocks are taken by the torsion bar.

Rear suspension is by semi-elliptic leaf springs, the springs being mounted on rubber bushed shackle pins. Double acting telescopic hydraulic shock absorbers are fitted to absorb road shocks and damper spring oscillations.

A rack and pinion steering is used. The layout is shown in

Fig.11.15 and it will be seen that the steering wheel is splined to the upper inner column which in turn is connected to the lower column by a flexible coupling. A second flexible coupling connects the lower column to the steering gearbox pinion. The pinion teeth mesh with those machined in the rack so that rotation of the pinion moves the rack from one side of the housing to the other. Located at either end of the rack are tie rods and ball joints attached to the suspension swivel pin steering arms.

2. Front hub bearings - removal and refitting

1 Jack up the front of the car and support on firmly based axle stands. Remove the wheel trim and the road wheel.
2 Drum brake models: Refer to Chapter 9 and back off the brake adjusters. Undo and remove the two countersunk screws securing the brake drum to the hub. Remove the brake drum. If it is tight tap around its circumference with a soft faced hammer.
3 Disc brake models: Refer to Chapter 9 and remove the disc brake caliper.
4 Using a wide blade screwdriver carefully ease off the grease cap.
5 Straighten the split pin ears and extract the split pin. Lift away the nut retainer and then undo and remove the hub nut. Withdraw the splined washer. The hub may now be drawn from the axle stub.
6 Remove the outer bearing cone.
7 Using a screwdriver ease out the oil seal noting that the lip is innermost. Lift away the inner bearing cone.
8 If the bearings are to be renewed carefully drift out the bearing

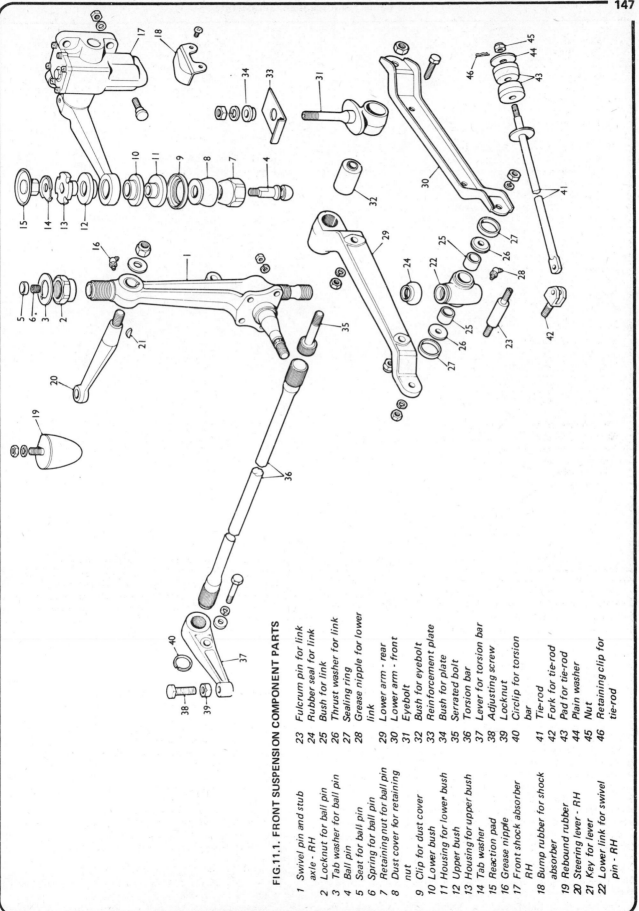

FIG.11.1. FRONT SUSPENSION COMPONENT PARTS

1 Swivel pin and stub axle - RH
2 Locknut for ball pin
3 Tab washer for ball pin
4 Ball pin
5 Seat for ball pin
6 Spring for ball pin
7 Retaining nut for ball pin
8 Dust cover for retaining nut
9 Clip for dust cover
10 Lower bush
11 Housing for lower bush
12 Upper bush
13 Housing for upper bush
14 Tab washer
15 Reaction pad
16 Grease nipple
17 Front shock absorber RH
18 Bump rubber for shock absorber
19 Rebound rubber
20 Steering lever - RH
21 Key for lever
22 Lower link for swivel pin - RH

23 Fulcrum pin for link
24 Rubber seal for link
25 Bush for link
26 Thrust washer for link
27 Sealing ring
28 Grease nipple for lower link
29 Lower arm - rear
30 Lower arm - front
31 Eyebolt
32 Bush for eyebolt
33 Reinforcement plate
34 Bush for plate
35 Serrated bolt
36 Torsion bar
37 Lever for torsion bar
38 Adjusting screw
39 Locknut
40 Circlip for torsion bar
41 Tie-rod
42 Fork for tie-rod
43 Pad for tie-rod
44 Plain washer
45 Nut
46 Retaining clip for tie-rod

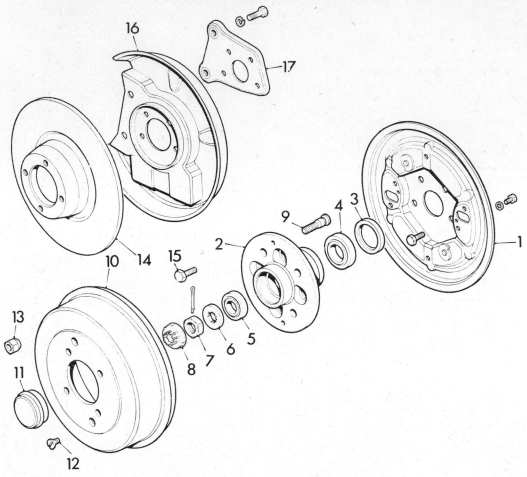

FIG.11.2. FRONT HUB COMPONENTS, DRUM AND DISC

1	Brake backplate	6	Splined washer
2	Wheel hub	7	Nut for stub axle
3	Oil seal for hub	8	Retainer for nut
4	Inner bearing	9	Wheel stud
5	Outer bearing	10	Brake - drum

11	Grease retaining cap	15	Bolt for brake disc to hub
12	Screw for brake-drum	16	Mud shield for disc
13	Wheel nut	17	Adaptor plate for brake caliper
14	Front brake disc - RH		

cups working from the inside of the hub.

9 Thoroughly wash all parts in paraffin and wipe dry using a non-fluffy rag.

10 Inspect the bearings for signs of rusting, pitting or overheating. If evident, a new set of bearings must be fitted.

11 Inspect the oil seal journal face of the stub axle shaft for signs of damage. If evident either polish with fine emery tape or if very bad a new stub axle will have to be fitted.

12 To reassemble, if new bearings are to be fitted carefully drift in the new bearing cups using a piece of tube of suitable diameter. Make sure they are fitted the correct way round with the tapers facing outwards.

13 Work some high melting point grease into the inner bearing cone and fit it into the hub.

14 Smear a new oil seal with a little Castrol GTX and fit it with the lip innermost using a tube of suitable diameter. The final fitted position should be flush with the flange of the hub.

15 Fit the hub to the axle stub. Work some high melting point grease into the outer bearing cone and fit it into the hub.

16 Refit the splined washer and nut.

17 It is now necessary to adjust the hub bearing end float and full information will be found in Section 3 of this Chapter.

18 Refit the grease cap, road wheel and wheel trim. Lower the front of the car to the ground.

3. Front hub bearings - adjustment

1 Jack up the front of the car and support on firmly based axle stands.

2 Remove the wheel trim road wheel and grease cap (Fig.11.3).

3 Straighten the split pin ears and extract the split pin. Lift away the hub nut retainer.

4 Back off the hub nut and spin the hub. Whilst it is spinning tighten the nut using a torque wrench set to 5 lb ft (0.69 Kg fm).

5 Stop the hub spinning and slacken the nut. Tighten the nut again but this time finger tight only.

6 Position the nut retainer so that half the split pin hole is covered by one of the arms of the retainer.

7 Slacken the nut and retainer until the split pin hole is fully uncovered.

8 Fit a new split pin and lock by opening the ears of the split pin and bending around the nut retainer.

9 Fit the grease cap and replace the road wheel and wheel trim.

10 It will be observed that the end float setting achieved can cause a considerable amount of movement when the tyre is 'rocked'. Do not reduce the end float any further provided it has been set correctly as described. The bearings must not on any account be pre-loaded.

FIG.11.3. FRONT HUB ASSEMBLY

1 Brake drum retaining screw
2 Grease cap
3 Split pin
4 Nut retainer
5 Nut
6 Splined washer
7 Hub
8 Outer bearing cone
9 Bearing cups
10 Inner bearing cone
11 Oil seal
A Drum brake grease cap
B Disc brake grease cap

Inset: Split pin replacement

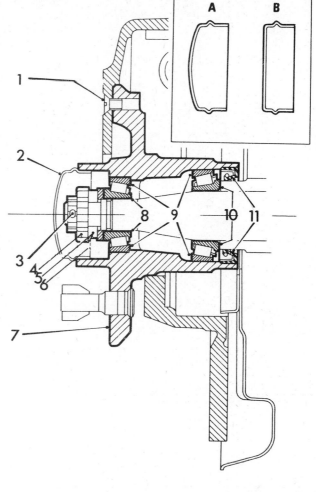

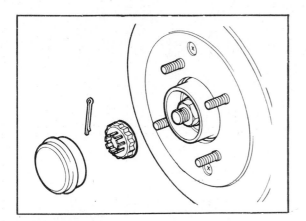

4. Lower suspension arm - removal and refitting

1 Jack up the front of the car and support on firmly based axle stands. Suitably support the suspension unit under the rear lower arm.
2 Remove the wheel trim and the road wheel.
3 Undo and remove the nut and spring washer from the eye bolt pin (Fig.11.4).
4 Undo and remove the front nut and spring washer from the swivel lower link pin.
5 Undo and remove the nut, bolt and spring washer retaining the tie-rod to the tie-rod fork.
6 Undo and remove the nut retaining the tie-rod fork to the lower suspension arms. Lift away the fork.
7 Undo the nut, bolt and spring washer that clamps the front and rear lower arms together.
8 The front lower suspension arm may now be lifted away.
9 Refer to Section 10 and remove the torsion bar.
10 Withdraw the eye bolt pin and then undo and remove the rear nut and spring washer from the swivel lower link pin.
11 The rear lower suspension arm may now be lifted away.
12 Refitting the lower suspension arm assembly is the reverse sequence to removal. In addition:
a) Tighten the rod fork nut to a torque wrench setting of 48 to 55 lb ft (6.6 to 7.6 Kg fm).
b) Tighten the tie-rod to fork nut to a torque wrench setting of 22 lb ft (3.0 Kg fm).

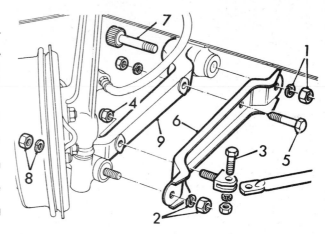

FIG.11.4. THE LOWER SUSPENSION ARM ASSEMBLY

1 Eyebolt pin nut
2 Lower link pin securing nut
3 Tie-rod securing bolt, nut
4 Tie-rod fork retaining nut
5 Lower arm clamp bolt, nut
6 Front lower suspension arm
7 Eyebolt pin
8 Swivel lower link pin nut
9 Lower suspension arm

5. Shock absorber - removal and refitting

Note: When retightening the reaction pad nut, a crowfoot adaptor (Leyland Part No. 18G1237) is required. If you do not have this adaptor, an open-ended spanner can be used, but you should arrange for your Leyland dealer to check the tightness of the nut after fitting.

1 Jack up the front of the car and support on firmly based axle stands. Suitably support the lower suspension arm.
2 Remove the wheel trim and road wheel.
3 Unlock the reaction pad nut. Using a mole wrench or 'C' spanner hold the upper bush housing and remove the nut (Fig. 11.5).
4 Lift away the lock washer, upper bush housing and upper bush.
5 Raise the shock absorber arm. Undo and remove the four nuts and plain washers that secure the shock absorber to its mounting.
6 Lift away the shock absorber.
7 Test the operation of the shock absorber by topping up the level if necessary and then moving the shock absorber arm up and down. If the action is weak or jerky then either the unit is worn or air has entered the operating cylinders. Move the arm up and down ten times and if the performance has not improved a new shock absorber must be obtained.
8 Inspect the shock absorber arm bushes for wear. If evident obtain new bushes.
9 Refitting the shock absorber is the reverse sequence to removal. In addition:
a) Always use a new reaction pad lock washer.
b) Tighten the reaction pad nut to a torque wrench setting of 35 - 40 lb ft (4.8 to 5.5 Kg fm), using the crowfoot adaptor.
c) Tighten the shock absorber retaining nuts to a torque wrench setting of 26 to 28 lb ft (3.5 to 3.8 Kg fm).

6. Swivel pin - removal and refitting

1 Refer to Section 5 and follow the instructions given in paragraphs 1 to 4 inclusive.
2 Raise the shock absorber arm.
3 Wipe the top of the brake master cylinder reservoir. Remove the cap and place a piece of thick polythene over the top. Refit the cap. This is to stop syphoning of fluid during subsequent operations.
4 Wipe the area around the flexible brake hose connection at the body mounted bracket. Hold the flexible hose metal end nut and undo and remove the metal pipe union nut. Undo and remove the flexible hose securing nut and star washer and draw the flexible hose from the bracket (Fig.11.6).
5 Remove the lower link pin rear nut and spring washer.
6 The swivel pin assembly may now be lifted away.
7 Refitting the swivel pin assembly is the reverse sequence to removal.

7. Swivel pin ball joint - removal and refitting

Note: When retightening the ball retainer locknut, a crowfoot adaptor (Leyland Part No. 18G1192) is required. If you do not have this adaptor, an open-ended spanner can be used, but you should arrange for your Leyland dealer to check the tightness of the nut after refitting (also see relevant Figure in Chapter 13).

1 Refer to Section 5 and follow the instructions given in paragraphs 1 to 4 inclusive.
2 Raise the shock absorber arm.
3 Remove the dust cover and retaining clip.
4 Unlock the tab washer and using an open ended spanner hold the locknut. With a ring spanner undo the ball pin retainer.
5 Lift away the ball pin, ball seat and spring. Finally remove the tab washer and locknut.
6 To reassemble first obtain a new tab washer. Pack the ball pin retainer with Castrol LM Grease.
7 Fit the tab washer and locknut and then replace the ball seat and spring. Refit the ball pin and its retainer.

8 Fully slacken the locknut and tighten the ball retainer until the torque required to produce articulation of the ball pin is 32 to 52 lb in (0.38 to 0.56 Kg fm).
9 Hold the ball retainer against rotation and tighten the locknut to a torque wrench setting of 70 - 80 lb ft (9.6 to 11.0 Kg fm) using the crowfoot adaptor.
10 Lock the retainer and the locknut with the tab washer.
11 Reassembly is now the reverse sequence to removal.

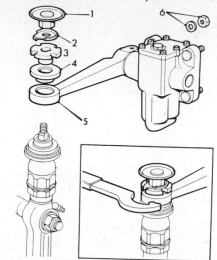

FIG.11.5. FRONT SHOCK ABSORBER REMOVAL

1 Reaction pad nut	4 Upper bush
2 Lock washer	5 Shock absorber arm
3 Upper bush housing	6 Nut and spring washer

Inset: 'C' spanner used to hold upper bush housing

FIG.11.6. LOWER SWIVEL PIN LINK REMOVAL

1 Drum retaining screw	8 Brake hydraulic hose
2 Grease cap	9 Brake backplate
3 Nut retainer and split pin	10 Sealing ring
4 Nut	11 Thrust washer
5 Splined washer	12 Lower link pin
6 Hub	13 Link pin securing nut and spring washer
7 Backplate retaining bolt and spring washer	14 Lower link
	15 Lower link bushes

8. Lower swivel pin link - removal and refitting

1   Jack up the front of the car and support on firmly based axle stands. Suitably support the rear lower suspension arm.

2   Remove the wheel trim and road wheel.

3   Drum brake models: Refer to Chapter 9 and back off the brake adjusters. Undo and remove the two countersunk screws securing the brake drum to the hub. Remove the brake drum. If it is tight tap around its circumference with a soft faced hammer.

4   Disc brake models: Refer to Chapter 9 and remove the disc brake caliper.

5   Using a wide blade screwdriver carefully ease off the grease cap (Fig.11.3).

6   Straighten the split pin ears and extract the split pin, lift away the nut retainer and then undo and remove the hub nut. Withdraw the splined washer.

7   The hub may now be drawn from the axle stub.

8   Wipe the top of the brake master cylinder reservoir. Remove the cap and place a piece of thin polythene over the top. Refit the cap. This is to stop syphoning of fluid during subsequent operations.

9   Wipe the area around the flexible brake hose connection at the body mounted bracket. Hold the flexible hose metal end nut and undo and remove the metal pipe union nut. Undo and remove the flexible hose secuirng nut and star washer and draw the flexible hose from the bracket.

10 Undo and remove the four nuts, bolts and spring washers securing the backplate or dust shield and caliper bracket to the swivel pin. Lift away the brake backplate or dust shield and caliper bracket.

11 Refer to Section 4 and remove the lower suspension arm.

12 Undo and remove the remaining nut and spring washer from the lower link pin.

13 Swing the swivel pin forwards and remove the rubber sealing rings and thrust washers from the lower link.

15 Unscrew and remove the lower link from the swivel pin.

16 Thoroughly wash all parts in paraffin and wipe dry using a non-fluffy rag.

17 Check for excessive wear across the thrust faces and in the threaded bore. If wear is excessive a new swivel link must be obtained.

18 Check the lower link chisels for wear and if this is evident new brushes should be fitted by a BLMC garage as it has to be ream finished. If an expanding reamer and micrometer are available however, the old bushes should be drifted out. Further instructions are given in paragraphs 22 and 23.

19 Inspect the thrust washers for signs of damage or wear which, if evident new thrust washers must be obtained.

20 Remove the grease nipple and ensure that both it and its hole are free from obstruction.

21 Obtain a new set of rubber sealing rings.

22 If new bushes are to be fitted these should be drifted or pressed in so that the oil groove is located as shown in Fig.11.7.

The bush oil groove blank ends should be towards the outside edge of the link.

23 Using the expanding reamer, line ream the new bushes to a finished size of 0.688 ± 0.005 inch (17.48 ± 0.013 mm).

24 Place the swivel in link and seal on the swivel pin and screw on the link. Engage the seal on the recessed shoulder of the link and screw the link fully onto the swivel pin.

25 Unscrew the link one complete turn.

26 Reassembly is now the reverse sequence to removal. In addition:

a) The backplate to hub or caliper bracket and dust shield retaining bolts should be tightened to a torque wrench setting of 35 to 42 lb ft (4.8 to 5.8 Kg fm).

b) Tighten the brake drum retaining screws to a torque wrench setting of 26 to 28 lb ft (3.5 to 3.8 Kg fm).

c) Refer to Section 3 and adjust the front hub bearing end float.

9. Eye bolt bush - removal and refitting

1   Refer to Section 10 and remove the torsion bar.

2   Undo and remove the nut and spring washer from the eye bolt pin (Fig.11.8).

3   Withdraw the eye bolt pin.

4   Draw the suspension assembly clear of the eye bolt.

5   Undo and remove the nut, spring washer and spacer from the eye bolt.

6   Lift away the eye bolt and, if fitted, the reinforcement plate.

7   The bush may be removed with pieces of suitable diameter tube, pressing it out in a bench vice.

8   To fit a new bush lubricate its outer surface with a little soapy water and press it in using the reverse procedure to removal.

9   Refitting the eye bolt is the reverse sequence to removal. In addition:

a) It is not necessary to fit the reinforcement plate when a later type eye bolt is being used. This is identifiable by having a 2.5 inch (63 mm) elliptical diameter.

b) The eye bolt retaining nut should be tightened to a torque wrench setting of 50 to 54 lb ft (6.9 to 7.4 Kg fm).

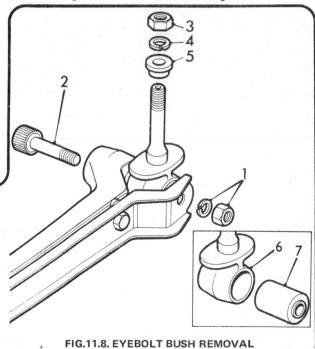

FIG.11.8. EYEBOLT BUSH REMOVAL

1	Eyebolt pin nut and	4	Spring washer
	spring washer	5	Spacer
2	Eyebolt	6	Eyebolt
3	Nut	7	Bush

FIG.11.7. CORRECT POSITION OF BUSH OIL GROOVE

10. Torsion bar - removal and refitting

1 Unscrew and remove the grease nipple from the swivel pin lower link (Fig.11.9).
2 Place a wooden block 8 inch (200 mm) thick on the floor under the lower suspension arm as near as possible to the brake backplate or disc brake dust shield as shown in Fig.11.9
3 Jack up the front of the car. Remove the wheel trim and road wheel.
4 Carefully lower the car until the weight of the suspension is placed on the wooden block.
5 Unlock the reaction pad nut. Using a mole wrench hold the upper bush housing and remove the nut.
6 Remove the upper bush housing and the upper bush.
7 Raise the shock absorber arm clear of the ball pin and lift away the lower bush.
8 Undo and remove the steering track rod ball pin nut.
9 Using a universal ball joint separator release the ball pin from the steering lever.
10 Jack up the front of the car so as to relieve the torsion bar load and yet the lower suspension arm is still just resting on the wooden block.
11 Undo and remove the bolt, spring washer and special washer that secures the torsion bar reaction lever onto the chassis member.
12 Remove the reaction lever from the chassis member and move the lever forwards along the torsion bar.
13 Release the nut that retains the eye bolt through the chassis member and make sure that the suspension lowers itself by ½ inch (12 mm).
14 Ease the torsion bar forwards until it clears the shoulder from the chassis housing. Lower the torsion bar and remove it in a rearwards direction.
15 Using a pair of circlip pliers remove the torsion bar circlip.
16 Slide off the reaction lever from the torsion bar.
17 Refitting the torsion bar is the reverse sequence to removal, in addition:
a) Once a torsion bar has been fitted and used on one side of the car it must not under any circumstances be used on the other side. This is because a torsion bar becomes handed once it has been in use. Torsion bars are only interchangeable when new.
b) Do not fit a torsion bar that is corroded or deeply scored as this will effect is realiability and in bad cases cause premature failure.
c) The reaction lever adjustment screw must be set to the mid way position of its travel and the locknut tightened before refitting.
d) Tighten the eye bolt nut to a torque wrench setting of 50 to 54 lb ft (6.9 to 7.4 Kg fm).
e) Tighten the reaction lever to chassis member bolt to 22 lb ft (3.0 Kg fm).
f) Tighten the track rod ball pin nut to a torque wrench setting of 2.7 to 3.3 Kg fm).
g) Tighten the reaction pad nut to 35—40 lb ft (4.8 to 5.5 Kg fm).
18 Refer to Section 25 and adjust the front suspension trim height if necessary.

11. Tie-rod - removal and refitting

1 Jack up the front of the car and support on firmly based axle stands.
2 Remove the wheel trim and road wheel.
3 Using a pair of pliers remove the tie-rod spring clip from the end of the tie-rod (Fig.11.10).
4 Undo and remove the locking nut and large plain washer.
5 Slide off the rubber outer pad.
6 Undo and remove the nut, spring washer and bolt that secures the tie-rod to the fork end.
7 Remove the rubber inner pad from the tie-rod.
8 Undo and remove the nut that secures the rod fork and lift

away the fork from the lower suspension arm.
9 Refitting the tie-rod is the reverse sequence to removal but the following additional points should be noted:
a) Inspect the two rubber pads and if they show signs of oil contamination, cracking or perishing obtain and fit a new pair of pads.
b) The tie-rod to fork nut should be tightened to a torque wrench setting of 22 lb ft (3.0 Kg fm).
c) Tighten the rod fork nut to a torque wrench setting of 48 to 55 lb ft (6.6 to 7.6 Kg fm).

12. Rear hub assembly - removal and refitting

1 Chock the front wheels, jack up the rear of the car and place on firmly based axle stands.
2 Remove the wheel trim and road wheel. Apply the handbrake
3 Undo and remove the axle shaft nut and washer.
4 Release the handbrake and refer to Chapter 9. Back off the brake adjuster. Remove the two countersunk screws that retain the brake drum and pull off the brake drum.
5 Using a universal puller and suitable thrust block pull the hub from the end of the axle shaft.
6 Remove the axle shaft key.
7 Refitting the rear hub assembly is the reverse sequence to removal. The axle shaft nut must be tightened to a torque wrench setting of 85 lb ft (11.7 Kg fm).

13. Rear road spring - removal and refitting

1 Refer to Section 14 and remove the road spring shackle plate (Fig.11.11).
2 Jack up the rear of the car and support on firmly based axle stands located under the main longitudinal chassis members. Support the weight of the axle on the side which the spring is to be removed.
3 Undo and remove the shock absorber locknut, plain nut and plain washer. Note the location of the lower bush in the shock absorber lower mounting plate and remove the lower bush.
4 Undo and remove the nut, spring washer and bolt that secures the front spring eye to the body mounted brackets.
5 Undo and remove the four nuts from the two 'U' bolts.
6 Carefully lower the spring and its mountings.
7 Remove the shock absorber mounting plate followed by the spring mounting plates and mounting rubbers. Note the fitted location of the spring mounting wedge.
8 Lift away the two 'U' bolts.
9 If the spring bushes are worn or have deteriorated they should be pressed out using suitable diameter tubes and a large bench vice.
10 Should the spring have considerably weakened or failed necessitating the fitting of a new one, rear springs must be renewed in pairs and not singly as the remaining spring will have settled slightly. Unless the springs have the same performance and characteristics road holding can be adversely affected.
11 Refitting the road spring is the reverse sequence to removal. In addition:
a) Tighten the upper shackle pin nuts to a torque wrench setting of 28 lb ft (3.9 Kg fm).
b) Tighten the spring eye bush bolt nuts to a torque wrench setting of 40 lb ft (5.5 Kg fm).
c) Tighten the 'U' bolt nuts to a torque wrench setting of 14 lb ft (1.9 Kg fm).
d) Tighten the shock absorber to spring bracket retaining nut to a torque wrench setting of 28 lb ft (3.9 Kg fm) and then secure by tightening the locknut.

14. Rear road spring shackles - removal and refitting

1 Chock the front wheels, jack up the rear of the car and place on firmly based axle stands located under the main longi-

FIG.11.9. TORSION BAR REMOVAL

1 Grease nipple
2 Wood block
3 Track rod ball pin nut
4 Eyebolt retaining nut
   and bush
5 Torsion bar
6 Reaction lever
7 Reaction lever retaining bolt, spring and special washer

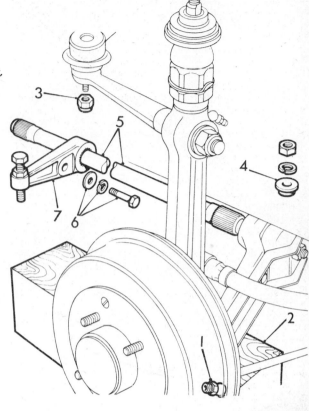

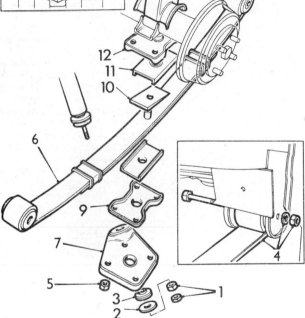

FIG.11.11. REAR SPRING REMOVAL

1 Shock absorber retaining nut and locknut
2 Plate washer
3 Lower bush
4 Forward spring eyebolt securing nut and spring washer
5 'U' bolt nut
6 Spring assembly
7 Shock absorber mounting plate
8 Spring mounting plate (lower)
9 Rubber pad
10 Wedge
11 Rubber pad
12 Spring mounting plate (upper)
13 Rubber bump stop
14 'U' bolts
15 Inset: Drifting in new shackle bush

FIG.11.10. TIE-ROD REMOVAL

1 Tie-rod fork
2 Tie-rod retaining bolt
3 Nut and spring washer
4 Tie-rod
5 Spring clip
6 Inner pad
7 Outer pad
8 Plain washer
9 Nut

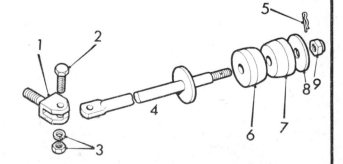

tudinal chassis member.

2   Remove the wheel trim and road wheel.

3   Undo and remove the nut and spring washer on each side of the upper shackle pin (Fig.11.12).

4   Undo and remove the nut and spring washer from the spring bush bolt.

5   Lift away the inner shackle plate.

6   Using a suitable diameter parallel pin punch partially drift out the spring bolt and then release the outer shackle plate from the upper pin.

7   Remove the upper shackle pin and lift away the two upper half bushes.

8   Inspect the bushes for signs of deterioration or oil contamination which, if evdient, new brakes should be obtained.

9   Refitting is the reverse sequence to removal. In addition:

a) Tighten the upper shackle pin nuts to a torque wrench setting of 28 lb ft (3.9 Kg fm).

b) Tighten the spring eye bush bolt nut to a torque wrench setting of 40 lb ft (5.5 Kg fm).

15. Bump stop - removal and refitting

1   Chock the front wheels, jack up the rear of the car and place on firmly based axle stands located under the main longitudinal chassis members.

2   Remove the wheel trim and road wheel.

3   Support the weight of the axle on the side to be worked upon.

4   Undo and remove the shock absorber locknut, plain nut, and plain washer. Note the location of the lower bush in the shock absorber mounting bracket and lift away the lower bush.

5   Undo and remove the fair 'U' bolt nuts.

6   Lift away the shock absorber mounting plate and spring locating bracket and rubber.

7   Lift away the bump stop and two 'U' bolts.

8   Refitting the bump stop rubber is the reverse sequence to

removal but the following additional points should be noted:

a) Check the condition of the spring mounting rubber and if its condition has deteriorated a new mounting rubber should be obtained and fitted.

b) The shock absorber to spring bracket retaining nut should be tightened to a torque wrench setting of 28 lb ft (3.9 Kg fm) and then locked with the locknut.

16. Rear shock absorber - removal and refitting

1   Undo and remove the shock absorber lower locknut and retaining nut (Fig.11.13).

2   Lift away the plain washer and note the position of the lower bush. Lift away the lower bush.

3   Contract the shock absorber thereby detaching it from the mounting bracket.

4   Note the position of the upper bush and then lift it away followed by the plain washer.

5   Undo and remove the nut, spring washer and bolt that fixes the upper part of the shock absorber to the body bracket. Lift away the shock absorber.

6   To test the shock absorber alternatively compress and extend it throughout its full movement. If the action is jerky or weak, either it is worn or there is air in the hydraulic cylinder. Continue to compress and extend it and if the action does not become more positive a new shock absorber should be obtained. If the shock absorber is showing signs of leaking it should be discarded as it is not possible to overhaul it.

7   Check the bushes and if they show signs of deterioration a new set of rubbers should be obtained.

8   Refitting the shock absorber is the reverse sequence to removal. In addition:

a) Tighten the shock absorber to body bracket retaining bolt nut to a torque wrench setting of 28 lb ft (3.9 Kg fm).

b) The shock absorber to spring bracket should be tightened to a torque wrench setting of 28 lb ft (3.9 Kg fm) and then locked.

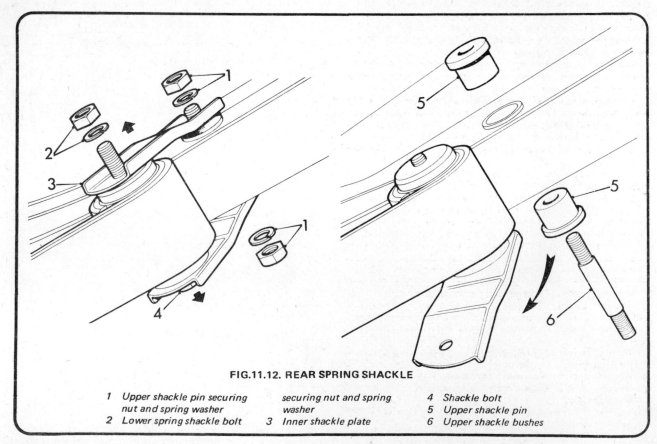

FIG.11.12. REAR SPRING SHACKLE

1 Upper shackle pin securing nut and spring washer	securing nut and spring washer	4 Shackle bolt
2 Lower spring shackle bolt	3 Inner shackle plate	5 Upper shackle pin
		6 Upper shackle bushes

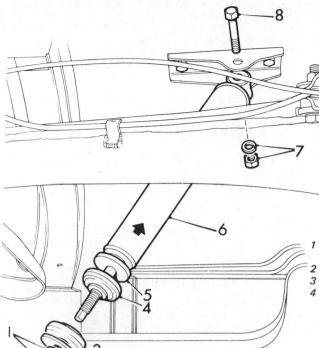

FIG.11.13. REAR SHOCK ABSORBER REMOVAL

1	Shock absorber retaining nut and locknut	5	Plate washer
2	Plate washer	6	Shock absorber
3	Lower bush	7	Upper mounting bolt securing nut and spring washer
4	Upper bush	8	Upper mounting bolt

17. Steering wheel - removal and refitting

1   Using a knife carefully prise the safety pad from the centre of the steering wheel (Fig.11.14).
2   Undo and remove the five self tapping screws that secure the switch cowls. Lift away the cowls from over the switch arms.
3   Undo and remove the nut and shakeproof washer that secures the steering wheel to the upper inner column.
4   With a centre punch mark the relative positions of the steering wheel hub and inner column so that they may be refitted in the same position.
5   With the palms of the hands behind the spokes and near to the centre hub thump the steering wheel from the steering inner column splines. If it is very tight it will be necessary to use a universal puller fitted with long feet and a suitable thrust block.
6   Refitting the steering wheel is the reverse sequence to removal. In addition:
a) The steering wheel securing nut should be tightened to a torque wrench setting of 43 to 50 lb ft (6.0 to 6.9 Kg fm).
b) When refitting the safety pad to the centre of the steering wheel the pins at each end of the pad must be located and inserted first. This will make sure that the width between the safety pad and steering wheel is equally spaced on either side of the pad.

18. Steering column top bush - removal and refitting

1   Refer to Section 17 and remove the steering wheel.
2   Slacken the screw that retains the combined switch mechanism and lift the switch mechanism over the top of the inner column.
3   Using a screwdriver ease the top bush from the inside of the outer column.
4   To refit the top bush first align the slots in the column bush with the depression in the outer column and ensure that the chamfered end of the bush enters the column first.
5   Using a suitable diameter metal drift carefully drive the top bush into position.
6   Refitting the combined switch mechanism and steering wheel is now the reverse sequence to removal.

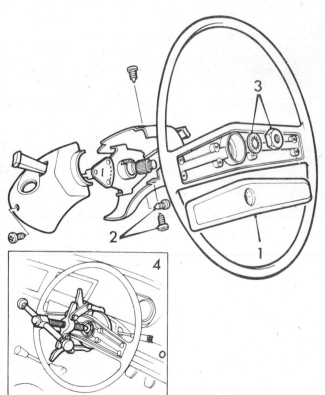

FIG.11.14. STEERING WHEEL REMOVAL

1	Safety pad		nut and shakeproof washer
2	Switch cowl securing screws	4	Using a universal puller to remove steering wheel
3	Steering wheel securing		

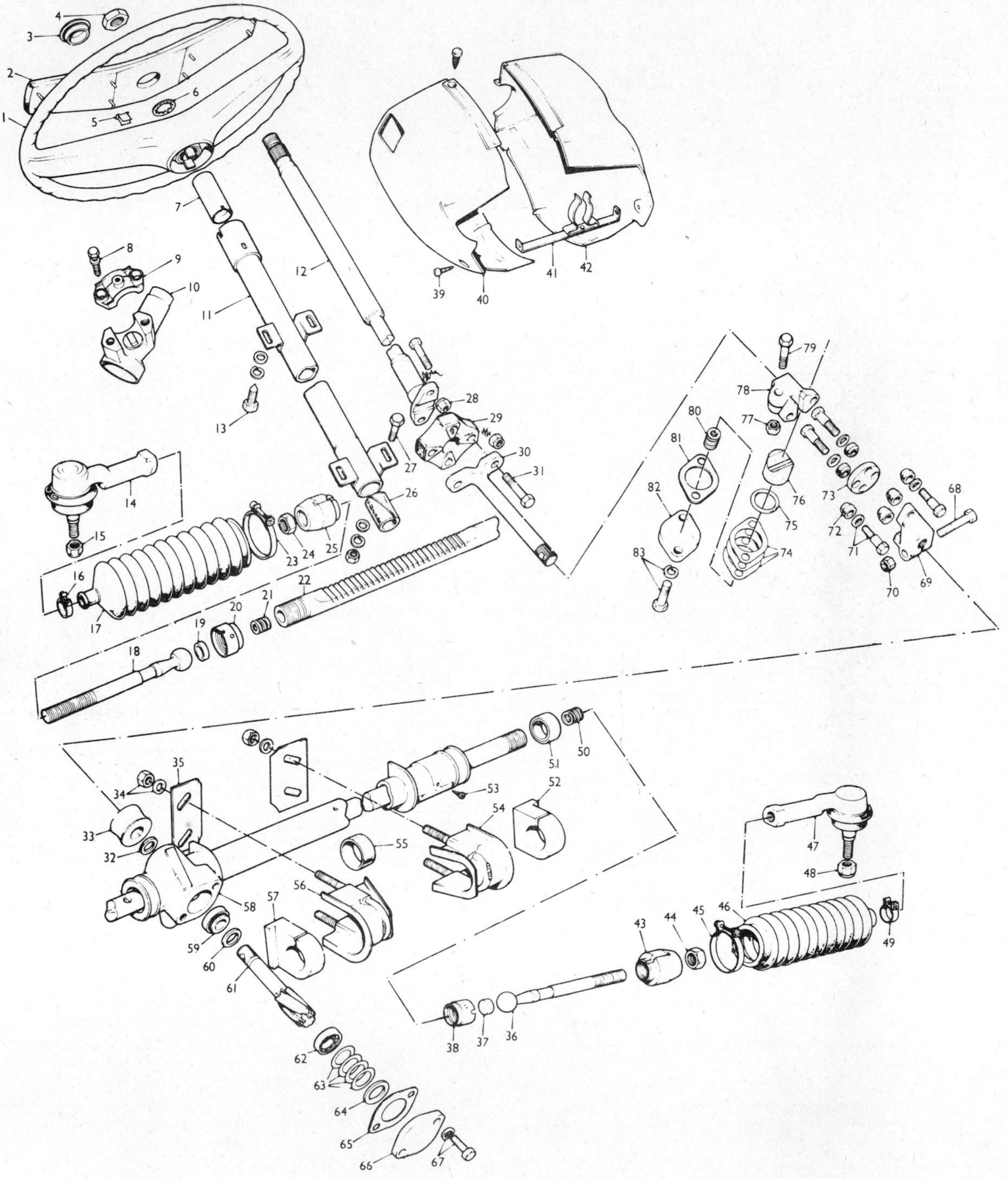
1
2
3
4
5
6
7
8
9
10
11
12
13
14
15
16
17
18
19
20
21
22
23
24
25
26
27
28
29
30
31
32
33
34
35
36
37
38
39
40
41
42
43
44
45
46
47
48
49
50
5.1
52
53
54
55
56
57
58
59
60
61
62
63
64
65
66
67
68
69
70
71
72
73
74
75
76
77
78
79
80
81
82
83

FIG.11.15. RACK AND PINION STEERING ASSEMBLY

1	Steering-wheel	22	Rack	43	Ball housing	65	Shim gasket - .010 in.
2	Safety pad	23	Clip - large	44	Locknut		(0.254 mm)
3	Motif	24	Locknut	45	Clip - large	66	End cover
4	Nut	25	Ball housing	46	Rack seal	67	Bolt and spring
5	Clip-safety pad to wheel	26	Lower bush	47	Tie-rod end		washer
6	Shakeproof washer	27	Bolt - plain and spring	48	Nut - self-locking	68	Bolt
7	Bush-upper		washer	49	Clip - small	69	Flexible joint - half
8	Shear bolt-steering lock	28	Nut	50	Thrust spring	70	Nut
9	Clamp plate	29	Flexible coupling	51	Rack bearing	71	Shouldered bolt
10	Steering lock	30	Column - lower	52	Rack mounting rubber	72	Rubber bush
11	Column outer - upper	31	Bolt	53	Screw - rack bearing	73	Joint plate
12	Column inner - upper	32	Pinion oil seal	54	Rack clamp	74	Shim
13	Screw - spring and	33	Sealing washer	55	Sealing rubber	75	'O' ring
	plain washer	34	Nut and plain washer	56	Rack clamp	76	Support yoke
14	Tie-rod end	35	Locating plate	57	Rack mounting rubber	77	Nut
15	Nut - self-locking	36	Tie-rod	58	Pinion housing	78	Flexible joint - half
16	Clip - small	37	Ball seat	59	Pinion bearing	79	Bolt
17	Rack seal	38	Locknut	60	Washer	80	Thrust spring
18	Tie-rod	39	Screw	61	Pinion	81	Joint
19	Ball seat	40	Cowl half	62	Pinion bearing	82	End cover
20	Locknut	41	Cowl support	63	Shim	83	Bolt and spring
	Thrust spring	42	Cowl half	64	Shim - .60 in. (1.524 mm)		washer

19. Steering column lock and ignition starter switch housing - removal and refitting

1　Refer to Section 17 and remove the steering wheel.

2　Refer to Chapter 12 and remove the lower facia panel.

3　Refer to Chapter 12 and remove the instrument panel.

4　Locate the multi pin terminal connector on the end of the wiring harness to the column lock and ignition starter switch and disconnect the cable connector (Fig.11.16).

5　Using either a drill or a drill and 'ease out' stud extractor remove the two special shear screws.

6　Lift away the clamp plate and the steering lock.

7　To refit, offer up the steering column lock and ignition switch and clamp plate so that the indent in the top of the column is lined up with the clamp plate grub screw.

8　Lightly tighten the two new shear screws and the one grub screw.

9　Check the operation of the lock to ensure that it operates correctly.

10　Slowly tighten the two shear bolts until the heads shear at the waisted point. This will normally occur at a torque wrench setting of 14 lb ft (1.94 Kg fm).

11　Reassembly is now the reverse sequence to removal.

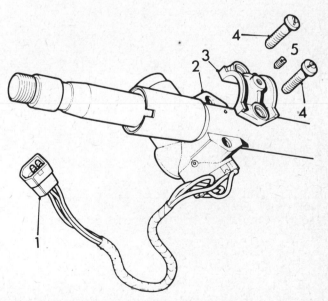

FIG.11.16. STEERING COLUMN LOCK AND IGNTION STARTER SWITCH HOUSING REMOVAL

1	Multi-pin connector	4	Shear bolts
2	Steering lock housing	5	Grub screw
3	Clamp plate		

20. Steering column universal joint coupling - removal and refitting

1 Refer to Section 21 and remove the upper steering column.
2 Undo and remove the pinch bolt and nut that secures the lower column to the rack pinion (Fig.11.17).
3 Lift away the lower steering column assembly.
4 Undo and remove the pinch bolt and nut that secures the lower column to the flexible joint.
5 Unlock and remove the four shouldered bolts from the flexible joint.
6 Lift away the rubber washers noting that the conical face mates with the countersunk face of the joint plate.
7 Lift away the plain washers from each of the four shouldered bolts.
8 Undo and remove the two nuts and bolts that retain the flexible coupling to the lower steering column.
9 Inspect the flexible couplings for signs of deterioration which if evident a new coupling must be obtained.
10 Refitting the couplings is the reverse sequence to removal. The upper flexible joint coupling bolts should be tightened to a torque wrench setting of 20 to 22 lb ft (2.77 to 3.04 Kg fm). If a new coupling has been fitted it will be necessary to break the band that compresses the coupling.

21. Upper steering column - removal and refitting

1 Refer to Section 17 and remove the steering wheel.
2 Refer to Chapter 12 and remove the lower facia panel.
3 Refer to Chapter 12 and remove the instrument panel.
4 Disconnect the multi pin connector on the end of the wiring harness to the switch mechanism at the harness connector.
5 Slacken the screw that retains the combined switch mechanism and lift the switch mechanism from over the top of the inner column.
6 Disconnect the multi pin connector on the end of the wiring harness to the ignition switch at the harness connector.
7 Undo and remove the two nuts and bolts that secure the upper column to the flexible coupling (Fig.11.18).
8 Undo and remove the two screws, plain and spring washers that secure the column to the upper support bracket.
9 Undo and remove the two locknuts, plain and spring washers that attach the column to the lower support bracket bolts.
10 Lift away the upper steering column.
11 To refit the upper steering column first engage the steering lock.
12 Centralise the steering rack by making sure the front wheels are in the straight ahead position.
13 Refitting is now the reverse sequence to removal. In addition:
a) The steering column mounting bolts should be tightened to a torque wrench setting of 14 to 18 lb ft (1.94 to 2.49 Kg fm).
b) The flexible joint coupling bolts should be tightened to a torque wrench setting of 20 to 22 lb ft (2.77 to 3.04 Kg fm).
c) If a new flexible coupling has been fitted it will be necessary to break the band that compresses the coupling. Lfit away the band.

22. Steering rack and pinion - removal and refitting

1 Refer to Chapter 12 and remove the lower facia panel.
2 Refer to Chapter 12 and remove the instrument panel.
3 Disconnect the steering column combined switch mechanism and ignition switch connections at the wiring harness multi pin connectors.
4 Undo and remove the two screws, plain and spring washers securing the steering column to the upper support bracket.
5 Undo and remove the two locknuts, plain and spring washers that secure the steering column to the lower support bracket.
6 Undo and remove the pinch bolt and nut securing the flexible joint to the steering rack pinion.
7 The steering column assembly may now be lifted away.

8 Carefully pull off the two heater rain water vent tubes from the front of the bulkhead.
9 Jack up the front of the car and support with firmly based axle stands located under the two longitudinal chassis members.
10 Undo and remove the nut that secures each tie-rod ball pin end. Using a universal ball joint separator detach the tie-rod ball pin ends from the steering levers (Fig.11.20).
11 Undo and remove the two nuts and plain washer securing each rack clamp bracket to the bulkhead. Make a note of the fitted position of the packing strip relative to the body panel. Lift away the packing strip.
12 The clamp brackets and rubber inserts may now be removed. The rubber inserts have slots cut in them to enable them to be removed from the rack tube.
13 The rack assembly may now be lifted from the car through the wheel arch opening.
14 Lift away the pinion seal from over the end of the pinion.
15 Refitting the steering rack and pinion assembly is the reverse sequence to removal. In addition:
a) Check the pinion seal and the two clamp bracket rubber inserts for signs of oil contamination or deterioration. If evident new rubbers must be obtained.
b) The rack clamp nuts should be tightened to a torque wrench setting of 20 to 22 lb ft (2.77 to 3.04 Kg fm).
c) The tie-rod ball pin nuts should be tightened to a torque wrench setting of 20 to 24 lb ft (2.77 to 3.3 Kg fm).
d) Tighten the lower flexible joint pinch bolt to a torque wrench setting of 6 to 8 lb ft (0.4 to 0.5 Kg fm).
16 It will now be necessary to check and reset the front wheel alignment. Further information will be found in Section 24.

23. Steering rack and pinion - dismantling, overhaul and re-assembly

1 Wash the outside of the rack and pinion assembly in paraffin or Gunk and wipe dry with a non-fluffy rag.
2 Slacken off the two tie-rod end locknuts and unscrew the two tie-rod ends as complete assemblies.
3 Unscrew and remove the two locknuts from the ends of the tie-rods.
4 Slacken the rack seal clips at either end of the rack assembly body. Remove the clips and two rack seals.
5 Using a small chisel carefully ease out the locknut indent from each of the ball joint housings.
6 Using two mole wrenches or one mole wrench and a soft metal drift hold the locknut and unscrew the ball joint housing from each end of the rack. Lift away the tie-rods.
7 Recover the ball cup and spring from each end of the rack.
8 Using a small chisel carefully ease out the locknut indent from the rack. Unscrew the locknuts.
9 Undo and remove the rack bearing pan head retaining screw located in the rack tube end as opposed to the pinion housing.
10 The bearing may now be removed from the rack housing.
11 Undo and remove the two bolts and spring washers that secure the rack yoke cover plate.
12 Lift away the cover plate, shims and joint washer.
13 Recover the rack support yoke from the pinion housing.
14 Remove the 'O' ring and thrust spring from the support yoke.
15 Undo and remove the two bolts and spring washers that secure the pinion end cover plate. Lift away the cover plate, shims and joint washer.
16 Carefully push out the pinion and the lower bearing. Note which way round the bearing is fitted.
17 The steering rack may now be withdrawn from the rack tube. Note which way round the rack is fitted in the rack tube.
18 Using a soft metal drift, tap out the upper pinion bearing and its washer. Note which way round the bearing is fitted.
19 Recover the pinion shaft oil seal from the pinion housing.
20 The steering rack assembly is now fully dismantled, Clean all the parts in paraffin and wipe dry with a non-fluffy rag.
21 Thoroughly inspect the rack and pinion teeth for signs of wear, cracks or damage. Check the ends of the rack for wear

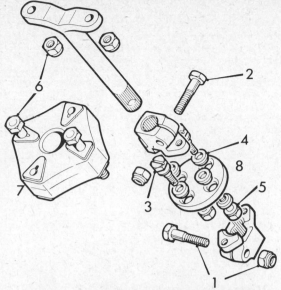

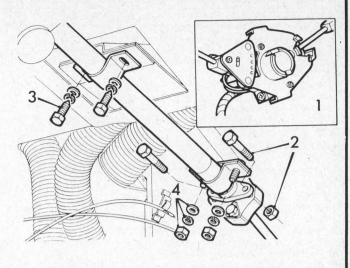

FIG.11.17. STEERING COLUMN UNIVERSAL JOINT COUPLINGS

1 Pinch bolt and locknut (upper)
2 Pinch bolt and locknut (lower)
3 Flexible joint shouldered bolt
4 Conical rubber washer
5 Plain washer
6 Flexible coupling securing locknut and bolt
7 Flexible coupling (upper)
8 Joint place

FIG.11.18. UPPER STEERING COLUMN REMOVAL

1 Combination switch
2 Upper column to flexible coupling bolt and locknut
3 Column to upper support bracket, bolt, plain and spring washer
4 Column to lower support bracket securing nuts and spring washer

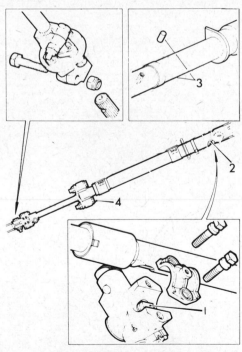

FIG.11.19. UPPER STEERING COLUMN ATTACHMENTS

1 Steering lock engagement sector
2 Slot in column
3 Steering rack centralisation
4 Lower universal coupling

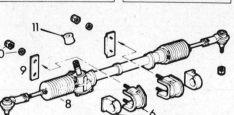

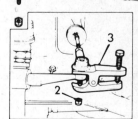

FIG.11.20. STEERING RACK REMOVAL

1 Pinch bolt and locknut
2 Tie-rod ball pin nut
3 Universal joint separator
4 Heater drain tubes
5 Rack clamp bracket packing strip
6 Rack clamp bracket
7 Rubber insert
8 Rack and pinion assembly
9 Plate
10 Bracket securing nut and spring washer
11 Pinion seal

especially where it moves in the bushes.

22 Examine the rubber gaiters for signs of cracking, perishing or other damage which if evident new gaiters must be obtained.

23 Inspect the ball ends and housings for wear which evident new parts will be necessary. Any other parts that show wear or damage must be renewed.

24 To reassemble first fit a new rack bearing into the rack housing so that the flats of the bearing are positioned offset to the bearing retaining screw hole.

25 Using a 0.119 inch (3.00 mm) diameter drill located in the retaining screw hole drill through the bearing. Clear away any swarf from the bearing and the housing.

26 Apply some non hardening oil resistant sealing compound to the brush retaining screw and refit the screw.

27 It is very important that the screw does not protrude into the bore of the bearing. Should this condition exist the end of the screw must be filed flat.

28 Fit the pinion washer to the pinion followed by the upper bearing. The thrust face must face towards the pinion washer.

29 Carefully fit the rack into the rack housing the correct way round as noted during dismantling.

30 Insert the pinion into the housing and then centralise the rack relative to the rack housing. Fit a peg into the centre location.

31 Position the pinion making sure the groove in the pinion serrations is facing and also parallel with the rack teeth.

32 Refit the lower bearing with the thrust face facing towards the pinion.

33 Replace the bearing shims and make sure that the bearing shim pack stands proud of the pinion housing. If necessary add new shims to achieve this condition.

34 Refit the pinion housing end cover but without the paper gasket. Secure in position with the two bolts and spring washers. The two bolts should only be tightened sufficiently to nip the end cover (Fig.11.20).

35 Using feeler gauges measure the gap between the pinion housing and the end cover. Make a note of this measurement.

36 Undo and remove the two pinion housing end cover securing bolts and spring washers. Lift away the end cover.

37 Adjust the number of shims in the end pack so as to obtain a 0.011 to 0.013 inch (0.279 to 0.330 mm) gap. A range of shims is available for this adjustment. Details may be found in the specifications at the beginning of this chapter.

38 It is important that the 0.060 inch (1.524 mm) shim is positioned next to the joint washer. Refit the shim pack, joint washer and end cover.

39 Apply a little non-hardening oil resistant sealing compound to the end cover securing bolts. Fit the two bolts and spring washers and tighten to a torque wrench setting of 12 to 15 lb ft (1.6 to 2.0 Kg fm).

40 Carefully fit a new pinion oil seal.

41 Replace the cover bolts and spring washers and gradually tighten these in a progressive manner whilst turning the pinion to and fro through 180° until it is just possible to rotate the pinion between the finger and thumb.

42 Using feeler gauges measure the gap between the cover and the housing (Fig.11.22).

43 Remove the cover and reassemble this time including the damper spring, a new 'O' ring oil seal and shims to the previous determined measurement plus 0.002 to 0.005 inch (0.05 to 0.13 mm).

44 Tighten the bolts that secure the yoke cover to a torque wrench setting of 12 to 15 lb ft (1.6 to 2.0 Kg fm).

45 Screw a new ball housing locknut onto each end of the rack to the limitssof the thread.

46 Insert the two thrust springs into the ends of the rack.

47 Fit each tie-rod into its ball housing and locate the ball cup against the thrust spring.

48 Slowly tighten the two ball housings until the tie-rod is just nipped.

49 Using a mole wrench and a soft metal drift carefully tighten the locknut onto the ball housing. Again check that the tie-rod is still pinched.

50 Next slacken the ball housing back by one eighth of a turn to allow full articulation of the tie-rods.

51 Fully tighten the locking ring to the housing. Whilst this is being done make sure the housing does not turn.

52 Using a centre punch or blunt chisel drive the ball housing edge of the locking ring into the locking slots of the ball housing and opposite into the locking slot of the rack.

53 Replace the two rack rubber seals and secure with the large clips to the housing. Position the two small clips and tighten on the pinion end.

54 Refit the tie-rod locknuts and then screw on each tie-rod end by an equal amount until the dimension between the two ball pin centres in 43.7 inches (110.9 cm). Tighten the locknuts sufficiently to prevent this initial setting being lost during refitting.

55 Using a squirt type oil can insert 1/3 pint (0.19 litre) of recommended grade oil through the pinion seal. Finally position the small seal clip and lightly tighten.

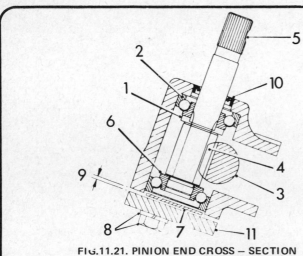

FIG.11.21. PINION END CROSS — SECTION

FIG.11.22. DAMPER COVER SHIM THICKNESS

1	Pinion washer	7	Shims
2	Upper bearing	8	Bolt and spring washer
3	Rack	9	Gap measurement
4	Pinion teeth	10	Pinion shaft oil
5	Pinion		seal
6	Lower bearing	11	End cover

1	Damper yoke	5	Damper spring
2	Shims and gasket	6	'O' ring seal
3	Cover plate	7	Gap measurement
4	Bolt and spring washer		

24. Front wheel alignment

The front wheels are correctly aligned when they are turning in at the front 1/16 inch (1.6 mm). It is important that this measurement is taken on a centre line drawn horizontally and parallel to the ground through the centre line of the hub. The exact point should be in the centre of the sidewall of the tyre and not on the wheel rim which could be distorted and therefore give inaccurate readings.

The adjustment is effected by loosening the locknut on each tie-rod ball joint and also slackening the rubber gaiter clip holding it to the tie-rod, both tie-rods then being turned equally until the adjustment is correct.

This is a job best left to a BLMC garage, as accurate alignment requires the use of special equipment. If the wheels are not in alignment, tyre wear will be heavy and uneven, and the steering be stiff and unresponsive.

25. Suspension trim height - adjustment

Before checking the front trim height of the car it must be prepared by removing the contents of the boot with the exception of the spare wheel. Ideally there should be two gallons of petrol in the tank. Check and adjust the tyre pressures as necessary. Stand the car on a level surface and measure the vertical distance between the underside of the wheel arch and the floor, this distance being taken through the centre line of the hub.

This height measurement should be 25.3/8 $\pm$ 1/4 inch (7.715 $\pm$ 0.064 mm) when the vehicle has been in service for a short while. However, if new torsion bars are fitted this dimension must be increased by 5/16 inch (7.94 mm) to allow for initial settling.

Coarse adjustment

This is applicable when there is a need to adjust the trim height by more than ¾ inch (19.05 mm) up to 1¼ inch (31.75 mm) down.

1 Apply the handbrake and chock the rear wheels. Jack up the front of the car and place on firmly based axle stands located under the front chassis members.
2 Remove the wheel trim and the road wheel.
3 Hold the upper bush housing with a mole wrench and unlock the reaction pad nut. Unscrew and remove the nut.
4 Lift away the lock washer, upper bush housing and the upper bush.
5 Undo and remove the steering track rod ball pin nut and using a universal ball joint separator detach the ball pin from the steering lever.
6 Raise the shock absorber arm and support the weight of the suspension on a wood block. The assembly must not be allowed to hang on the brake flexible hydraulic hose.
7 Mark the relative position of the torsion bar lever and car body with a scriber. Do not mark the torsion bar.
8 Ease the lever forwards out of mesh with the torsion bar splines and reposition it one spline up or down.
9 Reassembling is now the reverse sequence to removal. It will now be necessary to make the final fine adjustment.

Fine adjustment

1 Refer to Fig.11.23 and remove the adjustment lever lockbolt, spring washer and spacer.
2 Slacken the adjuster screw locknut and turn the adjuster screw in a clockwise direction to increase the trim height or anti-clockwise to decrease the trim height. Retighten the locknut.

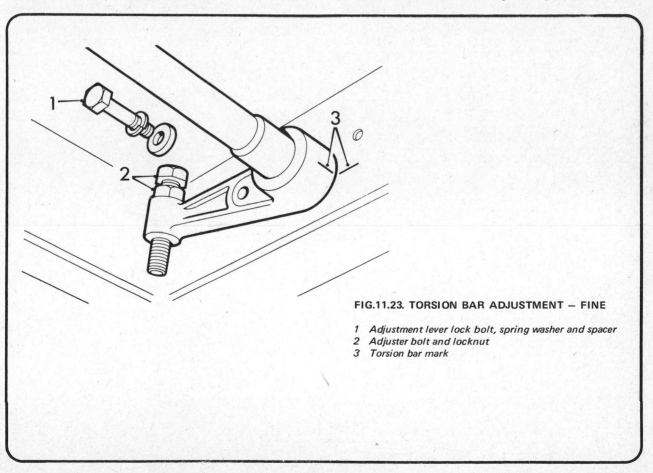

FIG.11.23. TORSION BAR ADJUSTMENT — FINE

1 Adjustment lever lock bolt, spring washer and spacer
2 Adjuster bolt and locknut
3 Torsion bar mark

Suspension and steering gear fault diagnosis is given overleaf (Page 162)

Symptom	Reason/s	Remedy
STEERING FEELS VAGUE, CAR WANDERS AND FLOATS AT SPEED		
General wear or damage	Tyre pressures uneven	Check pressures and adjust as necessary.
	Shock absorbers worn	Test, and replace if worn.
	Steering gear ball joints badly worn	Fit new ball joints.
	Suspension geometry incorrect	Check and rectify.
	Steering mechanism free play excessive	Adjust or overhaul steering mechanism.
	Front suspension and rear suspension pick-up points out of alignment or badly worn	Normally caused by poor repair work after a serious accident. Extensive rebuilding necessary.
	Front suspension lacking grease	Check condition and grease or replace worn parts and re-grease.
STIFF AND HEAVY STEERING		
Lack of maintenance or accident damage	Tyre pressures too low	Check pressures and inflate tyres.
	No grease in steering rack	Top up steering rack.
	No grease in steering ball joints	Replace.
	Front wheel toe-in incorrect	Check and reset toe-in.
	Suspension geometry incorrect	Check and rectify.
	Steering gear incorrectly adjusted too tightly	Check and re-adjust steering gear.
	Steering column badly misaligned	Determine cause and rectify (usually due to bad repair after severe accident damage and difficult to correct).
WHEEL WOBBLE AND VIBRATION		
General wear or damage	Wheel nuts loose	Check and tighten as necessary.
	Front wheels and tyres out of balance	Balance wheels and tyres and add weights as necessary.
	Steering ball joints badly worn	Replace steering gear ball joints.
	Hub bearings badly worn	Remove and fit new hub bearings.
	Steering gear free play excessive	Adjust and overhaul steering gear.
	Front torsion bars weak or broken	Inspect and renew as necessary.

Chapter 12 Bodywork and underframe

Contents

1. General description

The combined body and underframe is of all welded stell construction. This makes a very strong and torsionally rigid shell.

The Marina 1.3 is either two door or four door. The door hinges are securely bolted to both the doors and body. The drivers door is locked from the outside by means of a key and all other doors may be locked from the inside.

The toughened safety glass is fitted to all windows; the windscreen has a specially toughened 'zone' in front of the driver. In the event of the windscreen shattering this 'zone' breaks into much larger pieces than the rest of the screen thus giving the driver much better vision than would otherwise be possible.

The front seats are of the adjustable bucket type whilst the rear seat is a bench seat, without a central arm rest.

For occupant safety all switches and controls are suitably recessed or positioned so that they cannot cause body harm. Provision is made for the fitting of either static or automatic seat belts.

The instruments are contained in two dials located above the steering column. A heater and ventilation system is fitted incorporating a full flow system with outlet ducts at instrument panel level.

2. Maintenance - body and chassis

1   The condition of the bodywork is of considerable importance as it is on this in the main that the second-hand value of the car will mainly depend. It is much more difficult to repair neglected bodywork than to renew mechanical assemblies. The hidden portions of the body, such as the wheel arches, the underframe and the engine compartment are equally important, although obviously not requiring such frequent attention as the immediately visible paintwork.

2   Once a year, or every 12,000 miles, it is advisable to visit a garage equipped to steam clean the body. This will take about 1½ hours. All traces of dirt and oil will be removed and the underside can then be inspected carefully for rust, damaged hydraulic pipes, frayed electrical wiring and similar maladies. The car should

be greased on completion of this job.

3   At the same time the engine compartment should be cleaned in a similar manner. If steam cleaning facilities are not available, then brush 'Gunk' or a similar cleaner over the whole of the engine, and engine compartment, with a stiff brush, working it well in where there is an accumulation of oil and dirt. Do not paint the ignition system, and protect it with oily rags when the 'Gunk' is washed off. As the 'Gunk' is washed away it will take with it all traces of oil and dirt, leaving the engine looking clean and bright.

4   The wheel arches should be given particular attention, as under sealing can easily come away here, and stones and dirt thrown up from the road wheels can soon cause the paint to chip and flake, and so allow rust to set in. If rust is found, clean down the bare metal with wet and dry paper. Paint on an anti-corrosive coating such as 'Kurust', or if preferred red lead, and renew the undercoating and top coat.

5   The bodywork should be washed once a week or when dirty. Thoroughly wet the car to soften the dirt, and then wash the car down with a soft sponge and plenty of clean water. If the surplus dirt is not washed off very gently it will in time wear the paint as surely as wet and dry paper. It is best to use a hose if this is available. Give the car a final wash down and then dry with a soft chamois leather to prevent the formation of spots.

6   Spots of tar and grease thrown up from the road can be removed by a rag dampened in petrol.

7   Once every three months, give the bodywork and chromium trim a thoroughly good wax polish. If a chromium cleaner is used to remove rust on any of the cars plated parts, remember that and cleaner also removes part of the chromium so use only when absolutely necessary.

3. Maintenance - upholstery and carpets

1   Remove the carpets or mats, and thoroughly vacuum clean the interior of the car every three months, or more frequently if necessary.

2   Beat out the carpets and vacuum clean them if they are very dirty. If the upholstery is soiled apply an upholstery cleaner with a damp sponge and wipe off with a clean dry cloth.

4. Body repairs - minor

1   Major damage must be repaired by a specialist body repair shop but there is no reason why you cannot successfully beat out, repair, and re-spray minor damage yourself. The essential items which the owner should gather together to ensure a really professional job are:—
a) A plastic filler such as Holts 'Cataloy'.
b) Paint whose colour matches exactly that of the bodywork, either in a can for application by a spray gun, or in an aerosol can.
c) Fine cutting paste.
d) Medium and fine grade wet and dry paper.

2   Never use a metal hammer to knock out small dents as the blows tend to scratch and distort the metal. Knock out the dent with a mallet or rawhide hammer and press on the underside of the dented surface a metal dolly or smooth wooden block roughly contoured to the normal shape of the damaged area.

3   After the worst of the damaged area has been knocked out, rub down the dent and surrounding area with medium wet and dry paper and thoroughly clean away all traces of dirt.

4   The plastic filler comprises a paste and hardener which must be thoroughly mixed together. Mix only a small portion at a time as the paste sets hard within five to fifteen minutes depending on the amount of hardener used.

5   Smooth on the filler with a knife or stiff plastic to the shape of the damaged portion and allow to thoroughly dry — a process which takes about six hours. After the filler has dried it is likely that it will have contracted slightly so spread on a second layer of filler if necessary.

6   Smooth down the filler with fine wet and dry paper wrapped round a suitable block of wood and continue until the whole area is perfectly smooth and it is impossible to feel where the filler joins the rest of the paintwork.

7   Spray on from an aerosol can, or with a spray gun, an anti-rust undercoat, smooth down with wet and dry paper and then spray on two coats of the final finishing using a circular motion.

8   When thoroughly dry polish the whole area with a fine cutting paste to smooth the re-sprayed areas into the remainder of the of the wing and to remove the small particles of spray paint which will have settled round the area.

9   This will leave the wing looking perfect with not a trace of the previous dent.

5. Body repairs - major

1   Because the body is built on the monocoque principle and is integral with the underframe, major damage must be repaired by specialists with the necessary welding and hydraulic straightening equipment.

2   If the damage is severe, it is vital that on completion of the repair the chassis is in correct alignment. Less severe damage may also have twisted or distorted the chassis although this may not be visible immediately. It is therefore always best on completion of repair to check for twist and squareness to make sure all is well.

3   To check for twist, position the car on a clean level floor, place a jack under each jacking point, raise the car and take off the wheels. Raise or lower the jacks until the sills are parallel with the ground. Depending where the damage occurred, using an accurate scale, take measurements at the suspension mounting points and if comparable readings are not obtained it is an indication that the body is twisted.

4   After checking for twist, check for squareness by taking a series of measurements on the floor. Drop a plumb line and bob weight from various mounting points on the underside of the body and mark these points on the floor with chalk. Draw a straight line between each point and measure and mark the middle of each line. A line drawn on the floor starting at the front and finishing at the rear should be quite straight and pass through the centres of the other lines. Diagonal measurements can also be made as a check for squareness.

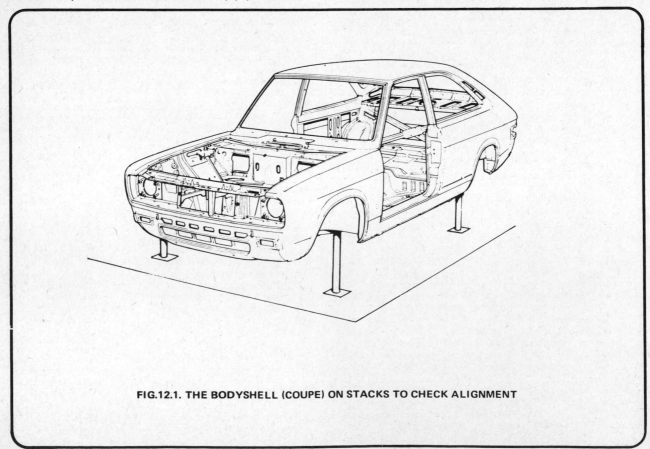

FIG.12.1. THE BODYSHELL (COUPE) ON STACKS TO CHECK ALIGNMENT

6. Maintenance - locks and hinges

Once every 6,000 miles (10,000 Km) or 6 months the door, bonnet and boot hinges should be oiled with a few drops of engine oil from an oil can. The door striker plates can be given a thin smear of grease to reduce wear and ensure free movement.

7. Door rattles - tracing and rectification

The most common cause of door rattles is a misaligned, loose or worn striker plate but other causes may be:
1) Loose door handles, window winder handles or door hinges.
2) Loose, worn or misaligned door lock components.
3) Loose or worn remote control mechanism.
Or an combination of these.
2 If the striker catch is worn as a result of door rattles renew it and adjust as described later in this Chapter.
3 Should the hinges be badly worn then they must be renewed.

8. Door - removal and refitting

1 Refer to Section 10 and remove the door trim panel.
2 Working inside the door mark the outline of the stiffener plate at each hinge position (Fig.12.2). An assistant should now take the weight of the door.
3 Undo and remove the locknuts and plain washers that secure the door to the hinge.
4 Lift away the stiffener plates and finally the door.
5 Refitting the door is the reverse sequence to removal. Should it be necessary to adjust the position of the door in the aperture leave the locknuts slightly loose and reposition the door by trial and error. Fully tighten the locknuts.

9. Door hinge - removal and refitting

1 Refer to Section 22 and remove the front parcel tray.
2 Using a wide blade screwdriver carefully ease back the side trim panel door seal and then the trim panel.
3 If the rear door hinges are to be removed, using a wide blade screwdriver ease back the 'B' post door seals. Undo and remove the carpet finisher retaining screws, slide the front seat forward and ease the trim panel retaining clips from the 'B' post. Hinge the trim panel up at the PVC lining crease. This will give access to the door hinge retaining nuts.
4 Undo and remove the locknuts and plain washers securing each hinge (Fig.12.2). Lift away the stiffener plates and finally the door hinges.
5 Refitting the door hinge is the reverse sequence to removal.

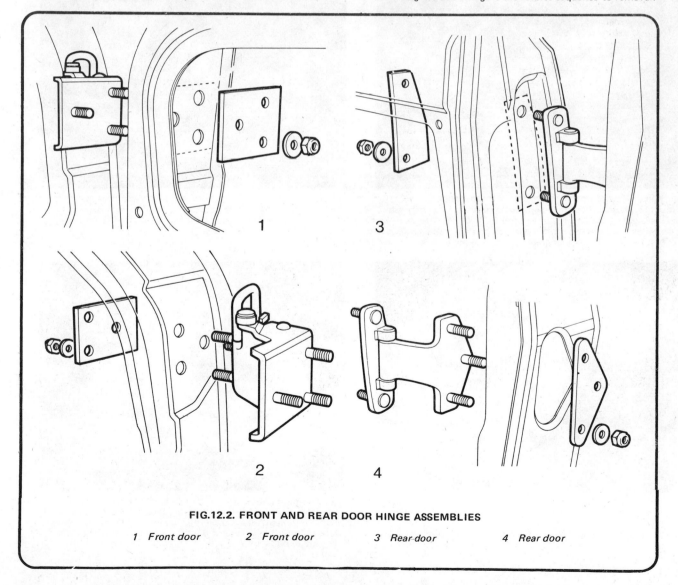

FIG.12.2. FRONT AND REAR DOOR HINGE ASSEMBLIES

| 1 Front door | 2 Front door | 3 Rear door | 4 Rear door |

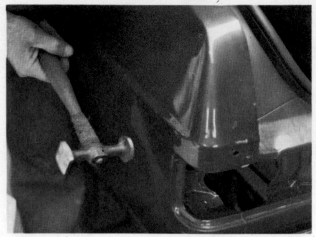

This sequence of photographs deals with the repair of the dent and scratch (above rear lamp) shown in this photo. The procedure will be similar for the repair of a hole. It should be noted that the procedures given here are simplified - more explicit instructions will be found in the text

In the case of a dent the first job - after removing surrounding trim - is to hammer out the dent where access is possible. This will minimise filling. Here, the large dent having been hammered out, the damaged area is being made slightly concave

Now all paint must be removed from the damaged area, by rubbing with coarse abrasive paper. Alternatively, a wire brush or abrasive pad can be used in a power drill. Where the repair area meets good paintwork, the edge of the paintwork should be 'feathered', using a finer grade of abrasive paper

In the case of a hole caused by rusting, all damaged sheet-metal should be cut away before proceeding to this stage. Here, the damaged area is being treated with rust remover and inhibitor before being filled

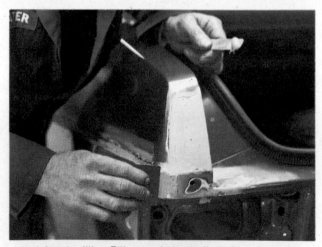

Mix the body filler according to its manufacturer's instructions. In the case of corrosion damage, it will be necessary to block off any large holes before filling - this can be done with zinc gauze or aluminium tape. Make sure the area is absolutely clean before ...

... applying the filler. Filler should be applied with a flexible applicator, as shown, for best results: the wooden spatula being used for confined areas. Apply thin layers of filler at 20-minute intervals, until the surface of the filler is slightly proud of the surrounding bodywork

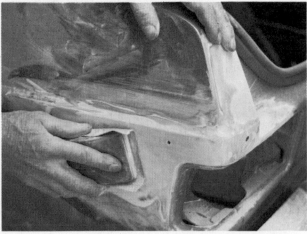

Initial shaping can be done with a Surform plane or Dreadnought file. Then, using progressively finer grades of wet-and-dry paper, wrapped around a sanding block, and copious amounts of clean water, rub-down the filler until really smooth and flat. Again, feather the edges of adjoining paintwork

The whole repair area can now be sprayed or brush-painted with primer. If spraying, ensure adjoining areas are protected from over-spray. Note that at least one-inch of the surrounding sound paintwork should be coated with primer. Primer has a 'thick' consistency, so will fill small imperfections

Again, using plenty of water, rub down the primer with a fine grade of wet-and-dry paper (400 grade is probably best) until it is really smooth and well blended into the surrounding paintwork. Any remaining imperfections can now be filled by carefully applied knifing stopper paste

When the stopper has hardened, rub-down the repair area again before applying the final coat of primer. Before rubbing-down this last coat of primer, ensure the repair area is blemish-free - use more stopper if necessary. To ensure that the surface of the primer is really smooth use some finishing compound

The top coat can now be applied. When working out of doors, pick a dry, warm and wind-free day. Ensure surrounding areas are protected from over-spray. Agitate the aerosol thoroughly, then spray the centre of the repair area, working outwards with a circular motion. Apply the paint as several thin coats.

After a period of about two-weeks, which the paint needs to harden fully, the surface of the repaired area can be 'cut' with a mild cutting compound prior to wax polishing. When carrying out bodywork repairs, remember that the quality of the finished job is proportional to the time and effort expended

10. Door trim panel and capping - removal and refitting

1 Wind the window up fully and note the position of the handle.
2 Undo and remove the screw and spacer that secures the window regulator handle. Lift away the handle (Fig.12.3).
3 Undo and remove the two screws that retain the arm rest. Lift away the arm rest.
4 With a screwdriver carefully slide the upper and lower bezels from the remote control door handle.
5 With a wide blade screwdriver or knife inserted between the trim panel and door carefully ease the trim panel clips from the door. Lift away the trim panel.
6 Should it be necessary to remove the trim capping, undo and remove the screws and shaped washers and unclip the trim capping from the door.
7 Refitting is the reverse sequence to removal. If the capping has been removed make sure that the door glass seal and wiper strip are correctly positioned.

11. Door exterior handle - removal and refitting

1 It is important to check that if the door lock is not operating correctly that the cause is not due to maladjustment. Full information on this will be found in Section 12.
2 Refer to Section 10 and remove the door trim.
3 Undo and remove the two nuts or screws, plain and shakeproof washers that secure the clamp bracket. Lift away the

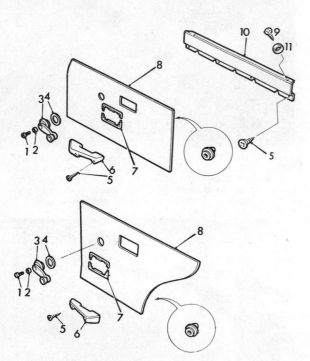

FIG.12.3. DOOR TRIM PANEL AND CAPPING

1	Screw	7	Upper and lower
2	Spacer		bezel
3	Window regulator handle	8	Trim panel
4	Bezel	9	Screw
5	Screw	10	Coupling
6	Arm rest	11	Shaped washer

clamp bracket.
4 Front door: Disconnect the private lock control rod clip from the locking bar cross shaft. Carefully unclip and detach the screwed rod at the exterior handle release lever.
5 Rear door only: Disconnect the screwed rod at the cross lever but do not alter the rod adjustment.
6 Lift away the handle assembly.
7 Refitting is the reverse sequence to removal. Lubricate all moving parts with Castrol GTX.

12. Door lock adjustment

Four adjustments may be made to the door locks and it will usually be found that any malfunction of a lock is caused by incorrect adjustment.

Exterior handle
1 Refer to Section 10 and remove the trim panel.
2 Close the door and partially operate the exterior release lever. Check that there is free movement of the lever before the point is reached where the transfer lever and its screwed rod move.
3 Operate the exterior release lever fully and check that the latch disc is released from the door striker before the lever is fully open.
4 To adjust, disconnect the screwed rod and screw in or out to achieve the correct setting.

Remote control
1 Refer to Section 10 and remove the trim panel.
2 Undo and remove the screw and slacken the control retaining screws.
3 Move the remote control assembly towards the latch unit. Retighten the retaining screws and make sure that the operating lever is against its stop 'A' (Fig.12.4 or 12.5).

Safety locking lever
Refer to Section 10 and remove the trim panel.

Front
1 Disconnect the long lock rod from the safety locking lever and then the short rod from the locking bar. Push the locking bar against its stop 'B' and move the safety locking lever to the locked position.
2 Refit the long rod in the safety locking lever and then press in the legs of the clip. Adjust the short rod so as to fit into the rod bush in the locking bar.
3 Release the safety locking lever and make sure that the operating lever is quite free to operate.

Rear
1 Disconnect the long lock rod from the safety locking lever and then the short lock rod from the locking lever.
2 Press the free wheeling operating lever against the stop 'D' and position the safety locking lever in the locked position.
3 Reconnect the long lock rod to the safety locking lever. Push in the legs of the clip and adjust the short rod to fit into the rod bush in the locking lever.
4 Release the safety locking lever and ensure that the operating tab aligns with the striker pin of the latch disc release lever.

Door striker
1 It is very important that the latch disc is in the open position. Also do not slam the door whilst any adjustment is being made otherwise damage may result.
2 Slacken the striker plate retaining screws until it is just sufficient to allow the door to close and latch.
3 Push the door inwards or pull it outwards without operating the release lever until the door is level with the body door aperture.
4 Open the door carefully and with a pencil round the striker plate to act as a datum.
5 Place the striker accurately by trial and error until the door can be closed easily without signs of lifting, dropping or rattling.
6 Close the door and make sure that the striker is not positioned too far in by pressing on the door. It should be possible to press the door in slightly as the seals are compressed.
7 Finally tighten the striker plate retaining screws.

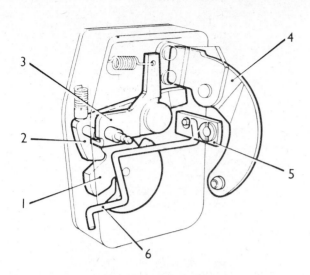
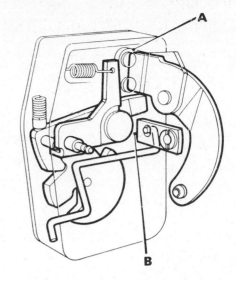

FIG.12.4. FRONT DOOR LOCK MECHANISM

1 Latch disc	lever	4 Operating lever	6 Locking bar cross
2 Latch disc release	3 Cross control lever	5 Locking bar	shaft

Positive stop A
Positive stop B

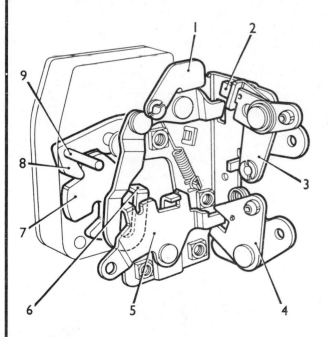
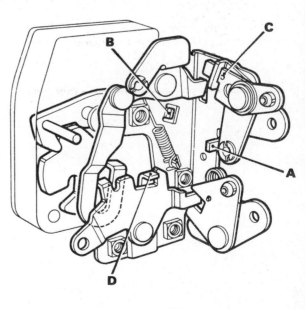

FIG.12.5. REAR DOOR LOCK MECHANISM

1 Corss-lever	3 Operating lever	lever	8 Latch disc release
2 Child safety inter-	4 Locking lever	6 Operating tab	lever
mediate lever	5 Free-wheeling actuating	7 Latch disc	9 Striker pin

Positive stop B and C
Positive stop A
Positive stop D

13. Door remote control handle - removal and refitting

It is important to check that if the door lock is not operating correctly that the cause is not due to maladjustment. Full information on this will be found in Section 12.

2 Refer to Section 10 and remove the door trim.

3 Undo and remove the three screws, shakeproof and plain washers that secure the remote control.

4 Undo and remove the lock screw.

5 Detach the long remote control lock rod from the safety locking lever.

6 Detach the remote control release rod from the operating lever.

7 Lift away the remote control assembly.

8 Front door only : Undo and remove the screw and plain washer that secures the glass channel. Detach the exterior handle transfer lever from the lifting stud of the cross control lever.

9 Rear door only: Detach the exterior handle screwed rod from the cross lever.

10 Detach the remote control release rod from the operating lever of the disc lock front door or free wheel assembly — rear door.

11 Detach the lock rod clip from the lock bar cross shaft.

12 Front door only: Detach the short lock rod from the locking bar.

13 Rear door only: Detach the short lock rod from the free wheel locking lever.

14 Using a pencil mark the position of the disc latch body on the door. Undo and remove the four screws that secure the disc latch and the free wheel from the rear door.

15 With a pencil mark the position of the door pillar and remove the two screws retaining the striker plate assembly. The striker plate may now be lifted away. The tapped stiffener plate is retained inside the door 'B' post by fan retaining tags.

16 Refitting the door remote control assembly is the reverse sequence to removal. Lubricate all moving parts with Castrol GTX.

14. Door private lock - removal and refitting

1 Refer to Section 11 and remove the door exterior handle.

2 Using a small screwdriver carefully remove the circlip and lift away the spring and special washers (Fig.12.8).

3 The lock barrel may now be removed.

4 Refitting is the reverse sequence to removal.

15. Door glass - removal and refitting

1 Refer to Section 10 and remove the door trim.

2 Lower the window until the glass regulator channel appears in the door inner panel aperture.

3 Undo and remove the four screws and spring washers that secure the regulator and lift away the regulator and lift away the regulator (Fig.12.9).

4 Front door: Carefully lower the glass to the bottom of the door.

5 Rear door: Raise the glass fully.

6 If the capping is fitted this should next be removed. Undo and remove the screws and shaped washers. Unclip the trim capping from the door.

7 Using a screwdriver carefully so as not to damage the paintwork spring off the six clips that retain the glass wiper strip. Lift away the wiper strip.

8 Carefully remove the window channel rubber by easing it out of the door glass aperture.

9 Using a drill of suitable diameter remove the 'pop' rivet that retains the top of the centre window channel.

10 Undo and remove the screw and plain washer that retains the bottom of the centre window channel.

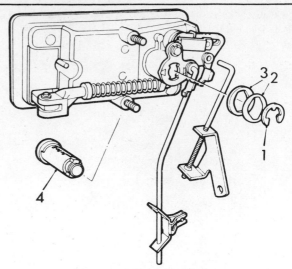

FIG.12.8. DOOR PRIVATE LOCK ASSEMBLY REMOVAL

1 Circlip	3 Shaped washer
2 Spring washer	4 Lock barrel

11 The window channel may now be removed by turning it through 90° and aligning the narrowest section with the glass aperture in the door.

12 Remove the door fixed or opening quarter light, whichever is fitted, and its sealing rubber.

13 The window glass may now be lifted out of the glass aperture.

14 Finally remove the regulator channel and its protective rubber from the glass.

15 Refitting the door glass is the reverse sequence to removal. If a new glass is to be fitted make sure that the regulator channel is refitted centrally on the door glass. Lubricate all moving parts with Castrol GTX.

16. Bonnet - removal and refitting

1 Open the bonnet and support on its stay.

2 With a pencil mark the outline of the hinge on the bonnet to assist correct refitting. If the hinge is to be removed also mark the inner panel as well.

3 An assistant should now take the weight of the bonnet. Undo and remove the bonnet to hinge retaining bolts, spring and plain washers at both hinges. Carefully lift away the bonnet over the front of the car (Fig.12.10).

4 Refitting is the reverse sequence to removal. Alignment in the body may be made by leaving the securing bolts slightly loose and repositioning by trial and error. The securing bolts must not be overtightened as they could damage the outer bonnet panel.

17. Bonnet lock - removal and refitting

1 Open the bonnet and support it on its stay.

2 Slacken the nut and detach the release cable from the trunnion located at the lock lever (Fig.12.11).

3 Detach the release cable and its clip from the bonnet lock.

4 Undo and remove the three bolts, plain and shakeproof washers securing the bonnet lock. Lift away the bonnet lock.

5 Undo and remove the two bolts, plain and shakeproof washers that secure the locking pin assembly to the underside of the bonnet.

6 Detach the return spring and remove the rivet that secures the safety catch.

7 Refitting is the reverse sequence to removal. It is now necessary to adjust the lock pin assembly until a clearance of 2 inches (50.8 mm) exists ('A' Fig.12.11) between the thimble and bonnet panel.

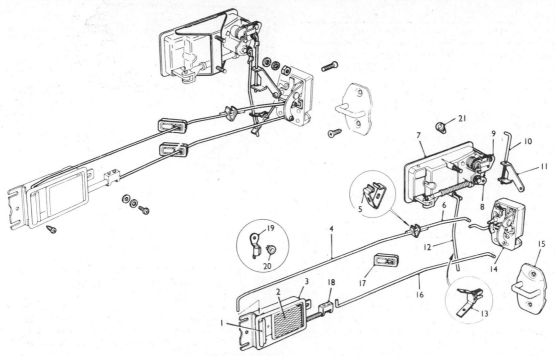

FIG.12.6. FRONT DOOR LOCK COMPONENT PARTS

1	Safety locking lever	7	Outside handle
2	Remote release handle	8	Lock barrel free-wheel lever
3	Remote control assembly	9	Outside handle release lever
4	Remote lock rod-long	10	Screwed rod
5	Remote lock rod clip	11	Transfer lever
6	Remote lock rod - short		
12	Lock rod (outside handle)	17	Door rod guide
13	Lock rod clip	18	Retaining clip
14	Disc lock assembly	19	Rod clip
15	Lock striker	20	Rod bush
16	Remote release rod	21	Rod bush (cross control lever)

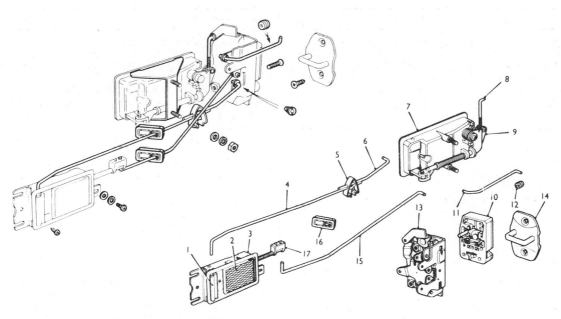

FIG.12.7. REAR DOOR LOCK COMPONENT PARTS

1	Safety locking lever	6	Remote lock rod - short
2	Remote release lever	7	Outside handle
3	Remote control assembly	8	Screwed rod
4	Remote lock rod-long	9	Outside handle release lever
5	Remote lock rod clip	10	Disc lock assembly
		11	Child safety lever rod
		12	Door grommet
		13	Free-wheel assembly
14	Lock striker		
15	Remote release rod		
16	Door rod guide		
17	Retaining clip		
18	Rod bush		

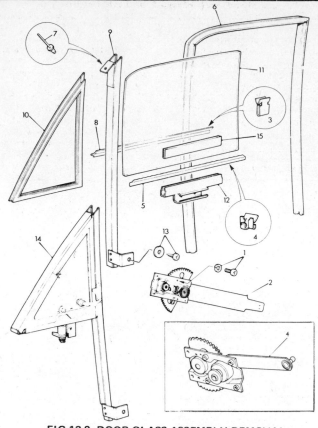

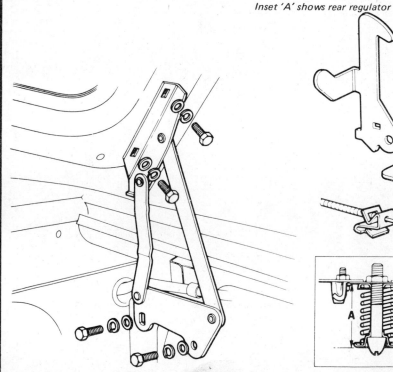

FIG.12.9. DOOR GLASS ASSEMBLY REMOVAL

1	Regulator securing bolt and spring washer	
2	Regulator	
3	Clip	
4	Clip	
5	Glass wiper strip	
6	Window channel rubber	
7	'Pop' rivet	
8	Glass outer weatherstrip	
9	Window channel	
10	Quarter light sealing rubber	
11	Door glass	
12	Regulator channel	
13	Channel securing screw and plain washer	
14	Opening quarter light assembly	
15	Protective rubber	

Inset 'A' shows rear regulator

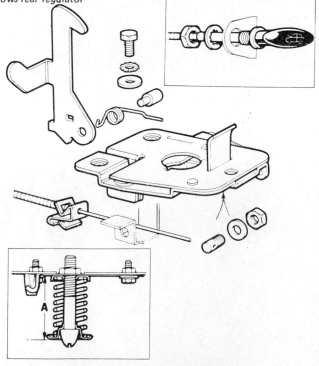

FIG.12.10. BONNET HINGE ASSEMBLY   **FIG.12.11. BONNET LOCK ASSEMBLY**

8 Carefully lower the bonnet and check the alignment of the pin thimble with the lock hole. If misaligned slacken the fixing bolts and move the assembly slightly. Retighten the fixing bolts.
9 Close the bonnet and check its alignment with the body wing panels. If necessary reposition the lock pin assembly.
10 The bonnet must contact the rubber stops. To adjust the position of the stops screw in or out as necessary.
11 Lubricate all moving parts and finally check the bonnet release operation.

18. Bonnet lock control cable - removal and refitting

1 Open the bonnet and support on its stay.
2 Slacken the nut and detach the release cable from the trunnion located at the lock lever (Fig.12.11).
3 Detach the release cable and its clip from the bonnet lock.
4 Release the outer control cable from its snap clamp and then unscrew and remove the screw that secures each clip to the wing valance. Lift away the two clips.
5 Undo and remove the nut and shakeproof washer that secures the outer cable to the body side bracket mounted below the facia panel.
6 Carefully withdraw the control cable assembly through the body grommet.
7 Refitting is the reverse sequence to removal. It is however, necessary to adjust the inner cable. Push the release knob in fully and make sure that the lock release lever is not pre-loaded by the release cable.
8 There must be a minimum movement of 0.5 in. (12.7 mm) prior to the release of the bonnet. To adjust, slacken the cable trunnion nut and re-adjust the cable so that the bonnet is released within 0.5 to 2.0 in. (12.7 to 50.8 mm) of cable movement.

19. Boot lid hinge - removal and refitting

1 Open the lid and using a pencil mark the position of the hinge relative to the luggage compartment lid.
2 Undo and remove the four bolts, spring and plain washers that secure the hinges to the lid. Lift away the lid over the back of the car. For this operation it is desirable to have the assistance of a second person.
3 To remove a hinge undo and remove the two nuts, plain and spring washers that secure each hinge to the body bracket. Lift away the hinge (Fig.12.12).
4 Refitting is the reverse sequence to removal but if adjustment is necessary leave the bolts securing the hinge to the lid slack.
5 Close the lid and adjust the position to ensure correct trim spacing. Open the lid and tighten the hinge bolts. Do not over-tighten as they could damage the outer lid panel.

20. Boot lid lock - removal and refitting

1 Using a pencil mark the outline of the lock catch plate on the lid under panel.
2 Undo and remove the three bolts, spring and plain washers that secure the lock catch (Fig.12.13).
3 Slacken the locknut and unscrew the spindle. Lift away the shakeproof washer, spindle striker and spring.
4 Break off the two retaining ears of the barrel housing spring retaining clip using a screwdriver and withdraw the barrel assembly and sealing gasket from outside the lid. A new clip will be necessary during reassembly.
5 Using a pencil mark the outline of the striker on the body panel.
6 Undo and remove the two bolts, spring and plain washers retaining the striker. Lift away the striker.
7 Refitting is the reverse sequence to removal. Lubricate all moving parts with Castrol GTX.

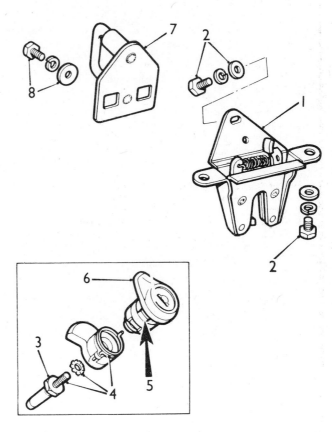

FIG.12.13. BOOT LOCK ASSEMBLY

1 Lock catch plate	5 Barrel housing spring
2 Bolt, spring and plain washer	6 Lock barrel assembly
3 Locknut	7 Striker
4 Shakeproof washer, spindle and spring	8 Bolt, spring and plain washer

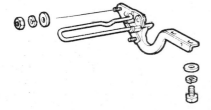

FIG.12.12. BOOT LID HINGE

21. Windscreen and rear window glass - removal and refitting

If you are unfortunate enough to have a windscreen shatter, fitting a replacement windscreen is one of the few jobs which the average owner is advised to leave to a professional. For the owner who wishes to do the job himself the following instructions are given:

1   Remove the wiper arms from their spindles using a screwdriver to lift the retaining clip from the spindle end and pull away.

2   Using a screwdriver very carefully prise up the end of the finisher strip and withdraw it from its slot in the rubber moulding (Fig.12.14).

3   The assistance of a second person should now be enlisted, ready to catch the glass when it is released from its aperture.

4   Working inside the car, commencing at one top corner, press the glass and ease it from its rubber moulding.

5   Remove the rubber moulding from the windscreen aperture.

6   Now is the time to remove all pieces of glass if the screen has shattered. Use a vacuum cleaner to extract as much as possible. Switch on the heater boots motor and adjust the controls to 'Screen defrost' but watch out for flying pieces of glass which might be blown out of the ducting.

7   Carefully inspect the rubber moulding for signs of splitting or deterioration. Clean all traces of sealing compound from the rubber moulding and windscreen aperture flange.

8   To refit the glass, first apply sealer between the rubber and glass.

9   Press a little 'Dum Dum' onto four or five inches of the body flange on either side of each corner.

10 Apply some 'Bostik' mastic sealer to the body flange.

11 With the rubber moulding correctly positioned on the glass it is now necessary to insert a piece of cord about 16 ft long all round the outer channel in the rubber surround which fits over the windscreen aperture flange. The two free ends of the cord should finish at either top of bottom centre and overlap each other by a minimum of 1 ft.

12 Offer the screen up to the aperture and get an assistant to press the rubber surround hard against the body flange. Slowly pull one end of the cord moving round the windscreen so drawing the lip over the windscreen flange on the body. If necessary use a piece of plastic or tapered wood to assist in locating the lip on the windscreen flange.

13 The finisher strip must next be fitted to the moulding and for this a special tool is required. An illustration of this tool is shown in Fig.12.14 and a handyman should be able to make up an equivalent using netting wire and a wooden file handle.

14 Fit the eye of the tool into the groove and feed in the finisher strip.

15 Push the tool around the complete length of the moulding, feeding the finisher into the channel as the eyelet opens it. The back half beds the finisher into the moulding.

16 Clean off traces of sealer using turpentine.

22. Parcel tray - removal and refitting

1   Refer to Fig.12.15 and undo and remove the screw and plain washer.

2   Undo and remove the nut, shakeproof washer, bolt and plain washer.

3   Remove the parcel tray from the inside of the car taking care not to damage the headlining or interior trim.

4   Refitting the parcel tray is the reverse sequence to removal.

23. Facia panel - removal and refitting

1   Refer to Section 32 and remove the instrument panel.

2   Refer to Section 25 and remove the glovebox.

3   Refer to Section 24 and remove the lower facia panel.

4   Undo and remove the six nuts, spring and plain washers that secure the facia to the windscreen lower panel (Fig.12.16).

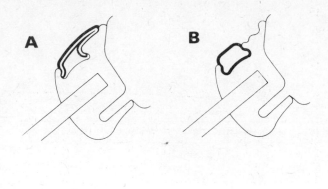

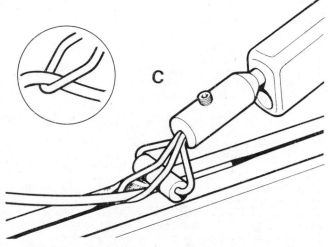

FIG.12.14. GLASS REMOVAL AND REFITTING

A and B Profile of two types of finisher strip in place
C Type of tool necessary to replace finisher

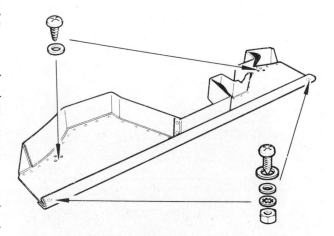

FIG.12.15. PARCEL SHELF ATTACHMENTS

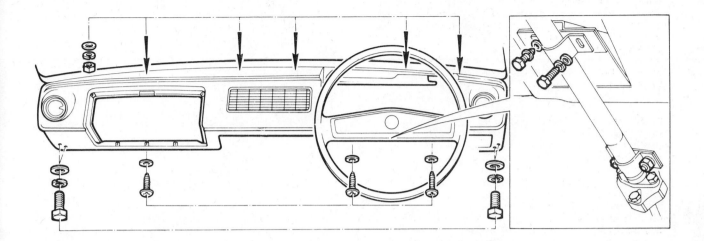

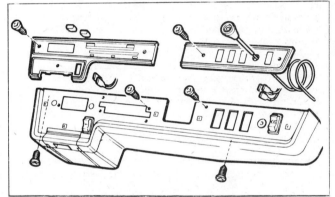

FIG.12.16. FACIA PANEL ASSEMBLY

Inset: Lower facia panel assembly

5 Undo and remove the three bolts that secure the facia panel to the lower rail.

6 Undo and remove the four bolts, plain and spring washers that secure the two outer brackets to the lower rail.

7 Undo and remove the two bolts, spring and plain washers that secure the upper steering column bracket.

8 Slacken the two nuts that secure the lower steering column bracket and remove the facia panel from the inside of the car taking care not to damage the headlining or interior trim.

9 Refitting the facia panel is the reverse sequence to removal.

24. Lower facia panel - removal and refitting

1 Open the bonnet and slacken the choke control cable clamp at the carburettor. Detach the control cable and pull out the choke control knob and inner cable.

2 Undo and remove the two self tapping screws that secure the right hand switch trim panel. Lift away the panel.

3 Undo and remove the three self tapping screws that secure the left hand switch trim panel. Lift away the panel.

4 Undo and remove the two screws that secure the heater controls.

5 Undo and remove the three screws that retain the facia lower panel.

6 Undo and remove the two self tapping screws that secure the facia lower panel brackets to the upper facia panel.

7 Carefully draw the panel forwards and make a note of the electrical cable connections at the rear of the heater and lighting switches. Detach the cable connectors from the rear of the switches.

8 The choke control outer cable and facia lower panel may now be lifted away from the inside of the car.

9 Refitting is the reverse sequence to removal.

25. Glovebox - removal and refitting

1 Open the glovebox lid. Undo and remove the three screws that secure the hinge and lower the lid (Fig.12.17).

2 Undo and remove the two screws that retain the glovebox compartment. Lift away the glovebox.

3 Undo and remove the two screws that secure the glovebox lid catch. Lift away the catch and spacer plates.

4 Refitting is the reverse sequence to removal.

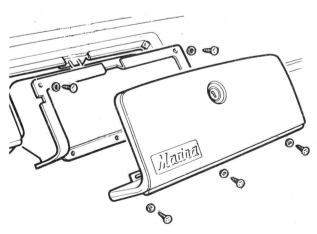

FIG.12.17. GLOVEBOX LID

26. Bumpers - removal and refitting

Front

1 Refer to Fig.12.18 and undo and remove the bolt, spring and plain washer and mounting rubber from each end of the bumper.
2 Undo and remove the bolts, spring and plain washer that secures each support bracket to the body.
3 Lift away the front bumper assembly.
4 Undo and remove the bolts, spring and plain washers securing each bracket to the bumper.
5 Refitting is the reverse sequence to removal.

Rear

The sequence for removing the rear bumper is basically identical to that for the front bumper with the exception that before the bumper support brackets are released, the electric cables to the number plate light must be disconnected.

27. Radiator grille - removal and refitting

1 Refer to Fig.12.19 and undo and remove the four self tapping screws and plain washers that secure the case to the body.
2 The grille and case may now be lifted upwards and forwards away from the front of the car.
3 To detach the grille from the case undo and remove the self-tapping screws and the plain washers.
4 Refitting is the reverse sequence to removal. Make sure that the rubber inserts are correctly positioned in the body panel cut-out and the locating pegs of the case are located in the centre of the rubber inserts.

28. Heater unit - removal and refitting

1 Refer to Section 24 and remove the lower facia panel.
2 Refer to Section 32 and remove the instrument panel.
3 Detach the demister duct tubes from the heater.
4 Refer to Chapter 2, Section 2 and completely drain the cooling system.

5 Slacken the two heater hose clips located at the front of the bulkhead and remove the two hoses (Fig.12.20).
6 Pull off the two plenum chamber drain tubes located at the front of the bulkhead.
7 Undo and remove the nut and spring washer that holds the top of the heater unit to the bulkhead.
8 Undo and remove the two bolts, spring and plain washers that hold the heater side brackets to the bulkhead.
9 Detach the heater motor cable terminals from the wiring harness connector.
10 Place some plastic sheeting on the floor to prevent water damaging the carpeting. Draw the top of the heater unit rearwards to clear the upper fixing stud.
11 Pull the lower section of the heater rearwards until the heater unit is tilted so that it can be removed from under the facia support rail in front of the passengers position. Lift away from inside the car.
12 Refitting is the reverse sequence to removal but there are several additional points to be noted to ensure a satisfactory and watertight job.
13 Undo and remove the three self tapping screws that secure the air intake grille to the bulkhead top panel. Lift away the grille.
14 Place the heater in the car and lift into position engaging the top stud with the hole in the bulkhead. Refit the securing spring washer and nut but leave loose.
15 Working through the air intake grille hole carefully work the seal over the grille housing panel. Always fit a new seal if the condition of the original one is suspect.

29. Heater fan and motor - removal and refitting

1 Refer to Section 28 and remove the heater unit.
2 Undo and remove the heater plenum chamber securing self-tapping screws and lift away the plenum chamber (Fig.12.21).
3 Undo and remove the three nuts and plain washers that secure the motor and fan assembly to the heater body. Lift away the motor.
4 If it is necessary to remove the fan, note which way round on the motor spindle it is fitted and remove the clip retaining the

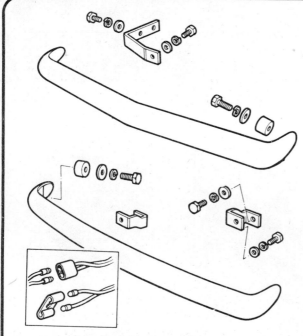

FIG.12.18. BUMPER ASSEMBLIES

Top: Front
Bottom: Rear (with number plate light connection)

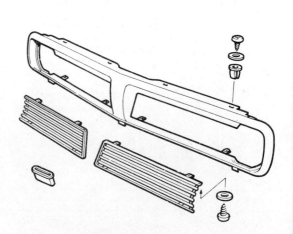

FIG.12.19. RADIATOR GRILLE ASSEMBLY

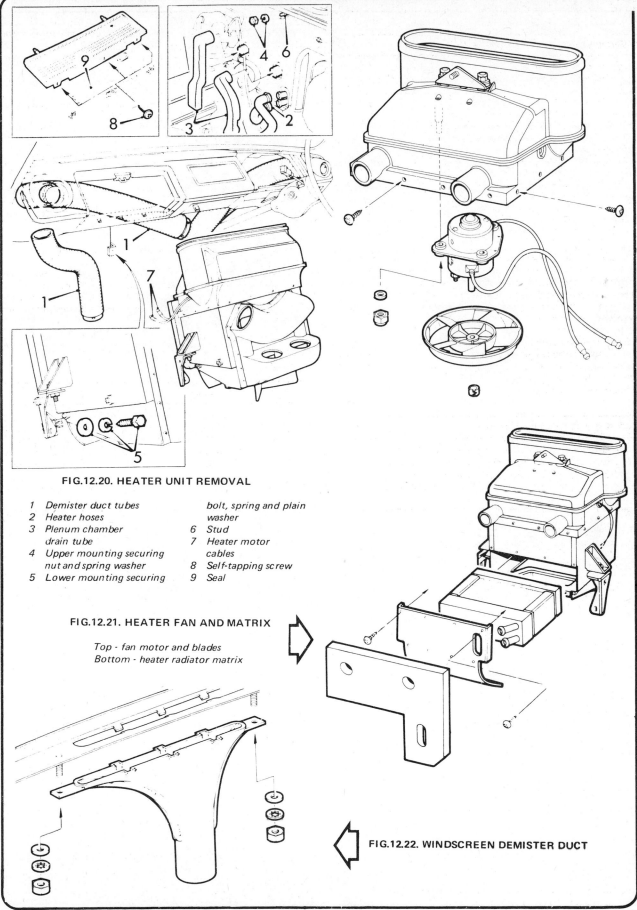

FIG.12.20. HEATER UNIT REMOVAL

1	Demister duct tubes		bolt, spring and plain
2	Heater hoses		washer
3	Plenum chamber	6	Stud
	drain tube	7	Heater motor
4	Upper mounting securing		cables
	nut and spring washer	8	Self-tapping screw
5	Lower mounting securing	9	Seal

FIG.12.21. HEATER FAN AND MATRIX

Top - fan motor and blades
Bottom - heater radiator matrix

FIG.12.22. WINDSCREEN DEMISTER DUCT

fan boss. Lift away the fan.
5   Refitting the heater fan and motor is the reverse sequence to removal. Before fitting a new motor always test it by placing the cable terminals on the battery terminals.

30. Heater matrix - removal and refitting

1   Refer to Section 28 and remove the heater unit.
2   Carefully remove the packing rubber from the forward end of the heater unit.
3   Undo and remove the screws securing the matrix cover plate to the heater body. Lift away the cover plate.
4   The heater matrix may now be slid out from its location in the heater body.
5   If the matrix is leaking or blocked follow the instructions given in Chapter 2, Section 6.
6   Refitting the heater matrix is the reverse sequence to removal.

31. Windscreen demister duct - removal and refitting

1   Refer to Section 32 and remove the instrument panel.
2   Refer to Section 25 and remove the glovebox.
3   Detach the tubes from the demister duct (Fig.12.22).
4   Working under the facia undo and remove the two nuts, shakeproof and plain washers that secure the duct in position.
5   Carefully raise the duct finisher to clear the bolts and lift away the duct.
6   Refitting the duct is the reverse sequence to removal.

32. Instrument panel - removal and refitting

1   Undo and remove the four crosshead screws, spring and plain washers that secure the instrument panel to the facia. Note that the two longest screws are located above the instruments (Fig.12.23).
2   Draw the instrument panel away from the facia panel.
3   Press the release lever on the speedometer cable connector and detach the speedometer cable.
4   Disconnect the electrical multi pin connector from the rear of the instrument panel. Completely lift away the instrument panel.
5   Refitting the instrument panel is the reverse sequence to removal.

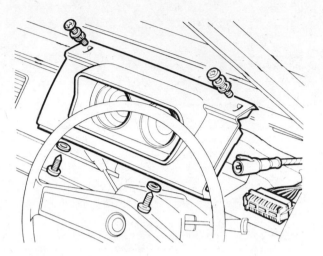

FIG.12.23. INSTRUMENT PANEL REMOVAL

Chapter 13 Supplement

1 Introduction

The purpose of this Chapter is to provide the Marina owner with information and procedures relative to new models introduced, and modifications made to the vehicles in the Marina range, since the original manual was published.

We have also taken this opportunity to incorporate coverage of the Austin/Morris Marina Vans, Pick-ups and Estate cars.

If your Marina was manufactured in, or after, the latter half of 1972, or if you have a Marina Van, Pick-up or Estate, the information in this Chapter should be used in conjunction with the other relevant parts of this manual whenever you are working on the car.

Note: The information given in this Chapter is presented in the same sequence as found in Chapters 1 to 12.

On the 1st August 1972 BLMC introduced the new range of 7 cwt and 10 cwt Vans based on the successful range of Marina models, and later followed a 10 cwt Pick-up. With these models an 1100 cc engine, previously used on other BLMC models, was introduced in the range and is used in some of the 7 cwt Vans. Other Vans and Pick-ups use the 1300 cc power unit, but this has a lower compression ratio than the one used in cars.

In the Van and Pick-up models, the engine and transmission layout is similar to that used in the Saloons, although there is some uprating of the suspension and rear axle.

From 1976 onwards some revised Specifications were issued for all models in the range; these Specifications are listed, and any amended workshop procedures are given. Also in 1976 the 1.3 Marina Estate car was introduced. For those of you who have later cars, first refer to the information in this Chapter; if no specific Specification or procedure is given, you should refer back to Chapters 1 to 12 for the appropriate information. In some instances, there is information included in this Chapter which applies also to earlier cars, but which was not previously available.

Contents

---

2 Specifications

Engine 1100 cc (Van only)

Manufacturer's type number	10V LC
Number of cylinders	4
Bore	2·543 in (64·58 mm)
Stroke	3·296 in (83·72 mm)
Capacity	1098 cc (67 cu in)
Firing order	1 – 3 – 4 – 2
Valve operation	Overhead by pushrod
Compression ratio	7·5 : 1
Oversize bores	+0·010 in (+0·254 mm), +0·020 in (+0·508 mm) +0·030 in (+0·762 mm), +0·040 in (+1·016 mm)
Torque	56 lbf ft at 2,600 rpm

Crankshaft

Main journal diameter	1·7505 to 1·7510 in (44·462 to 44·475 mm)
Minimum regrind diameter	1·7104 to 1·7110 in (43·444 to 43·459 mm)
Crankpin journal diameter	1·6254 to 1·6259 in (41·285 to 41·297 mm)
Minimum regrind diameter	1·5854 to 1·5859 in (40·269 to 40·281 mm)
Crankshaft endthrust	Taken on thrust washers at centre main bearing
Crankshaft endfloat	0·002 to 0·003 in (0·051 to 0·076 mm)

Main bearings
Number and type . . . . 3 thin wall type
Material . . . . Steel backed, reticular tin-aluminium AS15
Width . . . . 1·057 to 1·067 in (26·847 to 27·101 mm)
Diametrical clearance . . . . 0·001 to 0·0027 in (0·025 to 0·068 mm)
Undersizes . . . . 0·010 in, 0·020 in, 0·030 in, 0·040 in
(0·254 mm, 0·508 mm, 0·762 mm, 1·016 mm)

Connecting rods
Type . . . . Diagonally split big-end, bushed small-end
Length between centres . . . . 5·748 to 5·752 in (145·99 to 146·10 mm)

Big-end bearings
Type and material . . . . Steel backed, reticular tin-aluminium
Length . . . . 0·870 to 0·880 in (22·098 to 22·352 mm)
Diametrical clearance . . . . 0·001 to 0·0025 in (0·025 to 0·063 mm)

Gudgeon pin
Type . . . . Plain, circlip retained
Fit in piston . . . . Hand push-fit at 16° C (60° F)
Fit in connecting rod . . . . Push-fit at room temperature
Diameter (outer) . . . . 0·6244 to 0·6247 in (15·859 to 15·867 mm)

Pistons
Type . . . . Aluminium, solid skirt, dished crown
Number of rings . . . . 4 (3 compression, 1 oil control)
Width of ring grooves:
    Top, second and third rings . . . . 0·0645 to 0·0655 in (1·638 to 1·663 mm)
    Oil control . . . . 0·1265 to 0·1275 in (3·213 to 3·238 mm)
Gudgeon pin bore . . . . 0·6247 to 0·6249 in (15·867 to 15·872 mm)

Piston rings
Compression rings:
    Type:
        Top . . . . Chrome
        Second and third . . . . Tapered, cast iron
    Width – Top, second and third . . . . 0·0615 to 0·0625 in (1·57 to 1·60 mm)
    Fitted gap:
        Top . . . . 0·007 to 0·012 in (0·177 to 0·304 mm)
        Second and third . . . . 0·007 to 0·012 in (0·177 to 0·304 mm)
    Ring to groove clearance:
        Top, second and third . . . . 0·0015 to 0·0035 in (0·04 to 0·09 mm)
Oil control ring:
    Type . . . . Duaflex
    Fitted gap:
        Rails . . . . 0·012 to 0·028 in (0·304 to 0·711 mm)
        Side spring . . . . 0·10 to 0·15 in (0·254 to 0·381 mm)

Camshaft
Journal diameters:
    Front . . . . 1·6655 to 1·6660 in (42·304 to 42·316 mm)
    Centre . . . . 1·62275 to 1·62325 in (41·218 to 41·231 mm)
    Rear . . . . 1·37275 to 1·37350 in (34·866 to 34·889 mm)
Bearing line inside diameter (reamed after fitting):
    Front . . . . 1·6670 to 1·6675 in (42·3418 to 42·3545 mm)
    Centre . . . . 1·62425 to 1·62475 in (41·2559 to 41·2686 mm)
    Rear . . . . 1·3745 to 1·3750 in (34·9123 to 34·9250 mm)
Bearings:
    Type . . . . White metal-lined, steel backed
Diametrical clearance . . . . 0·001 to 0·002 in (0·02 to 0·05 mm)
Endthrust . . . . Taken on locating plate
Endfloat . . . . 0·003 to 0·007 in (0·07 to 0·18 mm)
Drive . . . . Single chain and gear from crankshaft
Timing chain . . . . 0·375 in (9·52 mm) pitch x 52 pitches
Cam lift . . . . 0·250 in (6·35 mm)

Rocker gear
Rocker shaft:
    Diameter . . . . 0·5615 to 0·5625 in (14·262 to 14·287 mm)
Rocker arm:
    Bore . . . . 0·686 to 0·687 in (17·42 to 17·45 mm)
    Bush inside diameter (reamed in position) . . . . 0·5630 to 0·5635 in (14·300 to 14·312 mm)

Tappets (cam followers)
Type .... Bucket
Outside diameter .... 0·81125 to 0·81175 in (20·60 to 20·62 mm)
Length .... 1·495 to 1·505 in (37·97 to 38·23 mm)

Valves
Seat angle:
    Inlet .... 45°
    Exhaust .... 45°
Head diameter:
    Inlet .... 1·151 to 1·156 in (29·23 to 29·36 mm)
    Exhaust .... 1·0 to 1·005 in (25·4 to 25·53 mm)
Stem diameter:
    Inlet .... 0·2793 to 0·2798 in (7·09 to 7·11 mm)
    Exhaust .... 0·2788 to 0·2793 in (7·08 to 7·09 mm)
Stem to guide clearance; inlet and exhaust .... 0·0015 to 0·0025 in (0·04 to 0·08 mm)
Valve lift; inlet and exhaust .... 0·318 in (8·07 mm)

Valve guides
Length; inlet and exhaust .... 1·531 in (38·894 mm)
Outside diameter; inlet and exhaust .... 0·4695 to 0·470 in (11·925 to 11·938 mm)
Inside diameter; inlet and exhaust .... 0·2813 to 0·2818 in (7·1450 to 7·1577 mm)
Fitted height above spring seat; inlet and exhaust .... 0·540 in (13·72 mm)
Interference fit in head; inlet and exhaust .... 0·0005 to 0·0015 in (0·0127 to 0·0381 mm)

Valve springs
Free length .... 1·750 in (44·45 mm)
Fitted length .... 1·296 in (32·94 mm)
Load at fitted length .... 52 lbf (23·5 kgf)
Number of working coils 4½

Valve timing and rocker (tappet) clearance
Timing marks .... Dimples on camshaft and crankshaft wheels
Rocker clearance:
    Cold .... 0·012 in (0·305 mm)
Inlet valve:
    Opens .... 5° BTDC
    Closes .... 45° ABDC
Exhaust valve:
    Opens .... 51° BBDC
    Closes .... 21° ATDC

Lubrication
System .... Wet sump, pressure fed
System pressure:
    Running .... 60 lbf/in² (4·21 kgf/cm²)
    Idling .... 15 lbf/in² (1·05 kgf/cm²)
Oil pump .... Internal gear, pin drive from camshaft
Capacity .... 1·75 gal (2·1 US gal) (8 litres) per minute at 1000 rpm
Oil filter .... Full flow; screw on, disposable element type
Bypass valve opens .... 8 to 12 lbf/in² (0·56 to 0·84 kgf/cm²)
Oil pressure relief valve .... 60 lbf/in² (4·21 kgf/cm²)
Relief valve spring:
    Free length .... 2·86 in (72·62 mm)
    Fitted length .... 2·156 in (54·77 mm)
    Load at fitted length .... 13 to 14 lbf (5·90 to 6·36 kgf)

Torque wrench settings

	lbf ft	kgf m
Big-end bolts (1975 onwards)	35	4·8
Main bearing cap bolts	60	8·3
Cylinder head nuts	40	5·5
Big-end cap nut (up to 1975)	45	6·22
Front mounting bolts	25	3·4
Rocker shaft nuts	25	3·4
Gearbox adaptor plate bolts	25	3·4
Flywheel securing bolts	40	5·5
Sump securing bolts	6	0·8
Oil pump securing bolts	9	1·2

Cooling system

Fan (Van)
Type .... Plastic

Number of blades:
    Standard . . . . 8 blades
    Hot countries . . . . 7 blades

Radiator
Type . . . . 7·5 GPI, 2 row, steel

Carburation

Carburettor (1100 Van)

	1972/73	1974 on
Type	SU HS2	SU HS4
Specification	AUD 368	AUD 627
Needle (standard)	AN	ABN
Piston spring	Red	Red
Jet size	0·090 in (2·29 mm)	0·090 in (2·29 mm)

Carburettor (1·3 LC engine, 1974 on)
Type . . . . SU HS4
Specification:
    Saloon . . . . AUD 541
    Van, Pick-up . . . . AUD 589
Needle (standard) . . . . AAZ
Piston spring . . . . Red
Jet size . . . . 0·090 in (2·29 mm)

Carburettor (1·3 HC engine, 1975 on)
Type . . . . SU HS4
Specification:
    Manual gearbox . . . . AUD 541 or AUD 670 (Capstat)
    Automatic transmission . . . . AUD 542 or FZX 1071 (Capstat)
Needle . . . . AAZ or ADG (Capstat)
Piston spring . . . . Red
Jet size . . . . 0·090 (2·29 mm)
Exhaust emission at idle speed:
    Without Capstat . . . . 3 to 4·5% CO
    With Capstat . . . . 3% CO
Engine idle speed . . . . 750 rpm
Fast idle speed . . . . 1300 rpm

Ignition system

Ignition timing
1100 Van:
    Stroboscopic at 1000 rpm (vacuum disconnected) . . . . 13° BTDC
    Static . . . . 8° BTDC
1·3 LC engine, 1974 on:
    Stroboscopic at 1000 rpm (vacuum disconnected) . . . . 12° BTDC
    Static . . . . 7° BTDC
1·3 HC engine, 1975 on:
    Stroboscopic at 1000 rpm . . . . 14° BTDC
    Static . . . . 9° BTDC

Distributor type
1100 Van, 1972/73 . . . . Lucas 25D4
    Dwell angle . . . . 60 ± 3°
1100 Van, 1974 on . . . . Lucas 45D4
    Dwell angle . . . . 51 ± 5°
1·3 LC engine, 1974 on . . . . Lucas 45D4
    Dwell angle . . . . 51 ± 5°
1·3 HC engine, 1975 on . . . . Lucas 43D4
    Dwell angle . . . . 51 ± 5°
Contact breaker points gap (all distributors) . . . . 0·014 to 0·016 in (0·35 to 0·40 mm)

Clutch

Van, Pick-up and 1976 onwards Saloons
Driven plate diameter . . . . 8·0 in (203 mm)

Automatic transmission

Type (1976 onwards) . . . . Borg Warner model 65

Fluid capacity (total) . . . . 11·5 pt (13·8 US pt) (6·54 litre)

Rear axle

Final drive ratio
7 cwt Van (up to 1976) . . . . 4·11 : 1
10 cwt Van and later 7 cwt Van . . . . 4·556 : 1

Braking system

Type (Van and Pickup)
Front brakes . . . . Twin leading shoe drum brakes
Rear brakes . . . . Leading and trailing shoe drum brakes

Master cylinder diameter
7 cwt Van (early models) . . . . 0·70 in (17·78 mm)
7 cwt Van (from chassis No. 'Morris 1509', Austin 1486') . . . . . . 0·75 in (19·05 mm)
1·3 – Saloon and Coupe with drum brakes:
    Servo:
        Early cars . . . . 0·75 in (19·05 mm)
        Later cars . . . . 0·70 in (17·78 mm)
    Non-Servo:
        Early cars . . . . 0·70 in (17·78 mm)
        Later cars . . . . 0·75 in (19·05 mm)
1·3 – Saloon and Coupe with front disc and servo . . . . 0·75 in (19·05 mm)
10 cwt Van:
    Servo . . . . 0·75 in (19·05 mm)
    Non-Servo . . . . 0·70 in (17·78 mm)

Front wheel cylinder diameter
1·3 – Saloon and Coupe and 10 cwt Van . . . . 0·75 in (19·05 mm)
1·3 – Saloon and Coupe from Chassis No. '172479' and
7 cwt Van from Chassis No. 'Morris 1590' and 'Austin 1486' . . . . 0·875 ln (22·22 mm)

Rear wheel cylinder diameter
With front drum brakes:
    1·3 Saloon and Coupe (early models) . . . . 0·700 in (17·78 mm)
    7 cwt Van to Chassis No. '1589' . . . . 0·620 in (15·74 mm)
    1·3 Saloon and Coupe from Chassis No. '172479' and
    7 cwt Van from Chassis No. 'Morris 1590' and 'Austin 1489' . 0·750 in (19·05 mm)
    10 cwt Van . . . . 0·750 in (1905 mm)
With front disc brakes:
    1·3 Saloon and Coupe . . . . 0·620 in (15·74 mm)
    1·3 Saloon and Coupe from Chassis No. '172479' . . . . 0·70 in (17·78 mm)

Electrical system

Control box fitment (dynamo models)
RB106 . . . . lhd models
RB340 . . . . rhd models

RB340
Maximum dynamo output . . . . 22 amps ± 1 amp
Cut-in voltage . . . . 12·7 – 13·3 volts
Drop-off current . . . . 9·5 – 11·0 volts
Reverse current . . . . 10 amps (max)
Voltage and current regulator air gap . . . . 0·022 ± 0·003 in (0·558 ± 0·076 mm)
Cut-out relay air gap . . . . 0·025 – 0·035 in (0·63 – 0·90 mm)

Alternator
Type . . . . Lucas 16ACR, 17ACR or 18ACR
Output at 14V and 6000 alternator rpm . . . . 16ACR – 34 amps; 17ACR –36 amps; 18ACR – 45 amps
Brush length (minimum) . . . . $\frac{5}{16}$ in (8 mm)
Winding resistance at 20° C (68° F):
    16ACR (purple winding identification) . . . . 3·3 ohms ± 5%
    17ACR (pink winding identification) . . . . 4·2 ohms ± 5%
    17ACR (green winding identification) . . . . 3·2 ohms ± 5%
    18ACR (green winding identification) . . . . 3·2 ohms ± 5%

Starter motor
Pre-engaged type (alternative to M35J pre-engaged type) 2M100
Brush spring tension . . . . 36 oz (1 kg)

Lock torque	14·4 lbf ft (2·02 kgf m) at 463 amps
Torque at 1000 rpm	7·3 lbf ft (1·02 kgf m) at 300 amps
Light running current	40 amps at 6000 rpm
Solenoid closing coil resistance	0·25 to 0·27 ohm
Solenoid holding coil resistance	0·76 to 0·80 ohm

Suspension and steering

Front suspension
Camber angle (1976 onwards) . . . .   0° 46′ positive

Tyre pressures

	Front	Rear
Saloon/Coupe:		
145–13 radial-ply tyres and 155–13 radial-ply tyres	26 lbf/in² (1·8 kgf/cm²)	28 lbf/in² (2·0 kgf/cm²)
Estate car:		
155–13 radial-ply tyres:		
Unladen	26 lbf/in² (1·8 kgf/cm²)	28 lbf/in² (2·0 kgf/cm²)
Laden	26 lbf/in² (1·8 kgf/cm²)	32 lbf/in² (2·25 kgf/cm²)
7 cwt Van:		
155SR–13 radial-ply tyres	24 lbf/in² (1·68 kgf/cm²)	32 lbf/in² (2·25 kgf/cm²)
10 cwt Van, 10 cwt Pick-up:		
155SR–13 radial-ply reinforced tyres:		
Unladen	24 lbf/in² (1·68 kgf/cm²)	30 lbf/in² (2·18 kgf/cm²)
Laden	24 lbf/in² (1·68 kgf/cm²)	40 lbf/in² (2·8 kgf/cm²)

---

3   Engine

1100 engine (Van only) – servicing
1   The 1100 cc engine fitted to the standard 7 cwt Van is the well proven BLMC 'A' series unit and may be considered to be the predecessor of the 1300 cc engine.
2   There are several minor differences between these two engines but suffice it to state that provided care is taken during dismantling, and note is made of any slight differences, no problems will arise if the instructions are followed for the 1300 cc engine.
3   Exploded views of this engine together with comprehensive specifications should answer any queries that the reader may have, but particular attention is drawn to the following.
4   *Pistons:* It will be seen from the illustration that circlips are used to retain the gudgeon pins. After these have been removed, it should be possible to press out the gudgeon pin but, if it is reluctant to move, the piston can be soaked in very hot water for a few minutes to allow the piston material to expand so that the gudgeon pin moves more freely.
5   *Piston rings:* It will be seen that the piston rings are slightly different in detail, in that instead of a one piece expander for the oil control ring, an expander and side spring are used.
6   *Flywheel, endplate and gasket:* There are minor differences in detail parts, and these are shown in the illustration.
7   *Big-end bearing and end cap:* There are minor differences in the detail parts, and these are shown in the illustration.
8   *Oil pump:* The oil pump is generally similar to the one used on the 1300 cc engine, but is attached by three bolts instead of four. The arrangement is shown in the illustration.
9   *Engine mountings:* Modified engine mountings are used on 1100 cc models, and are as shown in the illustration.

Engine modifications for later models
10   All 1100 cc and 1300 cc can have cylinder liners fitted in the event of subsequent rebores being made up to the maximum limit. As with some of the other major engine repair operations, this is a specialist job and must be carried out by a suitably equipped automobile engineering workshop.

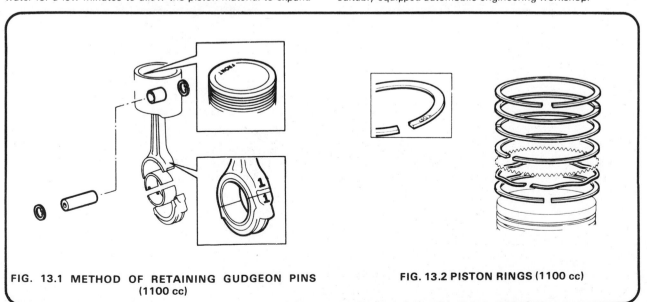

FIG. 13.1 METHOD OF RETAINING GUDGEON PINS (1100 cc)   **FIG. 13.2 PISTON RINGS (1100 cc)**

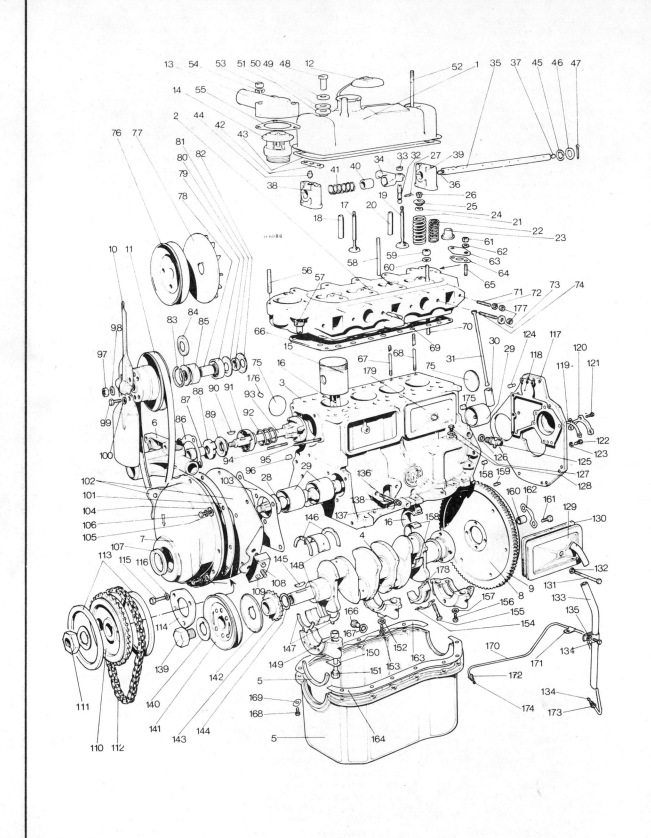

FIG. 13.3 EXPLODED VIEW OF 'A' SERIES ENGINE (TYPICAL)

1 Cover – rocker gear
2 Cylinder head
3 Block – cylinder
4 Crankshaft
5 Sump
6 Water pump body
7 Cover – cylinder block front
8 Flywheel
9 Starter ring
10 Fan blade
11 Fan belt
12 Oil filler cap
13 Elbow – water outlet
14 Thermostat
15 Piston assembly
16 Connecting rod
17 Exhaust valve
18 Exhaust valve guide
19 Inlet valve
20 Inlet valve guide
21 Outer valve spring
22 Inner valve spring
23 Shroud for valve guide
24 Valve packing ring
25 Valve spring cup
26 Valve cotter
27 Valve cotter circlip
28 Camshaft
29 Camshaft bearing liners
30 Tappet
31 Pushrod
32 Tappet adjusting screw
33 Locknut
34 Rocker (bushed)
35 Valve rocker shaft (plugged)
36 Rocker shaft plug (screwed)
37 Rocker shaft plug (plain)
38 Rocker shaft bracket (tapped)
39 Rocker shaft bracket (plain)
40 Rocker bush
41 Rocker spacing spring
42 Rocker shaft bracket plate
43 Cover joint gasket
44 Rocker shaft locating screw
45 Spring washer
46 Washer
47 Split pin
48 Nut
49 Cup washer
50 Distance piece
51 Cover bush
52 Rocker bracket long stud
53 Nut
54 Spring washer
55 Elbow joint gasket
56 Water outlet elbow stud
57 By-pass adaptor
58 Rocker bracket stud (short)
59 Cylinder head nut
60 Washer

61 Cover nut
62 Spring washer
63 Cover plate
64 Cover plate joint gasket
65 Cover plate stud
66 Cylinder head gasket
67 Cylinder head stud (short)
68 Cylinder head stud (long)
69 Exhaust manifold stud (medium)
70 Cylinder head stud (long)
71 Exhaust manifold stud (short)
72 Small washer
73 Large clamping washer
74 Exhaust manifold stud (long)
75 Core plug
76 Dynamo pulley
77 Dynamo fan
78 Bearing distance piece
79 Bearing
80 Outer retainer for felt
81 Felt
82 Inner retainer for felt
83 Retainer circlip
84 Bearing grease retainer
85 Bearing
86 Water pump gasket
87 Distance piece
88 Seal
89 Seal rubber
90 Pulley key
91 Spring locating cup
92 Spring
93 Spindle with vane
94 Water pump body stud (short)
95 Water pump body stud (long)
96 Oil gallery plug
97 Spindle nut
98 Spindle washer
99 Screw to pulley
100 Spring washer
101 Cover gasket
102 Front bearer plate
103 Bearer plate joint gasket
104 Plain washer
105 Spring washer
106 Front bearer plate screw
107 Cover felt
108 Rubber front mounting block
109 Block attachment bolt
110 Camshaft sprocket (upper)
111 Sprocket nut
112 Camshaft drive chain
113 Tensioner rings
114 Locking plate
115 Plate to crankcase screw
116 Shakeproof washer

117 Gearbox bearer plate
118 Joint gasket to block
119 Cover joint washer
120 Rear cover
121 Cover screw
122 Screw to block
123 Spring washer
124 Dowel (top) to block
125 Drain tap (water)
126 Tap washer
127 Oil priming plug
128 Copper washer
129 Block front side cover (with elbow)
130 Side cover gasket
131 Screw to block
132 Fibre washer
133 Fume vent pipe (with clip)
134 Clip screw
135 Spring washer
136 Stud (blanking plate)
137 Nut
138 Washer
139 Pulley retaining bolt
140 Lockwasher
141 Crankshaft pulley
142 Oil thrower
143 Crankshaft sprocket
144 Packing washer
145 Crankshaft key
146 Upper thrust washers
147 Lower thrust washers
148 Main bearing
149 Main bearing cap dowel
150 Lockwasher
151 Bearing cap bolt
152 Shakeproof washer
153 Bearing cap screw
154 Lockwasher for bolts
155 Cap bolt
156 Bearing cap screw
157 Shakeproof washer
158 Big end bearing
159 Dowel
160 First motion shaft bush
161 Flywheel to crank-shaft screw
162 Lockwasher
163 Sump right-hand gasket
164 Sump left-hand gasket
165 Main bearing cap seal
166 Sump drain plug
167 Drain plug washer
168 Screw
169 Washer
170 Ignition control pipe
171 Pipe clip
172 Pipe nut (distributor end)
173 Pipe nut (carburettor end)
174 Pipe olive
175 Oil gallery plug
176 Oil pressure relief-valve passage plug
177 Stud nuts
178 Big end cap
179 Block rear side cover

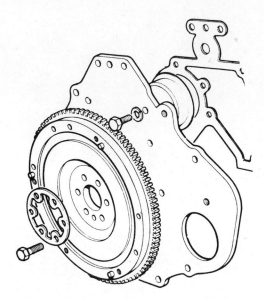

FIG. 13.4 FLYWHEEL, ENDPLATE AND GASKET (1100 cc)

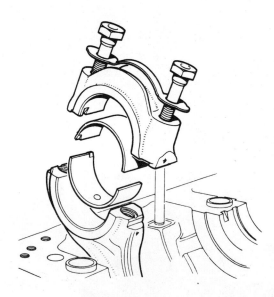

**FIG. 13.5 BIG-END BEARING AND END CAP DETAIL
(1100 cc)**

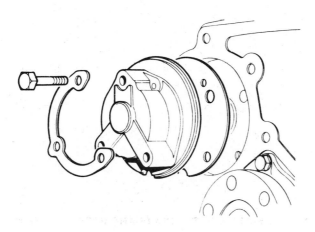

FIG. 13.7 OIL PUMP REMOVAL (1100 cc)

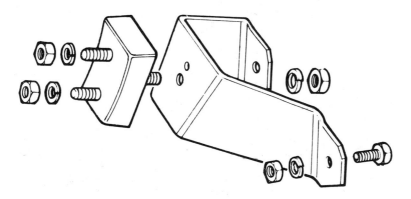

FIG. 13.8 ENGINE FRONT MOUNTING (1100 cc)

4 Cooling system

Cooling system – general

1   Later models have a modified thermostat housing although there is no difference in procedure for removing and refitting it.
2   The sequence for removal of the radiator and shroud is basically similar to that described in Section 5, of Chapter 2, but it will be necessary to remove the screws securing the shroud panel to the radiator bracket. Also undo and remove the nuts and washers that secure the radiator shroud top panel (Fig. 13.9).
3   Refitting the shroud and radiator is the reverse sequence to removal. Don't forget to refer to Chapter 2, Section 4 when refilling the system.

5 Fuel system

Carburettors

1   In addition to the SU HS4 carburettor described in Chapter 3, two other carburettors have been introduced.
2   Early model Vans used the SU HS2 carburettor which , apart from its overall size, is almost identical to the HS4 type described in Chapter 2. The arrangement is shown in Fig. 13.11.
3   Later carburettors fitted to some of the Saloons and Estate cars may be of the HS4 capstat type. The capstat is a modified jet assembly, but this carburettor also has a different method of idle speed adjustment with a seal to prevent unauthorized interference. Dismantling procedures on this carburettor are essentially the same as for the earlier HS4 type but it is recommended that the idle speed and mixture screw settings are noted before dismantling, and that the adjustments are checked by a BLMC dealer after reassembly and refitting. The carburettor details are shown in Fig. 13.12.
4   On cars for some markets, an induction heater coil is clamped around the carburettor suction chamber as an aid for cold starting. Apart from an electrical connection which has to be detached before the carburettor is removed, the carburettor is similar to others fitted to cars covered by this Manual.

Fuel pump

5   Alternative fuel pumps are used on later models and, although different in appearance, removal and refitting procedures have not altered. Later SU pumps do not have a filter, but filters are still used on the AC pumps. The later type AC pump cannot be dismantled for repair and, in the event of failure, must be replaced by a new one.

Fuel tank – removal and refitting

   Paragraphs 6 to 15 are applicable to Saloon models from chassis number '153500' up to 1976 models, all Estate cars up to 1976 models, all Vans and Pick-ups.
6   Disconnect the battery.
7   Chock the front wheels, raise the rear of the car and support it on stands located under the rear axle.
8   Unscrew the fuel tank drain plug and drain the contents of the fuel tank into a container of suitable capacity, taking suitable safety precautions.
9   Disconnect the electrical connection from the fuel tank sender unit.
10 Compress the retaining clip and remove the fuel pipe flexible hose from the fuel tank.
11 Compress the retaining clip and disconnect the vent pipe from the fuel tank.
12 On Van models release the filler pipe grommet from the body panel cut-out.
13 Remove the screws, spring washers and support plates securing the tank.
14 Lower the tank and remove from under the car. **Note:** The

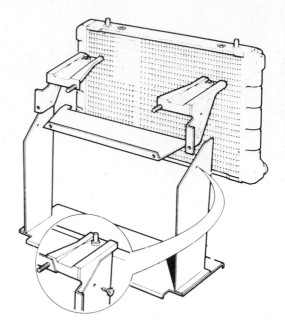

FIG. 13.9 RADIATOR AND SHROUD ASSEMBLY

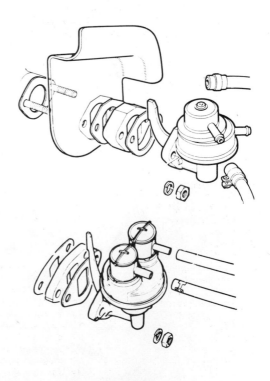

FIG. 13.10 ALTERNATIVE TYPES OF FUEL PUMP

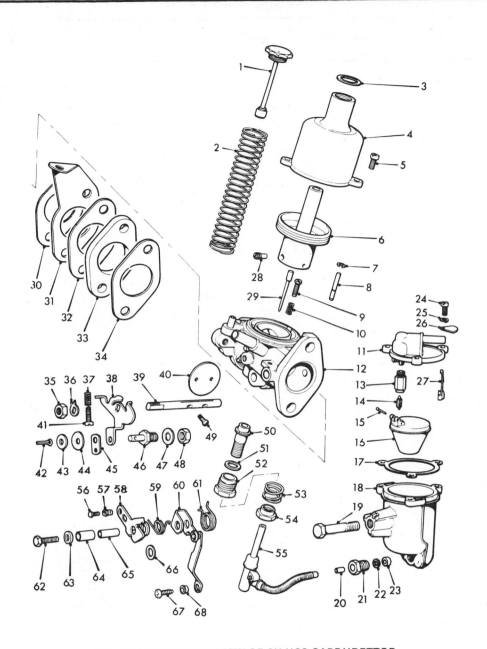

FIG. 13.11 EXPLODED VIEW OF SU HS2 CARBURETTOR

1 Piston damper	18 Float chamber	35 Nut	52 Jet locating nut
2 Spring	19 Bolt	36 Lock washer	53 Spring
3 Sealing washer	20 Ferrule	37 Fast idle screw spring	54 Jet adjusting nut
4 Piston chamber	21 Sleeve nut	38 Throttle return lever	55 Jet assembly
5 Screw	22 Washer	39 Throttle spindle	56 Choke cable screw
6 Piston	23 Gland	40 Throttle disc assembly	57 Retainer
7 Circlip	24 Screw	41 Fast idle screw	58 Cam lever
8 Piston lifting pin	25 Spring washer	42 Split pin	59 Spring
9 Throttle adjusting screw	26 Identification tag	43 Washer	60 Pick-up lever
10 Spring for throttle	27 Baffle plate	44 Concave washer	61 Spring
adjusting screw	28 Locking screw	45 Anchor tag	62 Pivot bolt
11 Float chamber lid	29 Needle	46 Throttle cable spindle	63 Distance washer
12 Body	30 Joint washer	47 Washer	64 Outer pivot bolt nut
13 Needle seat	31 Bracket	48 Nut	65 Inner pivot bolt nut
14 Needle	32 Joint washer	49 Screw	66 Washer
15 Hinge pin	33 Insulator block	50 Jet bearing	67 Screw
16 Float	34 Joint washer	51 Sealing washer	68 Bush
17 Joint washer			

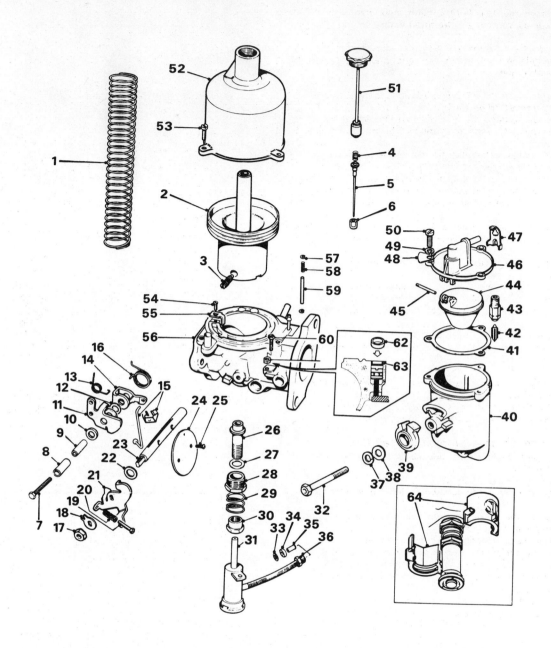

FIG. 13.12 EXPLODED VIEW OF SU HS4 CAPSTAT CARBURETTOR

1 Spring	17 Nut	33 Washer	49 Spring washer
2 Piston	18 Lockwasher	34 Gland	50 Screw
3 Locking screw	19 Fast idle screw	35 Ferrule	51 Piston damper
4 Spring for needle	20 Fast idle screw spring	36 Sleeve nut	52 Piston chamber
5 Needle	21 Throttle return lever	37 Spring washer	53 Screw
6 Needle support guide	22 Washer throttle spindle	38 Washer	54 Screw
7 Pivot bolt	23 Throttle spindle	39 Spacer	55 Suction chamber piston guide
8 Outer pivot bolt tube	24 Throttle disc asembly	40 Float chamber	56 Carburettor body
9 Inner pivot bolt tube	25 Screw	41 Joint washer	57 Circlip
10 Distance washer	26 Jet bearing	42 Needle	58 Spring
11 Cam lever	27 Sealing washer	43 Seat	59 Lifting pin
12 Washer	28 Jet locating nut	44 Float	60 Throttle adjusting screw
13 Spring	29 Spring	45 Hinge pin	61 Locknut
14 Pick-up lever	30 Jet adjusting nut	46 Lid	62 Throttle adjusting screw housing seal
15 Pick-up rod	31 Capstat assembly	47 Baffle plate	63 Fitted position of seal
16 Spring	32 Bolt	48 Specification label	64 Jet adjusting nut seal

Saloon models fuel tank is fitted with a non-vented type filler cap whereas all Van models are fitted with a vented type filler cap.

15 Refitting the fuel tank is the reverse sequence to removal. On Van models ensure that the filler vent pipe is routed over the rear chassis member.

Paragraphs 16 to 25 are applicable to all Saloons and Estate cars from 1976 onwards.

16 If possible, reduce the fuel level to a minimum by normal usage; alternatively, syphon as much fuel out of the tank as possible.

17 Chock front wheels, raise the rear of the car and support it on stands located under the rear axle.

18 Remove the filler neck clamp retaining screw then loosen the clamp neck screw. Rotate the clamp clear of the body.

19 Spring back the clip attaching the pipe to the filler cover hinge.

20 On Saloons only, remove the four self-tapping screws retaining the pipe protective cover. Remove the protective cover and pull the pipe into the luggage compartment.

21 Remove the electrical connection from the tank unit, then detach the flexible fuel pipe.

22 Remove the screws, spring washers and support plates securing the tank, then lower the tank a little.

23 Where applicable, disconnect the second pipe from the tank.

24 Remove the filler neck clamp, and remove the tank.

25 Refitting is the reverse of the removal procedure, but the following should be noted:

    a)   *On Estate cars make sure that the flexible pipe is above the chassis member.*

    b)   *On Saloon models use a sealing compound to prevent water entering the luggage compartment.*

Fuel tank vent pipe – removal and refitting

Paragraphs 26 to 33 are applicable to cars up to chassis number '148627'.

26 Remove the rear seat squab.

27 Undo and remove the screw securing the vent pipe clip to the body.

28 Compress the retaining clips and disconnect the flexible hose from the tank and vent pipe.

29 Working inside the boot, remove the tank vent pipe.

30 Remove the filler vent pipe from the tank connection.

31 Release the pipe from the plastic retainer.

32 Unclip and remove the rubber retaining band, and lift away the filler vent pipe.

33 Refitting the filler vent pipe is the reverse sequence to removal but the following additional points should be noted:

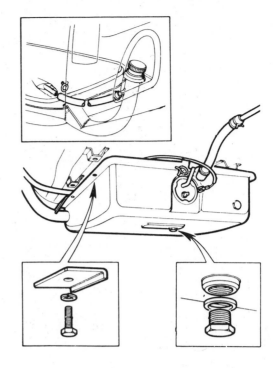

FIG. 13.13 FUEL TANK ATTACHMENTS – TYPICAL FOR EARLY MODELS, VANS AND PICK-UPS

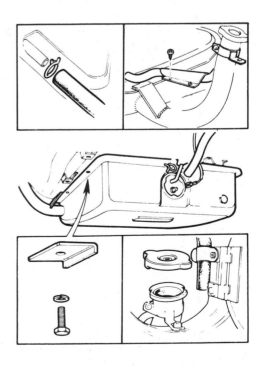

FIG. 13.14 THE FILTER ON THE AC FUEL PUMP

FIG. 13.15 FUEL TANK ATTACHMENTS – TYPICAL FOR LATER SALOON AND ESTATE CARS

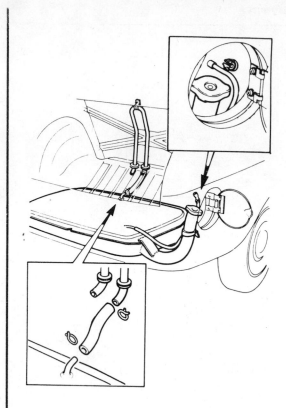

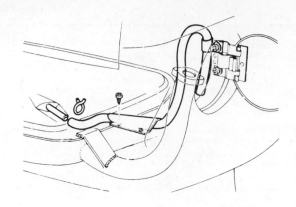

FIG. 13.17 FUEL TANK VENT PIPE (LATER MODELS)

FIG. 13.16 FUEL TANK VENT PIPE (EARLY MODELS)

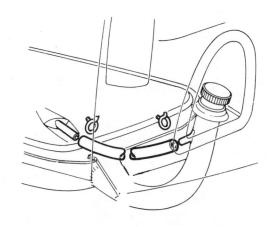

FIG. 13.18 FUEL TANK VENT PIPE (VAN AND PICK-UP)

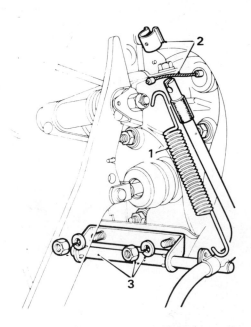

FIG. 13.19 THROTTLE PEDAL ARRANGEMENT

1   Spring (some models)   3   Bracket, nut and washer
2   Throttle cable and clip

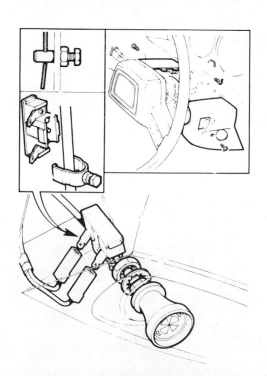

FIG. 13.20 CHOKE CABLE REMOVAL – SALOON AND ESTATE CAR

a) Inspect the filler vent pipe for damage and ensure that it has not perished or become porous.

b) Blow through the pipe and ensure the end restrictor is not blocked.

c) To prevent entry of water into the boot the area surrounding the vent pipe grommets should be sealed with a suitable sealing compound.

Paragraphs 34 to 38 are applicable to cars from chassis number '153599' and Pick-ups and all Vans.

34 Compress the retaining clips and disconnect the pipe from the fuel tank.

35 *Saloon models:* Undo and remove the four self-tapping screws securing the pipe protective cover. Lift away the protective cover.

36 *Saloon models:* Spring back the clip retaining the pipe to the filler cover hinge or remove the screw and washer holding the pipe clamp to the hinge.

37 Remove the vent pipe.

38 Refitting the vent pipe is the reverse sequence to removal but the following additional points should be noted:

a) On Estate cars and Vans, the pipe must be located over the top of the chassis member.

b) On Saloon models, to prevent the entry of water into the boot, the protective cover fixings screws and pipe entry area of the compartment floor should be sealed using a suitable sealing compound.

Throttle pedal – removal and refitting

39 There are minor differences on later models, and in some cases there is an additional spring which has to be detached. In other respects, removal and refitting procedures have not been altered. The arrangement is shown in Fig. 13.19.

Choke cable – removal and refitting

Van and Pick-up

40 Although a different type of dash panel is used on Vans and Pick-ups, the removal and refitting procedure is similar to that described in Chapter 3 for early models.

Saloon and Estate car

41 Detach the cable at the carburettor, then unclip it from the throttle cable.

42 If the cable only is to be removed, pull it through the grommet, then unscrew the cable securing nut from behind the left-hand cowl and pull out the cable. If the warning light switch is to removed, first follow the procedure in paragraphs 43 to 45 before removing the cable.

43 Remove the screw and take off the right-hand steering column cowl, then remove the three screws and take off the left-hand cowl.

44 Where applicable, loosen the locknut and release the clamp screw securing the switch to the cable.

45 Slide the switch along the cable and disconnect the wires, then pull the cable through the body grommet.

46 Refitting is the reverse of the removal procedure, but note the following:

a) A shakeproof washer is used with the cable securing nut.

b) The large locating pip on the switch body locates in the hole nearest the control knob.

c) Ensure that the choke control has 0.06 in (2 mm) free movement.

---

6   Ignition system

Lucas 43D4 and 45D4 distributors – dismantling and reassembly

The 43D4 and 45D4 distributors are a later type, but are generally similar to the 23D4 and 25D4 type although they do

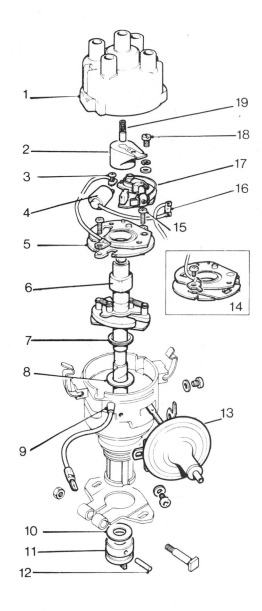

FIG. 13.21 45D4 DISTRIBUTOR – EXPLODED VIEW

The 43D4 distributor is similar, but no vacuum unit is fitted

1	Distributor cap	11	Drive dog
2	Rotor	12	Parallel pin
3	Earth tag	13	Vacuum unit (45D4 only)
4	Capacitor (condenser)	14	Baseplate (early type)
5	Base and bearing plate	15	Baseplate retaining screws
6	Spindle	16	LT lead
7	Nylon spacer	17	Contact set
8	Steel washer	18	Fixed contact retaining screw
9	Grommet	19	Carbon brush
10	Thrust washer		

not have a vernier adjuster. This means that for any adjustment of ignition timing it will be necessary to loosen the clamping plate screws so that the distributor can be turned (clockwise to advance, anti-clockwise to retard). Also, the 43D4 does not have a vacuum advance unit.

1   Remove the distributor as described in Chapter 4.

2   Spring back the clips and remove the cover. Remove the rotor arm and cam oiling pad.

3   Where applicable, remove the two screws and remove the vacuum unit. Note the two prongs protruding downwards from the baseplate straddling one of the screws, then carefully detach the operating arm from the movable plate.

4   Push the grommet and LT lead through into the body, then remove the backplate retaining screw(s).

5   On early type distributors, carefully lever the baseplate from the retaining groove in the body.

6   Remove the base and bearing plate assembly.

7   Note the position of the offset drive dog relative to the rotor (or rotor locating cut-out in the top of the cam spindle), then carefully drive out the drive dog parallel pin.

8   Remove the drive dog and thrust washer; note that the raised pips face the drive dog.

9   Remove the centre spindle, and the automatic advance weights and springs. Take off the steel washer and nylon spacer.

10 Push the moving contact spring towards the centre, and unclip the LT lead.

11 Remove the earth tag and capacitor retaining screw.

12 Remove the screw, spring washer and flat washer, and take off the fixed contact assembly.

13 Inspection of the distributor parts is basically as described in Chapter 4 Section 8, but if any of the moving parts are worn or damaged a new distributor must be obtained as no repairs of this type are possible. Do not dismantle the automatic advance mechanism, other than to remove the control springs. Also check that the spring between the fixed and moving plates is in a satisfactory condition.

14 Reassembly is basically the reverse of the removal procedure, but lubricate the pivots of the weights and springs with Rocal MP (Molypad), and put a trace of general purpose grease or petroleum jelly on the cam profile. Apply a few drops of engine oil to the lubrication pad.

15 On early type distributors, ensure that the baseplate is pressed against the register in the body of the distributor so that the chamfered edge engages the undercut. Measure across the centre of the distributor at right angles to the slot in the baseplate, then tighten the securing screw and re-measure. If

the measurement has increased by 0.006 in (0.152 mm) or more, a new baseplate must be used.

16 When refitting the drive dog to a new spindle, a $\frac{3}{16}$ in (4.76 mm) hole is required for the pin. Tap the drive end of the distributor dog to flatten the pips on the washer to obtain the correct amount of endfloat.

Contact breaker points – renewal and adjustment

17 Remove the distributor cap and rotor as described in the previous paragraphs.

18 Remove the contact plate securing screw, and the spring and flat washers.

19 Press the contact breaker spring from the insulated post, then release the terminal plate and remove the contact set.

20 Refitting is the reverse of the removal procedure, but, where new points are being used, wipe the contact faces with a petrol moistened cloth to remove any protective treatment. Adjustment of the points gap is described in Chapter 4, Section 2.

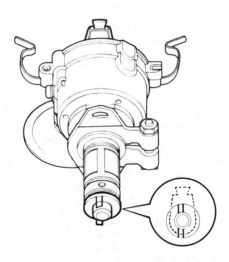

FIG. 13.22 POSITION OF DRIVE DOG RELATIVE TO ROTOR

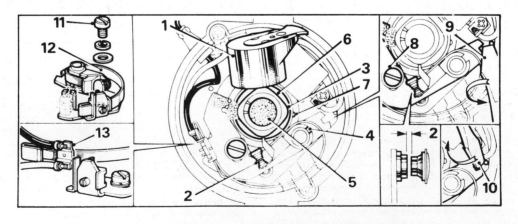

FIG. 13.23 SERVICING 43D4 and 45D4 DISTRIBUTORS

1 Rotor	5 Felt pad	9 Points gap adjustment : anti-clockwise to increase	11 Contact set securing screw
2 Contact points gap	6 Lubrication gap	10 Points gap adjustment : clockwise to decrease	12 Contact set
3 Cam	7 Lubrication holes (2)		13 Terminal plate
4 Pivot post	8 Contact set securing screw		

7   Gearbox and automatic transmission

Gearbox – modifications for later models

1   There is only one major modification to the gearbox on later models, and that is to preload the layshaft by means of three springs at the forward end of the gearbox. These are held in compression when the clutch bellhousing is fitted.

2   In association with this modification, O-rings are deleted from the front end of the gearbox where the selector shaft and selector fork shaft pass through.

3   The procedures given in Chapter 6 are still applicable to the later type gearbox, but the three layshaft preload springs must not be forgotten. The component parts are shown in Fig. 13.28.

Automatic transmission – general

4   The Borg Warner Model 65 automatic transmission is available on later models as an optional extra. It is a lightweight version of the earlier Borg Warner Model 35, and due to the resighting of the hydraulic control unit to within the sump, the unsightly bulge in the transmission tunnel which was associated with former versions is no longer necessary. The system comprises two main components.

    a)   A three element hydrokinetic to., ⌐ converter coupling capable of torque multiplication at an infinitely variable ratio between 2 : 1 and 1 : 1.

    b)   A torque/speed responsive hydraulic epicyclic gearbox comprising a planetary gearset providing three forward ratios and one reverse ratio.

Selection of the required ratio is by means of a T-lever, mounted on the gearbox tunnel, which has a fixed quadrant with the selector positions 'P', 'R', 'N', 'D', '2', '1' marked.

It is not possible to start the engine unless the selector is in the 'P' or 'N' positions. This prevents inadvertent movement of the vehicle and is controlled by an inhibitor switch mounted on the transmission unit.

The gate is suitably shaped to prevent accidental engagement of '1', '2', 'R' or 'P' positions.

5   If the car has to be towed for any reason, the selector lever should be at 'N' and an additional $1\frac{1}{2}$ to 2 pints (2 to $2\frac{1}{2}$ US pints) (0.85 to 1.14 litres) of fluid added. The car should be towed no faster than 30 mph (48 km/h) and no further than 40 miles (64 km). If the transmission is faulty these conditions do not apply, but it is then essential to either disconnect the propeller shaft or raise the rear wheels. It is not possible to tow-start or push-start a car with automatic transmission.

6   Due to the complexity of the automatic transmission it is not recommended that stripping the unit is attempted. Where the unit is known to be faulty, and the fault cannot be rectified by following the procedures given in the following paragraphs, the repair should be entrusted to a Leyland or automatic transmission specialist.

Automatic transmission – fluid level check

7   Make sure that the car is on a level surface then apply the handbrake and move the selector lever to 'P'. Let the engine idle for at least two minutes then, while still idling, pull out the dipstick and wipe it clean with a lint-free cloth or tissue. Insert the dipstick and draw it out again, noting the level.

8   If the engine was started from cold, the level should be up to 'H' mark on the 'cold'scale on the dipstick. If the engine is hot (after at least 30 minutes of running) the level should be up to the 'H' mark of the 'hot' scale. Add fluid of the correct type (**NOT** Dexron type) down the dipstick/filler tube to bring it up to the correct level. The difference between the 'H' and 'L' marks corresponds to $\frac{3}{4}$ pint (1.0 US pint) (0.43 litres). Take great care that no dirt enters the transmission when topping up or internal damage will occur.

Automatic transmission – removal and refitting

9   Although the rear mounting is slightly different, and more

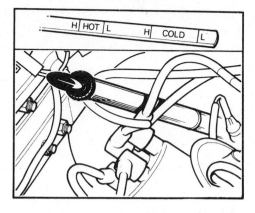

FIG. 13.24 AUTOMATIC TRANSMISSION DIPSTICK AND FILLER TUBE

bolts are used to attach the transmission to the engine, the removal and refitting procedures are virtually identical to those given in Chapter 6, Section 11. It should be noted, however, that the total fluid capacity is $11\frac{1}{2}$ pt (13.8 US pt) (6.54 litre), and that there may be no earth cable attached to the transmission. There is also a rubber stop adjacent to the engine mounting bracket; the locknut on the bolt must be slackened and the rubber stop moved well clear of the engine mounting bracket when the transmission is being removed.

10   When refitting, follow the reverse of the removal procedure, but take note of the following points:

    a)   Align the torque converter and front pump driving dogs and slots horizontally.

    b)   Carefully align the transmission to locate the input shaft and driving dogs.

    c)   Make sure that the propeller shaft is correctly aligned when it is refitted (refer to Chapter 7 as necessary).

    d)   Adjust the rubber stop to obtain 0.020 to 0.060 in (0.5 to 1.5 mm) clearance between the front face of the stop and the rear face of the engine mounting bracket, then tighten the locknut.

    e)   Refill the transmission up to the 'M' mark on the 'cold' scale, run the engine and then select each gear in turn. Now check the fluid level as described in Section 14.

Hand selector lever assembly – removal and refitting

11   Slacken the locking collar and unscrew the selector lever knob.

12   Remove the selector gate cover (three screws) and the front carpet.

13   Remove the self-tapping screws and take off the selector gate housing.

14   Disconnect the selector panel illumination lamp leads at the snap connectors.

15   Ease off the housing, and disconnect the selector rod from the selector lever.

16   If it should be necessary to dismantle the lever assembly, refer to Fig. 13.26 where the parts are shown in the order of dismantling. When reassembling, lubricate the rubbing, pivoting and sliding surface with a general purpose grease, and adjust the selector lever nut and bolt to eliminate free play between the yoke and spindle.

Selector rod – removal, refitting and adjustment

17   With the handbrake applied, select 'N' then push the clip from the levers. This will free the selector rod from the gearbox and hand levers.

18   When refitting, slacken the selector rod locknut, check that the gearbox lever and the hand lever are both at 'N', then refit

the selector rod and clip to the hand lever 'N' on the transmission is the third position from fully forward).

19 Adjust the length of the rod by loosening the locknut and turning the short rod until it can be located in the gearbox selector lever.

20 Tighten the locknut and refit the remaining clip.

21 To check whether any further adjustment is needed, start the engine with 'N' selected, then select 'D'. As the car moves forward, select 'N' and check that disconnection of the drive can be felt. Repeat this with 'N', then 'R' selected. If any further adjustment is required it is done by altering the length of the short rod as already described.

Starter inhibitor/reverse light switch — removal and refitting

22 Apply the handbrake and chock the wheels, then raise the car for access to the left-hand side of the transmission. **Don't attempt to start the car now until the switch has been refitted.**

23 Unsolder the leads from the switch terminals, noting the lead colours.

24 Remove the thread protector, then remove the single screw and washer securing the switch.

25 Refitting is the reverse of the removal procedure. No adjustment is required.

Rear extension oil seal — renewal

26 Drive the car on to a ramp or have jacks available. Chock the wheels and select 'N'.

27 Remove the propeller shaft flange connection and support the weight of the shaft.

28 Whilst restraining the flange from turning, unscrew the locking nut then pull the flange off.

29 Prise out the existing oil seal.

30 Make sure that the seal recess is clean, then lubricate a new seal with transmission fluid and drive it in squarely.

31 Refit the remaining items in the reverse order to removal; tighten the shaft locknut to 58 lbf ft (8.0 kgf m).

Transmission sump — draining and refilling

32 Drive the vehicle on to a ramp or have available adequate jacks to provide access to the underside of the car.

33 Select 'P' and apply the handbrake.

34 Raise the ramp or jacks.

35 *Models with a drain plug:* Wipe around the drain plug and then remove it; drain the contents into a container of at least 11.5 pt (13.8 US pt) (6.54 litre) capacity.

36 *Models without a drain plug:* Unscrew the dipstick/filler pipe at the union on the lower sidewall of the sump, and allow the oil to drain into a container of at least 11.5 pt (13.8 US pt/6.54 litre) capacity. Unscrew the sump bolts, then remove

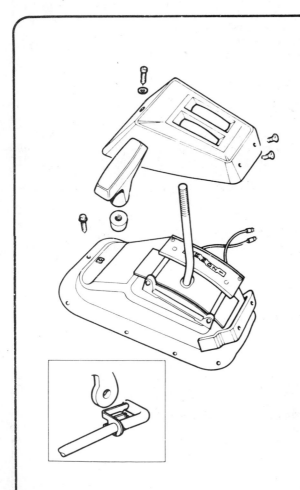

FIG. 13.25 REMOVING HAND SELECTOR LEVER

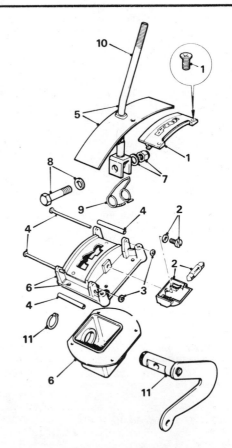

FIG. 13.26 DISMANTLING HAND SELECTOR LEVER

1	Screws and graphics plate	7	Locknut and washer
2	Light assembly	8	Bolt and washer
3	Retaining clips	9	Spring
4	Pins and rollers	10	Selector lever
5	Slide and grommet	11	Circlip and shaft
6	Gate casting		

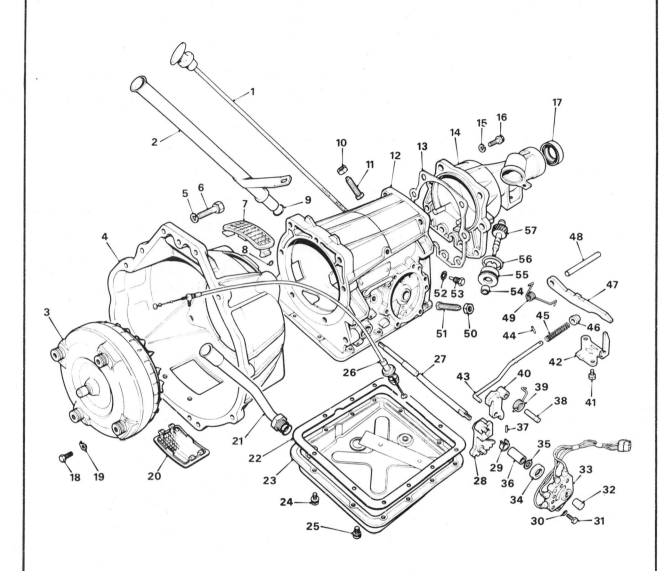

FIG. 13.27 BORG WARNER MODEL 65 AUTOMATIC TRANSMISSION – EXTERNAL COMPONENTS

1 Dipstick	20 Stoneguard	39 Spring
2 Filler tube	21 Filler tube (lower)	40 Parking pawl lever
3 Converter assembly	22 Gasket	41 Bolt
4 Converter housing	23 Oil pan assembly	42 Cam plate
5 Spring washer	24 Bolt	43 Parking brake rod
6 Bolt	25 Drain plug	44 Pin
7 Stoneguard	26 Downshift cable assembly	45 Spring
8 O-ring for manual control shaft	27 Manual control shaft	46 Parking pawl cam
9 O-ring	28 Manual detent lever	47 Parking pawl
10 Locknut	29 Spring clip	48 Pin
11 Rear brake band adjusting screw	30 Washer	49 Spring
12 Case assembly	31 Bolt	50 Locknut
13 Gasket	32 Thread protector	51 Front brake band adjusting screw
14 Rear extension housing	33 Starter inhibitor/reverse lamp switch	52 Lockwasher
15 Spring washer	34 Oil seal	53 Centre support locating bolt
16 Bolt	35 Washer	54 Pinion oil seal
17 Rear oil seal	36 Spacer	55 Speedometer pinion housing
18 Bolt	37 Pin	56 O-ring
19 Lockwasher	38 Pin	57 Speedometer pinion

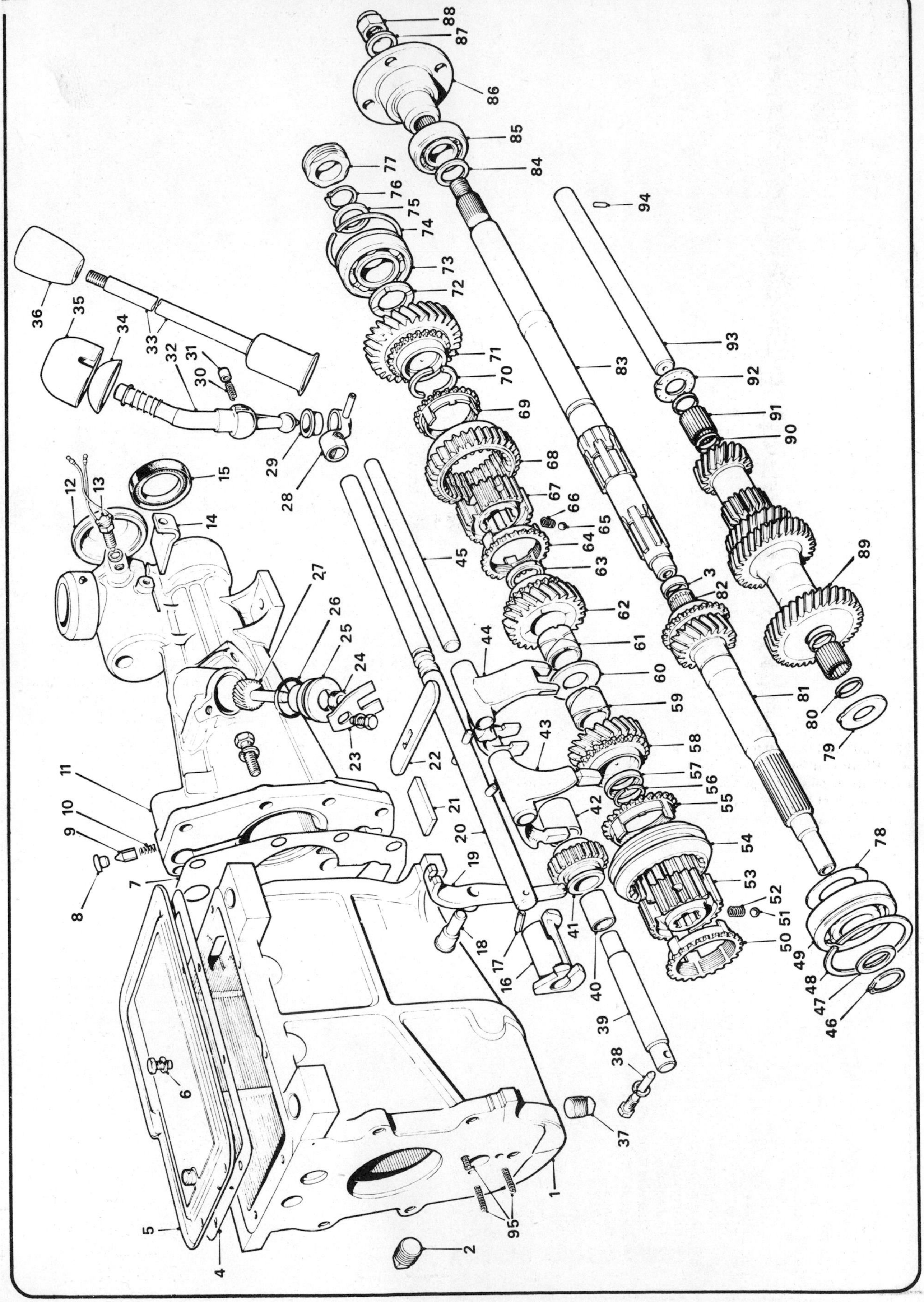
1
2
3
4
5
6
7
8
9
10
11
12
13
14
15
16
17
18
19
20
21
22
23
24
25
26
27
28
29
30
31
32
33
34
35
36
37
38
39
40
41
42
43
44
45
46
47
48
49
50
51
52
53
54
55
56
57
58
59
60
61
62
63
64
65
66
67
68
69
70
71
72
73
74
75
76
77
78
79
80
81
82
83
84
85
86
87
88
89
90
91
92
93
94
95

FIG. 13.28 LATER TYPE GEARBOX

1 Gearbox casing
2 Oil filler level plug
3 O-ring
4 Gasket
5 Top cover
6 Top cover bolt
7 Gasket
8 Plug
9 Detent plunger
10 Detent spring
11 Rear extension
12 End cover
13 Reversing light switch
14 Reverse lift plate
15 Oil seal
16 Interlock spool
17 Selector shaft roll pin
18 Reverse operating lever pin
19 Reverse operating lever
20 Gear selector shaft
21 Magnet
22 Interlock spool plate
23 Retaining clip
24 Seal
25 Housing
26 O-ring
27 Speedometer pinion
28 Gear lever yoke
29 Seat
30 Spring
31 Anti-rattle plunger
32 Lower gearchange lever
33 Upper gearchange lever
34 Dust cover washer
35 Dust cover
36 Knob
37 Drain plug
38 Reverse idler spindle locating screw
39 Reverse idler spindle
40 Reverse idler gear bush
41 Reverse idler gear
42 Reverse idler distance piece
43 3rd and 4th speed selector forks
44 1st and 2nd speed selector forks
45 Selector fork shaft
46 Circlip
47 Backing washer
48 Snap-ring
49 Ball bearing
50 Synchromesh cup
51 Ball
52 Spring
53 3rd and 4th speed synchromesh hub
54 3rd and 4th speed operating sleeve
55 Synchromesh cup
56 Mainshaft circlip
57 3rd speed gear thrust washer
58 3rd speed gear
59 Gear bush
60 Selective washer
61 Gear bush
62 2nd speed gear
63 Thrust washer
64 Synchromesh cup
65 Ball
66 Spring
67 1st and 2nd speed operating sleeve
68 Mainshaft reverse gear
69 Synchromesh cup
70 Split collar
71 1st speed gear
72 Thrust washer
73 Mainshaft centre bearing
74 Snap-ring
75 Selective washer
76 Circlip
77 Speedometer gear
78 Oil slinger
79 Front thrust washer
80 Bearing outer retaining ring
81 1st motion shaft
82 Needle-roller bearing
83 Mainshaft
84 Washer
85 Ball bearing
86 Drive flange
87 Washer
88 Self locking nut
89 Laygear cluster
90 Bearing inner retaining ring
91 Needle rollers
92 Thrust washer
93 Layshaft
94 Layshaft dowel
95 Laygear pre-load springs

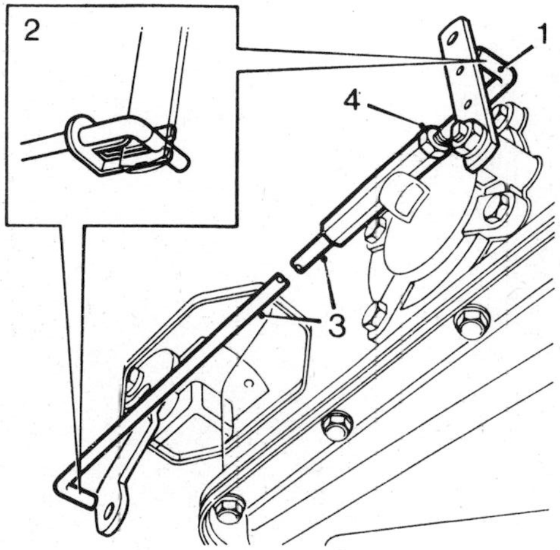

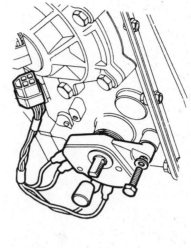

FIG. 13.29 SELECTOR ROD REMOVAL

1 Short rod
2 Retaining clip in position
3 Selector rod
4 Locknut

FIG. 13.30 STARTER INHIBITOR/REVERSE LIGHT SWITCH

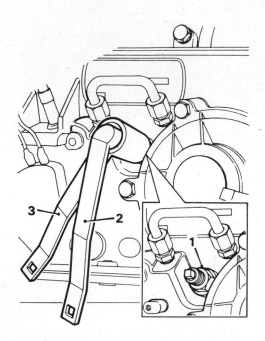

FIG. 13.31 FRONT BRAKE BAND ADJUSTMENT

1   *Locknut*   3   *Locknut holding tool*
2   *Adjuster turning tool*

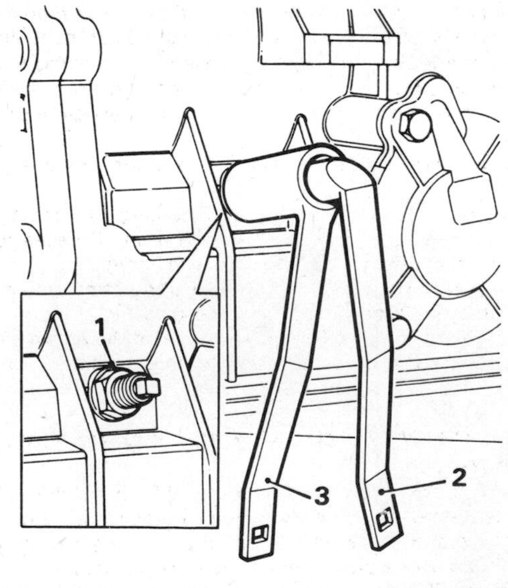

FIG. 13.32 REAR BRAKE BAND ADJUSTMENT

1   *Locknut*   3   *Locknut holding tool*
2   *Adjuster turning tool*

the sump and its gasket.

37 Refitting is a straightforward reverse of the removal procedure, using a new gasket or joint washer as necessary. Add fluid
to bring it up to the 'H' mark on the 'cold' scale, then run the
engine and select each gear in turn. Now check the fluid level as
described in paragraphs 7 and 8.

Front brake band – adjustment

38 Slacken the locknut on the adjustment screw then torque
tighten the screw to 5 lbf ft (0.7 kgf m).
39 Back the screw off $\frac{3}{4}$ of a turn then hold it stationary in this
position whilst tightening the locknut to a torque of 35 lbf ft
(4.8 kgf m).

Rear brake band – adjustment

40 Slacken the adjuster locknut.
41 Torque tighten the screw to 5 lbf ft (0.7 kgf m) then back it
off $\frac{3}{4}$ of a turn.
42 Hold the screw stationary in this position and tighten the
locknut to a torque of 35 lbf ft (4.8 kg f m).

Automatic transmission – fault diagnosis

Stall test: This test can only be satisfactorily carried out with an
engine which is in good condition and capable of developing full
power. It will be necessary to connect an external tachometer to
the engine in order to check the engine speed.
43 Run the engine until its normal operating temperature is
achieved.
44 Chock the wheels and apply both foot and handbrakes.
45 Select '1' or 'R' and depress the throttle to the 'kick-down'
position for a period not exceeding 10 seconds (to avoid overheating the transmission). Note the tachometer reading which
should be 1600 to 1900 rpm. If the reading is lower than 1250
rpm suspect stator slip in the torque converter; if the reading is
1300 to 1600 rpm, the engine is not developing full power; if
the reading is over 2000 rpm, suspect brake band or clutch slip
in the transmission unit.
46 If the test is to be repeated, allow 10 to 15 minutes for the
transmission fluid heat to dissipate.
Converter diagnosis: Refer to Chapter 6, Section 16.

---

8   Propeller shaft

Propeller shaft universal joint – renewal

On later models, it is possible to renew the universal joints
on the propeller shaft by reference to the following procedure.
1   Clean away all traces of dirt from the whole assembly , then
mark the two yokes to ensure the correct relationship when
reassembling . Remove the circlips which hold each set of
needle roller bearings in position. On the front joint, also
unscrew the grease nipple. If the circlip is tight, tap the face of
the bearing cup inside it which may be jamming it in its groove.
2   The bearing should come out if the edges of the yoke ears
are tapped with a mallet. If, however, they are very tight, it
should be possible to shift them by pressing them between the
jaws of a vice, using two distance pieces. Two different size
socket spanners are ideal, and it will be possible to force one
out sufficiently far to enable it to be gripped by another suitable
tool (pliers or vice again) and drawn out. Take care not to
damage the yokes. An alternative method of removing the bearings is to use a socket and hammer as illustrated in the photo. If
the bearings have seized up or worn so badly that the holes in
the yokes are oval, then a new yoke will be needed – and if this
is on the propeller shaft then that will have to be acquired too,
as the whole assembly is balanced and parts are not supplied
separately.
3   New bearings will be supplied with new seals and circlips.
Make sure the needles are correctly in position and the cup $\frac{1}{3}$
full of grease.
4   Fit the spider to the propeller shaft yoke.
5   Engage the spider trunnion in the bearing cup and insert the

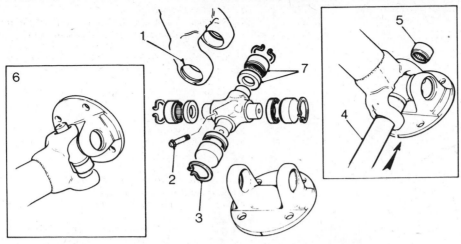

FIG. 13.33 PROPELLER SHAFT JOINT RENEWAL

1 *Alignment mark*	3 *Circlip*	5 *Bearing housing*	7 *Bearing and oil seal*
2 *Grease nipple (front joint)*	4 *Drift or socket spanner*	6 *Joint removal*	

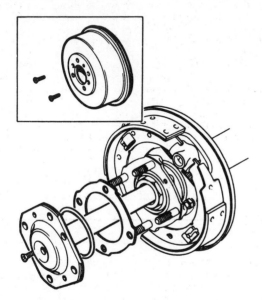

FIG. 13.34 REAR AXLE SHAFT REMOVAL (10 CWT VAN AND PICK-UP)

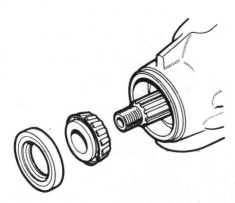

FIG. 13.35 PINION OIL SEAL AND BEARING (10 CWT VAN AND PICK-UP)

cup into the yoke.

6   Fit the opposite bearing cup to the yoke and carefully press both cups into position, ensuring that the spider trunnion engages the cups and that the needle bearings are not displaced.

7   Using two flat-faced adaptors of slightly smaller diameter than the bearing cups, press the cups into the yoke until they reach the lower land of the circlip grooves. Do not press the bearing cups below this point or damage may be caused to the cups and seals.

8   Fit the circlips.

9   Rear axle

Axle shaft, bearing and oil seal (10 cwt Van and Pick-up) – removal and refitting

1   Chock the front wheels, jack-up the rear of the vehicle and support on firmly based axle stands. Remove the roadwheel. Note that if the axleshaft is removed with the vehicle on an even keel, it is likely that oil will run out from the differential and contaminate the brake linings. If only one shaft is being removed then jack-up that side of the vehicle only. If both shafts are being removed drain the oil from the differential before proceeding further.

2   Release the handbrake and slacken the brake adjusters right off.

3   Unscrew the two crosshead countersunk brake drum retaining screws and pull off the brake drum. If necessary tap the brake drum off with a wooden or hide hammer.

4   Unscrew the single shaft flange locating screw and pull the axle shaft, by its flange, out from the axle casing.

5   Refitting of the axleshafts is a reversal of the above process. Always renew the paper washers to ensure that no oil leaks develop.

Pinion oil seal (10 cwt Van and Pick-up – removal and refitting

6   If oil is leaking from the front of the differential nose piece it will be necessary to renew the pinion oil seal. If a pit is not available jack-up and chock-up the rear of the van. It is much easier to do this job over a pit, or with the car on a ramp.

7   Refer to Chapter 7, and disconnect the propeller shaft from the rear axle.

8   If the oil seal is being renewed with the differential nose piece in position, drain the oil and check that the handbrake is firmly on, to prevent the pinion flange moving.

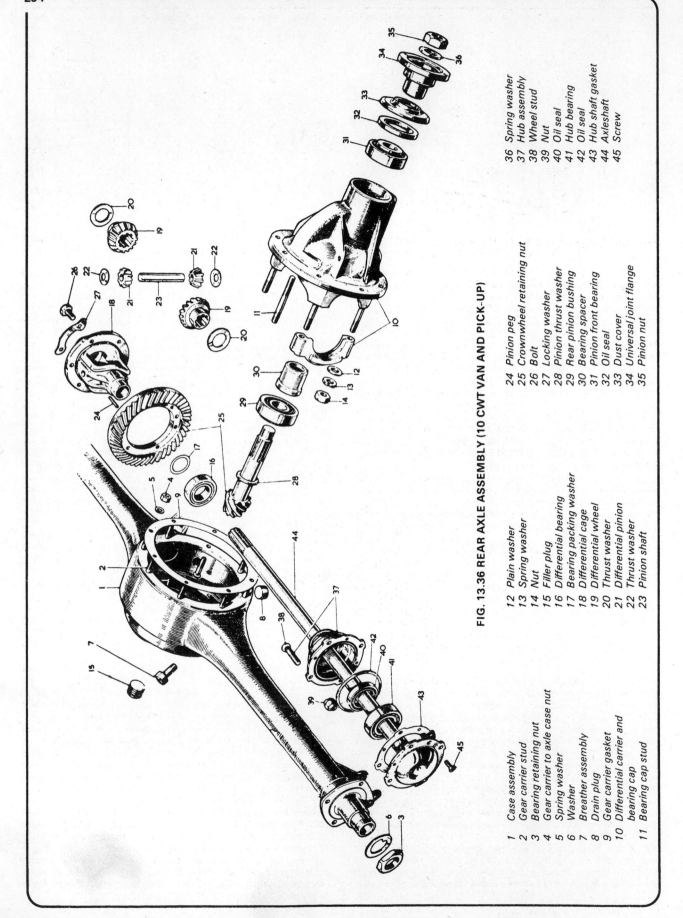

FIG. 13.36 REAR AXLE ASSEMBLY (10 CWT VAN AND PICK-UP)

1 Case assembly
2 Gear carrier stud
3 Bearing retaining nut
4 Gear carrier to axle case nut
5 Spring washer
6 Washer
7 Breather assembly
8 Drain plug
9 Gear carrier gasket
10 Differential carrier and bearing cap
11 Bearing cap stud

12 Plain washer
13 Spring washer
14 Nut
15 Filler plug
16 Differential bearing
17 Bearing packing washer
18 Differential cage
19 Differential wheel
20 Thrust washer
21 Differential pinion
22 Thrust washer
23 Pinion shaft

24 Pinion peg
25 Crownwheel retaining nut
26 Bolt
27 Locking washer
28 Pinion thrust washer
29 Rear pinion bushing
30 Bearing spacer
31 Pinion front bearing
32 Oil seal
33 Dust cover
34 Universal joint flange
35 Pinion nut

36 Spring washer
37 Hub assembly
38 Wheel stud
39 Nut
40 Oil seal
41 Hub bearing
42 Oil seal
43 Hub shaft gasket
44 Axleshaft
45 Screw

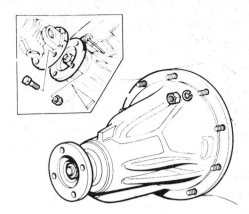

FIG. 13.37 DIFFERENTIAL HOUSING REMOVAL (10 CWT VAN AND PICK-UP)

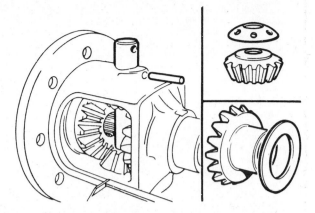

FIG. 13.38 DIFFERENTIAL CARRIER COMPONENTS REMOVAL (10 CWT VAN AND PICK-UP)

9   Unscrew the nut in the centre of the pinion drive flange. Although it is tightened to a torque of 140 lbf ft (19.36 kgf m) it can be removed fairly easily with a long extension arm fitted to the appropriate socket spanner. Remove the nut and spring washer.

10 Pull off the splined drive flange, which may prove a little stubborn, in which case it should be tapped with a hide mallet from the rear (the pressed steel end cover), and prise out the oil seal with a screwdriver taking care not to damage the lip of its seating.

11 Refitting is a reversal of the above procedure. **Note**: the new seal must be pushed into the differential nose piece with the edge of the sealing ring inwards. Take great care not to damage the edge of the oil seal when refitting the end cover and drive flange. Smear the face of the flange which bears against the oil seal lightly with oil before driving the flange onto its splines.

Differential assembly (10 cwt Van and Pick-up) — removal and refitting

12 Refer to paragraphs 1 to 5, and remove the axleshafts.

13 Refer to Chapter 7, and disconnect the propeller shaft from the rear axle.

14 Remove the ring of nuts and spring washers which join the differential nose piece to the axle casing, and pull the nose piece complete with differential assembly out of the casing.

15 Carefully clean down the inside of the axle casing, fit a new nose piece to casing joint, and then fit the exchange or rebuilt differential assembly. Refitting is a reversal of the removal procedure.

16 Refill the differential with the correct grade of oil and run the axle in slowly for the first 500 miles, (800 km) and then change the oil when it is hot.

Differential assembly (10 cwt Van and Pick-up) — dismantling, inspection, reassembly and adjustment

17 Most garages will prefer to renew the complete differential carrier assembly as a unit if it is worn, rather than to dismantle the unit to renew any damaged or worn parts. To do this job 'according to the book' requires the use of special and expensive tools which the majority of garages do not have, and probably, do not have the skilled mechanics who know how these tools should be used.

18 The primary object of these special tools is to ensure that noise is kept to a minimum. If any increase in noise cannot be tolerated (providing that the rear rear axle is not already noisy due to a defective part), then it is best to purchase an exchange, built-up differential unit.

19 If the possibility of a slight increase in noise can be tolerated, then it is quite possible to successfully recondition the rear axle without these special tools. The differential assembly should be stripped and examined in the following fashion:

20 Remove the differential assembly from the rear axle as detailed in the preceding paragraphs.

21 With the differential assembly on the bench begin dismantling the unit by unscrewing the nuts holding the differential bearing caps in place. Ensure that the caps are marked to ensure correct refitting.

22 Pull off the caps and then lever out the differential unit complete with crownwheel and differential gears.

23 Check the differential bearings for side play and, if present, draw them off the differential cage together with any shims fitted between the inner ring of each bearing and the cage.

24 Six high tensile steel bolts hold the crownwheel to the differential cage. Knock back the tabs of the locking washers, and undo and remove the bolts.

25 Professional fitters use a special tool for holding the pinion flange stationary while the nut in the centre of the flange is unscrewed. As it is tightened to a torque of 140 lbf ft (19.36 kgf m) it will require considerable force to move it. As the average owner will not have the use of this tool use the following alternative method. Clamp the pinion flange in a vice and then undo the nut. Any damage caused to the edge of the flange by the vice should be carefully filed smooth.

26 With the nut and spring washer removed, pull off the splined pinion flange (tap the end of the pinion shaft if the flange appears stuck), and remove the pressed end cover and oil seal.

27 Drift the pinion shaft rearwards out of the nose piece. With it will come the inner race and rollers of the rear bearing, the bearing spacer and shims. The old bearing spacer can be thrown away as a new spacer which has not been compressed must always be used. The outer race and front bearing will be left in the nose piece. With the pinion shaft removed the rear outer race can be quite easily extracted.

28 The inner race of the front bearing can now be tapped out and then the outer race extracted.

29 The inner race of the rear bearing is a press fit on the pinion shaft, and must be drifted off carefully. Remove the thrust washer under the pinion gear head, and retain for future use.

30 Check the rollers and races for general wear, score marks, and pitting and renew these components as necessary.

31 Examine the teeth of the crownwheel and pinion for pitting, score marks, chipping, and general wear. If a new crownwheel and pinion is required a mated crownwheel and pinion must be fitted. It is asking for trouble to renew one without the other.

32 Tap out the pinion peg from the crownwheel side of the differential cage to free the pinion shaft which is then driven out. Note that the hole into which the peg fits is slightly tapered, and the opposite end may be lightly peened over and should be cleared with a 0.125 in (3.175 mm) drill.

33 Extract the pinions, wheels, and thrust washers from the differential cage. Check them for wear and renew as necessary. Refitting of the pinion is a reversal of the above process. **Note**:

after the peg has been inserted, the larger end of the hole should be lightly peened over to retain the pin in position.

34 Refit the thrust washer on the pinion shaft and then fit the inner race of the rear bearing. It is quite satisfactory to drift the rear bearing on with a piece of steel tubing 12 to 15 in (300 – 350 mm) long with sufficient internal diameter to just fit over the pinion shaft. With one end of the tube bearing against the race, tap the top end of the tube with a hammer – so driving the bearing squarely down the shaft and hard up against the underside of the thrust washer.

35 Slip a new bearing spacer over the pinion shaft and fit the outer race of the front and rear bearings to the differential nose piece.

36 Insert the pinion shaft forwards into the differential nose piece from inside the casing and then drop the front inner bearing race and rollers into place.

37 Lubricate the bearings with the correct grade of rear axle oil. Fit a new oil seal with the edge of the sealing ring facing inwards. A block of wood is useful for ensuring the seal is driven on squarely.

38 With the seal in position, refit the dust cover, lubricate the underside of the pinion flange (which bears against the oil seal) and drive the flange onto the splines with a hide hammer.

39 Refit the spring washer and with the flange held securely in a vice tighten the flange nut to 140 lbf ft (19.26 kgf m).

40 To obtain the correct pinion bearing preload it is first essential to have renewed the bearing spacer. The correct preload should be 11 to 13 lbf in (0.91 kgf cm). Measure this with a spring balance hooked into one of the drive flange holes. As these holes are 1.5 in (38.1 mm) from the shaft axis a pull of 8 lbf (0.56 kgf) is the correct preload figure using this method. If the preload is too great, use a thinner thrust washer. If too high, use a thicker thrust washer. Renew the bearing spacer each time as it must never be compressed twice.

41 Refit the shims and differential bearings to the differential cage.

42 Ensure that the crownwheel and cage are scrupulously clean and then bolt the crownwheel to the differential cage flange, tightening the six high tensile steel bolts down to a torque of 60 lbf ft (8.30 kgf m). Turn up the tabs on the locking washers.

43 Measure the backlash at the edge of the pinion flange. The reading should be 0.0312 – 0.125 in (0.794 – 1.588 mm). Also check the meshing of the crownwheel and pinion by smearing 'engineer's blue' on the crownwheel and then turning the pinion. The contact mark should appear right in the middle of the crownwheel teeth. If the mark appears on the toe or the heel of the crownwheel teeth them shims must be moved from one side of the differential bearings to the other until the marks are in the correct position.

44 The differential unit can now be refitted to the axle casing.

10 Braking system

Brake master cylinder (Lockheed) – dismantling and reassembly

1 Remove the master cylinder as described in Chapter 9, Section 11.

2 Remove the dust cover shield and the dust cover, then take out the circlip, washer and piston assembly.

3 Remove the curved washer and the main piston seal.

4 Remove the return spring from the cylinder bore.

5 Remove the secondary piston seal.

6 Clean all the parts using clean brake fluid or methylated spirit.

7 Examine the parts for wear, scoring and corrosion; if any is found, renew the part because repair is impracticable.

8 Reassemble the master cylinder using new seals. Smear the seals and all sliding parts with brake fluid when reassembling. Take care with the piston seal; don't use any force when fitting it, and only use your fingers. Make sure that the piston curved washer is fitted with it's domed side nearest the piston.

9 After refitting the master cylinder, don't forget to bleed the hydraulic system as described in Chapter 9, Section 3.

Brake pedal assembly – removal and refitting

10 The procedure is as described in Chapter 9, Section 22, except that it is no longer necessary to remove the complete instrument panel and parcel tray. It is, however, necessary to remove the face vent hose.

11 If the pedal assembly is to be dismantled, although there is a modified return spring arrangement, the general instructions in Chapter 9, Section 22 still apply. The assembly is shown in Fig. 13.39.

Dual master cylinder – removal and refitting

12 This is essentially the same procedure as described in Chapter 9, Section 11, but note the O-ring seal at the flange attachment.

Dual master cylinder – dismantling and reassembly

13 With the master cylinder removed from the car, unscrew the filler cap, then carefully lever out the baffle and sealing washer.

14 Remove the clips and take out the reservoir fixing pins. Pull off the reservoir.

15 Take the two reservoir seals out of the body, noting their fitted positions.

16 With the master cylinder clamped in a vice, push in the plunger and withdraw the secondary plunger stop pin.

17 Remove the circlip from the cylinder bore, and withdraw the primary plunger assembly.

18 If necessary, apply air pressure at the secondary outlet port, and remove the secondary plunger assembly.

19 Remove the two vacuum seals and spacers from the primary plunger, followed by the spring, seal retainer, recuperating seal and washer.

20 Remove the spring, seal retainer, recuperating seal and washer from the secondary plunger, followed by the two seals; note which way round these are fitted.

21 Clean all the parts in clean brake fluid or methylated spirit. Check that all the ports are unobstructed. Check the parts for corrosion, wear and scoring; if any is found, renew the part because repair is impracticable.

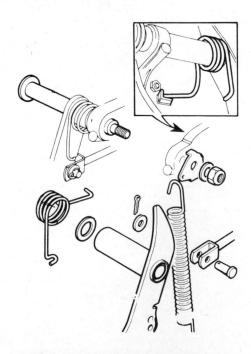

FIG. 13.39 BRAKE PEDAL ASSEMBLY

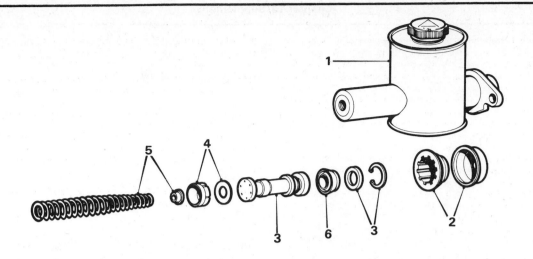

FIG. 13.40 LOCKHEED BRAKE MASTER CYLINDER COMPONENTS

1	Master cylinder	3	Circlip, washer and piston assembly	5	Return spring
2	Shield and dust cover	4	Curved washer and main piston seal	6	Secondary seal

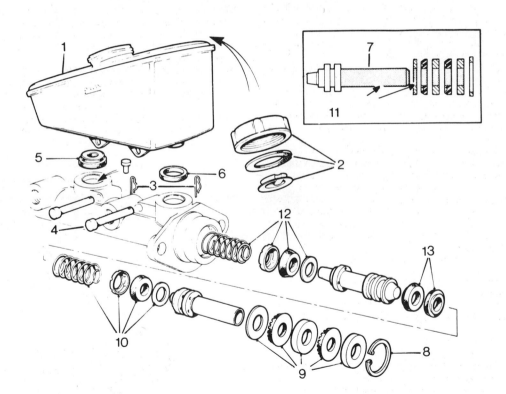

FIG. 13.41 DISMANTLING DUAL MASTER CYLINDER

1	Master cylinder reservoir	9	Vacuum seals and spacers
2	Filler cap, baffle and washer	10	Spring, seal retainer, recuperating seal and washer
3	Clips	11	Primary plunger assembly. Lubricate with special grease
4	Fixing pins		where arrowed
5	Seal	12	Spring, seal retainer, recuperating seal and washer
6	Seal	13	Secondary plunger seals
7	Plunger		
8	Circlip		

22 Reassemble the master cylinder using new seals, by reversing the dismantling procedure. Pay attention to the following points:

   a) *Unscrew all seals and sliding parts in new brake fluid when assembling*
   b) *Press the plunger fully down the cylinder bore to allow the secondary plunger stop pin to be fitted.*
   c) *Note that the secondary plunger return spring is the larger of the two.*
   d) *Lubricate the vacuum seals, spacers and plunger (see arrows in Fig 13.41 inset) with the special grease provided with the seal kit.*

11A Electrical system (standard equipment)

Regulator unit (RB 340) – checking and adjustment

1 The regulator requires very little attention during its service life, and if there should be any reason to suspect its correct functioning, tests of all circuits should be made to ensure that they are not the reason for the trouble.

2 These checks include the tension of the fan belt, to make sure it is not slipping and so providing only a very low charge rate. The battery should be carefully checked for possible low charge rate due to a faulty cell, or corroded battery connections.

3 The leads from the generator may have been crossed during refitting, and if this is the case, then the regulator points will have stuck together as soon as the generator starts to charge. Check for loose or broken leads from the generator to the regulator.

4 If, after a thorough check, it is considered advisable to test the regulator, this should be carried out by an electrician who is well acquainted with the correct method, using test bench equipment.

Voltage regulator

5 Pull off the Lucas connections from the two adjacent control box terminals 'B'. To start the engine it will now be necessary to join together the ignition and battery leads with a suitable wire.

6 Connect a 0-20 volt voltmeter between terminal 'D' on the control box and terminal 'WL'. Start the engine and run it at 3000 rpm. The reading on the voltmeter should be steady and lie between the limits detailed in the Specifications.

7 If the reading is unsteady this may be due to dirty contacts. If the reading is outside the specified limits stop the engine and adjust the voltage regulator in the following manner:

8 Take off the control box cover and start and run the engine at 3000 rpm. Using the correct Lucas tool, turn the voltage adjustment cam anti-clockwise to raise the setting and clockwise to lower it. To check that the setting is correct, stop the engine, and then start it and run it at 3000 rpm, noting the reading. Refit the cover and the connections to the 'WL' and 'D' terminals.

Current regulator

9 The output from the current regulator should equal the maximum output from the dynamo which is 22 amps. To test this it is necessary to bypass the cut-out by holding the contacts together.

10 Remove the cover from the control box and with a bulldog clip hold the cut-out contacts together.

11 Pull off the wires from the adjacent terminals 'B' and connect a 0 - 40 moving-coil ammeter to one of the terminals and to the leads.

12 All the other connections, including the ignition must be made to the battery.

13 Turn on all the lights and other electrical accessories and run the engine at 3000 rpm. The ammeter should give a steady reading between 19 and 22 amps. If the needle flickers it is likely that the points are dirty. If the reading is too low, turn the special Lucas tool clockwise to raise the setting and anti-clockwise to lower it.

Cut-out

14 Check the voltage required to operate the cut-out connecting a voltmeter between the control box terminals 'D' and 'WL'. Remove the control box cover, start the engine and gradually increase its speed until the cut-out closes. This should occur when the reading is between 12.7 to 13.3 volts.

15 If the reading is outside these limits turn the cut-out adjusting cam by means of the adjusting tool, a fraction at a time, clockwise to raise the voltage and anti-clockwise to lower it.

16 To adjust the drop-off voltage, bend the fixed contact blade carefully. The adjustment to the cut-out should be completed within 30 seconds of starting the engine as otherwise heat build-up from the shunt-coil will affect the readings.

17 If the cut-out fails to work, clean the contacts, and if there is still no response, renew the cut-out and regulator unit.

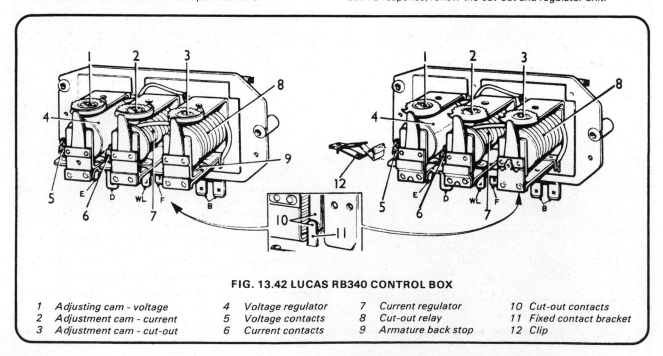

FIG. 13.42 LUCAS RB340 CONTROL BOX

1 *Adjusting cam - voltage*	4 *Voltage regulator*	7 *Current regulator*	10 *Cut-out contacts*
2 *Adjustment cam - current*	5 *Voltage contacts*	8 *Cut-out relay*	11 *Fixed contact bracket*
3 *Adjustment cam - cut-out*	6 *Current contacts*	9 *Armature back stop*	12 *Clip*

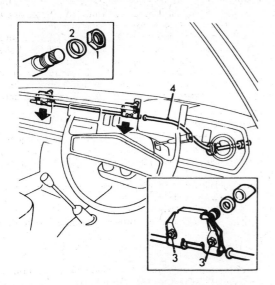

FIG. 13.43 WHEELBOX AND DRIVE CABLE REMOVAL

1　Nut　　　　3　Nut
2　Spacer　　　4　Drive tube

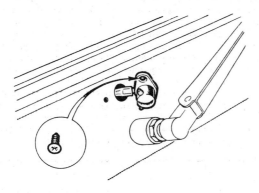

FIG. 13.44 TAILGATE WASHER JET REMOVAL

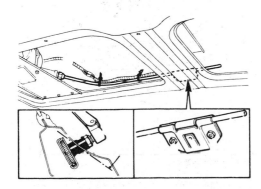

FIG. 13.45 TAILGATE WIPER WHEELBOX AND RACK TUBES

Windscreen wiper wheelboxes and drive cable (Van and Pick-up) – removal and refitting

18　Remove the demister ducts and then the wiper motor and drive.
19　Undo and remove the nuts securing the wheelboxes.
20　Lift away the spacers.
21　Slacken the nuts clamping the wheelbox plates on the right-hand side and lift away both wheelboxes from underneath the facia panel.
22　Recover the spacer from each wheelbox.
23　Remove the shaped drive tube from the engine side of the bulkhead by pulling it through the two cable straps and bulkhead grommet.
24　Refitting the wheelboxes and cable drive is the reverse sequence to removal.

Tailgate screen washers (Estate car)
Pump - removal and refitting
25　Remove the spare wheel, then drill out the rivets so that the pump can be removed. Note the earth leads.
26　Disconnect the wiring connector, then remove the inlet and outlet tubes.
27　Refitting is the reverse of the removal procedure. Either use pop rivets or self-tapping screws to secure the pump bracket to the mounting bracket.

Washer jet – removal and refitting
28　Remove the securing screws, then manoeuvre the jet sideways so that it can be pulled out and the feed pipe attached.
29　Refitting is straightforward. Adjust the jet to spray at the top of the tailgate glass.

Tailgate wiper motor (Estate car) – dismantling and reassembly

30　Remove the tailgate wiper arm and the tailgate trim pad.
31　Remove the motor electrical connector, then unscrew the rack retaining tube nut from the motor ferrule.
32　Support the mounting plate, then remove the six screws and pull away the cable rack from the tube.
33　Slacken the mounting strap screw and remove the motor, then remove the gearbox cover (four screws).
34　To remove the rack, first remove the circlip and washer, then withdraw the connecting rod and washer from the crank-pin.
35　Lift out the crosshead and remove the cable rack assembly.
36　Remove the circlip and washer from the gear shaft; withdraw the gear, but make sure that the end of the shaft is not burred.
37　Remove the dished washer.
38　Reassembly and refitting are the reverse of the dismantling and removal procedures, but the following points should be noted:

　　a)　Use Ragosine Listate grease or an equivalent to lubricate the gear teeth, worn gear, connecting rod and pin, crosshead slide and cable rack.
　　b)　Use Shell Turbo 41 oil or an equivalent to lubricate the bearing bushes, gearwheel shaft and crankpin.
　　c)　If a new gearwheel is being used, make sure that when the motor is in the 'Park' position (cable rack retracted), the cam is opposite the crankpin.
　　d)　Note that the dished washer is fitted with the concave side towards the gearwheel.
　　e)　Note that the larger of the two washers is fitted beneath the crankpin.
　　f)　When refitting the wiper arm, ensure that the motor is in the 'Park' position to obtain a satisfactory sweep.

Tailgate wiper wheelbox and rack tubes – removal and refitting

39　Remove the wiper arm and tailgate trim pad.
40　Remove the wiring clips, then unscrew the rack tube ferrule at the motor.

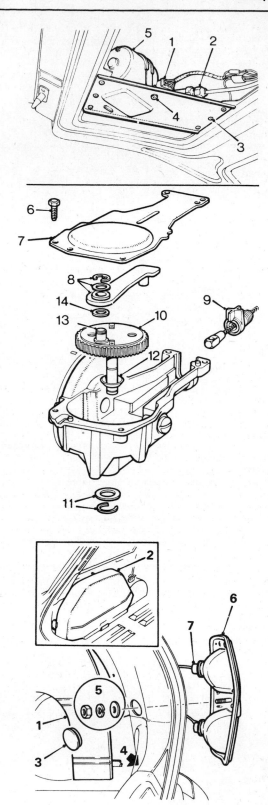

FIG. 13.46 TAILGATE WIPER REMOVAL

1	Connector	8	Circlip, washer
2	Retaining nut on ferrule		and connecting rod
3	Screws	9	Crosshead
4	Screw	10	Gear
5	Motor assembly	11	Circlip and washer
6	Screw	12	Dished washer
7	Gearbox cover	13	Crankpin
		14	Large washer

41 Loosen the wheelbox cover retaining nuts.

42 Remove the spindle nut and spacer, then remove the wheelbox assembly from inside the panel.

43 Remove the spacer from the wheelbox and take out the rack tubes.

44 Check the condition of the moving parts and renew as necessary, then refit the parts in the reverse order to removal. Note the following points:

  a) Lubricate the wheel teeth with Ragosine Listate grease or an equivalent.

  b) With the rack tubes free, insert the rack and turn the spindle to engage the wheel.

  c) Ensure that the spacers are fitted with the angle towards the glass.

  d) Align the rack tubes then tighten the wheelbox cover plate.

Windscreen washer pump (Van and Pick-up) — removal and refitting

45 Carefully unscrew the pump securing bezel by tapping round with a screwdriver.

46 Lift away the bezel and withdraw the pump plunger.

47 Lift away the washer pump from behind the facia panel and disconnect the two tubes from the rear of the pump. Note which way round the tubes are fitted for correct refitting.

48 Refitting the windscreen washer pump is the reverse sequence to removal.

Front flasher repeater lamp — removal and refitting

49 For access to the bulb, remove the screw and take off the lens.

50 If the lamp is to be removed, detach the leads at the connector then remove the retaining nuts. Note the earth lead clipped to one of the studs.

51 Refitting is straightforward; note the lens retaining clip which must be engaged before the lens is fitted.

Stop, tail and flasher lights — removal and refitting
Later Saloons

52 The information given in Chapter 10, Section 35 is applicable, except that there are three bulbs instead of two.

Estate car

53 For access to the bulbs, remove the rear compartment trim pad (right-hand side) or spare wheel (left-hand side).

54 Pull out the bulb holder and remove the appropriate bulb.

55 To remove the lamp assembly, remove the rubber plug then, with the opening in the body directly below the lamp covered, remove the nut, spring washer and flat washer retaining the lamp assembly.

56 Detach the lamp assembly, and remove the lens (six screws), if necessary.

57 Refitting is the reverse of the removal procedure. Note that the flasher lens laps over the stop and tail lens. When refitting bulb holders, note the slot(s) which must align with the locating tongue(s).

Van

58 Undo and remove the screws at the top and bottom of the light cluster and lift away the cover.

59 Pull out the bulb holder and detach the bulb which has a

FIG. 13.47 STOP, TAIL AND FLASHER LAMP – ESTATE CAR

1	Trim pad (right-hand side)	5	Nut and washers
2	Spare wheel cover (left-hand side)	6	Lamp assembly
3	Rubber plug	7	Bulb holder
4	Opening in body		

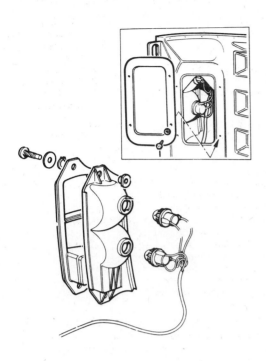

FIG. 13.48 REAR LIGHT CLUSTER COMPONENTS (VAN)

bayonet fixing.

60 To remove the light cluster assembly undo and remove the two screws and nylon nuts securing the assembly to the body.

61 Lift away the light, lens and rubber sealing washer.

62 Refitting the light cluster assembly and bulb is the reverse sequence to removal.

Pick-up

63 Remove the access panel (four screws) and take out the bulb holders.

64 To remove the lamp assembly, remove the two screws and fibre washers followed by the two circlips and their studs.

65 Reassembly and refitting is the reverse of the removal procedure. A new lens seal should be used if the existing one is damaged, with a little adhesive used to hold it in place.

Number plate light – removal and refitting

Van

66 Disconnect the wires at the snap connectors located behind the light unit.

67 Undo and remove the two nuts and spring washers securing the light unit to the body.

68 Lift the light assembly complete with rubber seal from the body.

69 Refitting the rear number plate light is the reverse sequence to removal.

Pick-up

70 Remove the nut on the cover, then take off the cover and lens so that the bulb can be removed.

71 To remove the complete light, detach the electrical leads and remove the eyelets from the cable ends.

72 Remove the two nuts and shakeproof washers then remove the lamp, pulling the cables through the lamp body grommet.

73 Refitting is the reverse of the removal procedure.

Estate car

74 Push the lamp body up out of the bumper, and remove the cap and lens for access to the bulb.

75 If the lamp is to be removed, disconnect the inline connectors.

76 Refitting is the reverse of the removal procedure, but make sure that the register on the lamp body lines up with the cut-out on the lens and in the bumper.

Reversing lights (flush mounted) – removal and refitting

77 Undo and remove the two screws securing the reversing light lens to the body. Recover the retaining clamps and rubber washers.

78 Lift away the lens.

79 The bulb is of the festoon type and is removed by unclipping from the two electrodes.

80 To remove the reversing light unit, disconnect the harness connector located inside the boot.

81 Undo and remove the two nuts securing the light to the body and lift away the light unit.

82 To refit the reversing light and bulb is the reverse sequence to removal. Before refitting the light unit fill the trough formed in the rear of the light body with some sealing compound.

Reversing light bulb (protruding type) – removal and refitting

83 Undo and remove the two screws securing the reversing light lens to the light body.

84 Lift away the lens and recover the gasket.

85 The bulb is of the festoon type and is removed by unclipping from the two electrodes.

86 To remove the reversing light unit undo and remove the lower fixing screw.

87 Disconnect the harness connector located in the luggage compartment.

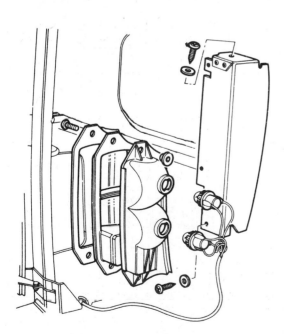

FIG. 13.49 REAR LIGHT CLUSTER COMPONENTS (PICK-UP)

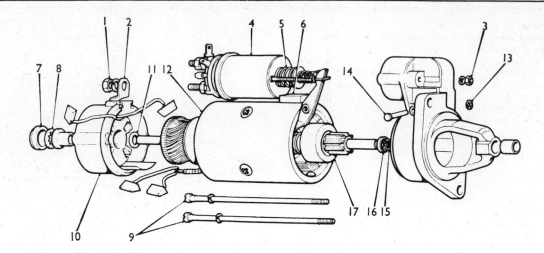

FIG. 13.50 2M100 PRE-ENGAGED STARTER MOTOR COMPONENT PARTS

1 Connecting link securing nut	5 Solenoid plunger and return spring	9 Through-bolts
2 Connecting link	6 Rubber block	10 Commutator end cover
3 Solenoid to drive end bracket securing nut	7 End cap seal	11 Thrust washer
4 Solenoid	8 Armature shaft retaining ring (spire nut)	12 Yoke
		13 Retaining ring (spire nut)

14 Pivot pin
15 Thrust collar jump ring
16 Thrust collar
17 Roller clutch drive

88 Undo and remove the two bolts, plain and spring washers and nuts securing the light body. Disconnect the earth lead.
89 Refitting the reversing light and bulb is the reverse sequence to removal.

Interior roof light (Saloon) – removal and refitting
90 For safety reasons, disconnect the battery.
91 Detach the light unit lens.
92 The bulb is of the festoon type and is removed by unclipping from the two electrodes.
93 Undo and remove the two screws securing the light unit to the roof panel.
94 Withdraw the light unit and detach the two wires from the rear.
95 Refitting the interior roof light and bulb is the reverse sequence to removal.

Interior roof light (Van and Pick-up) – removal and refitting
96 For safety reasons, disconnect the battery.
97 Squeeze the lens at the top and bottom and detach the lens.
98 The bulb is of the festoon type and is removed by unclipping from the two electrodes.
99 Push out the wire terminals from the light terminals.
100 Undo and remove the two screws securing the light unit to the body.
101 Withdraw the light from its location on the body.
102 Refitting the interior roof light and bulb is the reverse sequence to removal.

Starter motor (2M100)
103 Although a different type of starter motor is fitted on some later models, the information given in Chapter 10 is still applicable. An exploded view of the starter motor is shown in Fig. 13.50.

Light switch – removal and refitting
Saloon, Coupe and Estate Car
104 Compress the retaining springs on the switch body, then press out the switch and disconnect the wiring.

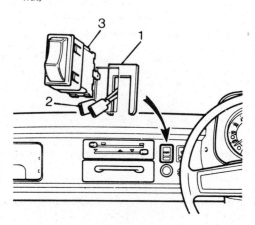

FIG. 13.51 HEATER FAN SWITCH REMOVAL (VAN AND PICK-UP)

1 Special tool   3 Switch
2 Switch leads

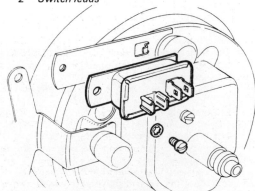

FIG. 13.52 VOLTAGE STABILIZER (VAN AND PICK-UP)

Van and Pick-up

105 Disconnect the battery earth lead, then detach the wires from the back of the switch.

106 Using a suitable tool to compress the springs on the sides of the switch, remove it. **Note:** Leyland tool 1862101 is made for this purpose, but it should not be difficult to make up something similar, or to improvise as described in Chapter 10, Section 40. The tool is shown in Fig. 13.51, being used for the heater switch on Vans and Pick-ups.

All models

107 Refitting is straightforward, the switch just snapping into place.

Heater fan switch – removal and refitting

Saloon and Estate Car

108 Press in the clips on the switch sides and push the switch out. Disconnect the wires.

Van and Pick-up

109 Disconnect the battery earth lead, then detach the wires from the back of the switch.

110 Using a suitable tool as shown in Fig. 13.51, compress the springs on the sides of the switch and remove it.

All models

111 Refitting is straightforward, the switch just snapping into place.

Instrument panel cowl (Van and Pick-up) – removal and refitting

112 Undo and remove the two screws and plain washers located on the sides of the cowl.

113 Lift away the cowl.

114 Refitting the instrument panel cowl is the reverse sequence to removal. Make sure that the front locating clip engages under the facia panel shroud.

Voltage stabilizer (Van and Pick-up) – removal and refitting

115 The voltage stabilizer is located at the rear of the speedometer head (Fig 13.52).

116 Remove the instrument panel cowl and speedometer head.

117 Undo and remove the two screws and shakeproof washers securing the stabiliser and lift away from its location.

118 Refitting the stabiliser is the reverse sequence to removal.

Speedometer (Van and Pick-up) – removal and refitting

119 For safety reasons, disconnect the battery.

120 Remove the instrument panel cowl.

121 Undo and remove the four screws and plain washers securing the speedometer head. Ease the instrument forwards.

122 Press the release lever on the speedometer cable connector and disconnect the speedometer cable.

123 Note the location of the various bulb holders and then detach (See Fig. 13.53 caption for identification).

124 Disconnect the light green shrouded lead from the 'B' connector on the rear of the voltage stabilizer.

125 Disconnect the light green spade connector from the 'I' connector of the voltage stabilizer and the opposite end connector from the fuel gauge.

126 Disconnect the green/black lead from the fuel gauge.

127 Undo and remove the nut and shakeproof washer securing the earth lead tag and disconnect the lead.

128 Lift away the speedometer head.

129 Refitting the speedometer head is the reverse sequence to removal.

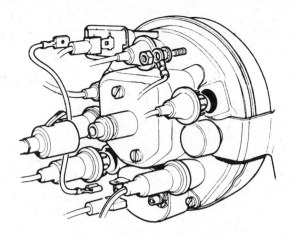

FIG. 13.53 REAR VIEW OF SPEEDOMETER HEAD (VAN AND PICK-UP)

Cable colour code

Main beam warning lamp	*Blue-white*
Panel lamps	*Red-green RH steering/ Red LH steering*
Oil pressure warning lamp	*White/White brown*
Ignition warning lamp	*Brown-yellow/White*
Direction indicator warning lamp	*Green-red/Green-white*

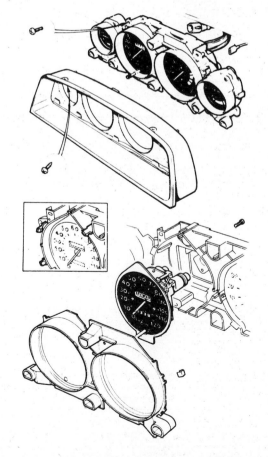

FIG. 13.54 SPEEDOMETER REMOVAL (SALOON AND ESTATE CAR)

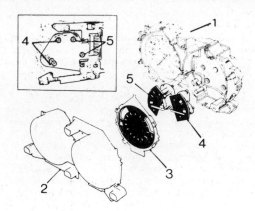

FIG. 13.55 FUEL AND TEMPERATURE GAUGES (SALOON AND ESTATE CAR)

1 Instrument housing   4 Temperature gauge
2 Lens   5 Fuel gauge
3 Face plate

Speedometer (Saloon and Estate car) – removal and refitting

130 For safety reasons, disconnect the battery.
131 Remove the two screws and withdraw the instrument cowl from the facia.
132 Remove the instrument pack retaining screws.
133 Press the locking lever on the speedometer cable ferrule from behind the facia, and detach the cable.
134 Pull the instrument pack forward and disconnect the electrical connectors.
135 Remove the retaining clips and take off the one-piece lens. Remove the instrument face plate.
136 Remove the two screws retaining the speedometer, and withdraw it from its housing.
137 Refitting is the reverse of the removal procedure.

Fuel gauge (Van and Pick-up) – removal and refitting

138 Remove the instrument panel cowl and speedometer head.
139 Undo and remove the two screws and shakeproof washers securing the fuel gauge and lift the unit away from its location.
140 Refitting the fuel gauge is the reverse sequence to removal.

Fuel and temperature gauges (Saloon and Estate car) – removal and refitting

141 Remove the instrument pack as described in paragraphs 130 to 137.
142 Release the one-piece lens from its clips, and remove it.
143 Remove the instrument face plate.
144 Remove the two nuts and wave washers securing the instrument(s).
145 Refitting instrument(s) is the reverse of the removal procedure.

11 B Electrical system (accessories)

Radios and tape players – fitting (general)

A radio or tape player is an expensive item to buy and will only give its best performance if fitted properly. It is useless to expect concert hall performance from a unit that is suspended from the dash panel on string with its speaker resting on the back seat or parcel shelf! If you do not wish to do the installa-

tion yourself there are many in-car entertainment specialists who can do the fitting for you.
Make sure the unit purchased is of the same polarity as the car, and ensure that units with adjustable polarity are correctly set before commencing installation.
It is difficult to give specific information with regard to fitting, as final positioning of the radio/tape player, speakers and aerial is entirely a matter of personal preference. However, the following paragraphs give guidelines to follow, which are relevant to all installations.

Radios
Most radios are a standardised size of 7 inches wide, by 2 inches deep - this ensures that they will fit into the radio aperture provided in most cars. If your car does not have such an aperture, then the radio must be fitted in a suitable position either in, or beneath, the dashpanel. Alternatively, a special console can be purchased which will fit between the dashpanel and the floor, or on the transmission tunnel. These consoles can also be used for additional switches and instrumentation if required. Where no radio aperture is provided, the following points should be borne in mind before deciding exactly where to fit the unit:
   a) *The unit must be within easy reach of the driver wearing a seat belt.*
   b) *The unit must not be mounted in close proximity to an electric tachometer, the ignition switch and its wiring, or the flasher unit and associated wiring.*
   c) *The unit must be mounted within reach of the aerial lead, and in such a place that the aerial lead will not have to be routed near the components detailed in the preceding paragraph 'b'.*
   d) *The unit should not be positioned in a place where it might cause injury to the car occupants in an accident; for instance, under the dashpanel above the driver's or passengers' legs.*
   e) *The unit must be fitted really securely.*
Some radios will have mounting brackets provided together with instructions: others will need to be fitted using drilled and slotted metal strips, bent to form mounting brackets - these strips are available from most accessory shops. The unit must be properly earthed, by fitting a separate earthing lead between the casing of the radio and the vehicle frame.
Use the radio manufacturers' instructions when wiring the radio into the vehicle's electrical system. If no instructions are available refer to the relevant wiring diagram to find the location of the radio 'feed' connection in the vehicle's wiring circuit. A 1-2 amp 'in-line' fuse must be fitted in the radio's 'feed' wire - a choke may also be necessary (see next Section).
The type of aerial used, and its fitted position is a matter of personal preference. In general the taller the aerial, the better the reception. It is best to fit a fully retractable aerial - especially, if a mechanical car-wash is used or if you live in an area where cars tend to be vandalised. In this respect electric aerials which are raised and lowered automatically when switching the radio on or off are convenient, but are more likely to give trouble than the manual type.
When choosing a site for the aerial the following points should be considered:
   a) *The aerial lead should be as short as possible - this means that the aerial should be mounted at the front of the car.*
   b) *The aerial must be mounted as far away from the distributor and HT leads as possible.*
   c) *The part of the aerial which protrudes beneath the mounting point must not foul the roadwheels, or anything else.*
   d) *If possible the aerial should be positioned so that the coaxial lead does not have to be routed through the engine compartment.*
   e) *The plane of the panel on which the aerial is mounted should not be so steeply angled that the aerial cannot be mounted vertically (in relation to the 'end-on' aspect of*

the car). Most aerials have a small amount of adjustment available.

Having decided on a mounting position, a relatively large hole will have to be made in the panel. The exact size of the hole will depend upon the specific aerial being fitted, although, generally, the hole required is of $\frac{3}{4}$ inch (19 mm) diameter. On metal bodied cars, a 'tank-cutter' of the relevant diameter is the best tool to use for making the hole. This tool needs a small diameter pilot hole drilled through the panel, through which, the tool clamping bolt is inserted. On GRP bodied cars, a 'hole-saw' is the best tool to use. Again, this tool will require the drilling of a small pilot hole. When the hole has been made the raw edges should be de-burred with a file and then painted, to prevent corrosion.

Fit the aerial according to the manufacturers' instructions. If the aerial is very tall, or if it protrudes beneath the mounting panel for a considerable distance it is a good idea to fit a stay between the aerial and the vehicle frame. This stay can be manufactured from the slotted and drilled metal strips previously mentioned. The stay should be securely screwed or bolted in place. For best reception it is advisable to fit an earth lead between the aerial and the vehicle frame - this is essential for GRP bodied cars.

It will probably be necessary to drill one or two holes through body-work panels in order to feed the aerial lead into the interior of the car. Where this is the case ensure that the holes are fitted with rubber grommets to protect the cable, and to stop possible entry of water.

Positioning and fitting of the speaker depends mainly on the type. Generally, the speaker is designed to fit directly into the aperture already provided in the car (usually in the shelf behind the rear seats, or in the top of the dashpanel). Where this is the case, fitting the speaker is just a matter of removing the protective grille from the aperture and screwing or bolting the speaker in place. Take great care not to damage the speaker diaphragm whilst doing this. It is a good idea to fit a 'gasket' between the speaker frame and the mounting panel, in order to prevent vibration - some speakers will already have such a gasket fitted.

If a 'pod' type speaker was supplied with the radio, the best acoustic results will normally be obtained by mounting it on the shelf behind the rear seat. The pod can be secured to the mounting panel with self-tapping screws.

When connecting a rear mounted speaker to the radio, the wires should be routed through the vehicle beneath the carpets or floor mats - preferably the middle, or along the side of the floorpan, where they will not be trodden on by passengers. Make the relevant connections as directed by the radio manufacturer.

By now you will have several yards of additional wiring in the car, use PCV tape to secure this wiring out of harm's way. Do not leave electrical leads dangling. Ensure that all new electrical connections are properly made (wires twisted together will not do) and completely secure.

The radio should now be working, but before you pack away your tools it will be necessary to 'trim' the radio to the aerial. If specific instructions are not provided by the radio manufacturer, proceed as follows. Find a station with a low signal strength on the medium-wave band, slowly, turn the trim screw of the radio in, or out, until the loudest reception of the selected station is obtained - the set is then trimmed to the aerial.

Tape players

Fitting instructions for both cartridge and cassette stereo tape players are the same and in general the same rules apply as when fitting a radio. Tape players are not usually prone to electrical interference like radios - although it can occur - so positioning is not so critical. If possible the player should be mounted on an 'even-keel'. Also, it must be possible for a driver wearing a seat belt to reach the unit in order to change or turn over tapes.

For the best results from speakers designed to be recessed into a panel, mount them so that the back of the speaker protrudes into an enclosed chamber within the car (eg; door interiors or the boot cavity).

To fit recessed type speakers in the front doors first check that there is sufficient room to mount the speakers in each door without it fouling the latch or window winding mechanism. Hold the speaker against the skin of the door, and draw a line around the periphery of the speaker. With the speaker removed draw a second 'cutting' line, within the first, to allow enough room for the entry of the speaker back, but at the same time providing a broad seat for the speaker flange. When you are sure that the 'cutting-in line' is correct, drill a series of holes around its periphery. Pass a hacksaw blade through one of the holes and then cut through the metal between the holes until the centre section of the panel falls out.

De-burr the edges of the hole and then paint the raw metal to prevent corrosion. Cut a corresponding hole in the door trim panel - ensuring that it will be completely covered by the speaker grille. Now drill a hole in the door edge and a corresponding hole in the door surround. These holes are to feed the speaker leads through - so fit grommets. Pass the speaker leads through the door trim, door skin and out through the holes in the side of the door and door surround. Refit the door trim panel and then secure the speaker to the door using self-tapping screws. **Note**: If the speaker is fitted with a shield to prevent water dripping on it, ensure that this shield is at the top.

Pod type speakers can be fastened to the shelf behind the rear seat, or anywhere else offering a corresponding mounting point on each side of the car. If the pod speakers are mounted on each side of the shelf behind the rear seat, it is a good idea to drill several large diameter holes through to the boot cavity beneath each speaker - this will improve the sound reproduction. Pod speakers sometimes offer a better reproduction quality if they face the rear window - which then acts as a reflector - so it is worthwhile to do a little experimenting before finally fixing the speaker.

Radios and tape players – suppression of interference (general)

To eliminate buzzes and other unwanted noises, costs very little and is not as difficult as sometimes thought. With a modicum of common sense and patience and following the instructions in the following paragraphs, interference can be virtually eliminated.

The first cause for concern is the generator. The noise this makes over the radio is like an electric mixer and the noise speeds up when you rev up (if you wish to prove the point, you can remove the drive-belt and try it). The remedy for this is simple; connect a 1.0 - 3.0 mf capacitor between earth, probably the bolt that holds down the generator base, and the *large* terminal on the dynamo or alternator. This is most important for if you connect it to the small terminal, you will probably damage the generator permanently (see Fig. 13.56).

A second common cause of electrical interference is the ignition system. Here a 1.0 ohm capacitor must be connected between earth and the 'SW' or '+' terminal on the coil (see Fig. 13.57). This may stop the tick-tick-tick sound that comes over the speaker. Next comes the spark itself.

There are several ways of curing interference from the ignition HT system. One is to use carbon film HT leads but these have a tendency to 'snap' inside and you don't know then, why you are firing on only half your cylinders. So the second, and more successful method is to use resistive spark plug caps (see Fig. 13.58) of about 10 000 ohm to 15 000 ohm resistance. If, due to lack of room ,these cannot be used, an alternative is to use 'in-line' suppressors (Fig. 13.58) - if the interference is not too bad, you may get away with only one suppressor in the coil to distributor line. If the interference does continue (a 'clacking' noise), then doctor all HT leads.

At this stage it is advisable to check that the radio is well earthed, also the aerial, and to see that the aerial plug is pushed well into the set and that the radio is properly trimmed (see pre-

216

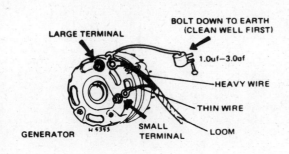

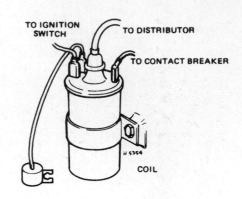

FIG. 13.56 THE CORRECT WAY TO CONNECT A CAPACITOR TO THE DYNAMO OR ALTERNATOR

FIG. 13.57 THE CAPACITOR MUST BE CONNECTED TO THE IGNITION SWITCH SIDE OF THE COIL

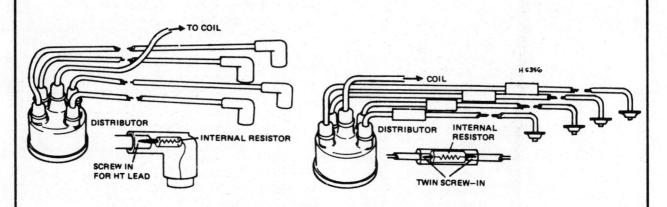

FIG. 13.58 IGNITION HT LEAD SUPPRESSORS

Left : Resistive spark plug caps   *Right: In-line suppressors*

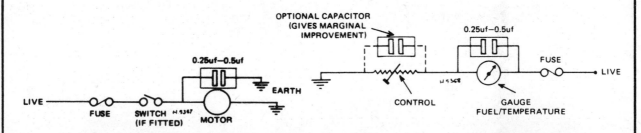

FIG. 13.59 CORRECT METHOD OF SUPPRESSING ELECTRIC MOTORS

FIG. 13.60 METHOD OF SUPPRESSING GAUGES AND CONTROL UNITS

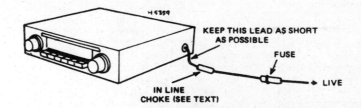

FIG. 13.61 ALL IN-LINE CHOKES SHOULD BE INSTALLED INTO THE SUPPLY LEAD AS CLOSE TO THE UNIT AS POSSIBLE

ceding Section). In addition, check that the wire which supplies the power to the set is as short as possible and does not wander all over the car. At this stage it is a good idea to check that the fuse is of the correct rating. For most sets this will be about 1 to 2 amps.

At this point the more usual causes of interference have been suppressed. If the problem still exists, a look at the cause of interference may help to pinpoint the component generating the stray electrical discharges.

The radio picks up electromagnetic waves in the air; now some are made by radio stations and other broadcasters and some, not wanted, are made by the car. The home made signals are produced by stray electrical discharges floating around the car. Common producers of these signals are electric motors; the windscreen wipers, electric screen washers, electric window winders, heater fan or an electric aerial, if fitted. Other sources of interference are electric fuel pumps, flashing turn signals, and instruments. The remedy for these cases is shown in Fig. 13.59 for an electric motor whose interference is not too bad and Fig. 13.60 for instrument suppression. Turn signals are not normally suppressed. In recent years, radio manufacturers have included in the line (live) of the radio, in addition to the fuse, an 'in-line' choke. If your installation lacks one of these, put one in as shown in Fig. 13.61.

All the foregoing components are available from radio shops or accessory shops. For a transistor radio, a 2A choke should be adequate. If you have an electric clock fitted this should be suppressed by connecting a 0.5 mf capacitor directly across it as shown for a motor in Fig. 13.59.

If after all this, you are still experiencing radio interference, first assess how bad it is, for the human ear can filter out unobtrusive unwanted noises quite easily. But if you are still adamant about eradicating the noise, then continue.

As a first step, a few 'experts' seem to favour a screen between the radio and the engine. This is OK as far as it goes, literally! - for the whole set is screened and if interference can get past that then a small piece of aluminium is not going to stop it.

A more sensible way of screening is to discover if interference is coming down the wires. First, take the live lead; interference can get between the set and the choke (hence the reason for keeping the wires short). One remedy here is to screen the wire and this is done by buying screened wire and fitting that. The loudspeaker lead could be screened also to prevent 'pick-up' getting back to the radio - although this is unlikely.

Without doubt, the worst source of radio interference comes from the ignition HT leads, even if they have been suppressed. The ideal way of suppressing these is to slide screening tubes over the leads themselves. As this is impractical, we can place an aluminium shield over the majority of the lead areas. In a vee - or twin-cam engine, this is relatively easy but for a straight engine the results are not particularly good.

Now for the really impossible cases, here are a few tips to try out. Where metal comes into contact with metal, an electrical disturbance is caused which is why good clean connections are essential. To remove interference due to overlapping or butting panels you must bridge the join with a wide braided earth strap (like that from the frame to the engine/transmission). The most common moving parts that could create noise and should be strapped are, in order of importance:

  a) Silencer to frame.
  b) Exhaust pipe to engine block and frame.
  c) Air cleaner to frame.
  d) Front and rear bumpers to frame.
  e) Steering column to frame.
  f) Bonnet and boot.
  g) Hood frame to frame on soft tops.

These faults are most pronounced when (1) the engine is idling, (2) labouring under load. Although the moving parts are already connected with nuts, bolts etc, these do tend to rust and corrode, thus creating a high resistance interference source.

If you have a 'ragged' sounding pulse when mobile, this could be wheel or tyre static. This can be cured by buying some anti-static powder and sprinkling it liberally inside the tyres.

If the interference takes the form of a high pitched screeching noise that changes its note when the car is in motion and only comes now and then, this could be related to the aerial, especially if it is of the telescopic or whip type. This source can be cured quite simply by pushing a small rubber ball on top of the aerial (yes, really!) as this breaks the electric field before it can form; but it would be much better to buy yourself a new aerial of a reputable brand. If, on the other hand, you are getting a loud rushing sound every time you brake, then this is brake static. This effect is most prominent on hot, dry days and is cured only by fitting a special kit, which is quite expensive.

In conclusion, it is pointed out that it is relatively easy, and therefore cheap to eliminate 95 per cent of all noises, but to eliminate the final 5 per cent is time and money consuming. It is up to the individual to decide if it is worth it. Please remember also, that you will not get concert hall performance from a cheap radio.

Finally at the beginning of this Section are mentioned tape players; these are not usually affected by interference but in a very bad case, the best remedies are the first three suggestions plus using a 3-5 amp choke in the 'live' line and in incurable cases screen the live and speaker wires.

Note: If your car is fitted with electronic ignition, then it is not recommended that either the spark plug resistors or the ignition coil capacitor be fitted as these may damage the system. Most electronic ignition units have built-in suppression and should, therefore, not cause interference.

---

12 Suspension and steering

Steering and suspension – general

1   Minor alterations have been made to the suspension on later models, but in general these do not affect the procedures already described in Chapter 11. It is important, however, to ensure that correct replacement parts are obtained when carrying out repairs, by quoting the car and body numbers (see page 6 of this Manual).
2   Special bolts are used on later cars for the steering coupling; more information on this will be found in paragraph 16.
3   A minor alternation to the procedures for the rear hub assembly on Saloons, Coupes, Estate cars and Vans is given in paragraphs 26 and 27.
4   Anti-roll bars are now fitted at the front and rear on Saloons and Coupes (paragraphs 6 to 15).
5   Revised mountings are now used for the swivel pin upper balljoints. Revised procedures are given in paragraphs 17 to 25, and are applicable where the shock absorber, swivel pin or balljoint are to be removed.

Anti-roll bar – removal and refitting
Front
6   Remove the two nuts and washers to release the end links.
7   Noting the fitted positions of the mountings, remove the securing screws.
8   Withdraw the anti-roll bar and remove the bushes.
9   Detach the lower ends of the links from the suspension arms.
10 Refitting is the reverse of the removal procedure, but note the 'L' mark on the left-hand side of the bar. Use a little rubber lubricant on the rubber bushes when refitting them.

Rear
11 Remove the two pivot bolts, nuts and washers securing the bushes to the chassis.
12 Disconnect the shock absorber lower mountings, and loosen the top ones so that the shock absorbers can be pushed to one side (refer to Chapter 11, Section 16 if necessary).
13 Remove the nuts, bolts and spring washers securing the

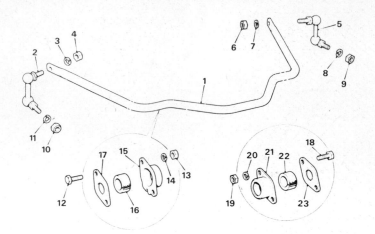

FIG. 13.62 FRONT ANTI-ROLL BAR COMPONENTS

1	Anti-roll bar	7	Spring washer	13	Nut	19	Nut
2	Link	8	Spring washer	14	Spring washer	20	Spring washer
3	Spring washer	9	Nut	15	Bearing carrier	21	Bearing carrier
4	Nut	10	Nut	16	Bearing	22	Bearing
5	Link	11	Spring washer	17	Bearing retainer	23	Bearing retainer
6	Nut	12	Bolt	18	Bolt		

anti-roll bar clamps. Unclip the clamps and remove the anti-roll bar.

14 Remove the rubbers, then loosen the locknuts and unscrew the end fittings.

15 Refitting is the reverse of the removal procedure. Adjust the positions of the end fittings to line up with the body holes. Tighten the pivot bolts to a torque of 48 to 55 lbf ft (6.6 to 7.6 kgf m) before tightening the end fitting locknuts.

Steering column universal joint coupling – removal and refitting

16 The procedure is generally as described in Chapter 11, Section 20, but the following should be noted:
  a) *On some cars, the flexible joint shouldered bolts are peened over. Where this is the case, they must not be disturbed.*
  b) *Where the flexible joint can be dismantled, it will be noted that two different types of bolts are used with either slotted he ʌls or crossheads. These will either have a square or s.ᴊouldered chamfer (Fig. 13.64). When retightening, the torque figure for the shouldered bolt is 6 to 9lbf ft (0.83 to 1.24 kgf m) and for the chamfered bolt is 8 to 12 lbf ft (1.1 to 1.6 kgf m). Use new locking wire to secure the bolts.*

Swivel pin balljoint – removal and refitting

Note: When retightening the reaction pad nut, a crowfoot adaptor (Leyland Part No. 1861237) is required; when retightening the ball retainer locknut a crowfoot adaptor (Leyland Part No. 1861192) is required. If you do not have these adaptors, open-ended spanners may be used, but you should arrange for your Leyland dealer to check the nut tightness after fitting.

17 Jack up the front of the car and support on firmly based axle stands.

18 Remove the wheel trim and roadwheel.

19 Unscrew the grease nipple from the swivel pin lower link, then support the weight of the lower suspension arm.

20 Unlock the reaction pad nut, then remove the lockwasher, upper bush housing and bush.

21 Using a balljoint separator or split wedges, separate the shock absorber arm from the balljoint pin.

22 Remove the balljoint dust cover and retaining clip.

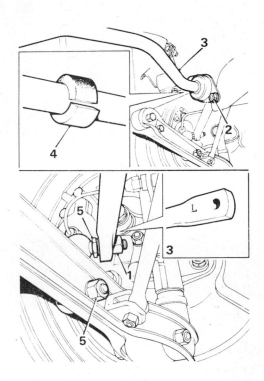

FIG. 13.63 FRONT ANTI-ROLL BAR REMOVAL

1	Retaining nut for link		identification mark
2	Nut	4	Bush
3	Anti-roll bar showing	5	Link and retaining nut

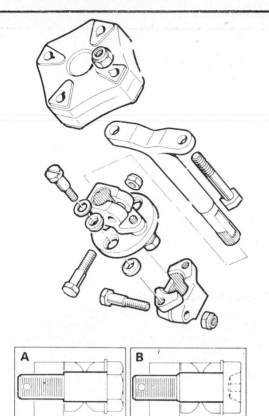

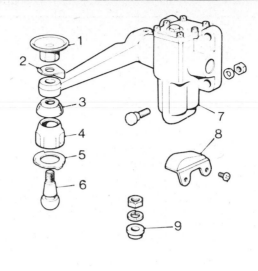

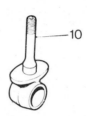

FIG. 13.64 LATER TYPE STEERING COUPLING

A Square shouldered bolt
B Chamfered shouldered bolt

FIG. 13.65 REVISED ARRANGEMENT FOR FRONT SUSPENSION SWIVEL (RIGHT-HAND SIDE SHOWN)

1	Reaction pad	6	Ball pin
2	Tab washer	7	Shock absorber
3	Dust cover	8	Bump rubber
4	Ball pin retaining nut	9	Bush
5	Tab washer	10	Eyebolt

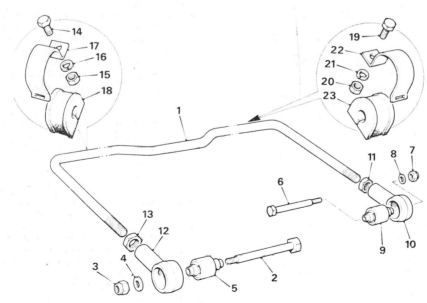

FIG. 13.66 REAR ANTI-ROLL BAR COMPONENTS

1	Anti-roll bar	7	Locknut	13	Locknut	19	Bolt
2	Bolt	8	Washer	14	Bolt	20	Nut
3	Locknut	9	Slotted bush	15	Nut	21	Spring washer
4	Washer	10	End fitting	16	Spring washer	22	Clamp
5	Slotted bush	11	Locknut	17	Clamp	23	Bearing
6	Bolt	12	End fitting	18	Bearing		

23 Using a suitable spanner to retain the locknut, remove the ballpin retainer.

24 Remove the ballpin, ballseat and spring, followed by the tab washer and locknut.

25 Refitting is basically the reverse of the removal procedure, but the following points should be noted:

    a) *Smear Duckhams Q 5468 grease or an equivalent on the ballpin spherical surface.*

    b) *Pack the ballpin retainer with a general purpose grease.*

    c) *Fully slacken the locknut, then tighten the ball retainer until the torque required to produce articulation of the ballpin is 32 to 52 lbf in (0.38 to 0.56 kgf m).*

    d) *Hold the ball retainer against rotation and tighten the locknut to a torque wrench setting of 70 to 80 lbf ft (9.6 to 11.0 kgf m) using the crowfoot adaptors.*

    e) *Tighten the reaction pad nut to a torque wrench setting of 35 to 40 lbf ft (4.8 to 5.5 kgf m) using the crowfoot adaptor.*

    f) *After fitting the grease nipple, grease the joint with a general purpose grease.*

Rear hub assembly – Saloon, Coupe, Estate car and 7 cwt Van

26 Removal procedures have not altered on this assembly but it should be noted that the procedure given in Chapter 11, Section 12 also applies to 7 cwt Vans and all Saloons, Coupes and Estate cars up to 1976 models.

27 From 1976, when refitting the halfshaft nut, make sure that the screw threads are clean then apply three drops of Loctite LT 270 to the nut threads and tighten it to a torque of 105 lbf ft (14.5 kgf m).

Rear hub assembly (10 cwt Van and Pick-up) – removal and refitting

28 Chock the front wheels, jack-up the rear of the vehicle and support on firmly based axle stands. Remove the roadwheel.

29 Remove the axleshaft, as described earlier in this Chapter.

30 Remove the bearing spacer.

31 Using a chisel knock back the tab of the locking washer.

32 Using a large box spanner remove the hub nut and keyed lockwasher.

33 Using a universal puller and suitable thrust block draw the hub assembly from the end of the axle.

34 Refitting the rear hub assembly is the reverse sequence to removal but the following additional points should be noted:

    a) *Carefully repack the bearing assembly with grease.*

    b) *If possible always use a new lockwasher.*

    c) *Drift the hub into position. The outer face of the bearing spacer should protrude from 0.001 - 0.004 in (0.025 - 0.102 mm) beyond the outer face of the hub when the bearing is fully seated.*

Rear hub assembly oil seal (10 cwt Van and Pick-up) – removal and refitting

35 Remove the rear hub assembly.

36 Using a suitable drift remove the bearing.

37 Prise out the oil seal.

38 Refitting the oil seal is the reverse sequence to removal but the following additional points should be noted:

    a) *When fitted the oil seal lip must face towards the bearing.*

    b) *Refit the bearing with its thrust face to the outside of the hub. The thrust face is the one with the maker's name and reference number stamped on.*

    c) *Carefully pack the bearings and the area between the oil seal and bearing with grease.*

13A Bodywork and underframe (exterior)

Sump guard – removal and refitting

1 Undo and remove the three screws and washers that

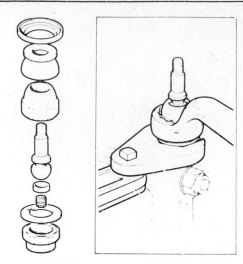

FIG. 13.67 USING THE CROWFOOT ADAPTOR WHEN REASSEMBLING THE BALLJOINT

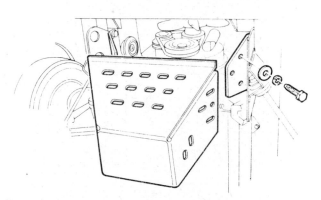

FIG. 13.68 THE SUMP GUARD

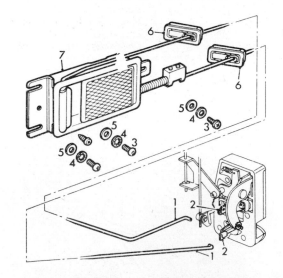

FIG. 13.69 DOOR LOCK REMOTE CONTROL (LATER SALOON, COUPE AND VAN)

1	Control rod	5	Plain washer
2	Spring retainer	6	Nylon guide
3	Screw	7	Remote control
4	Shakeproof washer		assembly

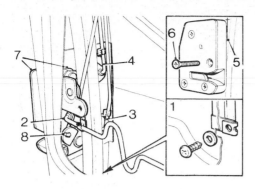

FIG. 13.70 FRONT DOOR LOCK REMOVAL

1 Glass channel screw	5 Door lock marking
2 Remote control operating link	6 Screws
3 Private lock operating link	7 Lock mechanism
4 Outside handle operating link	8 Locking link

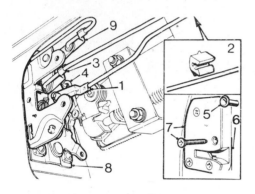

FIG. 13.71 REAR DOOR LOCK REMOVAL

1 Retainer	5 Knob
2 Clip	6 Door lock marking
3 Retainer	7 Screws and lock mechanism
4 Outside handle	8 Lock mechanism
operating link	9 Child safety operating link

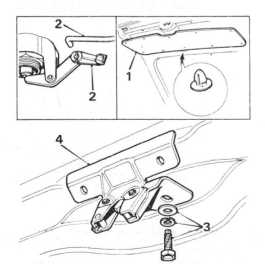

FIG. 13.72 TAILGATE LOCK MECHANISM

1 Trim pad	3 Screw and washers
2 Retainer and operating rod	4 Lock assembly

secure each side of the guard to the mounting brackets (Fig. 13.68).
2 Lift away the sump guard from under the front of the car.
3 Refitting the sump is the reverse sequence to removal.

Early type door lock remote control – modifications
4 These door locks were modified slightly prior to introduction of the later type referred to in paragraphs 5 to 11. The modifications will be apparent when Fig. 13.69 is compared with the original illustration. The servicing procedures are not affected to any great extent.

Later type side door locks (Saloon and Estate car) – removal and refitting
5 With the door glass fully raised, remove the trim pad. Also remove the adhesive cover where necessary.

Front door
6 Unclip the retainers and detach the operating links from the lock mechanism, private lock, door outside handle and remote control.

Rear door
7 Unclip the retainers and detach the operating links from the lock mechanism and door panel clip. Detach the locking link from the lock mechanism then unscrew the knob from the child safety operating link.

All models
8 Using a pencil, mark the lock position relative to the door then remove the four retaining screws.
9 Withdraw the mechanism and locking link through the aperture in the door.

Rear doors
10 Unclip the retainer so that the child operating link can be detached from the lock mechanism.

All models
11 Refitting is the reverse of the removal procedure, but adjust the outside handle so that, with the lock in the open position, the cranked end of the link is aligned with the bush in the lock mechanism operating lever.

Rear quarter trim pad and capping – removal and refitting
12 Remove the rear seat and cushion.
13 Undo and remove the two screws securing the arm rest and lift away the arm rest.
14 Unclip and remove the trim pad.
15 Undo and remove the screws and unclip the trim capping from the body.
16 Refitting the rear quarter trim pad and capping is the reverse sequence to removal.

Tailgate lock mechanism (Estate Car) – removal and refitting
Door lock
17 Remove the trim panel by carefully prising it away.
18 Unclip the retainer and detach the operating rod from the outside handle mechanism.
19 Remove the three screws and spring washers to release the lock assembly.
20 Refitting is the reverse of the removal procedure.

Door outside handle
21 Follow the procedure in paragraphs 17 and 18.

22 Unscrew the nut to release the operating lever assembly and handle.
23 Refitting is the reverse of the removal procedure.

Private lock
24 Remove the outside handle as described earlier then remove the circlip so that the lock parts can be removed.
25 Refitting is the reverse of the removal procedure.

Tail door lock (Van) – removal and refitting

26 Undo and remove the two screws that secure the lock to the door.
27 Lift the lock off the square shank of the outside handle.
28 Slide the locking bars out of their guides one at a time.
29 Detach the lock and bar assembly, noting the positions of the lock and the locking bars.
30 Refitting the lock and locking bars is the reverse sequence to removal. Lubricate all moving parts with a little engine oil.

Tail door exterior handle (Van) – removal and refitting.

31 Refer to paragraphs 26 to 30, and remove the tail door lock assembly.
32 Undo and remove the two nuts that secure the handle to the door.
33 Lift away the handle and recover the rubber seal.
34 Refitting the exterior handle is the reverse sequence to removal. Make sure that the handle points downwards when the door lock is in the locked position.

Tailgate – removal and refitting

35 In all essential details this is similar to the bonnet removal procedure given in Chapter 12, Section 16.
36 If the tailgate hinges are also to be removed, remove the rear interior light, noting the earth lead beneath one fixing screw.
37 Detach the rear panel headlining, and retain the fasteners.
38 Detach the courtesy light switch bracket and disconnect the wire.
39 Using a pencil, mark the hinge positions then remove the four screws to release the hinge and tension bar at each side.
40 Refitting is the reverse of the removal procedure.

Tailboard (Pick-up) – removal and refitting

41 Detach the number plate leads from the body harness connections.
42 With the tailboard supported, remove the two stay bracket screws.
43 Remove the two hinge retaining screws and washers, then remove the tailboard.
44 If necessary, remove the number plate lamp and mounting plate assembly. Remove the grommets, bump stop, badge and rubbing strip (five screws).
45 Refitting is the reverse of the removal procedure. If the badge was removed, new blind fittings will have to be obtained.

Tail door seal (Van) – removal and refitting

46 Carefully lever off the clips (where fitted) securing the seal to the door inner edge at the bottom and top. (Fig 13.75).
47 Carefully ease out the snap-in plugs retaining the seal to the door.
48 Detach the seal from the door.
49 Refitting the seal is the reverse sequence to removal. Apply a little adhesive to the seal at the corners of the door.

Tail doors (Van) – removal and refitting

50 Support the weight of the door.
51 Undo and remove the two nuts and flat washers that secure the top hinge to the door.

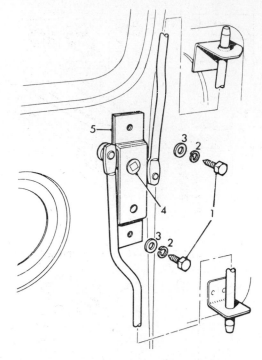

FIG. 13.73 TAIL DOOR LOCK ATTACHMENTS (VAN)

1 Screw	4 Squared shank location
2 Spring washer	5 Lock and bar assembly
3 Plain washer	

52 Undo and remove the two nuts and flat washers that secure the bottom hinge and friction stay bracket to the door.
53 Lift back the friction stay bracket from the hinge studs.
54 Lift away the door from the hinges.
55 Refitting the tail doors is the reverse sequence to removal. Do not, however, tighten the hinge securing nuts fully yet.
56 Close the door and check that there is an even distance between the outer edges of the door and the body line.
57 With the right-hand door check that the locking bars engage in their sockets in the body when the door handle is operated.
58 Finally when all is well, tighten the hinge retaining nuts.

Tail door hinges (Van) – removal and refitting

59 Refer to paragraphs 50 to 58 and remove the door.
60 Undo and remove the screw at the top and bottom of the tail light cluster. Lift away the cover.
61 Undo and remove the two nuts, plain washers and plate securing each hinge to the body (Fig. 13.76).
62 Lift away the tail door hinges.
63 Refitting the tail door hinges is the reverse sequence to removal. Do not tighten the securing nuts fully until the door adjustment has been checked as described in paragraphs 56 to 58.

Tail door check stay (Van) – removal and refitting

64 Undo and remove the screw and nut that secures the stay to its body mounted bracket.
65 Support the weight of the door.
66 Undo and remove the two nuts and plain washers that secure the stay to the lower door hinge.
67 Lift away the stay assembly.
68 Refitting the tail door check stay is the reverse sequence to removal. Adjust the pivot nut so that a pull of about 2.0 lbf (0.90 kgf) is required at the outer edge of the door to open and close the door.

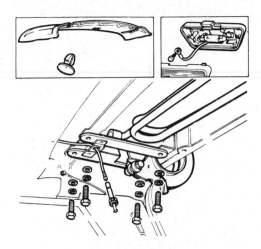

FIG. 13.74 TAILGATE DOOR HINGES

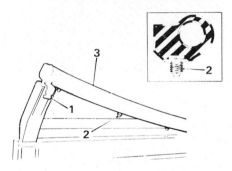

FIG. 13.75 TAIL DOOR SEAL (VAN)

1   Clip   3   Seal
2   Snap-in plug

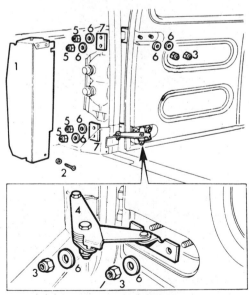

FIG. 13.76 DOOR CHECK STAY AND HINGE ASSEMBLY ATTACHMENTS (VAN)

1   Cover   5   Self-locking nut
2   Screw   6   Plain washer
3   Self-locking nut   7   Plate
4   Door check stay

Quarter light and sealing rubber — removal and refitting

69   To remove the quarter light assembly from the body simply push it out from the inside of the car. Make sure that someone is on the outside ready to catch it.

70   Remove the finisher strip from the sealing rubber.

71   Remove the sealing rubber from the glass.

72   Carefully inspect the sealing rubber for signs of damage or hardening; if evident obtain a new sealing rubber.

73   If the original glass or sealing rubber is to be re-used first clean off all the old sealer.

74   Inject some sealer into the glass channel of the sealing rubber.

75   Fit the sealing rubber to the glass.

76   Lubricate the finisher channel of the seal and its surrounding area with a little washing-up liquid.

77   Insert the end of the finisher into the seal at the centre point of the curve.

78   Continue by feeding the finisher in at this point and pushing it along the rubber in its fitted position until the end of the seal slot is reached.

79   Position the remaining finisher over the seal slot and tap it into position with the palm of the hand until the upper glass corner is reached.

80   Using a soft-faced hammer strike the outside edge of the straight length of finisher, aiming the blow towards the glass.

81   Apply some sealer to the outside face of the quarter light aperture in the body.

82   Insert a cord into the body flange groove of the sealing rubber.

83   Hold the glass and rubber against the aperture and use the cord to pull the rubber lip over the body flange from inside the car.

84   Apply pressure against the outside of the glass to ensure that the sealing rubber settles correctly into the body flange.

Tail door glass (Van) — removal and refitting

85   Working on the outside of the door carefully lever out the top corner of the window glass.

86   Ease out the glass and rubber assembly from the aperture in the door (Fig 13.77).

87   Remove the rubber surround from the glass.

88   Remove all sealing compound from the rubber surround, glass and window aperture.

89   To refit first fit the rubber surround to the glass and smear the inside of the retaining lip of the rubber surround with a little washing-up liquid.

90   Insert some cord into the groove in the retaining lip of the rubber surround.

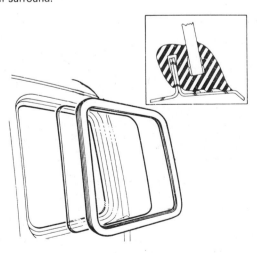

FIG. 13.77 TAIL DOOR GLASS (VAN)

91 Offer up the glass and rubber surround to the aperture and, with an assistant pushing on the glass, pull the cord through from the inside of the door.

92 Check that the glass and rubber surround lips are correctly located in the aperture and then seal the rubber surround to the door and also to the glass with a little sealer.

Back light glass (Pick-up) — removal and refitting

93 The procedure is similar to that described for the Van tail door glass except that it is better to apply the sealer to the outside face of the window aperture before the glass is fitted.

Bodyside glass and tailgate door glass (Estate Car) — removal and refitting

94 With an assistant ready to support the glass on the outside, press out the glass, rubber surround and finisher strip as an assembly.

95 Remove the finisher and rubber surround.

96 If the original glass or surround is to be used again, remove all traces of sealing compound.

97 Refit the rubber surround to the glass and seal it on its outer face.

98 Apply a little diluted washing-up liquid to the groove in the surround, then fit the finisher and joint covers.

99 Put a little sealer in the middle groove of the surround and around the outer face of the window aperture.

100 Refit the glass as described in paragraphs 90 to 91.

Front quarter light glass — removal and refitting

101 This Section is applicable to the quarter light assembly without a metal frame around the glass.

102 Undo and remove the special screw and protective washer securing the glass to the upper pivot.

103 Lift away the glass.

104 If it is necessary to remove the catch, drift out the catch handle roll pin and lift away the handle.

105 Remove the plunger, wave washer and spring.

106 Unscrew and remove the nut and washer.

107 Lift the catch body fom the glass.

108 Refitting the catch and glass is the reverse to removal.

Rear quarter bumper (Van and Pick-up) — removal and refitting

109 Undo and remove the two screws that secure the bumper bracket to the rear face of the body (Fig 13.80).

110 Undo and remove the two screws that secure the bumper bracket to the side of the body. Note that the larger screw is fitted to the forward fixing point.

111 Lift away the rear quarter bumper and recover the rubber packing pieces. The thicker packing piece is fitted to the forward fixing point.

112 Refitting the rear quarter bumper is the reverse sequence to removal.

13B Bodywork and underframe (interior)

Facia (Saloon and Estate Car) — removal and refitting

1 Disconnect the battery, then remove the steering wheel as described in Chapter 11, the instrument pack as described in Section 11A, paragraphs 130 to 137 of this Chapter, and the glovebox as described in paragraphs 34 to 38 of this Section.

2 Remove the two nuts, washers and screws and the single clip retaining the parcel shelf.

3 Disconnect the face level vent air tubes.

4 Remove the steering column bridge piece (two screws).

5 Remove the heater control knobs, then remove the two screws retaining the heater controls.

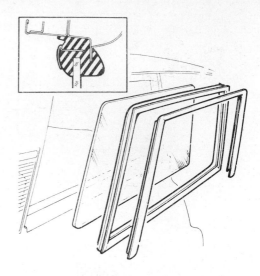

FIG. 13.78 BODY SIDE GLASS (ESTATE CAR)

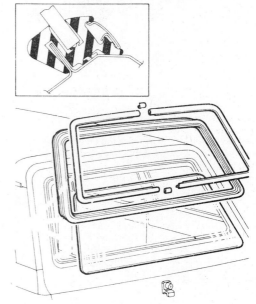

FIG. 13.79 TAILGATE DOOR GLASS (ESTATE CAR)

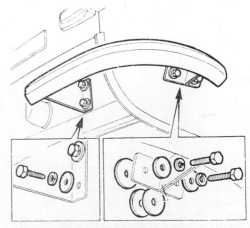

FIG. 13.80 REAR QUARTER BUMPER ATTACHMENTS (VAN AND PICK-UP)

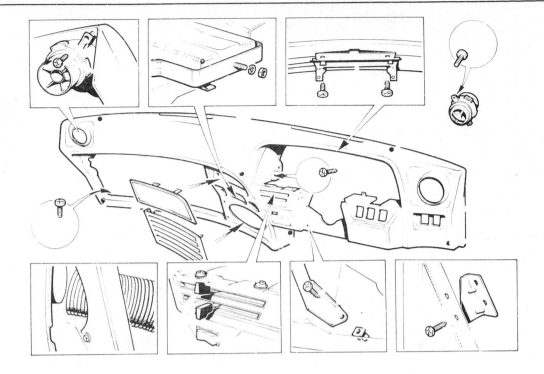

FIG. 13.81 FACIA PANEL ATTACHMENTS (SALOON AND ESTATE CAR)

6   Release all the facia panel switches (see Section 11A) and remove the connectors.

7   Where applicable, disconnect the cigar lighter leads.

8   Remove the five facia panel securing screws and the three securing nuts.

9   Press down on the centre of the panel then ease it from its retaining clips and lift it out.

10   If further dismantling is required, remove the four screws and release the two face level vents.

11   Remove the glovebox hinge brackets (two screws), then remove the nut and washer from the ashtray clip; remove the ashtray.

12   Where applicable, unscrew the cigar lighter body from the rear and withdraw the assembly.

13   Prise out the speaker grille and remove its fixings, then remove the radio blank.

14   Remove the instrument pack support bracket (two screws).

15   Drill out the two pop rivets to release the facia panel stud clip fasteners.

16   Remove the spire nuts for the instrument and face level vent fixings.

17   Remove the steering column bridge and glovebox plastic nut fixings.

18   Reassembly and refitting is the reverse of the dismantling and removal procedures.

Facia (Van and Pick-up) – removal and refitting

19   Refer to the relevant paragraphs and remove the instrument cowl, speedometer head, glovebox and windscreen demister ducts.

20   Undo and remove the nut and washer that secures the ashtray clamp plate. Lift away the clamp plate and pull out the ashtray assembly (Fig. 13.82).

21   Undo and remove the four screws that secure the cowl for the steering lock and steering column switches. Lift away the two halves of the cowl.

22   Carefully unclip the cowl support bracket.

23   Slacken the cable trunnion screw that secures the choke cable to the carburettor linkage and withdraw the cable from

the trunnion. Recover the cable trunnion screw assembly.

24   Remove the heater or fresh air control knobs from the levers.

25   Pull off the heater or fresh air control trim panel.

26   Undo and remove the two screws that secure the control assembly.

27   Undo and remove the two nuts and bolts, plain and spring washers that secure the facia to the outer support bracket.

28   Undo and remove the three screws, spring and plain washers that secure the facia to the support stays.

29   Undo and remove the six nuts, spring and plain washers that secure the facia to the studs on the windscreen lower panel.

30   Partially remove the facia and detach the windscreen washer pump securing bezel. Make a note of and disconnect the electrical connections to the switches.

31   Remove the facia whilst pulling the choke cable through its grommet on the scuttle.

32   If a new facia panel is being fitted transfer all switches, windscreen washer, choke control cable, face vents and all screw fixings from the old facia panel.

33   Refitting the facia panel is the reverse sequence to removal.

Glovebox (Saloon and Estate car) – removal and refitting

34   Open the lid and disconnect the hinge stay .

35   Remove the lower hinge bracket screws and loosen the upper ones.

36   Ease the lid from the right-hand hinge and remove it.

37   Remove the striker plate (two screws) followed by the glovebox itself (two more screws).

38   Refitting is the reverse of the removal procedure.

Glovebox (Van and Pick-up) – removal and refitting

39   Detach the air hose from the rear of the facia vent.

40   Undo and remove the two screws that secure each side of the glovebox to the facia.

41   Remove the glovebox from the rear of the facia.

42   Refitting the facia is the reverse sequence to removal.

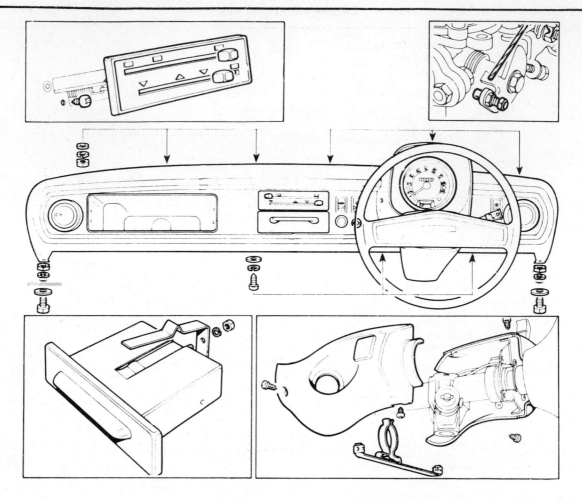

FIG. 13.82 FACIA PANEL ATTACHMENTS (VAN AND PICK-UP)

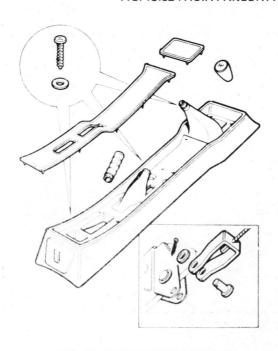

FIG. 13.83 CONSOLE ASSEMBLY

FIG. 13.84 FRONT SEATS AND MOUNTINGS (2-DOOR MODELS)

Lower inset shows handbrake link that must be detached before removal of the console.

Console assembly – removal and refitting
43 Carefully remove the two inset trim panels.
44 Unscrew the gearchange lever knob.
45 Remove the handbrake lever grip.
46 Undo and remove the screws and plain washers that secure the console assembly (Fig. 13.83).
47 Withdraw the split pin, washer and clevis pin securing the cable to the handbrake lever.
48 Raise the handbrake lever to the vertical position and lift away the console assembly.
49 Refitting the console assembly is the reverse sequence to removal.

Rear parcel tray – removal and refitting
50 Remove the rear seat squab and cushion.
51 Working inside the boot, push up the rear parcel tray and release it from its retaining clips.
52 Refitting the rear parcel tray is the reverse sequence to removal.

Front seats (standard type) – removal and refitting
Two-door models
53 Undo and remove the two bolts and spring washers that secure each bracket to the car floor panel.
54 Undo and remove the nuts retaining the lock-down bar.
55 Lift away the front seat and lock bar.

Four-door models
56 Undo and remove the locknut and dished washer that secures each front stud to the car floor panel.
57 Undo and remove the locknut and plain washer retaining each rear stud to the car floor panel. Note that on early cars a shaped washer is fitted.
58 Lift away the front seat. Note that on later cars a 1.5 in (38 mm) diameter plain washer is fitted between the spacer and the inside floor on the rear fixing studs only.

All models
59 Refitting the front seat is the reverse sequence to removal. It is recommended that on early four door cars the curved washer under the floor panel on the rear fixing only is discarded and a plain washer fitted. Also inside the car, a 1.5 in (38 mm) diameter plain washer should be fitted between the spacers and the floor panel. The spacer must still be fitted with the curved side away from the seat runner.

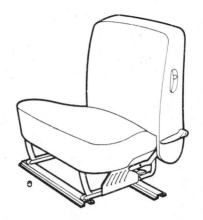

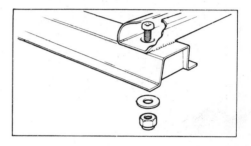

FIG. 13.85 CONTROLLED MOVEMENT TYPE SEATS AND MOUNTINGS

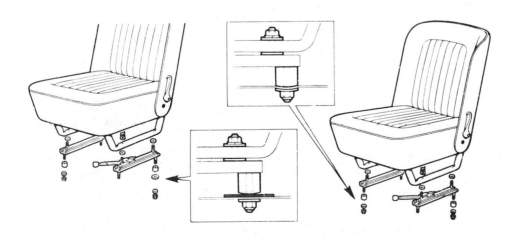

FIG. 13.86 FRONT SEAT ASSEMBLY SHOWING MOUNTINGS (4-DOOR MODELS, VAN AND PICK-UP)

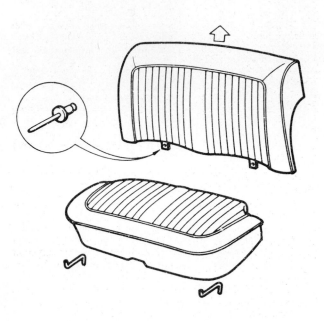

FIG. 13.87 REAR SEAT SQUAB AND CUSHION

Front seats (controlled-movement type) – removal and refitting

60 Move the seat fully forwards, and working under the car, undo and remove the two locknuts and large plain washer securing the seat rear fixing studs.

61 Move the seat fully forwards and, again from under the car, undo and remove the two locknuts and large plain washer securing the seat front fixing studs.

62 Lift away the front seat assembly.

63 Refitting the front seat is the reverse sequence to removal.

Rear seat squab and cushion – removal and refitting

64 Release the two cushion retaining clips and lift away the seat cushion.

65 Undo the two screws securing the arm rest and lift away the arm rest.

66 Using a drill remove the two rivet heads retaining the squab brackets. Remove the head only, as if the drill passes through the body the brake pipes could be damaged (Fig. 13.87).

67 Raise the squab to release it from the back panel retaining hooks and lift away the squab.

68 Refitting the rear seat cushion and squab is the reverse sequence to removal. Always use pop rivets and **not** self-tapping screws which could damage the brake pipes.

Windscreen demister duct (Saloon and Estate car) – removal and refitting

69 Remove the instrument panel and facia panel as described earlier in this Chapter.

70 Disconnect the duct tubes then remove the nuts and washers so that the ducts can be taken out.

71 Refitting is the reverse of the removal procedure.

Windscreen demister duct (Van and Pick-up) – removal and refitting

72 Remove the instrument cowl, speedometer and glove compartment.

73 Pull off the demister tubes from the demister ducts.

74 Undo and remove the nuts, washers and screws securing the demister duct and lift away the duct.

75 Refitting the demister duct is the reverse sequence to removal.

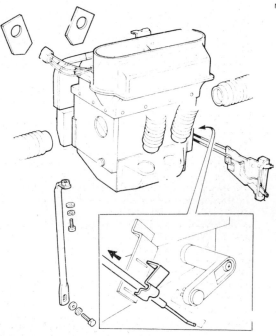

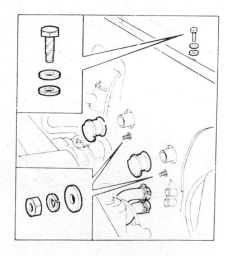

FIG. 13.88 HEATER UNIT ATTACHMENTS (SALOON AND ESTATE CAR)

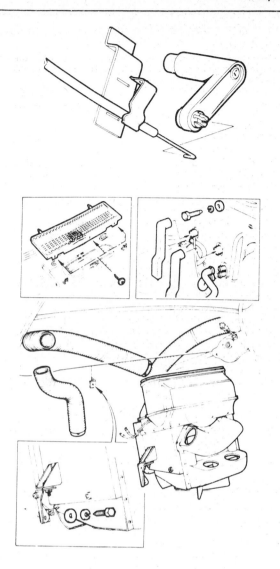

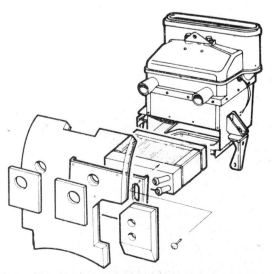

FIG. 13.89 HEATER UNIT ATTACHMENTS (VAN AND PICK-UP)

FIG. 13.90 HEATER UNIT SHOWING MATRIX REMOVED

Heater unit (Saloon and Estate) – removal and refitting

76 Drain the cooling system as described in Chapter 2.

77 Remove the instrument panel and facia panel as described earlier in this Chapter.

78 Disconnect the four heater tubes, then remove both demister tubes and the tube above the parcel shelf (Fig. 13.88).

79 Remove the fusebox, then remove the screws and take out the parcel shelf.

80 Disconnect the heater motor wires at the harness connector.

81 Remove the passenger side facia support tray.

82 Disconnect the two water hoses from the heater and plug the heater pipes to prevent spillage.

83 Remove the plenum drain caps.

84 Remove the two nuts, spring washers and flat washers securing the heater brackets to the bulkhead.

85 Remove the bolt, flat washer and sealing washer securing the heater to the windscreen panel.

86 Pull the heater rearwards and away from its mounting.

87 Release the outer cable retaining clips then detach the inner cables from the levers.

88 Remove the seal pads and insulation pad from the heater.

89 Refitting is the reverse of the removal procedure, but make sure that the heater levers and controls are in the 'Off' position then pull on the outer cable to remove slackness before fastening them with the clips.

Heater unit (Van and Pick-up) – removal and refitting

90 Remove the windscreen demister ducts.

91 Release the clip securing each outer cable to the bracket on the heater body.

92 Remove each inner cable from its plastic retainer in the control levers (Fig. 13.89).

93 Disconnect and remove the tubes from the heater.

94 Drain the cooling system as described in Chapter 2.

95 Remove the two plenum chamber drain tubes.

96 Remove the screw, plain and spring washers that secure the top of the heater unit to the bulkhead.

97 Remove the two bolts and washers securing the heater unit side brackets to the bulkhead.

98 Make a note of and disconnect the heater motor leads from the harness connector.

99 Pull the lower section of the heater rearwards until it is tilted over and can be withdrawn under the facia support rail on the passengers side. To stop staining of the carpets place some polythene sheeting on the floor.

100 To refit the heater, first undo and remove the three screws that secure the air intake grille to the body. Lift away the grille.

101 Place the heater in the vehicle and loosely fit the two bolts and washers securing the heater side brackets to the bulkhead.

102 Working through the air intake grille, work the seal over the grille housing.

103 Refitting the heater is now the reverse sequence to removal.

Heater matrix – removal and refitting

104 Remove the heater unit as described in the previous paragraphs. On Van and Pick-up models also remove the packing rubbers and felt.

105 Undo and remove the matrix cover plate securing the screws and lift away the matrix cover plate.

106 The matrix may now be slid out from the heater unit.

107 Refitting the heater matrix is the reverse sequence to removal.

Heater fan and motor – removal and refitting

108 Remove the heater unit as described in the previous paragraphs.

109 Remove the securing screws and lift the plenum chamber

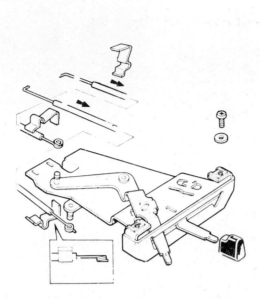

FIG. 13.91 HEATER CONTROLS (SALOON AND ESTATE CAR)

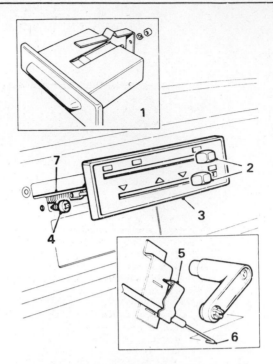

FIG. 13.92 HEATER CONTROLS (VAN AND PICK-UP)

1	Ashtray assembly	5	Clip
2	Control knob	6	Inner cable
3	Escutcheon	7	Heater control and
4	Screw		cable assembly

clear of the heater body.

110 Remove the three nuts and washers, and lift off the motor and fan assembly.

111 Remove the fan boss retaining clip and take off the fan.

112 Refitting is the reverse of the removal procedure.

Heater control cables (Saloon and Estate car) — removal and refitting

113 Remove the instrument cowl and the heater control knobs.

114 Remove the retaining screws and pull the control assembly down and out of the facia.

115 Release the outer cable retaining clips then detach the inner cables from the levers on the heater unit.

116 Remove the heater controls, then release the clips to free the outer cables from the control plate.

117 Refitting is the reverse of the removal procedure, but note that the inner cable ends at the heater end point in opposite directions. Make sure that the clips at the heater end of the cables are fitted approximately $\frac{1}{16}$ in (1 mm) from the outer cable

end, and that all slackness is removed from the outer cables at the control unit end before the clips are fitted.

Heater controls (Van and Pick-up) — removal and refitting

118 Undo and remove the nut and washer securing the ashtray clamp plate; lift away the clamp plate and pull out the ashtray assembly (Fig. 13.91.).

119 Pull the heater control knobs from the levers.

120 Remove the heater control assembly escutcheon.

121 Undo and remove the two screws securing the heater control quadrant to the facia panel.

122 Release the clip retaining each outer cable to the brackets on the heater body.

123 Remove the inner cable from its plastic retainer in the control levers.

124 Finally remove the heater control and cable assembly from below the facia panel.

125 Refitting is the reverse of the removal procedure.

FIG. 13.93 WIRING DIAGRAM (LEFT-HAND DRIVE MODELS WITH DYNAMO)

1 Dynamo
2 Control box (RB340)
3 Battery
4 Starter solenoid
5 Starter motor
6 Lighting switch
7 Dip switch
8 Headlamp high beam
9 Headlamp low beam
10 Main beam warning lamp
11 RH sidelamp
12 LH sidelamp
14 Panel lamps
15 Number plate lamps
16 Stop lamps
17 RH tail lamps
18 Stop lamp switch
19 Fuse unit
20 Interior light
21 Door switch
22 LH tail lamp
23 Horns
24 Horn push
25 Flasher unit
26 Direction indicator switch
27 Direction indicator warning light
28 RH front flasher
29 LH front flasher
30 RH rear flasher
31 LH rear flasher
32 Heater switch
33 Heater motor
34 Fuel gauge
35 Fuel gauge tank unit
36 Wiper switch

37 Wiper motor
38 Ignition switch
39 Ignition coil
40 Distributor
42 Oil pressure switch
43 Oil pressure warning light
44 Ignition warning light
45 Headlamp flasher switch
46 Water temperature gauge
47 Water temperature transmitter
49 Reverse lamp switch (if fitted)
50 Reverse lamps (if fitted)
57 Cigar lighter (if fitted)
60 Radio (if fitted)
64 Voltage stabilizer
65 Luggage compartment light switch
     (if fitted)
66 Luggage compartment lamp (if fitted)
67 Line fuse
75 Automatic gearbox safety switch
     (if fitted)
76 Automatic gearbox quadrant lamp
     (if fitted)
77 Electric screen washer motor
78 Electric screen washer switch
95 Tachometer (if fitted)
110 RH repeater flasher lamp
111 LH repeater flasher lamp
115 Rear window demist switch (if fitted)
116 Rear window demist warning light
     (if fitted)
150 Rear window demist warning light
     (if fitted)
158 Printed circuit instrument panel

Cable colour code

N	Brown	G	Green	W	White
U	Blue	LG	Light Green	Y	Yellow
R	Red	O	Orange	B	Black
P	Purple				

When a cable has two colour code letters the first denotes the main
colour and the second denotes the tracer colour

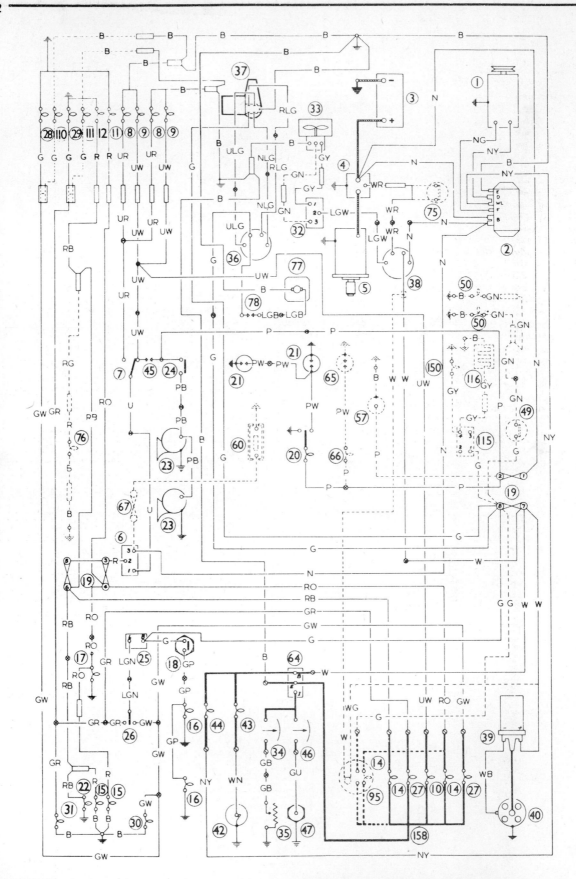

FIG. 13.93 WIRING DIAGRAM (LEFT-HAND DRIVE MODELS WITH DYNAMO)

1

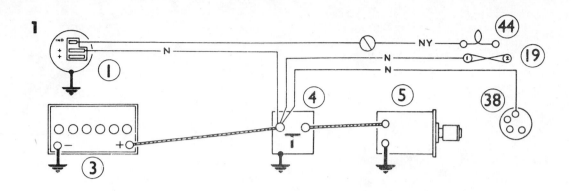

2

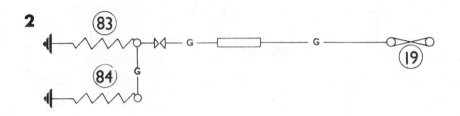

3

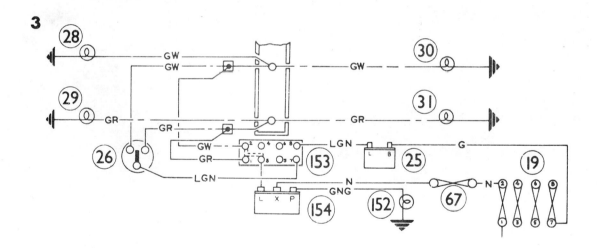

4

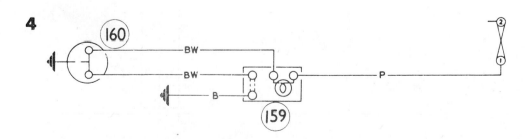

FIG. 13.94 **WIRING DIAGRAMS** – alternator, carburettor heater and thermostat, hazard warning, split braking circuits

FIG. 13.94 WIRING DIAGRAMS – alternator, carburettor heater and thermostat,
hazard warning, split braking circuits

1   Alternator circuit

1	Alternator	19	Fuse unit
3	Control box	38	Ignition switch
4	Starter solenoid	44	Ignition warning lamp
5	Starter motor		

2   Carburettor heater and thermostat circuit

19 Fuse unit

84 Suction chamber heater

83 Induction heater and
   thermostat

3   Hazard warning circuit

19	Fuse unit	31	LH rear direction indicator
25	Flasher unit	67	Line fuse
26	Direction indicator switch	152	Hazard warning lamp
28	RH front direction indicator	153	Hazard warning switch
29	LH front direction indicator	154	Hazard warning flasher unit
30	RH rear direction indicator		

4   Split braking circuit

159 Split braking test switch   160 Split braking shuttle valve

Cable colour code

N	Brown	P	Purple	Y	Yellow
U	Blue	G	Green	B	Black
R	Red	LG	Light Green	NY	Brown Yellow
O	Orange	W	White		

When a cable has two colour code letters the first denotes the main
colour the second denotes the tracer colour

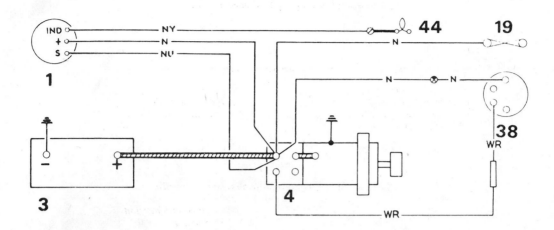

FIG. 13.95 WIRING DIAGRAM (MODELS WITH ALTERNATOR AND PRE-ENGAGED STARTER)

1	Alternator	4	Starter solenoid	38	Ignition switch
3	Battery	19	Fuse unit	44	Ignition warning lamp

FIG. 13.96 WIRING DIAGRAM – SALOON AND ESTATE CAR, RIGHT-HAND DRIVE

1 Alternator
3 Battery
4 Starter solenoid ⎤ Pre-engaged
5 Starter motor ⎦ starter
6 Light switch
7 Dip switch
8 Headlamp dip beam
9 Headlamp main beam
10 Main beam warning light
11 RH sidelamp
12 LH sidelamp
14 Panel lamps
15 Number plate lamps
16 Stop lamps
17 RH tail lamp
18 Stop lamp switch
19 Fuse unit
20 Interior lamp
21 Door switch
22 LH tail lamp
23 Horn(s)
24 Horn push
25 Flasher unit
26 Direction indicator switch
27 Direction indicator warning lamp
28 RH front direction indicator
29 LH front direction indicator
30 RH rear direction indicator
31 LH rear direction indicator
32 Heater blower motor switch
33 Heater motor
34 Fuel gauge
35 Fuel gauge sender unit
36 Wiper switch
37 Wiper motor
38 Ignition switch
39 Coil
40 Distributor
42 Oil pressure switch
43 Oil pressure warning lamp

44 Ignition warning lamp
45 Headlamp flasher switch
46 Water temperature gauge
47 Water temperature sender unit
49 Reversing lamp switch
50 Reversing lamps
56 Clock
57 Cigar lighter
59 Interior light switch
60 Radio
64 Voltage stabilizer
65 Luggage compartment lamp switch
66 Luggage compartment lamp
67 Line fuse
76 Automatic gearbox quadrant lamp
77 Screen washer motor
83 Induction heater and thermostat
105 Rear interior lamp – Estate
110 Repeater flasher lamps
111 Rear interior lamp switch –
      Estate
113 Inner headlamp – RH
114 Inner headlamp – LH
115 Heated rear window switch
116 Heated rear window unit
118 Wiper/washer switch
131 Reversing lamp and automatic
      inhibitor switch
150 Hazard rear window warning lamp
152 Hazard warning lamp
153 Hazard warning switch
154 Hazard warning flasher unit
158 Printed circuit instrument panel
159 Split braking test switch
160 Split braking shuttle valve
164 Ballast resistor (coil)
270 Tailgate wiper motor ⎤
271 Tailgate washer motor ⎬ Estate
272 Tailgate wipe/wash switch ⎦

CABLE COLOUR CODE

B	Black	O	Orange	U	Blue
G	Green	P	Purple	W	White
K	Pink	R	Red	Y	Yellow
N	Brown	S	Slate	LG	Light Green

When a cable has two colour code letters the first denotes
the main colour and the second denotes the tracer colour.

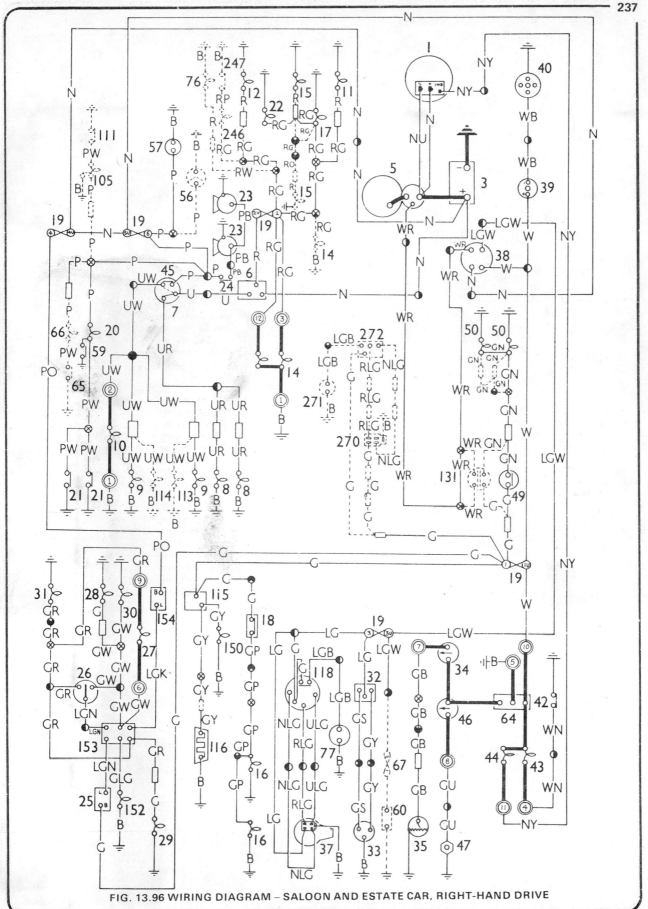

FIG. 13.96 WIRING DIAGRAM — SALOON AND ESTATE CAR, RIGHT-HAND DRIVE

**FIG. 13.97 WIRING DIAGRAM – SALOON AND ESTATE
CAR, LEFT-HAND DRIVE.**

1   Alternator
3   Battery
4   Starter solenoid) Pre-engaged
5   Starter motor   ) starter
6   Light switch
7   Dip switch
8   Headlamp dip beam
9   Headlamp main beam
10 Main beam warning light
11 RH sidelamp
12 LH sidelamp
14 Panel lamps
15 Number plate lamps
16 Stop lamps
17 RH tail lamp
18 Stop lamp switch
19 Fuse unit
20 Interior lamp
21 Door switch
22 LH tail lamp
23 Horn(s)
24 Horn push
25 Flasher unit
26 Direction indicator switch
27 Direction indicator warning lamp
28 RH front direction indicator
29 LH front direction indicator
30 RH rear direction indicator
31 LH rear direction indicator
32 Heater blower motor switch
33 Heater motor
34 Fuel gauge
35 Fuel gauge sender unit
36 Wiper switch
37 Wiper motor
38 Ignition switch
39 Coil
40 Distributor
42 Oil pressure switch
43 Oil pressure warning lamp

44 Ignition warning lamp
45 Headlamp flasher switch
46 Water temperature gauge
47 Water temperature sender unit
49 Reversing lamp switch
50 Reversing lamps
56 Clock
57 Cigar lighter
59 Interior light switch
60 Radio
64 Voltage stabilizer
65 Luggage compartment lamp switch
66 Luggage compartment lamp
67 Line fuse
76 Automatic gearbox quadrant lamp
77 Screen washer motor
83 Induction heater and thermostat
105 Rear interior lamp – Estate
110 Repeater flasher lamps
111 Rear interior lamp switch –
      Estate
113 Inner headlamp – RH
114 Inner headlamp – LH
115 Heated rear window switch
116 Heated rear window unit
118 Wiper/washer switch
131 Reversing lamp and automatic
      inhibitor switch
150 Hazard rear window warning lamp
152 Hazard warning lamp
153 Hazard warning switch
154 Hazard warning flasher unit
158 Printed circuit instrument panel
159 Split braking test switch
160 Split braking shuttle valve
164 Ballast resistor (coil)
270 Tailgate wiper motor
271 Tailgate washer motor) Estate
272 Tailgate wipe/wash switch)

CABLE COLOUR CODE

B	Black	O	Orange	U	Blue
G	Green	P	Purple	W	White
K	Pink	R	Red	Y	Yellow
N	Brown	S	Slate	LG	Light Green

When a cable has two colour code letters the first denotes
the main colour and the second denotes the tracer colour.

accurate job on the non-sealed type carburettor.

First the engine must be at normal operating temperature, so let it tick over for a few minutes. Then stop the engine and remove the air cleaner. Only two adjustments are provided on the SU carburettor; idling speed's governed by the throttle adjusting screw and the mixture strength by the jet adjusting screw. The SU carburettor's correctly adjusted for the whole engine revolution range when the idling mixture strength is correct.

On single carburettor models first set the engine to run at the correct speed (see *Vital Statistics*) by adjusting the idling screw. Then check the mixture strength by lifting the piston off the carburettor approximately $\frac{1}{32}$ in with the piston lifting pin. One of three things should happen:

(a) if the speed of the engine increases appreciably, the mixture's too rich;

(b) if the engine speed decreases immediately, the mixture's too weak;

(c) if the engine speed increases very slightly, the mixture's correct.

To enrich the mixture, screw the adjusting nut at the bottom of the carburettor down (it has a right-hand thread) one flat at a time; to weaken the mixture screw the adjusting nut up. Check the mixture strength after each turn and, if the engine idling speed is affected, correct it with the idle speed screw.

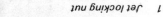

S.U. carburettor adjusting points

1 Jet locking nut
2 Jet adjusting nut
3 Piston lifting pin
4 Idling speed adjusting screw
5 Fast idle speed adjusting screw

Twin S.U. carburettor linkage arrangement

1 Dashpot oil level
2 Throttle spindle interconnecting clamp bolts
3 Jet control interconnecting clamp bolts

71

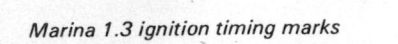
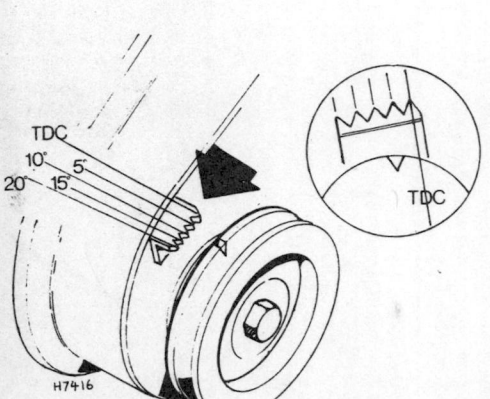
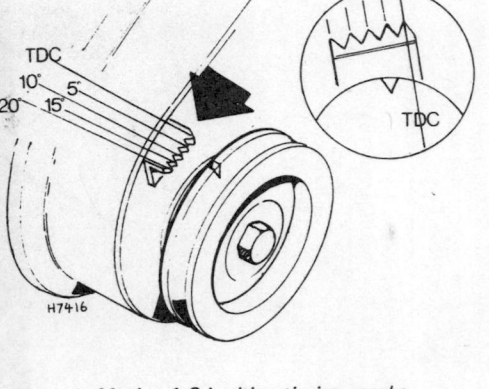

Marina 1.3 ignition timing marks

Marina 1.8 ignition timing marks

distributor clockwise to advance the ignition, anti-clockwise to retard the ignition (where a micrometer adjustment is fitted to the distributor it's possible to make a small adjustment without slackening the clamp bolts).

Tighten the clamp bolts again and recheck the setting with the timing light. Now increase the engine speed slowly whilst still looking at the timing marks, and you should see the timing advance in response to the centrifugal weights in the distributor. With the engine held at a steady speed, get someone to reconnect the vacuum pipe, and the ignition should advance immediately; this will show that the vacuum advance system's working correctly. Finally switch off the engine and disconnect the timing light.

6. Check carburettor idling and mixture settings

Before making any adjustments on the carburettor(s) unscrew the piston damper(s) on top of the piston chamber(s) and check the oil level, which should be 0.5 in (13 mm) above the top of the hollow piston rod.b use a small diameter length of wood or metal to make the check. Top it up as necessary with clean engine oil and then refit the piston damper(s).

All Marina models are fitted with a single carburettor with the exception of TC, GT, and HL versions which have twin carburettors. Some late Mk.2 models are fitted with sealed idling and/or mixture adjusters and it's suggested that on these, the work is entrusted to a Leyland garage which will have the necessary exhaust gas analyser to make an accurate check.

It's possible to make an adjustment without any instruments at all, but an engine tachometer and 'Colortune' kit will help you to make a much more

light comes on again - the crankshaft pulley notch should be aligned with the corresponding pointer. Switch off the ignition, disconnect the timing light, and refit the distributor cap.

Using a stroboscopic timing light is an easier and more accurate way of checking your ignition timing. First of all connect the light to the engine in accordance with the manufacturer's instructions. Start the engine and run it at the correct speed given in the *Vital Statistics*.

With the distributor vacuum pipe disconnected and plugged, point the timing light towards the timing marks and check that it's right. On 1.3 models you'll probably need an assistant as you'll have to observe the timing marks from underneath the front of the car. If adjustment is needed, stop the engine, slacken the distributor clamp bolts, and turn the complete

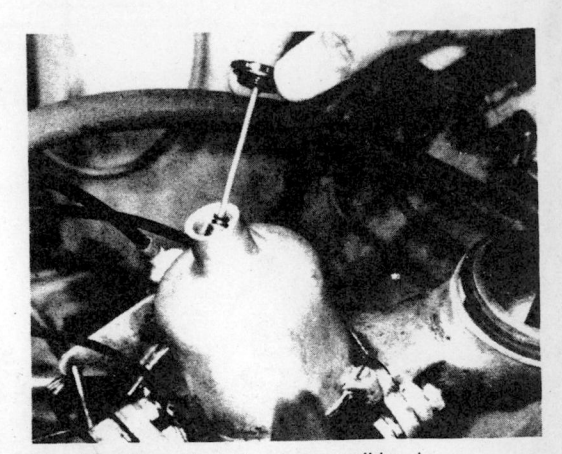

Checking the carburettor damper oil level

70

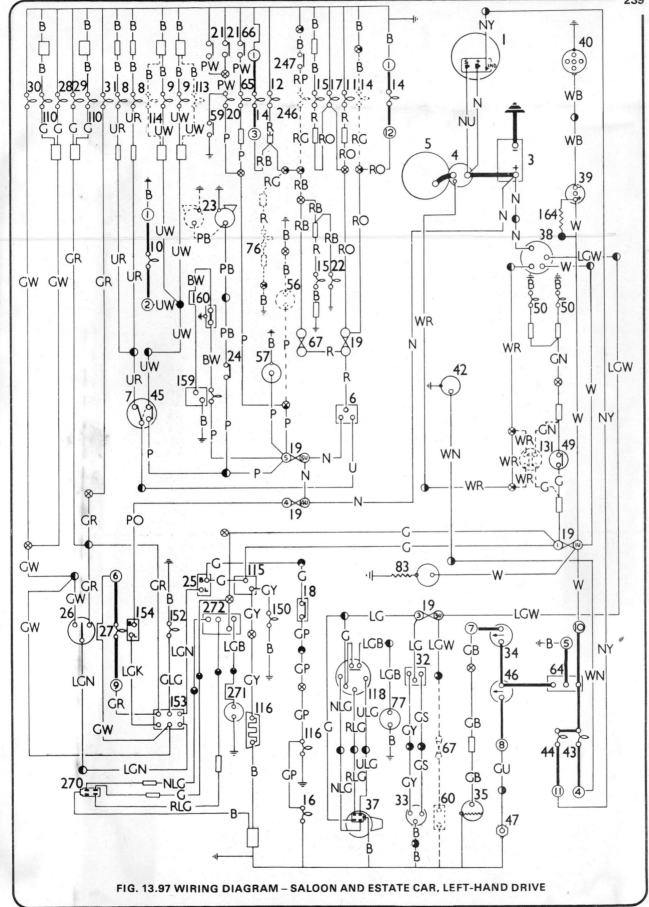

FIG. 13.97 WIRING DIAGRAM – SALOON AND ESTATE CAR, LEFT-HAND DRIVE

FIG. 13.98 WIRING DIAGRAM – VAN AND PICK-UP

1	Alternator	44	Ignition warning lamp
3	Battery	45	Headlamp flasher switch
4	Starter solenoid ⎞ Pre-engaged	46	Water temperature gauge
5	Starter motor ⎠ starter	47	Water temperature sender unit
6	Light switch	49	Reversing lamp switch
7	Dip switch	50	Reversing lamps
8	Headlamp dip beam	56	Clock
9	Headlamp main beam	57	Cigar lighter
10	Main beam warning light	59	Interior light switch
11	RH sidelamp	60	Radio
12	LH sidelamp	64	Voltage stabilizer
14	Panel lamps	65	Luggage compartment lamp switch
15	Number plate lamps	66	Luggage compartment lamp
16	Stop lamps	67	Line fuse
17	RH tail lamp	76	Automatic gearbox quadrant lamp
18	Stop lamp switch	77	Screen washer motor
19	Fuse unit	83	Induction heater and thermostat
20	Interior lamp	105	Rear interior lamp – Estate
21	Door switch	110	Repeater flasher lamps
22	LH tail lamp	111	Rear interior lamp switch – Estate
23	Horn(s)	113	Inner headlamp – RH
24	Horn push	114	Inner headlamp – LH
25	Flasher unit	115	Heated rear window switch
26	Direction indicator switch	116	Heated rear window unit
27	Direction indicator warning lamp	118	Wiper/washer switch
28	RH front direction indicator	131	Reversing lamp and automatic inhibitor switch
29	LH front direction indicator	150	Hazard rear window warning lamp
30	RH rear direction indicator	152	Hazard warning lamp
31	LH rear direction indicator	153	Hazard warning switch
32	Heater blower motor switch	154	Hazard warning flasher unit
33	Heater motor	158	Printed circuit instrument panel
34	Fuel gauge	159	Split braking test switch
35	Fuel gauge sender unit	160	Split braking shuttle valve
36	Wiper switch	164	Ballast resistor (coil)
37	Wiper motor	270	Tailgate wiper motor ⎞
38	Ignition switch	271	Tailgate washer motor ⎟ Estate
39	Coil	272	Tailgate wipe/wash switch ⎠
40	Distributor		
42	Oil pressure switch		
43	Oil pressure warning lamp		

CABLE COLOUR CODE

B	Black	O	Orange	U	Blue
G	Green	P	Purple	W	White
K	Pink	R	Red	Y	Yellow
N	Brown	S	Slate	LG	Light Green

When a cable has two colour code letters the first denotes
the main colour and the second denotes the tracer colour.

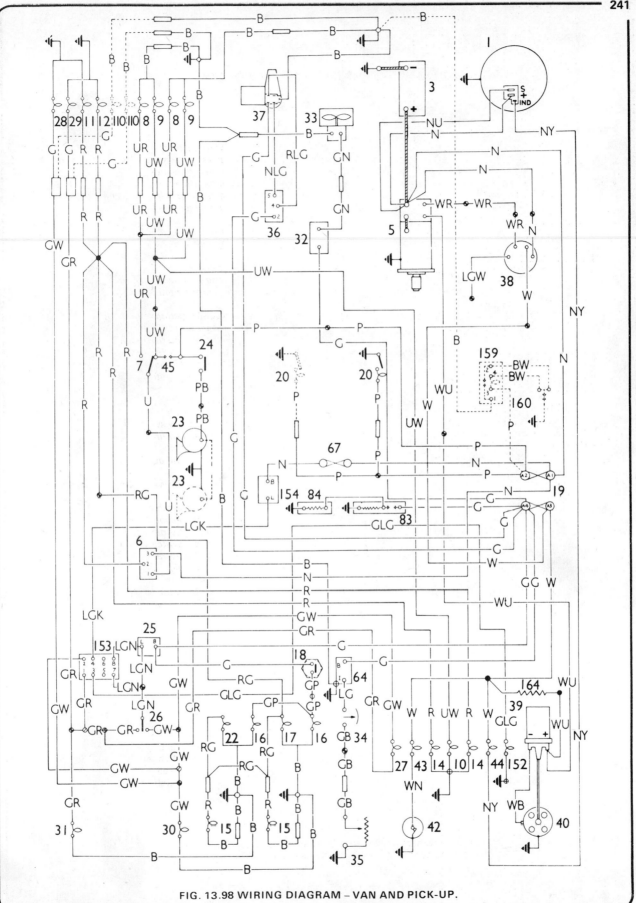

FIG. 13.98 WIRING DIAGRAM – VAN AND PICK-UP.

Metric conversion tables

Inches	Decimals	Millimetres	Millimetres to Inches		Inches to Millimetres	
			mm	Inches	Inches	mm
1/64	0.015625	0.3969	0.01	0.00039	0.001	0.0254
1/32	0.03125	0.7937	0.02	0.00079	0.002	0.0508
3/64	0.046875	1.1906	0.03	0.00118	0.003	0.0762
1/16	0.0625	1.5875	0.04	0.00157	0.004	0.1016
5/64	0.078125	1.9844	0.05	0.00197	0.005	0.1270
3/32	0.09375	2.3812	0.06	0.00236	0.006	0.1524
7/64	0.109375	2.7781	0.07	0.00276	0.007	0.1778
1/8	0.125	3.1750	0.08	0.00315	0.008	0.2032
9/64	0.140625	3.5719	0.09	0.00354	0.009	0.2286
5/32	0.15625	3.9687	0.1	0.00394	0.01	0.254
11/64	0.171875	4.3656	0.2	0.00787	0.02	0.508
3/16	0.1875	4.7625	0.3	0.01181	0.03	0.762
13/64	0.203125	5.1594	0.4	0.01575	0.04	1.016
7/32	0.21875	5.5562	0.5	0.01969	0.05	1.270
15/64	0.234375	5.9531	0.6	0.02362	0.06	1.524
1/4	0.25	6.3500	0.7	0.02756	0.07	1.778
17/64	0.265625	6.7469	0.8	0.03150	0.08	2.032
9/32	0.28125	7.1437	0.9	0.03543	0.09	2.286
19/64	0.296875	7.5406	1	0.03937	0.1	2.54
5/16	0.3125	7.9375	2	0.07874	0.2	5.08
21/64	0.328125	8.3344	3	0.11811	0.3	7.62
11/32	0.34375	8.7312	4	0.15748	0.4	10.16
23/64	0.359375	9.1281	5	0.19685	0.5	12.70
3/8	0.375	9.5250	6	0.23622	0.6	15.24
25/64	0.390625	9.9219	7	0.27559	0.7	17.78
13/32	0.40625	10.3187	8	0.31496	0.8	20.32
27/64	0.421875	10.7156	9	0.35433	0.9	22.86
7/16	0.4375	11.1125	10	0.39370	1	25.4
29/64	0.453125	11.5094	11	0.43307	2	50.8
15/32	0.46875	11.9062	12	0.47244	3	76.2
31/64	0.48375	12.3031	13	0.51181	4	101.6
1/2	0.5	12.7000	14	0.55118	5	127.0
33/64	0.515625	13.0969	15	0.59055	6	152.4
17/32	0.53125	13.4937	16	0.62992	7	177.8
35/64	0.546875	13.8906	17	0.66929	8	203.2
9/16	0.5625	14.2875	18	0.70866	9	228.6
37/64	0.578125	14.6844	19	0.74803	10	254.0
19/32	0.59375	15.0812	20	0.78740	11	279.4
39/64	0.609375	15.4781	21	0.82677	12	304.8
5/8	0.625	15.8750	22	0.86614	13	330.2
41/64	0.640625	16.2719	23	0.90551	14	355.6
21/32	0.65625	16.6687	24	0.94488	15	381.0
43/64	0.671875	17.0656	25	0.98425	16	406.4
11/16	0.6875	17.4625	26	1.02362	17	431.8
45/64	0.703125	17.8594	27	1.06299	18	457.2
23/32	0.71875	18.2562	28	1.10236	19	482.6
47/64	0.734375	18.6531	29	1.14173	20	508.0
3/4	0.75	19.0500	30	1.18110	21	533.4
49/64	0.765625	19.4469	31	1.22047	22	558.8
25/32	0.78125	19.8437	32	1.25984	23	584.2
51/64	0.796875	20.2406	33	1.29921	24	609.6
13/16	0.8125	20.6375	34	1.33858	25	635.0
53/64	0.828125	21.0344	35	1.37795	26	660.4
27/32	0.84375	21.4312	36	1.41732	27	685.8
55/64	0.859375	21.8281	37	1.4567	28	711.2
7/8	0.875	22.2250	38	1.4961	29	736.6
57/64	0.890625	22.6219	39	1.5354	30	762.0
29/32	0.90625	23.0187	40	1.5748	31	787.4
59/64	0.921875	23.4156	41	1.6142	32	812.8
15/16	0.9375	23.8125	42	1.6535	33	838.2
61/64	0.953125	24.2094	43	1.6929	34	863.6
31/32	0.96875	24.6062	44	1.7323	35	889.0
63/64	0.984375	25.0031	45	1.7717	36	914.4

Index

Printed by
Haynes Publishing Group
Sparkford Yeovil Somerset
England